SOVIET COMMUNISTS IN POWER

Soviet Communists in Power

A Study of Moscow during the Civil War, 1918–21

Richard Sakwa

Lecturer in Soviet Government and Politics
University of Kent at Canterbury

St. Martin's Press   New York

947.084
S15s

© Richard Sakwa, 1988

First published in the United States of America in 1988

Printed in Hong Kong

ISBN 0–312–01582–8

Library of Congress Cataloging-in-Publication Data
Sakwa, Richard.
Soviet communists in power: a study of Moscow during the civil
war, 1918–21/Richard Sakwa.
p. cm.
Bibliography: p.
Includes index.
ISBN 0–312–01582–8:$30.00 (est.)
1. Communism—Soviet Union—History.   2. Soviet Union—History-
-Revolution, 1917–1921.   3. Moscow (R.S.F.S.R.)-
-History—1917–1921.   4. Moscow (R.S.F.S.R.)—Politics and
government.   I. Title
HX313.S165 1987   87–24167
335.43'0947—dc19   CIP

To my mother and father

To my mother and father

Contents

List of Tables

Glossary of Russian Terms and Abbreviations

In the text

Cheka	see Vecheka
ChON	*Chasti osobogo naznacheniya* (special purpose party units)
Glavk	*Glavnyi komitet* (central directorate of a branch of industry)
Glavpolitprosvet	*Glavnoe politicheskoe upravlenie prosveshcheniya* (Chief Administration for Political Education under Narkompros)
Glavpolitput'	*Glavnoe politicheskoe upravlenie putei soobshcheniya* (Chief Political Administration under Narkomput')
Gubkom	*Gubernskii komitet* (provincial party committee)
Ispolkom (or EC)	*Ispolnitel'nyi komitet* (executive committee of a soviet)
(L) SR	*(Levye) sotsialisty-revolyutsionery* ((Left) Socialist-Revolutionaries)
MG (or) SNKh	*Moskovskii gubernskii (gorodskoi) sovet narodnogo khozyaistva* (Moscow *Guberniya* (City) Economic Council)
M (G) SPS	*Moskovskii (gubernskii) sovet professional'nykh soyuzov* (Moscow (*Guberniya*) Trade Union Council)
MK	*Moskovskii komitet* (Moscow Committee, of the Bolshevik Party)
MOB	*Moskovskoe oblastnoe byuro* (Moscow *Oblast* Bureau, of the Bolshevik Party)
MOSNK	*Moskovskii oblastnoi sovet narodnykh komissarov* (Moscow *Oblast* Council of Peoples Commissars)
MOSNKh	*Moskovskii oblastnoi sovet narodnogo khozyaistva* (Moscow *Oblast* Economic Council)
MPO	*Moskovskaya partiinaya organizatsiya* (Moscow Party Organisation)

xi

MRC	Military Revolutionary Committee, active October–December 1917
MREK	*Moskovskii raionnyi ekonomicheskii komitet* (Moscow *Raion* Economic Committee)
Narkompros	*Narodnyi komissariat prosveshcheniya* (People's Commissariat of Enlightenment)
Narkomput'	*Narodnyi komissariat putei soobshcheniya* (People's Commissariat of Transport)
NEP	*Novaya ekonomicheskaya politika* (New Economic Policy)
Proletcult	*Proletkul't (Proletarskaya kul'tura)* (Proletarian Culture Movement)
Rabkrin (RKI)	*Narodnyi komissariat raboche-krest'yanskoi inspektsii* (People's Commissariat of Workers' and Peasants' Inspection)
RK	*Raionnyi komitet (Raion* Committee, of the Bolshevik Party)
RKP (b)	*Rossiiskaya kommunisticheskaya partiya (bol'shevikov)* (Russian Communist Party (Bolsheviks))
RKSM (Komsomol)	*Rossiiskii kommunisticheskii soyuz molodezhı (Komosol)* (Russian Communist League of Youth)
RPO	*Raionnaya partiinaya organizatsiya* (Raion Party Organisation)
Sovnarkhoz (SNKh)	*Sovet narodnogo khozyaistva* (Economic Council)
Sovnarkom (SNK)	*Sovet narodnykh komissarov* (Council of People's Commissars)
Tsektran	Central Committee of Rail and Water Workers' Trade Union
TsK	*Tsentral'nyi komitet* (Central Committee, of the Party)
Vecheka	*Vserossiiskaya chrezvychainaya komissiya* (All-Russian Commission for the Struggle Against Counter-Revolution, Sabotage and Speculation, abbreviated to Cheka)
VSNKh	*Vysshii sovet narodnogo khozyaistva* (Supreme Economic Council)
VTsIK	*Vserossiiskii tsentral'nyi ispolnitel'nyi komitet* (All-Russian Central Executive Committee, of the soviets)

VTsSPS — *Vserossiiskii tsentral'nyi sovet profsoyuzov* (All-Russian Central Trade Union Council)

Zhenotdel — *Zhenskii otdel* (Women's Department, of the Bolshevik Party)

In the notes

KM — *Krasnaya Moskva: sbornik statei* (Moscow, 1920)

KT — *Kommunisticheskii trud*

P — *Pravda*

PR — *Proletarskaya revolyutsiya*

PSS — *Polnoe sobranie sochinenii*

SV — *Sotsialisticheskii vestnik*

TsGAOR — *Tsentral'nyi gosudarstvennyi arkhiv oktyabr'skoi revolyutsii.* In archival citations the name is followed by fond/opis'/edinitsa khraneniya/list number.

VI KPSS — *Voprosy istorii KPSS*

VIMS — *Vechernie izvestiya Moskovskogo soveta*

General Information

Dates

All dates up to and including 31 January 1918 are according to the old style Julian calendar: following a 13 day gap all dates from 14 February 1918 are on the new style Gregorian calendar.

Weights

1 *pood* = ca. 36lb = ca. 16.5kg
1 *funt* = 1/40th *pood* = 0.41 kg

Territorial divisions

Oblast   Region
Guberniya   Province
Raion   Urban borough
Uezd   Rural administrative division
Uchastok   Ward

The Raions of Moscow

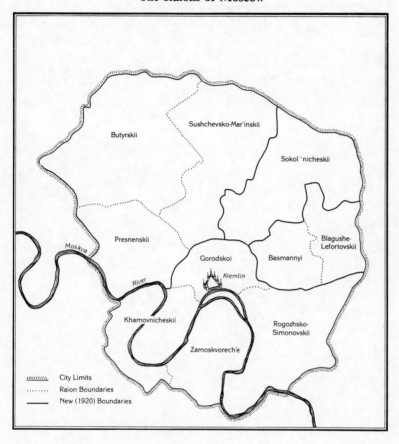

Preface

The Bolsheviks were the first to tread the path of communists in power. They have now been followed by a number of revolutions in which the patterns of power and authority that they established have to a greater or lesser extent been emulated. The Bolshevik revolution appears to present a viable path of development and have an applicability far beyond the country of its birth. However, on coming to power in Russia in October 1917 the Bolsheviks had no clear idea of what the dynamics of the new system would involve. The transition from a movement seeking power to one ultimately in control of a vast area stretching from Eastern Europe to the Pacific was accompanied by major organisational and ideological restructuring of the movement itself. It is the purpose of this study to analyse these changes by looking at the organisation and development of Bolshevik power in the first years after the achievement of power. It concentrates on the period known as war communism, from mid-1918 to early 1921. This was the crucial testing-time for the formation of the Soviet system. Despite many changes, the basic features which emerged at that time remain at the heart of Soviet-type politics. No single factor determined the shape of the new regime, but among the important influences were Bolshevik ideology, the legacy of Russia's political culture, and the circumstances of the time – hunger, economic dislocation and war. The problem for the historian is to balance the role of ideology and the impact of circumstances in the establishment of the Bolshevik form of socialism in Russia. In looking at these questions our view will be limited to a single city, Moscow, the heart of Russia and the new capital of the Soviet republic from March 1918.

The ideology itself was not an absolute law covering every detail, to which the Bolsheviks had to submit; but neither was it so flexible when treating of the fundamental relationships that were to hold under the new regime. The ideology provided the framework for the solution of the economic and political issues facing the new regime. While the Bolsheviks had no prescription for the details of the society that they were planning to build, certain key features were unassailable, stemming from the very fact that a new society was to be built. On coming to power the revolutionaries had two operative models: the future society known as communism; and the transitional society on the road to the final goal known as socialism and in the short term accompanied by the dictatorship of the proletariat. Corresponding to these stages two general organisational and ideological complexes can be defined: the communist project which dealt with the ultimate ends of the revolution; and the Bolshevik project which concentrated on the short-term exigencies of staying in power and transforming society in preparation for the second phase. The Bolshevik project subordinated some of the basic principles of the communist project to immediate necessities. The leaders of the movement were forced to judge the pace and timing of the transformation and hence the applicability of one or another principle at any time. Socialism in Russia became what the Bolsheviks defined it as, since no one knew what communism would be like, and fewer still had any idea of the features of the transitional period. In this respect Karl Marx's analysis of the state was the crucial legacy to V. I. Lenin. While thoroughly critical of the bourgeois state, Marx retained a high regard for the idea of the state, once shorn of its existing inadequacies. The Bolsheviks were to become among the most effective state-builders in history. The Bolshevik party under Lenin developed as the kernel of the new state in which Marx's rudimentary analysis of socialist political institutions was internalised and then generalised to the new system. The existence of some type of political democracy in the party and the new system was not excluded, and at various times within the party it burst out with exuberance. But democracy, socialist or otherwise, was not the main concern of the movement, and instead it focused on a programme of economic and social measures designed to inaugurate socialist relations.

A few months after coming to power in October 1917 the Bolsheviks were faced with full-scale civil war. From mid-1918 their military response was accompanied by the elaboration of a series of measures that came to be known as war communism, which lasted until March 1921. The debate over the nature of war communism reflects the larger debate over the nature of Soviet power. Was war communism a programme for the introduction of socialism, or was it a means to finesse Russia's alleged backwardness by employing non-capitalist ways of developing the economy? In other words, was the point socialism or 'modernisation'? This dilemma was the practical consequence of the divergence between the communist project, which combined ends and means and where economic goals were the means to serve a vision of human emancipation – from exploitation, inequality and alienation; and the Bolshevik project, which was more limited and concentrated on maintaining power and laying the basis for socialism, and not the building of socialism itself. This divergence is part of the explanation for the apparent contradiction between ideology and pragmatism in the first phase of Soviet power. This tension was the source of the lively debates of the civil war years. While the ultimate objectives of the communist revolution were in broad outline understood, the means of achieving them were less clear-cut. Indeed, the whole initial period of Bolshevik power was a highly unstable compromise between ultimate aims and immediate objectives. This is what gives the years before Stalin's consolidation of power their special interest. The state capitalist period of early 1918 clearly subordinated the politics of socialism to the imperatives of economic development (and regime survival), and was attacked on these grounds by a group of radical Bolsheviks known as the Left Communists. War communism, though accompanied by a radical rhetoric, continued the restructuring of the communist project. War communism was a peculiar amalgam of grandiose Utopian aspirations for the rapid implementation of the communist programme balanced by no less profound concessions to the harsh realities of the time. The economic collapse and the heightened passions aroused by the revolution and the civil war even encouraged the belief that in one fell swoop such 'leftovers' of the old system as money, which was becoming worthless anyway, could be abolished and a natural, or moneyless, economy instituted. But the economic collapse itself forced the implementation of highly unsocialist measures in the factories in order to maintain at least a minimum level of production to supply the Red Army. During war communism the communist project took on a Bolshevik guise as Marxist ideology became Sovietised under the impact of Russian conditions, Leninist organisational practice, and bitter class and civil war.

The bulk of this book analyses the internal organisational and ideological development of the first Leninist regime in power. Of equal importance were the relations between regime and society, whose theoretical background is discussed in chapter one. What was to be the position of civil society under the revolutionary state of the transition period? This was not, as such, discussed by Marx. The Russian revolution was above all concerned with achieving economic and social justice. It succeeded in almost entirely eliminating private commodity production, but at the price of political democracy in the sense understood before 1917. The socialism of the war communist period insisted on the primacy of the economic revolution and was dominated by the idea that once private property was eliminated freedom would somehow inevitably ensue. The October revolution laid the foundations of a new political culture whose features were moulded to fit in with the aims of the economic revolution. The destruction of the capitalist state led to the elimination not only of bourgeois civil society but also of an autonomous civil society in general. Cultural and political autonomy were repudiated together with capitalist economic exploitation. This development can be theoretically traced back to the lapses and lacunae of Marx's rather undeveloped notion of the transition to socialism and his insistence on the priority of the economic and social tasks of the revolution. To this extent we can say that Marxist ideology had a profound effect not only on the course but also on the forms of the Bolshevik revolution.

This book is primarily a study of the city of Moscow during the civil war and will aim to show how the processes described above developed in practice. The city can be seen as a microcosm of the changes that took place in the country at large. Because of its overwhelming importance as the seat of Bolshevik power it was also a crucible in which key processes for the rest of the country were developed. Here were concentrated some of the major industrial resources of Soviet power, the largest concentration of workers, and the biggest communist party organisation. The issues raised by the first chapter will be analysed in the body of the text. We will look at how these factors were played out successively in the economy, labour relations, the party and society, and then appraised by the Bolsheviks themselves in the intense intellectual debate of 1920 and early 1921. The work will consider the development of the centralised Soviet state in its local context. Among the questions considered are the degree to which the war or the attempt to eliminate commodity relations enhanced the powers of the centralised state; the nature of the internal metamorphosis of the Moscow party; the definition of its relationship to society; and the failure of the intra-party reform movements in 1920–21. The basic questions posed are the nature of war communism, how it worked in practice, and the role of the party in the new system.

This book is not a complete history of the city of Moscow during the civil war. Much is omitted or only cursorily mentioned, including cultural life and organisation, non-Bolshevik movements and parties, and society and social life. The emphasis is on political and economic developments, and other aspects are discussed only in so far as they contribute to the main theme of the emergence of a highly complex new power system. It was in this period that the main outlines of the Soviet system of power were established, and it is the belief of this work that detailed study of a single city helps us to understand the processes which determined the forms that this took. On the basis of such an understanding the later developments in the Soviet polity can be better comprehended.

This study is based on my doctoral dissertation entitled 'The Communist Party and War Communism in Moscow, 1918–1921', presented to the Centre for Russian and East European Studies, University of Birmingham, in Spring 1984. If within every fat thesis a thin book is struggling to emerge, then this book once again testifies to the difficulty of slimming! All those associated with the initial work are once again thanked: the Social Science Research Council; the British Council; various librarians in Moscow and Britain and in particular Ms Jenny Brine at the Baykov Library at the University of Birmingham. My special thanks go to Professor R. W. Davies, whose assistance in supervising the dissertation has now been compounded by great patience in overseeing the metamorphosis of a fat thesis into a slightly less fat book.

London   RICHARD SAKWA

There are two types of socialism . . . There is neutral socialism, which organises the nourishment of humanity and of purposeful economic life, which solves the problems of daily bread without pretending to replace heavenly bread with earthly bread. This type of socialism has enormous significance in the life of contemporary humanity and will play a large role in future history, but in the ultimate, religious sense it is neutral; it only clears the ground on which the most various flowers will grow up. This socialism does not pretend to be a dogma, does not try to replace religion; it acts within the social sphere . . . [The second type, the socialism which lays claim to replacing religion] is not the organisation of economic life, the satisfaction of humanity's economic requirements; it is not the shortening of the working day or the increasing of wages. It is an entire dogma, a solution to the question of the meaning of life, the purpose of history. It is the preaching of socialist morality, socialist philosophy, socialist science, and socialist art. It is the subordination of all aspects of life to daily bread.

Nikolai Berdyaev, *Socialism as Religion* (1906), in Martha Bohachevsky-Chemiak and Bernice Glatzer Rosenthal (eds), *A Revolution of the Spirit: Crisis of Value in Russia, 1890–1918* (Newtonsville, MA.: Oriental Research Partners, 1982) pp. 114–15.

1 Introduction

THE COMMUNIST PROJECT AND ITS CRITIQUE

When the Bolsheviks came to power in Russia in October 1917 they knew only the outlines of the society that they wished to build. Although Karl Marx talked of the working class having 'no ideals to realise, but to set free the elements of the new society',[1] he provided a broad outline of what the communist project would entail. These reflected a vision of man and society and of the process of change itself. On coming to power in October 1917 the Bolsheviks debated the options and chose policies within the Marxist framework. Marx's aversion to blueprints of the future society was shared by the Bolsheviks, but the latter, in the heat of a revolution conducted within the framework of Marx's social analysis of capitalist society, were forced to face up to the problem of applying the general principles of Marxism to a country which of all the major European states was perhaps the least prepared economically and politically for the attempt.

In studying the city of Moscow during war communism, the features of Marx's political thought of interest to us are the nature of the transitional period from capitalism to communism and the relationship of state to society. The question here focuses on the ambiguity within Marxist thought between 'smashing' the state or consolidating it, a problem which is central to Lenin's thought and practice in power. Radoslav Selucky summarised the issue thus: Marx's economic model of socialism was highly centralised, the political model highly decentralised.[2] The economic model outlined in the *Communist Manifesto* of 1848 called for state control over finances, communications and the means of production.[3] Marx's ambiguous treatment of the Paris commune of 1871 highlighted the decentralised political model. In effect the state was abolished, or at least transmuted from master to servant of society. Its key features were the use of universal suffrage with representatives recallable at any time, and these representatives were to be paid workmen's wages. The commune was a working rather than a parliamentary body. In Marxist theory the commune represents the highest aspiration towards direct democracy. If 'the state was alienated social power', an 'appalling parasitic growth', then the commune signified the return to the social body of the functions of management previously usurped by the state. It was the political form 'under which to

1

work out the economic emancipation of labour'.[4] But does Marx's analysis of the commune really negate his earlier unabashed statism of the *Communist Manifesto*?

Within the context of Marx's own logic the problem would be considered as falsely posed. His work contained a social and political model, and the basic dichotomy was, as Marx pointed out, the Hegelian separation of state and civil society: man is bifurcated into the *citoyen* (altruistic) and *bourgeois* (egotist). This duality was the 'hallmark of modernity' for Marx,[5] and on it was built his class theory. If in his 1843 critique of G. W. F. Hegel's *Philosophy of Rights*, Marx argued that civil society underlay the state, his view of this *bürgerliche Gesellschaft* soon changed from that of the classical political economists, who saw it as a 'society of free self-interested economic men interacting as equals in the market place', into an arena of the great class division between capital and labour.[6] Civil society for Marx, therefore, was ultimately reducible to economic classes and relationships: 'the anatomy of civil society is to be sought in political economy'.[7] In other words, civil society was defined as 'the product, not the condition, of capitalism and bourgeois development'.[8] In his critique of Hegel 'Marx postulated that civil society was the foundation of the state and economics the foundation of civil society'. It was an 'economic interpretation of politics'[9] in which Marx's ambivalence about the political institutions of capitalist democracy influenced the political characterisation of the socialist project. The two spheres would be integrated in the new society by 'abolishing the difference between the state and civil society'. The state would not 'wither away' as Friedrich Engels put it: it would be transcended through the achievement of a genuine universality incorporating civil society.[10] The key difficulty with Marx's resolution of the relationship between the state and society lay in his definition of civil society. The politics attending such a transcendence and the political institutions that would effect it were left unexplored. By defining politics in economic terms, Marx's view of the commune, and indeed Lenin's approach to the same problem in *The State and Revolution*, retained a statist heart.[11] The commune allegedly took back all the 'forces hitherto absorbed by the State parasite feeding upon, and clogging the free movement of society',[12] but the problem remained of how to reconcile 'the positive abolition of democracy'[13] with the concrete practice of politics or, as A. J. Polan puts it, creating 'the institutions of an emancipated society'.[14]

The resolution of this issue was a crucial part of the debate over paths for the transition to socialism. Put briefly, Marx argued that between capitalism and communism there would be an intervening stage of 'lower communism', conventionally called socialism, in which somewhat different principles were to operate than those relevant to the communist stage. A double set of values was introduced into the communist project whose dissonance provoked the major debates over ideology and organisation in the early years of Soviet power. Marx's reticence about the features of the future communist society is also evident in his brief though vivid description of the intermediate phase. Following the revolution there would be a 'political transition period in which the state can be nothing but the revolutionary dictatorship of the proletariat'.[15] This stage, 'stamped with the birth marks of the old society', is a fairly grim vision of unrestrained political authority marked by relative material scarcity in which all are made employees of the state. The political form of the dictatorship of the proletariat was left open but it contained an irreconcilable contradiction between enhanced state power to suppress capitalist opposition and elements of the commune state, the negation of state power. It was this proletarian state, and not the capitalist one, which was ultimately designed to wither away as it completed its allotted tasks. This approach laid the basis for the class reductionism and economism of the Bolshevik regime. R. C. Tucker argues that Marx was very much a political thinker but with a peculiar slant: 'His vision of the political saw the productive process itself as the prime field of power relations between man and man'.[16] This reduced politics to the struggle of economic and social forces and contained only a perfunctory theory of political institutions.

Critiques of this view focus on the relative autonomy of the state with respect to the productive system, and therefore by implication of civil society. Antonio Gramsci's major achievement was to modify 'The Marxist assumption that the institutions of modern civil society and the class relations of the capitalist mode of production are one and the same . . .'[17] in shifting the ideological elements of civil society away from the economic base into the relatively autonomous sphere of the superstructural realm of authority relations. Within the terms of what Gramsci called the 'historical block' (the combination of the economic system and the associated political and cultural features) a certain decoupling took place between civil society and class relations. In the new 'historical block' established by the Bolshevik regime this division was realised neither theoretically nor practically and an integrated system of power emerged. The abolition of private property in itself did not eliminate the source of exploitation. This system, however, while claiming to be based on class relations, in practice generated a system of power which was largely independent both of its class base and of society as a whole. Analyses of this phenomenon begin with Weberian studies of bureaucracy and, in keeping with the non-capitalist nature of the new regime, encompass systems where capitalist and bourgeois systems of rule do not apply. In this respect Alvin Gouldner argues that Marx himself was aware of the destructive potential of his own analysis of the idea of an oriental mode of production (OMP). The OMP suggested a social dynamic at variance with those which he argued were operative in Western European capitalist societies: one in which power was not derivative of classes based on a mode of production but, on the contrary, classes derived from the activities of the state.[18]

The defining characteristic of the Soviet regime as it emerged from the civil war by 1921 was its overarching statism. The sources of this massive enhancement of state power have long been a matter of debate. Proponents of a continuity in political culture between Tsarism and the Soviet regime, such as G. Konrad and I. Szelenyi, argue that in Russia the prolonged military threat led to the emergence of a militarised state with a bloated central bureaucratic authority which limited the emergence of groups (peasant, noble or merchant) based on property and hence engendered only an eviscerated civil society.[19] The argument put forward in the previous pages suggests that ideological factors were perhaps more important. After the revolution the Marxist regime eliminated the bourgeoisie, the proprietary class however poorly developed, and the state took over the management of production. A new bureaucracy emerged, reminiscent of the OMP, 'which plunges the rest of society into a new and more debilitating dependence'.[20] In consequence, civil society was left profoundly weakened *vis à vis* the state. The development of the socialist state bureaucracy, which according to Gouldner became a new ruling class, was not the result so much of any *a priori* statist intention of Marx but it 'was, nonetheless, in part *structured* by Marx's theoretical commitment'.[21] The abolition of class antagonisms did not lead to the demise of the state. As Jean Cohen put it, 'The crucial step beyond orthodox Marxism is the theorisation of the political/administrative system as a *source* of stratification and power rather than a mere reflection of socio-economic inequalities'.[22] Hence the Soviet regime was a new system of stratification and dominance based on political rather than economic categories.

The mode of production and the power relations of a particular society are not automatically reducible to each other. The tendency to see all 'social organisations as dependent on the mode of production'[23] devalued the role of semi-autonomous social structures. In the absence of a developed theory of politics this engendered a powerful tendency towards *dirigisme* (authoritarianism). The economistic approach to the relationship between the state and civil society suggested that the overcoming of class conflict would result in the necessary elimination of pluralism itself. Under the Bolsheviks, the Marxist 'tendency to view society as if it were a factory run by the state'[24] led almost from the first to the extension of the labour discipline of the factory to the whole of society. The new labour relations undermined cultural and ideological autonomy. In this respect, Neil Harding characterises the Soviet regime as an organic labour state, a variant of the oriental mode of production. The elimination of the 'distinctions between citizen and worker, republic and mode of production' meant that 'the dictatorship of the proletariat proclaimed the end of politics'.[25] Socialism was defined in terms of the logic of production, implicitly in Marx and in practice by Lenin. As Jean Cohen argues, 'Ironically, Marx's attempt to reunify civil society and state and thus, to recreate the conditions of possibility of a lost political praxis, leads to the dissolution of the rich opposition between state and civil society in statism. It is political interaction, not the state, that withers away. As the administrative instance of society, the state now absorbs the logic of production of capitalist society'.[26]

Hegel's concept of the *bürgerliche Gesellschaft*, or civil society, was sensitive to the role of particularities, whereas Marx stressed its negative features as a spawning ground for new types of oppression and class relations.[27] While Hegel sought a system of institutional mediations within civil society to prevent disintegration into the egotistical pursuit of self-interest, Marx rejected this option and developed a model of a civil society irrevocably fragmented into socio-economic classes with a state emanating from these class divisions. As José Casanova puts it: 'Once all institutions of civil society are deemed unacceptable, the solution can be only in some form of reunification of political and social life by abolishing both'.[28] Marx's idea of integral communism had no time for particularities of any sort and entailed not only a 'positive abolition of democracy' but also of politics itself since politics is largely about particularities. Pluralism was considered no more than the reflection of a divided society. Moreover, Marx's derogatory attitude to the institutional framework of liberal democracy had obvious implications for the post-revolutionary settlement. The Bolsheviks were hostages to fortune in the absence of a concept of politics which could give guidance once the proletariat had liberated itself from the power of capital. Would there be freedom irrespective of the political forms that accompanied the emancipation?[29] The destruction of private exploitation (the capitalist system) rendered both the political processes of the bourgeois world and the sphere of civil society superfluous. Society would, as it were, stand naked without the whole body of laws, courts and the bastions of partial interests typical of the bourgeois system. The baby of civil society was thrown out with the bathwater of capitalist exploitation. But what resources would society have to defend itself if the state did not disappear and, indeed, was predicated to increase its power while the dictatorship of the proletariat defeated its class enemies. In this light the period following the Bolsheviks coming to power was nothing other than a sustained assault not only against the capitalist system and the bourgeois state but also against civil society.

The above considerations have clear relevance for an analysis of the establishment of the communist system in Moscow after October 1917. On coming to power the Bolsheviks were faced with the concrete politics of the transitional period but had at their disposal an ideological legacy which contained the seeds of many future problems. There was no blueprint, but there was a mode of discourse which restricted the options. The major debates within the party after coming to power and the issues raised by the coalitionists and the Left Communists, the Democratic Centralists and the Workers' Opposition, indicate that there was no inevitability about the institutional arrangements within the new regime, but of the relations between the regime and society there was less doubt. How could society and sections of the party interact and maintain dialogue with the new state, which claimed to represent the interests of the proletariat, when both the political framework and social structures which could validate such an interaction had been 'positively abolished'? The Trade Union and party debates of 1920 can be seen as partial revolts against the commune idea of the destruction of integrative and mediating social structures in the socialist state. During the civil war the unions, together with the soviets and other mass organisations, were denied the possibility of becoming the kernel of a regenerated civil society within the framework of socialist property relations.

The communist project rejected the piecemeal amelioration of society as untenable and, in the name of universal values and of a universal class, called for the wholesale transformation of society. The political topography of the future society was left vague, but in the meantime the dictatorship of the proletariat entailed the maximisation of state power, while the commune idea posited the destruction of intermediary institutions in society. The project's social features entailed the end of the division of labour and of private property. The individual would be reintegrated into society, classes would disappear, and so ultimately would the state as governance became the administration of things. Under communism civil society would disappear since it was assumed that under capitalism it served as the sphere in which private property was defended. As mystifying and alienated social relations disappeared, so would the need for an autonomous sphere of particularities. The abolition of the bourgeois state would be tantamount to the abolition of civil society. It was this vision of integral communism which was implemented in Moscow during the civil war.

THE DEVELOPMENT OF BOLSHEVISM

The elements of the communist project derived from Marx, but its specific features when applied to Russia came from Lenin. Bolshevism was a development of the Russian revolutionary tradition and its most radical expression. The background to its emergence was the debate over strategies for Russian economic development. While Marx basically accepted, with modification, the Populist argument that Russia could move to socialism on the basis of its communal peasant traditions, the Russian Marxists from the 1880s insisted that Russia would have to take the path of capitalism and only then move on to socialism. The industrial growth of the Russian Empire in the nineteenth century, and in particular during the 'take-off' period of the 1890s, seemed to support the contention that the future lay with the working class and not the peasantry. The railway network centred on Moscow developed rapidly, new heavy industries were developed, and the major local industry of textiles was increasingly mechanised. Moscow's working class had nearly doubled in size since 1879 but still in 1900 the peasant face of the city remained in the unique 'fusion of peasant traditions and industrial development'.[30] Marxist views were further encouraged by the high degree of militancy of the work force as expressed by a rising curve in the number of strikes to 1905, and on the eve of the First World War.[31] Against this background the Russian Social-Democratic Workers' Party was formed in 1898. Soon after, in 1903, at its II Congress, the movement split between a Bolshevik and a Menshevik wing. Lenin dated the existence of Bolshevism as an identifiable current from 1903[32] and this was both an organisational and ideological judgement. The 'social problematic'[33] of Bolshevism itself was as important a factor in the changes Moscow underwent during the civil war as Russia's alleged backwardness or the revolution's battle to survive in isolation. Leninism itself focuses on the level of political practice: it is a theory of politics within the context of the abolition of politics. Five key theoretical positions can be identified which define Bolshevism as a distinctive current.

The first of these was organisation, the issue which divided them from the Mensheviks in 1903 because of an apparently trivial dispute over the qualifications of membership but reflecting profound differences on the role of the party in the socialist movement. Marx himself had little to say about the organisation of revolutionary parties, but the problem was posed as one of the working class 'in itself' (economically crucial and developing its own traditions) becoming aware of its strength as a class 'for itself' (able to claim its due).[34] Lenin's concept of political, rather than cultural, hegemony was reflected in his *What is to be Done?* (1902) in which he established the idea of consciousness coming from outside to the working class. This political leadership was identified with a radically new type of party. Already in this formulation of the role of consciousness the later division between the revolutionary party and the working class was present, and indeed the idea that the bourgeoisie has 'ideology' whereas the working class has 'consciousness'. The refusal or inability of the working class in ordinary circumstances to become a class 'for itself' belies the notion of a hegemonic and politically undifferentiated working class. Instead, the Bolshevik party claimed to represent the ideological 'for itself' aspect of the working class and hence once in power the organisational aspect as well. The possible consequences of the 1903 formulation on committed party membership, as opposed to the looser concept propounded by the Mensheviks, were already drawn by Leon Trotsky and Rosa Luxemburg in 1904–5: the danger of the party and its leadership substituting for the movement as a whole. The Bolshevik project was an attempt to introduce an 'integral politics' combining the economic demands of the workers and the struggle for political power, and this integration took place at the level of the party. As Mihaly Vajda points out, 'The concept of class consciousness and the Bolshevik conception of the party are one and the same'.[35] Bolshevik organisational dominance rested on the belief that their ideology reflected the nature of the world in a process which C. A. Linden has argued equated 'total knowledge with total power' to enable Lenin to produce a 'structure of ideocratic power'.[36]

It was with the concept of the tightly organised conspiratorial organisation that the Bolsheviks came to power in 1917. In practice, of course, the Bolshevik party up to 1918 was by no means as well organised or centralised as its declarations and leadership might have wished. Following the defeat of the 1905 revolution the Bolsheviks used both legal and illegal forms of organisation, but the latter in Moscow was very small with only 150 members in late 1909 and had almost disappeared by 1910.[37] Infiltrated by police spies, the city's Bolshevik organisation was repeatedly destroyed. Attempts to create a city-wide organisation in 1915 were foiled by the Okhrana (Tsarist security police), and when a temporary Moscow committee was formed later in the year all its members were arrested.[38] The organisation was frequently split over such major questions as methods of opposing the First World War, and during the eight months of the Provisional Government in 1917 it was racked by various disagreements over its attitude to coalition with the Mensheviks and to the government itself. Several leading Moscow city Bolsheviks, such as V. P. Nogin and P. G. Smidovich, were initially strongly in favour of some sort of agreement with the Mensheviks.[39]

The second distinguishing feature of the Bolsheviks was their ideas over the nature and time-scale of the transition to socialism in Russia. The Bolsheviks stressed that given the weak development of Russia's bourgeoisie and the strong role of the state in industrial development, the timetable of the revolution could be speeded up. Trotsky, who joined the Bolsheviks in 1917, argued that the pusillanimity of the Russian bourgeoisie would make it unlikely that they would lead a bourgeois revolution. Hence it would have to be made by the working class, the only significant revolutionary force, which could then go on to achieve the proletarian revolution – the theory of the permanent, or uninterrupted, revolution. After the irruption of the working class on to the stage of Russian political history in the revolution of 1905 Lenin developed a similar strategy. The proletariat in Russia, he argued in his 1915 pamphlet *Imperialism, the Highest Stage of Capitalism*, could strike the first blow against capitalism. The socialist revolution could begin in Russia, he insisted, but its success would depend on an alliance with the peasantry in their struggle for land and peace, and on the support of the international proletariat as the revolution spread to the West. The revolution in Russia would be made not by the national bourgeoisie but the proletariat. In other words, the political revolution would precede the social revolution.[40] This was the logic that led to Lenin's April Theses of 1917 which claimed that socialism was on the immediate agenda in Russia, and which so shocked Lev Kamenev and other 'moderate' Bolshevik leaders and forced Nogin and Smidovich to abandon their ideas of coalition with the Mensheviks. As the Mensheviks pointed out, this was a revolution made in too much of a hurry. They argued that the working class needed time to develop both numerically (in itself) and in its ability to engender its own hegemony (for itself). Otherwise others, primarily intellectuals, would rule in the name of the working class and the workers would remain as far from their own class power as ever. The attempt to force the pace of the revolution on 'unprepared soil', as they put it, would inevitably lead to distortions and dictatorship as the revolutionaries would be forced to create their own social base by taking over the role of the capitalists as industrialisers. The Menshevik concept of revolution stressed the more peaceful path of revolutionary change through alliance and the establishment of proletarian hegemony rather than dictatorship.[41] The burden of the Menshevik critique was to be borne out following the Bolsheviks coming to power.

The third key aspect of Bolshevik ideology in power was the separation of socialism and democracy (defined in liberal democratic terms),[42] a corollary of the division between politics and economics in the communist project. The Bolshevik contempt for the liberal idea of negative freedoms was derived from Marx,[43] and this was tied to the nature of the revolutionary process that they envisaged. The affinity between Leninism and the insurrectionary ideas, themselves derived from Auguste Blanqui, of the revolutionary Peter Tkachev has often been noted.[44] As Michael Lowy acerbically notes in discussing Georg Lukács, who in his youthful Hegelian phase saw the Bolsheviks 'as the inheritors of the dreaded Raskolnikov', any morality which talks of service to the revolution as the only morality is 'an infinite trivialisation of the revolution'.[45]

The fourth key aspect of Bolshevism was its emergence as a 'type of anti-state of the working class'.[46] It was, in a sense, a state in exile, and even though it participated in contemporary institutions – the movement to withdraw from Tsarist representative institutions (recall-ism) was defeated – it was not really part of the political processes of the time, and in this sense recallism remained in operation in the ideological sphere. The party's illegal status, especially during the First World War, magnified what were already to some extent innate tendencies within the Bolshevik movement: uncompromising hostility to the autocracy and the institutions of bourgeois democracy. This prolonged recallism meant that the Bolsheviks were in politics, but not of it, before 1917. Once in power, the anti-state proceeded to become the only state. This applied as much to the cultural sphere as to the political. Timothy W. Luke argues that the Bolsheviks attempted to stage a 'modern popular reformation' to create the conditions for socialism and economic development. Bolshevism emerged as a new civil religion based on secular development to replace old work habits and religious prejudices,[47] and represented a radical negation of Russian social traditions.

The fifth main area of policy debate which defined the Bolsheviks was their general appreciation of the state. For Lenin, the First World War saw the consolidation of the imperialist capitalist states in which finance capital predominated over industrial capital. If the state was to break its links with capitalist imperialism, then it would lose its exploitative character. Against this the younger Marxist intellectual Nikolai Bukharin argued that the modern bourgeois industrial state 'was an entirely new socio-political formation caused by the growth of finance capital', which led to the monopoly interpenetration of the state and the economic system to create state capitalism. In other words, the bourgeoisie and the state were merging,[48] and the process had gone the furthest in Germany with its war economy of 'state socialism'. The anarchy of capitalist production had given way to the centralisation and direction of the imperialist state. Both Lenin's and Nikolai Bukharin's concept of imperialism implied that the bourgeois systems themselves were being eroded from within. Hence the ever more transparent contradiction between the capitalist state and the proletariat would inevitably, and soon, lead to the socialist revolution which would take over and utilise the super-centralised industrial organisation of state capitalism, but under the auspices of the socialist political apparatus. The debt of the Bolshevik regime to the German war state was explicitly acknowledged by Lenin during the state capitalist period of March – April 1918.[49] A key aspect of this analysis was the disappearance of powerful intermediary forces between the state and the proletariat. In other words, from the horrors of the First World War a theory emerged which posed a stark choice between the capitalist imperialist state and the proletariat. This explicitly jettisoned something that allegedly had been declining anyway: bourgeois democracy, and with it the concept of civil society. The notion, undermined by Marx, was finally killed off by the theory of imperialism.[50] This was to have major theoretical and practical implications once the Bolsheviks came to power.

Lenin's *State and Revolution* tackled the problem of the state from a different angle. It is often considered to be the most Utopian interpretation of Marx's theory of the state, concerned in particular with the transitional role of the dictatorship of the proletariat. In it he seems to present a vision of a society managing its own affairs on the model of the Paris commune. On examination, however, the work displays the same ambivalence about the role of the state as Marx's own analysis, and contains a highly simplistic notion of administration which collapses the particularities of modern society into the mythical notion of the unity of the people.[51] The basic problem once again is the division between extreme political democracy and economic centralisation. Moreover, as in the war communist vision of society outlined in Nikolai Bukharin's and Evgenii Preobrazhenskii's *ABC of Communism* in 1919, the Communist Party, the most important political institution, is barely given a mention. There is the further problem of the relationship of the commune state to the dictatorship of the proletariat. Was the latter the antithesis of the commune, a development of it, or a different stage of a single process? Engels called the commune the dictatorship of the proletariat,[52] but the two concepts represented different, though not incompatible, perspectives on the transitional period. One stressed the maximisation of state power; the other the extension of participation in direct democracy. Was Lenin justified in identifying the dictatorship of the transitional period with the dictatorship of the proletariat as described by Marx?[53] The dictatorship of the proletariat, according to Marx, would be supported by the vast majority of the population and hence could get its unpleasant tasks over fairly quickly.[54] The problem was, if it was established in a country without the support of a majority, its coercive features would be intensified and last a considerable time. The commune concept was itself host to a variety of contradictions which ultimately reduce to the fact that at one and the same time it was to be both 'a state and a non-state'.[55] The absence of a developed concept of politics in Marx was here compounded by the problem of distinguishing between 'opposition to the transition' (counter-revolution) and 'opposition within the transition' (for example, the various oppositions within the Bolshevik party).[56] The concept of the commune state in Lenin's hands represented not only a challenge to the bourgeois state but also to the existence of a viable civil society. The contradictions within the theory of the commune state and the dictatorship of the proletariat, and the double set of values in the communist project, provoked the debates and established the terrain for contemporary evaluations of the first period of Soviet power.

It is in the context of these necessarily brief considerations on the communist project and the development of Bolshevism that a balance can begin to be drawn between the respective roles of ideology and pragmatism in the practice of Bolshevism in power. This question is considered in the following chapters but the following points should be borne in mind. First, as noted above on page 4, the idea of continuity between the autocracy and the Soviet regime is based on the apparent similarity of patterns of state dominance over society. Such a view would draw a line from Peter the Great to Joseph Stalin. However, the inner dynamics of the two systems are so much at variance, the patterns of authority so different, and the ideological bases of the respective societies so much the antithesis of each other that it would be far-fetched to suggest that they are systemically similar. Second, the Russian legacy was not a constant but changed over time. Marc Raeff argues that within the *ancien régime* since the middle of the nineteenth century a series of multifold 'transformations' had been taking place which are not adequately explained either by the optimistic liberal view that Russia was becoming a more constitutional regime, or by the socialist and radical view that all hopes for evolution were blocked. Instead, he argues, the 'era of the great reforms' inaugurated by Alexander II, followed by the counter-reforms of his successors, saw the emergence of a stasis between the body social and the incapacity of the autocracy and the intellectuals to guide society. The gap between the two led to a petrification which was finally resolved by the smashing of the system.[57] Third, the question of civil society in Tsarist Russia is a two-edged sword. On the one hand, Richard Pipes and others insist on its limited development[58] and hence support the continuity school. On the other hand, while the level of development of the economy and of civil society are highly contentious issues, several recent studies have suggested that Russia on the eve of the 1917 revolutions had generated a powerful civil society.[59] The very ebullience of democracy in 1917 would support this thesis, though the fact that the democracy of that year differed from Western liberal democracy and took a peculiarly Russian form has tended to shield its achievements from Western observers. This leads on to the fourth point: late Tsarism could be said to have suffered from a profound cultural crisis. No adequate way could be found of developing a politics which would effectively express the profound developments in society. The reasons for this failure are as much intellectual as social, and indeed, the source of the failure in part lay with the intellectuals. This, at least, was the view of Nikolai Berdyaev, who argued that they were predisposed 'for communism' by their thirst for social righteousness and equality, the integrated outlook, their sectarianism, and a certain authoritarianism in regard to society.[60] As Theodore Dan puts it, 'Russian democratic thought was never liberal or purely political. A political protest against the autocracy was interwoven with the social protest against the principles of the capitalist economy'.[61] From this point of view the Bolsheviks were the heirs to Russia's revolutionary tradition which by the late nineteenth century, in its socialist guise, had become increasingly prepared to use violence. In this respect Linden argues that Lenin fused the despotic potential within Marxism and the authoritarianism of the Russian political tradition.[62] Fifth, according to Zygmunt Bauman, since the emergence of the Soviet system took place largely in isolation, and was not imposed by a foreign power, the arguments in favour of the role of ideology should be tempered: '. . . the maturation of the socialist utopia into its Soviet form [was] not set in motion nor shaped solely by the logic of the doctrine'.[63] It could be argued that this reasoning leads to quite the opposite conclusion: the fact that the regime developed its policies in isolation permitted their ideological proclivities full reign, tempered only by the force of domestic circumstances. And sixth, the radical nature of the break in October 1917 should not be underestimated. The reasoning which minimises the role of ideology suggests that Russia's peculiar backwardness, with a weakly developed economy and civil society, somehow subverted the ideology and forced the Bolsheviks to adapt to circumstances and in the process were subverted by them. Whatever the previous level of development of civil society, the Bolshevik regime destroyed not only the old state system but also the features of civil society as it had developed not only as part of the bourgeois system but also within the workers' movement and ultimately within the Bolshevik party itself. More than circumstances were responsible for such profound changes. The radical strengthening of the state and its ideology smashed the emerging balance between state and society. The original communist project was refined by the Bolsheviks under the two-fold impact of the Russian revolutionary tradition and the circumstances of the time. The refining, however, repudiated no major principle of the original project but instead gave it form. N. N. Bazhenov called the resulting system 'integral socialism',[64] the fusion of politics and ideology, and it is to the creation of this that we now turn.

BOLSHEVISM COMES TO POWER

The Bolsheviks came to power in Moscow on 2 November 1917 after ten days of sporadic fighting. While the overturn was relatively easy in Petrograd, the seat of the Provisional Government, in Moscow the revolution from the first took the form of civil war. Antonio Gramsci's well-known adage that 'In Russia the State was everything, civil society primordial and gelatinous',[65] has to be modified. The bourgeois state in Moscow did have secondary lines of defence in the ramparts of civil society and they would take several years to destroy. The relatively developed and sophisticated conditions in the city even affected the Bolshevik party itself.

This might well have been the 'first revolution with a programme'[66] for the total transformation of society, but the immediate perspectives were unchartered territory. Marx had been loath to provide a detailed programme for the transitional period, and this disinclination was shared by Lenin. In the debate in July 1917 over the review of the original party programme of 1903, Lenin successfully fought off the challenge, led by Bukharin and the left in the Bolshevik party's Moscow *Oblast* Bureau (MOB), to include a detailed outline of the transitional measures to socialism.[67] Lenin insisted that the party should keep its options open to take into account changing circumstances, whereas the left thought more in terms of ideological principle and wished to see them made binding by enshrining them in the programme. The rapid success of the Bolshevik takeover, however, left all sides equally confused. Once in control of the city the local Bolsheviks such as A. I. Rykov, V. P. Nogin, Nikolai Bukharin, P. G. Smidovich, N. Osinskii, G. I. Lomov and E. N. Ignatov had no idea of what the slogan 'all power to the soviets' was to mean in practice.[68] The absence of a clear-cut short-term programme was reflected in the vacillations of the city party organisation before, during and after the revolution, and in the prolonged debates over coalition that followed the transfer of power. In these debates the Moscow city Bolsheviks usually took a moderate line of compromise as they sought some form of alliance with non-Bolshevik democratic forces. In other words, they attempted to broaden Lenin's concept of hegemony.

Once in power, the Bolsheviks combined Marxist theory, the concepts of party organisation outlined above, and pragmatic responses to the problem of retaining power and implementing the theory in circumstances that daily deteriorated. Nevertheless, the very conditions that had permitted the Bolsheviks to come to power gave them a period in which to consolidate that power. Mihaly Vajda comments that it was the 'backward' Russian conditions themselves which made it possible to experiment with their concept of socialism, entailing the total destruction of bourgeois society,[69] but equal weight should probably be given to the immediate political confusion and the increasingly catastrophic economic conditions. The Bolshevik party itself was riven by various interpretations of the immediate tasks. For convenience, three interlocking models of the policies appropriate for the transition to socialism can be identified between November 1917 and mid-1918: (1) the coalitionists; (2) the Leninists; and (3) the Left Communists. Ultimately a synthesis of these positions emerged in the form of war communism.

Following the revolution the Moscow moderates put up a vigorous rearguard action to maintain elements of coalition in the city. They advocated the so-called 'third path' between extreme Bolshevism and counter-revolution, where moderate Bolsheviks, some internationally-minded Mensheviks (that is, those against the war), and what were to become the Left Socialist-Revolutionaries (LSRs), could unite on a coalition programme for the transition to socialism.[70] The coalition debate raised fundamental issues over the nature of power in the revolutionary state. While few of the moderates took issue with the fundamentals of the Bolshevik project, disagreement arose over the speed and scale of the immediate tasks. Coalition implied the use of some elements of the old state, which in Moscow above all meant the *raion dumas* (district councils) and a flexible attitude towards the Constituent Assembly, a position which did not necessarily imply a long-term role for particularities in the new society. Purely soviet power, as proposed by the Leninists, meant their complete and immediate rejection. The coalitionists' views harked back to an earlier stage of the revolution, when, for example, even the radicals of the Moscow *Oblast* Bureau in their proposals for the political structure of Russia to be incorporated in the new party programme called for a democratic republic with a parliament and made no mention of destroying the bourgeois state at all.[71] Times had changed, however, and the coalitionists' political ideas predated the shift inaugurated by Lenin's *State and Revolution* and its insistence on the need to smash the old state. From the resolution of the coalition debate came the future alignment of war communism: an increasingly powerful Soviet state applying radical measures to defeat its opponents in the field, factory, institution and society, and ultimately within the party itself. The ability of the party leadership to exert party discipline and defeat the coalitionists in Moscow and elsewhere testifies to the effectiveness of party discipline even at this early stage.

The hostility with which the moves were attacked by Lenin, and the rapid termination of any search for a broad coalition (other than with the LSRs) in favour of vigorous class war, stemmed from his fundamental analysis of the epoch of imperialism and the absence in his thought of the need to win over civil society, which in his view was both doomed and unnecessary. Such a policy set the regime on the road to irreconcilable class war and thence civil war. The economic crisis led to intensified pressure from the workers themselves for the state to take over the factories, prompted as much by the desire to secure funding and jobs as by ideological considerations.[72] This social pressure for radical policies needs to be seen within the broader political context. For Lenin, the period coincided with the lower phase of the revolution, the socialist phase of the dictatorship of the proletariat aimed at the expropriation of the landlords and the bourgeoisie,[73] but even he initially thought that the emphasis would be on the commune idea of the self-organisation of the new society, and entertained the idea that the republic of soviets could somehow accommodate the Constituent Assembly. However, once it became clear that the Bolsheviks had failed to obtain a majority in the Assembly elections, his views changed. In Moscow they achieved a majority with 48 per cent of the vote on a turnout of about 777 000, or 66 per cent of the total electorate of about 1 110 000,[74] but nationally the Socialist-Revolutionaries (SRs) maintained their support among the peasantry. On 6 December 1917 Lenin's theses on the Assembly made clear that the bourgeois revolution in Russia was over, and that the path ahead led to socialism. He insisted that a republic of soviets was a higher form of democracy than a bourgeois republic with its Constituent Assembly,[75] and on 6 January 1918 the Assembly was dissolved. In the debate in March 1918 over changing the name of the party to the Russian Communist Party, Lenin insisted that the change would symbolise the commitment to build socialism in the country.

How long this transitional period would last no one could tell. In the debate at the VII Party Congress in March 1918 over the new party programme, Lenin once again fought off the challenge by Bukharin to introduce a detailed analysis of socialism and communism and on the withering away of the state.[76] His understandable reluctance to talk prematurely about the end of the socialist state, however, hindered the emergence of concrete policies against which to measure progress towards the agreed goal. The unwillingness to talk in terms of 'blueprints' and specific commitments to the organisational form of the 'institutions of the emancipated society' gave a free hand to the leadership to define both practical and theoretical programmes. It was a concept of politics which freed the revolutionary process from the control of programmatic statements. The Bolsheviks, in line with the ideas of *State and Revolution*, proceeded to smash the old state and to create the institutions of the proletarian dictatorship. Though Lenin decisively rejected the idea that the bourgeois state could be used, the commune idea of a new and truly democratic state power provided the practical key for Lenin to have a state and not have one at the same time. It was an approach which called for the maximum participation of the working class while providing no institutional restraints on the power of the leadership. The Leninist solution to the immediate problem of political power combined Marxist theory and pragmatism. If *State and Revolution* stressed political participation in the revolutionary state, the economic programme enunciated by Lenin in, for example, his *The Impending Catastrophe and How to Combat It* of mid-September 1917 emphasised the role of the state in economic organisation.[77] The ideology of Bolshevism at that stage coincided with the demands of factory workers for state intervention to maintain economic life. Following the Treaty of Brest–Litovsk of 3 March 1918 the initial 'Red Guard assault against capital' gave way to the economic compromise of the state capitalist 'breathing space' period. Under the control of the socialist state Lenin's plan envisaged certain concessions to capitalism in the form of joint-stock companies and the application of capitalist methods to restore the economy. This stage ended with the beginning of the general nationalisation of industry by the decree of 28 June 1918. Lenin saw the state capitalist compromise as a period in which socialism (the state) and capitalism (industry) would coexist to allow the development of industry. In other words, in practice Lenin effected the division mentioned above between the Marxian economic and political models, between capitalism as a developer of productive forces and the bourgeois system of social relations. Capitalism as a way of developing German-type monopoly industry was acceptable; but the bourgeoise and its political system were not. Hence the period prior to June 1918 saw the consolidation of the socialist regime as the institutions of bourgeois democracy were eliminated, but permitted compromise on the economic level within the terms of the Marxian development model. While there was to be no compromise with the political institutions of the bourgeoisie, Lenin allowed compromise with the economic institutions of capitalism. Lenin attempted a delinkage between the bourgeoisie and capitalism and explicitly stated that the new Bolshevik political state would co-operate with the economic parts of capitalist society. Instead of destroying capitalism while developing the potential of liberal democracy and extending it to the economic sphere, an extraordinary reversal took place as the political liberation of the individual was sacrificed to the attempt to create a modern industrial state.[78]

The contradiction between the economic democracy for workers suggested by the Bolshevik revolution and the actual developments in economic policy during the state capitalist period were pointed out by proponents of the third model of socialism, the Left Communists. Their stronghold was in the Moscow *oblast* party organisation, led by MOB, which already prior to the revolution had urged the rapid seizure of power. After the revolution they called for a revolutionary war rather than accept the economically disastrous, in their view, terms of the Brest–Litovsk peace treaty with Germany in March 1918. In domestic policy their programme urged the rapid development of socialist measures: the immediate nationalisation of industry and the implementation of what they called working-class policies, directed above all against the employment of bourgeois economic specialists. If the coalitionists had been marked by caution and the search for alliances, the Left Communists were stamped with impatience and the insistence on a pure class line. It was this view, stripped of its emphasis on the democratic participation of the working class in political and economic institutions, that came to dominate during war communism. In his *Programme of the Communists* of May 1918 Bukharin had already argued for the maximum development of state power even if the revolution spread to other countries. The state would crush the bourgeoisie, nationalise economic activity, impose strict labour discipline, impose compulsory labour duty, and money would ultimately disappear as relations within the vast state mechanism became simplified.[79] This vision was the classic war communist fusion of the commune idea, the abolition of politics, and the dictatorship of the proletariat. His vision was largely implemented in the next three years and his better known *Economics of the Transition Period* of 1920 only repeated most of these points.

THE POLITICS AND IDEOLOGY OF WAR COMMUNISM

By mid-1918 the state capitalist compromise between economic accommodation and political radicalism was under increasing strain. The Left Communists attacked what they considered the betrayal of working class interests by the capitalists, specialists and the peasantry, but it was the economic, supply and military crisis which acted as the catalyst for the implementation of their calls for a crusade against them. Food shortages in the cities provoked the intensification of class war in the countryside in order to obtain supplies. The Bolshevik response to these problems led to the promotion of radical policies which together came to be known as war communism, lasting from about mid-1918 to March 1921. The genesis of this system and the manner of its implementation at this time are crucial issues in understanding the nature of the Soviet system. The key question revolves around the issue of whether war communism was a conscious attempt to move rapidly into the realm of communism or whether it was largely a response to the requirements of fighting a civil war in twentieth-century conditions. In other words, the problem is how to strike the correct balance between ideology and pragmatism, theory and necessity. A classic Western view stresses that war communism was 'a compound of war emergency and socialist dogmatism'.[80] The problem remains, however, of evaluating how far war communism was a coherent if forced application of traditional socialist precepts, above all aimed at the elimination of commodity production and bourgeois political relations,[81] or how far it was, as Maurice Dobb and the standard Soviet interpretations since the 1930s put it, 'an improvisation in face of economic scarcity and military urgency in conditions of exhausting civil war'.[82] The civil war coincided with massive social, economic and political changes which made up the system of war communism, but the development of policies was as much dependent on such factors as ideological preconceptions, food shortages and economic breakdown as they were on the war itself.

The ensemble of policies that made up war communism are disputed. Lenin stressed the requisitioning of grain from the peasantry, the extreme economic policies of nationalisation and the abolition of commodity exchange. The emphasis on the economic aspect of war communism, however, reinforces the view that the measures were a response to immediate crises and that they were adopted for much the same reasons as the state forged the German war economy between 1914–18: to win the war. But if war communism is seen as a combination of economic and political measures, then the ideological nature of the period emerges more clearly. We will seek to demonstrate that war communism was more than an economic system, whether introduced as a pragmatic response to circumstances or as a dogmatic exercise in socialist fundamentalism. It was a complex system of economic and political relationships which together created a novel social formation. The civil war acted as the catalyst hastening the formation of the new system. War communism was not simply an interruption in the development of the revolution whose progress was continued in early 1921. Many of the features of war communism, such as the limitations on 'bourgeois democracy' and the methods of the assault against capitalism, were already apparent before war communism. While the transition to the New Economic Policy (NEP) from March 1921 saw the dismantling of some aspects of the economic edifice of war communism, the political system associated with it was strengthened. At the same time the economic compromises of the NEP, such as the tax in kind on the peasants, the relaxation of trade, and some small private ownership, lasted about seven years in all and were swept away in the return of war communist-type policies at the end of the 1920s. In this respect the war communism model was an enduring component in the development of the Soviet system. This is not surprising given that the basic problem remained the same over the first years of Soviet power: how to build integral socialism in the absence, as the Mensheviks and others pointed out, of suffient economic resources to sustain that attempt. Hence the tension in this transitional period between the attempt to build socialism and the need to create the preconditions for that attempt. As Lenin put it later, because of the petty bourgeois nature of the country they needed several years to *prepare* for the transition to communism, to be achieved not by enthusiasm directly but through the use of enthusiasm.[83] It is this tension which is sometimes seen as a conflict between ideology and pragmatism. Instead of abundance the regime faced scarcity in the human and material resources available to build their vision of socialism. From this 'organisation of scarcity'[84] flowed extreme economic and political centralisation. War communism was, as Moshe Lewin put it, 'a harsh rationing system'[85] which could not provide adequate material incentives and hence relied on revolutionary enthusiasm reinforced by coercion. We will analyse war communism by looking in turn at the historiography of three related aspects: the civil war; the economic system; and the political system.

The civil war

The appellation 'war communism' only gained currency after the civil war as part of the attempt to ascribe the ultra-radical phase of Bolshevism to the exigencies of the wartime emergency. Lenin himself first used the term in his notes in late March 1921.[86] During the war there was unanimity in the party that the policies being implemented were in accordance with the general principles of Marxism and Bolshevism. Later, once some of the more extreme measures of the period had been repudiated, it was argued that they had been adopted because of the imperatives of war. In this way the policies, and their excesses, could be justified. The idea developed that if there had not been a war then Bolshevism in Russia would have been able to be more accommodating, more democratic. The war was thus seen as the executioner of a more liberal Bolshevism. While the war certainly had a major impact, the above argument is flawed in several respects. In the first place, the war was not some sort of elemental disaster visited upon the Bolshevik regime in Russia, but was both cause and result of Bolshevik policies themselves. This can be seen most clearly in the debate over when the civil war began. A traditional Soviet study argues that the period of the 'triumphal march' of the October revolution should be considered as the first stage of the civil war,[87] and the lull in spring 1918 was simply a 'breathing space' between wars.[88] In late 1917 Bukharin argued that 'the proletarian party well understood the objective inevitability of civil war',[89] and in many respects the Bolshevik programme of power was based on this idea, as Lenin himself admitted in March 1918.[90] Not surprisingly, this evoked a response first seen in the battles on the streets of Moscow in October 1917, then in the prolonged strike of civil servants, teachers and others which lasted until early 1918, and ultimately on the field of battle. It is difficult to establish precisely when the civil war in the cities became transformed into a civil war of armies because, as David Footman puts it: 'The fighting began untidily and haphazardly'.[91] The Bolshevik offensives on the Ukraine and the Don in early 1918 were followed by the German advance of February 1918 which was only halted by the humiliating Bolshevik concessions in the Treaty of Brest–Litovsk. The revolt of the Czechoslovak Legion on 25 May 1918 is often considered to be the beginning of full-scale military activity. There followed a succession of campaigns: Allied landings in Murmansk and elsewhere from June 1918; Admiral Kolchak's advance in Siberia up to April 1919, and his defeat by July of that year; the three-pronged offensive from the south in July 1919 launched by General A. I. Denikin and the Volunteer Army which came to within 250 miles of Moscow in October, but which was repulsed in November; a period of near peace in early 1920; a national revolutionary war with Poland from April 1920 which saw the Red Army at the gates of Warsaw in July and the signing of an armistice on 12 October 1920. By the end of 1920 Baron Wrangel's forces in the Crimea and Nestor Makhno's Green Army of peasant anarchists in the Ukraine had been defeated. There remained only the mopping-up operations of the so-called 'small civil war' of peasant uprisings, conspiracies, and urban anti-Bolshevik disturbances which continued into 1921. In all this, as Lenin put it in December 1919, the war was a 'continuation of revolutionary policies'.[92]

At the same time, two points about the war should be stressed. First, the relatively limited scale of foreign intervention. While at one stage or another fourteen countries were involved, the actual numbers and resources committed to the war against Bolshevism were fairly small. Evan Mawdsley comments that 'Allied commitments to Russia were tiny and confined to distant outlands'.[93] It was largely a real 'civil' war. Second, the problem of when the civil war began reflects the nature of the war as largely a series of separate campaigns which only with hindsight appear as a series of battles in a larger 'civil war'. The ease of the Bolshevik victory in October 1917 was belied by the delayed resistance to their rule breaking out in sporadic revolts. But this resistance was not co-ordinated from a single White headquarters comparable to the Bol-shevik's integrated military command structure, and neither did they have a unified coherent social or political programme around which the anti-Bolshevik forces could rally or attract the mass of the peasants. The sporadic nature of the fighting was mirrored by shifts in Bolshevik internal policy, such as the launching of the red terror in September 1918 and the attempts to restrain it in early 1920.

The problem of when the civil war ended is nearly as complicated as when it began. Confusion surrounding the issue is engendered by the fact that this war was both military and social. The continued assault against Moscow's Menshevik trade unionists into 1921, for example, was as much part of the struggle to establish Bolshevik hegemony as the battles in the field, and this indeed is how it was seen by the Bolshevik leaders themselves at the time.[94] Both in the sense of civil war as social war and as military battles the war had various phases and periods, but it cannot be seen as a steady escalation of conventional warfare culminating in the Bolshevik victories in the field by late 1920. It is even difficult to see the military war as sandwiched within the longer struggle, as Roy Medvedev does,[95] since the military campaigns of one sort or another began on the day of the revolution itself. The events are best seen as a revolutionary war restricted to Russia in which armies in the field fought in conjunction with political and ideological campaigns in the rear. Bolshevik success in the military war was as much assured by their mastery in the political and social struggle as it was by their ability to recreate a centralised military and state machine.

The economic system

The problem of when the civil war began is associated with the question of when the system of war communism began. Naum Jasny, for example, suggests that it lasted from the October revolution to 21 March 1921.[96] There is little doubt when it ended: from March 1921 a series of economic measures were introduced which came to be known as the NEP (New Economic Policy). Such a periodisation weakens the traditional view that war communism began in mid-1918 and suggests that the term 'war communism' itself is not only misleading but tendentious as well. It implies that the system of that time was simply a series of measures designed to win the civil war with which in chronological terms it coincided. War communism was a period of experimentation in the attempt to implement certain maximalist aims on the road to a Utopian conception of the new society. In April–May 1918 there were economic concessions which ended with the beginning of full-scale civil war. On this basis it is argued that war communism was primarily an economic system provoked by the war alone, and that it was a deviation from the programme of 1918. I.A. Gladkov writes:

> War communism was not an economically essential phase in the development of the socialist revolution. It is not an economic policy which corresponds to the economic tasks of the dictatorship of the proletariat, the building of socialism. Therefore, after the liquidation of foreign intervention and the victorious end of the civil war the proletarian dictatorship made the transition from the policy of war communism to the New Economic Policy, whose key points were announced and implemented in early 1918.[97]

This classic view of the civil war interrupting the implementation of Lenin's basically NEPist policies of early 1918 minimises the distinctive features of war communism and relegates them to temporary measures as a function of the war. It should be noted, however, that Stalin himself was not wholly satisfied with the identification of war communism and the civil war on the grounds that the civil war had already begun in October 1917 and was only accompanied by war communism later: 'it is quite possible to imagine civil war without the application of the methods of war communism'.[98] From the first days of Bolshevik power there was only a weak correlation between the extent of 'peace' and the mildness or severity of Bolshevik rule, between the intensity of the war and the intensity of proto-war communist measures. Economic difficulties even without war might well have sufficed to introduce war communism.

Was war communism an aberration or did it flow logically from the ideological armoury of Bolshevism? Considered in ideological terms there was little to distinguish the 'breathing space' (April–May 1918) from the war communism that followed. Roy Medvedev identifies specific policies that anticipated the later period, such as in food supply and state intervention in industry.[99] Laszlo Szamuely points out that Lenin's theoretical conception of the state capitalist period was in harmony with war communist ideology, but differed only in its practical application.[100] As Silvana Malle puts it, 'There were some constants, like centralisation of economic decisions, collective commodity–exchange, and the ability to make use of financial means of control, which preceded the major involvement in war and prepared the way for some later economic developments'.[101] In other words, the breathing space period had little in common with NEP, and to its protagonists war communism was both an ideologically desirable state of affairs and increasingly a necessary practical solution to the mounting problems.

Once launched, the participants in the great drama of war communism were convinced that it represented not a temporary response to military crisis but the direct implementation of communism. Lenin's vigorous defence of war communism at the time was very much based on his view of it as an economic category, above all the suspension of economic relations with the peasantry who were forced to give up their grain as a 'loan' to feed hungry workers and soldiers.[102] Leon Trotsky's major defence of war communism hinged on the fusion of the political and economic in what he called a Labour State.[103] Bukharin became war communism's chief theoretical exponent and in his *The Theory of the Dictatorship of the Proletariat* of 1919 he lauded the powers of the new state, claiming that the theory of a temporary dictatorship of the proletariat 'can be found almost in its entirety in Marx's work' and that its fundamental purpose was as a 'means of *economic* revolution'.[104] Economics and politics were thus merged into one. These arguments were systematised in his *Economics of the Transition Period*, published in May 1920, and provided the most cogent analysis of war communism during its brief existence. In the transition to socialism, he argued, not only the economic readiness of a country should be taken into consideration but also its human and political maturity. In other words, the socialist state, not eschewing coercion against the old order and in its own factories, could create the conditions for the 'building of socialism'.[105] Marx's economic categories were given a thoroughly political significance and a political gnosis was employed in which the state itself creates the new social relations.[106] The work therefore illustrates the 'economistic deviation of Marxism' whereby the social relations of production are subordinated to the development of the productive forces.[107] It was 'a restriction of the category of social relations of production to property relations alone'.[108] Hence nationalised industry could simply be labelled socialist industry. The ownership of productive forces allegedly determined its social essence. War communism took this concept to the absolute extreme. It was an extension of the 'capture' idea of the state[109] to employ the socialist economic and state infrastructure for new purposes without fundamentally altering social relations. On the basis of the circumstances at the time Bukharin, and with him Trotsky, developed a strategy based on coercion which provided a model for the later development of industry. Put another way, war communism was not so much a response to exogenous circumstances as a specific programme for the introduction of socialism in which, as Szamuely points out, every one of its features had its own ideological basis.[110]

The circumstances surrounding the dissolution of war communism and the introduction of NEP cast further light on war communism. As Szamuely hints, if Lenin defined NEP as a 'retreat', as a 'concession to the peasantry', and argued that it would 'last long but not forever', then what was the preferred economic model against which to set the retreat if not war communism?[111] In his pamphlet 'The Tax in Kind' (21 April 1921) Lenin argued that war communism had been forced by 'war and ruin' and had only been a 'temporary measure'.[112] This came after widespread disturbances in the country and months of bitter conflict in the party over democracy and the trade unions, and at the X Party Congress a few weeks earlier Lenin had flayed the oppositions. Lenin's position contained the seeds of the opposed interpretations of war communism: as both necessary and perverse.[113] Lenin's analysis at the VII Moscow *guberniya* Party Conference in October 1921 argued that it had been an attempt to achieve socialism by the quickest possible route forced by the 'logic of the struggle', and that it had failed, and this is crucial, because:

> The political situation in spring 1921 showed us that on a range of economic questions we had to retreat to a position of state capitalism, to shift from 'storming' to a position of 'siege'.[114]

In other words, the aims of war communism had been correct but the methods employed to achieve them had had to be adjusted when faced with the political, and not so much the economic, crisis of spring 1921.

One of the earliest attempts to rehabilitate war communism from Lenin's critique was made by L. Kritsman. His defensive account of the period emphasised the positive programme aimed at eliminating commodity production on the basis of several main principles: class exclusivity, the labour principle enacted through the obligation to work, the collective principle enshrined in collegiality, and the principle of rationality which was to sweep away the old mystified social relations.[115] While exalting war communism as an expression of the immanent tendencies of the proletarian revolution, which in the period 1918–20 led to the formation of what he called the proletarian-natural economic structure, Kritsman had no illusions about the actual practice of the system. The transformation took place, he argued, on a basis unprepared by capitalist development and using unsuitable materials (petty bourgeois and small capitalist forms) leading to the inevitable deformation of the proletarian–natural economy, such as its split into a legal and illegal part and the growth of bureaucracy. In sum, he argued:

> The period 1918–20, war communism, can be seen not as the transition to socialism but as the organisation of the 'rear', not the organisation of socialism but as the organisation of the war, i.e., a simulated transition to socialism.[116]

Kritsman has therefore been able to transcend the rather sterile debate over the supposed opposition between ideology and expediency in the development of war communism: it was both. The inherent tendencies of the October revolution were revealed by the civil war, which caused the deformation of the proletarian revolution beyond what was economically feasible (as Lenin had recognised during the breathing space period) in order to destroy the internal resources of the counter-revolution. The civil war only accelerated the development of what was implicit in the very act and manner of the Bolsheviks coming to power. His account therefore contains some of Lenin's contradictory evaluations of war communism, but stresses its inner logic.

While recent Soviet historical writing avoids some of the more dogmatic assertions of Stalinist historiography on the random nature of war communism, there remains a tendency to regard it as an aberration coming between the proto-NEP of early 1918 and the NEP itself, and forced by war alone. The question then arises that if this was indeed the case, why then was the opportunity afforded by the breathing space of the first months of 1920, after the victories over Kolchak and Denikin and the onset of the Polish war, not used to relax war communist policies, but instead saw their intensification and the militarisation of labour? E. G. Gimpel'son quite rightly argues that the military situation was still unclear, and that some of the more fantastic notions for the intensification of war communism, such as the expropriation of the *kulaks* raised at the IX Party Congress in March 1920, were rejected.[117] This does not answer the question of why, when strategies for peacetime development were being discussed, no serious attempt was made to review the aptness of war communist policies, for example, in relation to the grain requisitioning policies. Szamuely suggests some of the answers: the economic policies of war communism established a 'momentary correspondence between the earlier theoretical assumptions about socialist economy and the everyday requirements of practice'; and since this economic organisation had proved effective in winning the war then why not apply it to the peaceful construction of socialism; and the victory itself seemed to prove that the theory had been correct.[118] It was to take further economic collapse and worker and peasant insurgency, together with dangerous conflict within the party, before the need for NEP became 'self-evident'. Instead, war communism was intensified at home and attempts were made to link the Russian economy with the relatively advanced German economy by waging a 'revolutionary war' to seize the Polish bridge.[119] As W. H. Chamberlin put it, the closing stages of war communism were marked by an increasing miasma of 'bureaucratic unreality' as ever more grandiose ideas, such as an integrated economic plan, were mooted in ever more miserable circumstances.[120]

The political system

The political crisis of 1920–21 had long been maturing in society and within the party against the excesses of war communism. The new socialist state was of a novel type not only because of the extraordinary powers that accrued to it but also because of the unprecedented role assigned to the communist party. The Bolshevik party in 1917 and early 1918 was not the monolithic, disciplined party of later myth,[121] though in comparison with its rivals it had greater internal discipline and was capable of more effective intervention in the politics of the time. In the first months of power the party as an effective organisation 'withered away', but as a political force it became supreme. The anti-state in waiting before 1917, after the revolution it absorbed the bulk of the country's effective political life. However, the remarkable feature of much contemporary theoretical writing was the almost total absence of serious analyses of the role of the party in the new system. In his works Bukharin barely mentioned the issue: in his view the soviets and the party became merged into a single apparatus of power.[122] The onset of the civil war, however, forced a reappraisal of the role of the communist party in the Soviet State. As part of this process the party's internal organisation was improved and its leading role in the state confirmed. Under the impetus of the transition to war communism the withering away of the party was halted, and in parallel with the radicalisation of the economic revolution a new model party was forged which drew its inspiration partly from the ideology developed by Lenin in the pre-revolutionary period, and partly from the organisational requirements of war communism itself. Robert Service has described this organisational rejuvenation of the party as an 'internal metamorphosis'.[123] But, as in the economic sphere, there was a large degree of continuity between the organisational precepts of the party before war communism and developments during the civil war. The common responses include:

no organisational unity or alliances with other parties or groups without Bolshevik supremacy; Bolshevik fractions owing primary allegiance to the party and not to the organisation in which they worked (soviets, trade unions, and so on); the principle of individual party member allegiance and subordination to the party above all else; hierarchical command structures designated by the term democratic centralism. At the same time in society, just as commodity relations were extirpated during war communism, so were 'islands of separatism' (Alfred Meyer) eliminated and the one-party state established.[124] Zygmunt Bauman argues that 'In the "primary accumulation of authority" period, the Party is set on the annihilation of elites which originated outside the party, and which owe their prestige and influence to a source other than the party'.[125] The Bolshevik party no longer fulfilled the political party's traditional role of mediating between state and society. Instead, it identified itself with the state and left society defenceless against the doubled authority of the party-state. The source of the party's authority was unproblematically identified with, in Trotsky's words, the revolutionary supremacy of the proletariat, and he now denied that any substitution had taken place.[126]

The organisational consolidation of the party once again raises the issue of the role of ideology and pragmatism. Explanations for the metamorphosis have been sought in process internal to the party: its organisational principles as developed by Lenin; its totalistic ideology; or the application of general sociological laws of functional differentiation found in all large bureaucratic organisations in modern industrial societies. E. H. Carr, for example, stresses the applicability of Robert Michels' 'iron law of oligarchy' to the party, exacerbated by the circumstances, but not 'peculiarly Russian or peculiarly Bolshevik'.[127] In contrast Avtorkhanov focuses on the distinctively Bolshevik political and ideological features of the establishment of its dictatorship over the working class and society. This dictatorship was not of the party as a whole, he argues, but of the Central Committee (TsK), then the Politburo and the Secretariat, but above all the group around Lenin and finally of Stalin himself. In short, he describes the technology of power and the development of the central party apparatus.[128] His work has little to say about the social and economic conditions that made possible the development of this power, nor does he analyse the sociology of the party that facilitated the rise to power of this group.

Others have stressed the 'external' factors such as the civil war, the revolution's continued isolation, Russia's bureaucratic and authoritarian heritage in a peasant society, and the ambitious tasks the party set itself in a culturally and economically backward country. In this vein J. R. Adelman argues that:

> The nature of the revolution and the civil war, not Leninist theory and pre-revolutionary experiences, were decisive forces in the creation of the party machine by 1921.[129]

Such an approach raises a series of questions on why, out of various responses, particular policies were adopted at specific times and not others. Ideology, if not always Leninist theory, constantly impinged on the choices made at various points of the civil war. This line also fails to establish a relationship between the economic revolution and the political consolidation. Moreover, as noted, the legacy of the pre-revolutionary regime is ambiguous: by 1917 a complex semi-industrial country had developed which in many respects, in the urban centres such as Moscow in particular, was little more retarded than many Western European countries. The very explosion of a distinctively Russian democracy in 1917 testified to the enormous development of civil society against which the Bolshevik revolution itself had to struggle long to contain. Bolshevik authoritarianism cannot be ascribed simply to the Tsarist legacy or to adverse circumstances.

The fact of considerable opposition to the emergence of an 'internal dictatorship' within the party suggests that certain ideological and organisational options remained open, even though, just as in society, no 'islands of separatism' would be tolerated. There was a general consensus over the principles of party dictatorship for the greater part of the war. But the way in which these principles were applied aroused increasing opposition, and by 1920 the consensus broke down and various groups emerged with alternative organisational precepts. Democratic centralism was extended to the rest of society[130] but at the same time it began to be interpreted increasingly restrictively within the party. Broadly speaking, the oppositions sought to establish ins-titutional safeguards to allow each unit in the Soviet state the exercise of its nominal prerogatives. The debates centred over the extent to which greater scope could be allowed for the working class organised in trade unions or the soviets, for the rank and file party member, and in general the extent to which the dictatorship of the proletariat, in the sense of centralised party and state control, could be relaxed. At issue was the question of whether integral communism would necessarily have to be accompanied by an integral state: whether there was scope for a socialist civil society within the communist project.

Both R. V. Daniels and Leonard Schapiro look at civil war

developments from the perspective of the oppositions. Daniels admits that late 1920 was the high point of 'communist liberalism' in the party, and that the reform movement achieved significant strength and some gains in its attempts to overcome the worst aspects of the centralisation imposed during the war. With Avtorkhanov, he argues that the party leadership and Lenin himself had specific objectives of their own – 'to maintain a firm hold of the party machinery'.[131] A similar view is held by Schapiro, and he recognised the importance of war communism, as distinct from the civil war, as the key to the victory of the party machine:

> Though war communism failed as a system of organising national economy, it helped lay the foundations for the dictatorship of the communist bureaucracy which was designed to replace the old machinery of state.[132]

The linkage between the economic system of war communism and the political developments associated with it must be stressed, but at the same time the dual nature of the revolution as discrete economic and political processes was reflected in the emergence of a powerful economic apparatus not completely integrated into the civilian state system dominated by the party. In this light, E. H. Carr's view that war communism was the 'product of a special emergency, and lacked a sufficiently solid social and economic basis to ensure its full survival'[133] must be modified, because the political system associated with it survived almost in its entirety.

The civil war and developments in the economy and the party have provoked a debate which continues to this day. War communism had a strong ideological component and in many ways represented, to contemporary and later Bolsheviks, a viable pattern of development. If Bukharin gave a practical exposition of war communism, Lukács presented the most cogent version of its extreme Utopianism. The years 1917–23 are seen as the period of 'original communism' peaking during the *belle époque* of the civil war.[134] Lukács' major work, *History and Class Consciousness*, of 1920–22, responded to the period of war communism with the theory of the dialectic of totality, a thoroughgoing vision of man, society and economy which could only change through a revolution of all aspects of social life.[135] Without taking into account this aspect, the inner dynamism of war communism as a period of Bolshevik ideological exaltation is obscured.

From 1921, even while a retreat on the economic front was taking place, the power of the new state was consolidated. As Lenin put it, an army in retreat required much more discipline than an advancing army in order to prevent a rout. War communist ideology was forced to accommodate itself to the perceived sordid realities of the NEP, but it revived to accompany the renewed assault against the peasantry at the end of the 1920s. War communism saw the massive consolidation of state power but there was no Hegelian transcending of capitalism but a direct political assault. The socialist state expanded both as a measure of the ambitious economic tasks it set itself and as a result of the underdeveloped theory of politics in the idea of the dictatorship of the proletariat and the commune state. The civil war encouraged the integration of the theory of the transitional period with the practice of Bolshevik power but there remained several points of tension. Far from the civil war being the exclusive cause of the political and economic system of war communism, it served rather to bring out the latent elements of the communist–Bolshevik project. War communism was a fusion of economic and political practice in which the role of the state was intensified over both the economy and society, but there remained a potential divergence between the political and economic dynamics of the new system which was later exploited by Stalin. The communist project of reintegrating state and society was achieved, but in a way that eliminated the sphere of civil society as it became subsumed into the state.

2 Society and Economy in Moscow

SOCIAL AND OCCUPATIONAL STRUCTURE

Moscow's social and economic structure changed with unprecedented rapidity during the civil war. The privations of war, economic collapse and Bolshevik policies combined to undermine the urban economy and previous social relationships. The population declined and the working class was weakened, but at the same time a centralised and bureaucratically administered economy and society emerged. No longer the capital since Peter the Great had built the new city of St Petersburg on the banks of the Neva in the North as a 'window on the West', Moscow had nevertheless remained the religious and cultural centre of Russia. While St Petersburg became the hub of the Tsarist bureaucracy, Moscow represented a more traditional and insular heritage.[1] Both cities underwent extensive industrialisation in the nineteenth century, but while in Petersburg foreign capital dominated as massive metal plants were built, Moscow saw greater native investment in smaller plants, primarily in the textile industry. Following the emancipation of the serfs in 1861, Moscow's population grew rapidly and nearly tripled in size to reach just over a million in 1897.[2] In the first years of the twentieth century the growth rate of the population was the fastest of any city in the world, and by 1917 it had peaked at over two million (see Table 2.1). In 1913 the city contained 6.5 per cent of Russia's 25 million urban dwellers, who themselves represented only 18 per cent of the empire's total population of 137 million.[3] The urban expansion took place with a minimum of regard for health and safety as factories seized strategic points on the rail or river networks and threw up ramshackle accommodation for their workers.

Industrial expansion attracted migrants to the city and served as the catalyst for urban growth, but industry was not the major employer in Moscow's urban economy. Population growth was not directly related to industrial expansion.[4] The tumultuous development meant that by 1912, 90 per cent of the city's 165 184 industrial workers had been born outside the city.[5] The economic growth was led by the textile industry, employing 36 per cent of workers in 1913, followed by the metal industry.[6] The ability of the municipal authorities to respond to the new

Table 2.1   Demography of Moscow city, 1913–21

(a) In absolute figures

	Average population	No. of births	No. of deaths	Natural change	Migration Net	Migration Percentage
1913	1 694 815	54 649	41 945	12 704	43 019	2.54
1914	1 754 900	54 373	40 741	13 632	46 453	2.65
1915	1 846 200	49 736	44 313	5 425	85 875	4.65
1916	1 940 200	44 402	44 576	− 174	93 826	4.83
1917 (Sept)	1 882 400	36 308	43 924	− 7 616	80 184	4.33
1918	1 684 800	24 900	50 360	− 25 460	− 142 140	8.47
1919	1 415 600	24 564	64 316	− 39 754	− 229 446	16.21
1920	1 120 000	23 929	40 633	− 16 704	− 278 896	24.90
1921	1 176 600	36 111	30 055	6 056	50 544	4.30

(b) Per 1000 population

	Marriages	Divorces	Births	Deaths	Natural change	Deaths per 100 up to 1 yr old
1913	6.0	–	32.2	24.7	7.5	28.5
1914	5.5	–	31.0	23.2	7.8	27.9
1915	4.1	–	26.9	24.0	2.9	30.3
1916	3.9	–	22.9	23.0	− 0.1	34.2
1917	5.4	–	19.6	23.7	− 4.1	35.5
1918	7.5	2.1	14.8	29.9	− 15.1	32.2
1919	17.4	3.4	17.4	45.4	− 28.0	33.0
1920	19.1	3.7	21.4	36.3	− 14.9	23.0
1921	16.9	5.1	30.7	25.5	5.1	24.8

Note: Migration columns are calculations.
Source: Statisticheskii spravochnik g. Moskvy i Moskovskoi gubernii, 1927g (Moscow, 1928) pp. 12–13.

circumstances was increasingly undermined by the Tsarist government as urban autonomy was eroded.[7] The population explosion, the lack of a developed urban infrastructure and the political exclusion of the majority of the population generated powerful social conflicts which when combined with Russia's disastrous and futile participation in the First World War led to the revolutions of 1917. During the civil war from 1918 earlier forms of social conflict gave way to a profound social crisis. The problem became one of survival in the competition for a share of the meagre resources of food, accommodation and fuel. New patterns of privilege and authority emerged which in turn stimulated a new terrain of political struggle and consciousness. By 1920 Moscow's population had fallen below the 1897 level, decreasing by 40 per cent during the civil war alone and by half since the peak of February 1917.[8] Nearly a quarter of the city's population left in the twelve-month period from mid-1919 (Table 2.1 (a)). The decrease was not spread evenly throughout the city, however, but reflected the emerging new social pattern. In the working-class suburbs the population halved, but in the bureaucratic centre there was little change.[9] In an interview with H. G. Wells in late 1920, Lenin was even prepared to consider that the decline of the cities under communism would be allowed to continue[10] – a radical solution to overcoming the division between town and country. The city had grown within the context of the development of capitalism, and the destruction of capitalism was marked by the decline of the city. But the de-urbanisation of the revolutionary period marked the collapse not only of the capitalist economy in particular, welcomed by all Bolsheviks, but of the industrial economy in general, something that they could not countenance as it would have meant the radical adoption of the Populists' peasant-based path to socialism for Russia. The villages took back the population that they had so recently given to the towns and the urban-based Bolshevik party was faced with the erosion of its physical and ideological heartlands.

Table 2.1 (b) shows some of the social effects of the wars. Perhaps the most surprising phenomenon is the astonishing rise in the marriage rate from 1917. The boom was fuelled by the change in the population balance in favour of women, the easier conditions of divorce, the introduction of extremely simple civil marriages, and perhaps the search for family security at a time of cataclysmic change. In just the first half of 1919 there were nearly as many civil marriages (9359) as in the whole of 1917, representing a 250 per cent increase if the population fall is taken into account.[11] At the same time the civil war saw the divorce rate double, but there was a small rise in the birthrate after the steady decline of the First World War. The demobilisation of 1918 and the high marriage rate played their part, but another factor was the campaign waged on health grounds from late 1918 against the enormous number of abortions carried out by Moscow doctors.[12] Abortion itself was legalised only in November 1920. Despite this, the birthrate fell far short of the death rate for every year of the civil war. The lack of food and amenities encouraged large numbers to leave the city, and hunger weakened the resistance of those who remained against disease and cold. The death rate began to rise in 1918 and reached the catastrophic level of 45.4 per 1000 in 1919, but this was still only about half that in the starving and isolated city of St Petersburg.[13] Infants and old people suffered particularly badly, but even workers by late 1919 officially took nearly twice as much sick leave as in 1917.[14] The typhus epidemic which struck the city in late 1918 peaked in March of the following year with nearly 12 000 cases reported, and a further outbreak in late 1919 was particularly virulent. Cholera was widespread due to contaminated water supplies.[15] In 1919 the number of deaths a day in the city averaged 170 compared to 128 in 1918.[16]

The shortage of food was one of the major factors driving people from the cities. Already in early 1918 Moscow was on the verge of starvation and at no time during the civil war did the daily calorie intake even of industrial workers, who received preferential rations, reach the recommended level of 3600.[17] The factory worker's diet was reportedly worse than that of office workers, and both were worse than that of the bourgeoise who could barter, at the peril of life and limb, precious knick-knacks for food in the markets. The periods of the worst food shortages corresponded to the most intense outbreaks of worker disturbances, though the disturbances cannot be entirely laid at the door of the shortages. Despite the decreased population the housing shortages in the city remained acute. The number of apartments in the city fell by nearly a fifth during the civil war[18] as buildings were gutted to provide firewood or consumed by fires ignited through the use of crude stoves and open grates. In the winter of 1919–20 alone, 850 buildings were burnt down.[19] Lack of maintenance rendered many houses uninhabitable, and in addition the burgeoning bureaucratic apparatus devoured living space as buildings were converted into offices, a particularly severe problem since the government's arrival from Petrograd in March 1918. The acute housing crisis at the end of the war was exacerbated by the growing flood of people coming to the city to escape the worsening famine on the Volga.[20] During the civil war Moscow lost some of its homogeneous ethnic character as more Russians than other nationalities fled to the villages and as the social revolution increased national mobility. The city took on a more cosmopolitan flavour with the proportion of national minorities rising from 4.8 per cent in 1912 to 15 per cent of the population in 1920. The lifting of residence restrictions in the Pale of Settlement saw the proportion of Jews rise seven-fold to reach 28 016 by 1920, the largest single minority (2.8 per cent of the population).[21] The wars gradually reduced the sex imbalance in the population caused by the earlier arrival of men to work in the factories. Between 1912 and 1920 over 80 per cent more men than women left the city as the men were called into the armies. Already by mid-1917, for the first time since the

Table 2.2   Sex structure and children in Moscow, 1912–20

| | | Women | | | Women per 1000 men | Children under 10 | per 1000 |
	Men	No.	Percentage	Total		No.	
1912	877 688	740 012	45.74	1 617 700	843	255 969	158
1917 (Sept)	919 728	934 698	50.40	1 854 426	1016	264 065	142
1918 (May)	836 694	877 328	51.13	1 716 022	1046	245 746	143
1920 (Aug)	498 077	529 259	51.51	1 027 336	1063	146 608	143

Source: Stat. spravochnik, p. 24.

beginning of the city's industrialisation, women made up over half the population (see Table 2.2). By 1920 Moscow had slipped to become only the nineteenth largest city in the world, and its reduced population suffered from hunger, disease and cold. And yet against this background a profound social transformation had been taking place.

Russian cities, and Moscow in particular, had a far higher proportion of independent people (that is, earning an income) than other European cities because of the pattern of urban migration. The influx of refugees from the Western provinces during the First World War and the closure of factories in 1917–18 offset the tendency for the working and non-working parts of the population to equalise. The situation changed dramatically during the civil war as the population fell and the remainder were pressed into employment. Between 1918 and 1920 the city lost nearly a third of its working population but over half of its dependent population, indicating that the majority of those who left were not employed, above all unemployed women and children. By 1920 the proportion of the working population had nearly reached pre-war levels (see Table 2.3). The civil war, therefore, returned Moscow to its earlier

Table 2.3   Working population of Moscow city

	Total population	Independent	Dependent	Percentage independent
1912	1 616 415	1 052 263	565 152	65.0
1918	1 716 022	935 098	780 924	54.5
1920	1 027 000	651 118	375 882	63.4

Note: The figure of 935 098 includes 89 003 unemployed: if this number is subtracted the percentage of independent people in 1918 falls to 49.3.
Sources: Vydro, *Naselenie Moskvy*, p. 39; *KM*, col. 167.

stage of economic development with a high proportion in employment.

The October revolution destroyed the old 'pyramid of inequality' as the occupational structure changed. This was most marked at the top and bottom of the scale with a fall of about two-thirds in the number of employers and service workers, including domestic servants. Office workers of one type or another fared well and as a proportion of the population increased from 15 per cent in 1918 to 21 per cent in 1920 (see Table 2.4). The industrial working class fell by 44 per cent from 155 026 in 1918 to 87 091 in 1920, but as a proportion of the working population it represented a decline of only 3.2 per cent to 13.4 per cent and of the total population a fall of only 0.61 per cent to 8.5 per cent.[22] The only

Table 2.4   Occupational structure of Moscow in 1918 and 1920

	1918 No.	1918 per 10 000	1920 No.	1920 per 10 000
A Manual workers				
Agriculture	1 535	18	2 469	38
Smelting	74	1	55	1
Metal	47 694	564	33 407	513
Wood	9 685	115	3 515	85
Paper	2 531	30	721	11
Printing	11 788	139	9 335	143
Textiles	32 266	381	10 992	169
Tailoring	32 182	380	23 329	358
Leather	14 260	169	8 801	135
Food	14 869	176	11 514	177
Chemicals	9 868	117	3 819	59
Glass/porcelain	877	10	391	6
Construction	12 696	150	10 763	165
Railways	11 091	131	18 041	277
Tramways	5 314	63	1 471	23
Water supply	101	1	131	2
Local transport	21 858	258	18 500	284
Power workers	5 686	67	2 185	33
Other workers	71 486	845	43 959	675
Total	305 861	3 615	205 427	3 154
B Non-industrial professions				
Service workers				
Hotels/restaurants	109 677	1 297	41 308	634
Hospital staff	10 837	128	5 520	85
Personal servants	7 964	94	–	–
Total	128 478	1 519	46 826	719

| | *1918* | | *1920* | |
	No.	*per 10 000*	No.	*per 10 000*
Employees				
Admin. + law	14 589	172	10 741	165
Technical staff	15 861	188	14 695	226
C'mce, econ. admin.	43 418	513	25 264	388
Accounts & records	30 980	366	30 733	472
General organisers (*tolkachi*)	50 959	602	58 185	893
Nurses and health	21 844	258	22 557	346
Teachers	27 033	320	16 634	255
Police	21 156	250	15 402	237
Communications	9 260	109	9 140	140
Other employees	23 327	276	20 024	308
Total	258 427	3 054	223 375	3 430
Liberal professions				
Technicians, doctors and senior teachers	577	7	3 402	52
Artists, lawyers	153	2	1 604	25
Religious	4 773	56	1 119	17
Total	5 503	65	6 125	94
Bosses (*khozyaev*)				
With hired labour	32 157	380	713	11
Independent	60 816	719	30 776	473
Total	92 973	1 099	31 489	484
Family helps				
On the land	no information		2 259	35
In industry	–	–	745	11
In commerce	–	–	168	3
Total	–	–	3 172	49
Other professions				
Rentiers	8 067	95	1 769	27
Declassed groups	1 416	17	422	7
Pensioned (state/admin)	10 678	126	35 202	540
Self-employment unknown	1 308	15	10 367	159
Others	33 384	395	87 105	1 337
Total	54 853	648	134 865	2 070
Total employed	846 095	10 000	651 281	10 000
Unemployed	89 003	–	–	–

Source: Statisticheskii ezhegodnik g. Moskvy i Moskovskoi gubernii, issue 2, 1914–25 (Moscow, 1927) pp. 52–3.

major beneficiaries of changes in occupational structure during the civil war, therefore, were office workers. The expansion was stimulated by the transfer of the capital and the growth of bureaucratic regulation. By 1920 every third working person was employed in an office. Over half the new posts were occupied by former factory workers[23] and hence represented a significant drain on the enterprises as their most committed, if not most able, workers left for the offices (see Chapter 6).

While the relative decline of the industrial working class is not all that large, its internal composition changed much more radically. Already during the First World War there was an enormous fluidity in the labour force, with nearly 100 per cent annual turnover between 1914 and 1918 as workers moved away from factories, between factories, and from one industry to another.[24] Moscow was much less successful than Petrograd in shielding its workers from the draft[25] and between 1914 and 1917 the number of industrial workers fell by 40 per cent because of departures for the front.[26] By September 1917 only about 20 per cent of the skilled metal workers were left in the city.[27] Productivity was adversely affected since to a large extent only those unsuitable for military service were left. Although some workers returned during the demobilisation of early 1918, the economic crisis once again reduced their numbers. In Butyrskii *raion*, for example, the number of workers plummeted from 20 000 in October 1917 to 5000 by April 1918.[28] Hence, the decline and 'declassing' of Moscow's proletariat began during the First World War but the process accelerated during the civil war. The supply, military and other demands on manpower above all fell on Moscow's industrial working class. In 1918 a fifth (3703) of all the workers sent to the countryside on supply detachments came from the city, but by 1920 this had risen to three-quarters with 8500 men sent.[29] The serious drain that this represented was noted by Bolshevik leaders such as Grigorii Zinoviev in Petrograd and Rykov, the chairman of the Supreme Economic Council (VSNKh).[30] However, a much more serious source of loss was the military mobilisations. Universal military conscription was introduced on 29 May 1918 and in the first major draft of 21–24 June 1918, 8000 Moscow workers were taken. The pressure steadily increased and in August–September alone there were 9 mobilisations.[31] By late 1918, 100 000 of the city's workers had joined the army, in the first five months of 1919, 55 000, and 49 000 between January and October 1920.[32] Over the whole course of the war the city sent just under 315 000 people to the front, many of whom failed to return. G. N. Mel'nichanskii, the leader of the Moscow trade unions for the greater part of the civil war, later noted that workers sent on supply detachments preferred to stay in the countryside where food was more abundant. Concurrently, many of the remaining workers were drawn into the illegal economy and speculation, the production of lighters and other goods for exchange, all of which had a debilitating effect on industry and class consciousness.[33] The declassing described here refers not only to changes in the size and composition of the working class, but also to changes in its relationship to the industrial economy. New economic and social relationships emerged as industry collapsed, and at the same time Moscow workers re-established their links not only with the countryside but also with the peasant economy.

The haemorrhage of workers intensified the changes in the composition of the working class begun by the First World War. In so far as recruitment took place, the departed workers were replaced by women, the urban petty bourgeoisie and peasants. In 1914, 27.6 per cent of Moscow's workers were women concentrated in certain industries such as textiles, where they made up three-quarters of the workforce. By 1917 over 80 per cent of textile workers were women and they comprised 37.6% of the industrial labour force.[34] Even the traditionally male-dominated metal and print industries saw the proportion of women rise to 20 per cent.[35] As male workers returned from the fronts the proportion of women fell slightly to 35.6 per cent in 1918,[36] but by 1920 it had risen to 42.7 per cent. The wars had, therefore, seen the proportion of women in Moscow's population rise by 5.5 per cent, but in industry it had risen by 15 per cent. By 1920, 52.5 per cent of all women were employed, compared to just over a quarter in 1914.[37] At the same time the introduction of compulsory labour duty absorbed the urban lower middle class into the factories. They ranged from clerks to those formerly employed in professions that no longer existed, such as lawyers, small financiers, and so on. By 1920 about 90 per cent of the workforce in the Bromlei and Guzhon (Serp i Molot) metal plants were peasants, most of whom came from the counties around Moscow.[38] We have noted the increased proportion of office workers in the city, and in the factories a similar process took place. A survey of Moscow's 13 811 food workers in September 1918 found that 18 per cent of them were office staff, and in some plants they nearly equalled the number of workers.[39] In May 1918, 16 657 (11.6 per cent) of the 143 309 people employed in industry were office workers, in June 1919, 18 973 (15.3 per cent) out of 124 183, and in June 1920, 15 474 (15.1 per cent) out of 102 837.[40] In a *raion* such as Rogozhsko-Simonovskii, with 32 metal plants and 12 textile mills, the number of workers from July 1919 fell by nearly a fifth to reach 16 433 by October, but over the same period the number of office workers, concentrated in the metal plants, had nearly doubled to reach 2918.[41] The pervading bureaucratism of the period was a phenomenon which embraced the factories as much as the state apparatus.

The changed size and composition of the workforce, with the induction of women, *déclassé* people and peasants, and the growth of the bureaucracy and the illegal economy, radically altered the political climate in the factories. A resolution of a general meeting of the Guzhon plant as early as 1 August 1918 drew an unfavourable comparison between its revolutionary steadfastness in 1905 and 1917 and the present:

> Then only workers were employed in the plant, but now it is completely different. The best comrades have either died . . . or gone to the front . . . We must turn the comrades away from the speculationist temper that is seizing them.[42]

A year later a report on another general meeting in the same plant noted that the meeting resembled less a workers' meeting than a gathering of 'traders from the Sukharevka' (the largest market in Moscow).[43] By 1920 the authorities had become increasingly alarmed by an emerging subclass of workers who had evaded all measures aimed at integrating them into the Soviet state system, and the literacy campaign of that year was designed not only to achieve an educational improvement but also the political integration of this section of society. Despite the official figures showing that 84.3 per cent of men and 67.9 per cent of women were literate,[44] the campaign revealed a desperate picture with over a quarter of a million people illiterate in March 1920.[45] In the working-class Basmannyi district over a third of the working population was either completely or partially illiterate.[46] Hunger and sickness, depopulation and crime, economic collapse and the growth of bureaucracy, all contributed to the emergence of new social and economic relationships during the civil war. But it was clear that as workers left for the countryside and the fronts the revolutionary enthusiasm of 1917 had given way to a grim struggle for physical survival.

THE WAR COMMUNIST ECONOMY IN MOSCOW

The State Economy

The civil war saw the collapse not only of the urban economy but also of the industrial economy. Moscow was hit particularly hard since it was one of the greatest centres of the Russian economy, with 11.7 per cent of all the enterprises and 11 per cent of all the workers in the Russian republic at the time of the industrial census of 31 August 1918.[47] There were 1190 enterprises covered by the census in the city, and another 1788, mainly textile plants, in the surrounding province where industrialists preferred to locate their enterprises beyond the control of the police, and sanitary and other regulations of the city.[48] During the First World War the working class became increasingly concentrated as the metal, engineering and chemical plants expanded, but still the striking feature of Moscow industry was the absence of such giant works as the Trubochnyi and Putilov plants in Petrograd. Neither was there an overwhelming concentration of workers in a single industry as in Petrograd, where the metal workers made up two-thirds of factory workers.[49] By 1918 a Moscow plant employed on average 154 workers, a third less than in Petrograd.[50] Nevertheless, while Moscow had an abundance of small enterprises, with 942 employing under 500 workers in mid-1918, they contained only 48 per cent of the total industrial working class and over half were employed in the 64 enterprises with over 500 workers.[51] Thus the traditional picture of the Moscow working class as a heavily fragmented group, the bulk of whom were allegedly textile mill hands, should be seen in perspective. But the large plants in Moscow were indeed 'islands in a sea of small and medium enterprises'.[52]

Cut off from the sources of raw materials by hostile armies and railway dislocation, with the problems compounded by general disorganisation and inefficiency, factories were gradually forced to cease production or to close. In particular, the decline in the supply of Donets coal could not be fully compensated by the increased use of the more accessible firewood or the intensified exploitation of coal from the Moscow Basin. By 1919 Moscow's consumption of energy had fallen to a third of the 1914 level (see Table 2.5). By late 1920 the number of industrial enterprises of all sorts had plummeted from 9000 before the war to 2560.[53] While the number of census (or larger) enterprises only fell by a tenth, over two-fifths of the industrial workers disappeared, with the greatest decline in the textile industry, followed by the chemical and food industries (see Table 2.6).[54] By 1920 average concentration had fallen to 82 workers per plant. By June 1920 nearly two-fifths of Moscow's enterprises were idle (see Table 2.6), and those still active were working at an average of 45–60 per cent of capacity.[55] The giant Danilovskii textile mill, for example, had largely ceased production by March 1919 and its 8000 workers had been transferred to cleaning and maintenance work.[56] The output of Moscow industry in 1918 was only half that of 1917, and during the civil war the precipitous decline

Table 2.5 The energy crisis in Moscow, 1913–20

	Donets coal	Moscow coal	Oil	Peat	Firewood
A	*Fuel supply to Moscow (incl. railways, in 1000 poods)*				
1913	54 336	150	22 732	4 442	84 380
1914	57 439	350	25 361	5 257	90 611
1915	31 500	1 000	22 000	2 800	96 048
1916	27 700	3 000	22 800	4 900	106 811
1917	23 400	5 700	23 200	4 800	122 564
1918	6 200	2 451	12 000	2 295	84 000
1919	1 500	2 750	4 000	1 180	94 000
1920	2 500	4 000	6 736	1 451	127 000

B	*Fuel energy consumption in Moscow (incl. railways, in 1000 poods; Donets coal equivalent taken at 7000 cal/kg; percentages in brackets)*				
1913	54 300(42.5)	100(–)	34 000(27.0)	2 100(1.5)	37 000(29.0)
1914	57 400(44.5)	200(–)	38 000(27.5)	2 500(2.0)	40 000(29.0)
1915	31 000(29.0)	600(0.5)	33 000(30.5)	1 300(1.0)	42 500(39.0)
1916	27 700(24.0)	1 800(2.0)	34 000(30.0)	2 300(2.0)	47 000(42.0)
1917	23 400(20.0)	3 400(3.0)	35 000(29.5)	2 300(2.0)	54 000(45.5)
1918	6 200(9.6)	1 100(2.4)	18 000(27.8)	1 000(1.5)	38 000(58.7)
1919	1 500(0.3)	1 240(3.0)	6 000(11.6)	550(1.0)	43 000(84.1)
1920	2 500(3.5)	1 800(2.9)	10 000(13.9)	670(0.9)	58 000(78.8)

Source: Byulleten' MSNKh, 9, 15 June 1921. p.9.

continued. By 1920 the production value of Moscow industry was only 15 per cent of the 1913 level (see Table 2.7), 2 per cent higher than the average for the rest of the country. Isolated from cotton-producing areas, the textile industry was hit the hardest (see Tables 2.6 and 2.7), and by October 1920 only ninety of the 253 small and medium mills administered by the local authorities were functioning.[57] The mills in the city were in slightly better shape than those in the rest of the country, with output at 7.4 per cent of the 1913 level (see Table 2.7) compared to 4 per cent nationally.[58] The metal industry was only producing 15 per cent of the 1913 level in 1920 (see Table 2.7), but the national average was only 3–4 per cent.[59] Production in the Guzhon plant had fallen by 98 per cent since 1913 with some 24 per cent of the workforce (see Table 2.8). The Guzhon plant was at the trough of its fortunes in the autumn of 1920 when it had 680 workers on its lists, though in practice only half that number were actually working.[60] In other plants the story was the same. The 700 workers in the Bromlei plant in October 1919 represented less than a third of the number employed three years previously.[61]

Table 2.6 Moscow industry in 1918 and 1920

| | 31 August 1918 | | | | 1 June 1920 | | | | | |
| | Enterprises | | Employed | | Enterprises | | | Employed | | |
	No.	Percentage	No.	Percentage	No.	Percentage	Percentage fall compared to 1918	No.	Percentage	Percentage fall compared to 1918
Metal	239	20.1	23 285	15.1	222	20.9	7.1	20 241	23.2	13.1
Textiles	182	15.3	40 372	26.0	177	16.6	2.8	14 178	16.2	64.9
Clothing	157	13.2	15 514	10.0	137	12.9	12.7	14 042	16.1	9.5
Food	130	10.9	16 944	10.9	111	10.4	14.6	12 949	14.8	23.6
Printing	145	12.2	12 987	7.8	123	11.6	15.2	10 675	12.2	11.7
Chemical	119	10.0	14 922	9.6	114	10.7	4.2	6 912	7.9	53.7
Others	218	18.3	31 908	20.6	179	16.9	17.9	8 366	9.6	73.8
Total	1 190	100	155 032	100	1 063	100	10.7	87 363	100	43.7
Total Working enterprises	951	75.9	142 853[a]	92.1	657	61.8	30.9	79 033	90.5	44.7
Of which Fully	409	34.4								
Partly	542	45.5								
Enterprises idle	239	20.1	12,179[a]	7.9	406	38.2		8 330	9.5	

[a] Figures from K. Leites, *Recent Economic Developments in Russia* (Oxford, 1922) p. 148.

Source: *KM*, cols. 177, 179.

Table 2.7 Value of gross production for 1913–21 (in 1000s gold rubles at average prices for 1913)[a]

	1913	1916	1917	1918	1919	1920	1921
Minerals	18 784	9 894	6 689	2 279	1 087	459	2 973
	3 555	2 395	1 519	238	73	61	238
Metal	115 898	256 431	178 675	56 266	19 132	11 960	14 502
	57 982	171 485	124 090	35 121	13 723	8 722	9 292
Wood	5 457	3 885	2 902	1 683	1 808	1 021	1 293
	5 047	3 615	2 688	1 529	1 655	882	891
Chemicals	100 954	152 531	134 723	80 301	39 407	11 569	12 881
	93 558	131 399	115 506	70 306	37 463	10 755	12 682
Food	188 141	140 533	92 094	55 968	33 145	32 894	41 951
	187 619	140 080	91 953	55 840	33 008	32 595	41 534
Leather	14 375	19 928	13 184	6 433	4 977	3 149	4 490
	12 921	16 872	10 267	3 696	3 808	2 449	3 631
Textiles	563 599	467 302	319 642	214 507	113 138	61 359	58 023
	143 208	115 921	76 264	49 855	21 638	10 621	18 473
Clothes/	18 353	43 314	44 026	21 512	16 913	14 782	15 307
toiletry	17 802	41 259	42 169	20 418	16 567	14 284	14 559
Printing	24 962	21 714	22 130	16 574	7 684	2 864	3 790
trades	23 614	20 471	20 727	15 491	7 281	2 723	3 712
Applied	2 739	2 495	2 129	1 549	964	1 034	1 104
art/science	2 446	2 117	2 069	1 417	781	865	964
Power/	14 380	27 872	26 512	14 207	2 396	3 096	9 701
water	8 990	10 508	8 935	4 825	1 833	1 726	5 610
Total (city and *guber-niya*)	1 067 642	1 145 899	842 706	471 279	240 651	144 187	166 015
Total (city)	556 742	656 122	496 207	258 736	137 830	85 683	111 586

[a] Upper sets of figures city and *guberniya*; lower sets city alone.

Source: Stat. ezhegodnik, p. 172.

It was against this stark and inhospitable background of industrial and social decline that the attempt was made to introduce the elements of the socialist economy in the city. Even before the 28 June 1918 decree nationalising industry, certain state economic regulatory bodies had been created. In overall control, the Supreme Economic Council (VSNKh) was formed in December 1917, and its local counterpart was the Moscow *Raion* Economic Committee (MREK), also formed in December 1917, though some earlier versions had existed. In tune with Moscow's more conciliatory attitude, MREK contained not only Mensheviks but also representatives from capitalist industry. Gradually, as Bolshevik power was consolidated and the time for

Table 2.8 The Guzhon (Serp i Molot) plant, 1913–21

| | Output | | | | Average cost per tonne | | Productivity per worker | | | | | Tonnes of conv'l fuel equiv. per tonne output |
| | Weight | | Value | | | | Average no. of workers | By weight | | By value | | |
	Tonnes 1913–14	Percentage of 1913–14	Pre-war rubles	Percentage of 1913–14	rubles	Percentage of 1913–14		Tonnes	Percentage of 1913–14	rubles	Percentage of 1913–14	1913–14
1913–14	79 237	100	12 933 000	100	163	100	3 683	21.0	100	3 506	100	0.77
1916–17	31 921	40.3	6 021 100	46.6	189	115.9	3 153	10.0	47.5	1 910	54.4	1.51
1917–18	21 539	27.2	4 407 600	34.1	205	125.8	2 685	8.0	38.1	1 643	46.8	1.05
1919	3 965	5.0	863 600	5.3	172	105.5	1 611	2.5	11.9	424	12.0	1.62
1920	1 629	2.0	245 700	2.0	151	92.6	875	2.0	9.5	281	8.0	1.83
1921	3 229	4.0	497 000	3.8	154	94.5	1 104	3.0	14.3	460	12.8	2.79

Source: TsGAOR, 7952/3/210/37.

economic compromises passed, such a coalition body became less viable, and at the II *Oblast* Economic Conference (20–25 May 1918) a Moscow *Oblast* Council of the Economy (MOSNKh) was formed. The majority of its leaders came from a trade union background, including Ya. E. Rudzutak (its first chairman) and S. Al'perovich, who headed it from July 1918.[62] It appears that the Left Communists dominated the work of the council up to the autumn of 1918.[63] The nationalisation decree of 28 June 1918 put an end to the state capitalist period where the old managements were under the supervision of workers' control committees, and national accounting and control through these economic bodies took its place. But even before the decree many Moscow enterprises had already been sequestered or nationalised in response to internal necessities and usually initiated by the workers themselves in a desperate attempt to keep the factories working. The exact number of these is not clear, but the usual figure of 200 is exaggerated.[64] Recent calculations show that by June 1918, twenty-three enterprises in the city were directly under control of MOSNKh and another fourteen under some form of state supervision, a total of thirty-seven of the largest enterprises.[65] Other enterprises were under their previous managements supervised by control commissions elected by the factory committees. The June decree officially nationalised all Moscow's large and much of its medium industry. The status of many hitherto sequestered enterprises began to be regularised and those which had been formally nationalised were now taken over by the economic bodies. The process was a gradual one, however. The Til'mans Screw Plant, for example, had been sequestered as early as 1915 and transferred to the Main Artillery Board,[66] and then to MREK with the sequestration order still in force. It was only formally nationalised in late 1918, however, and MOSNKh appointed a new board to replace the one installed by MREK in March of that year. Worker and trade union representation on the board was now formalised.[67] Full nationalisation was particularly slow in the heterogeneous textile industry. A general textile body was formed under MOSNKh in summer 1918 under Rudzutak, and by November 1918 forty of the largest mills had been surveyed, but only eighteen nationalised, including the Trekhgornaya and Danilovskii enterprises. A number of smaller mills were amalgamated and nationalised, but the final nationalisation of Moscow's textile industry was only completed in the summer of 1919.[68] Over 600 city enterprises had been taken over by the state by the end of 1918.[69]

It was easier to nationalise the plants, however, than to find an effective way of running them. The nationalisation process signified the end of co-operation with capitalists and therefore complemented the struggle being waged on the field of battle, but, as Rykov, the chairman of VSNKh, pointed out at the II Congress of Economic Councils (19–27 December 1918), the major task of organising industry still remained.[70] The nationalisation process was both an element in the struggle against capitalism and an essential component of the original Marxist idea of the concentration of all economic resources in the hands of the state. As Lenin vividly put it at the congress: 'the whole economy of the country [must] be held in one fist'.[71] The congress laid the foundations for further economic centralisation under VSNKh and its *glavki* (directorates). The emergence of a powerful economic state came to overshadow not only the trade unions but also the local soviets.

With the great concentration of industry in the Moscow region it was felt by the autumn of 1918 that MOSNKh, covering 15 *gubernii* (provinces), was inadequate to serve the specific needs of the city. Such arguments were bolstered by the general move towards centralisation at the time as part of the battle against *oblastnichestvo* (regionalism), in which the regional tier was abolished in the party, economy and government. In a debate of September 1918 in the Moscow Soviet a representative of MOSNKh argued that it duplicated the work of VSNKh, appointing a board to an enterprise, and a few days later VSNKh appointed another. Above all there was enormous financial confusion.[72] At one stage there were six economic councils (*sovnarkhozy*) covering Moscow, swamping the factory committees, the boards and themselves in paperwork.[73] The session resolved to form a city economic council (MGorSNKh) with the rights of a *guberniya sovnarkhoz*[74] which by December 1918, under the chairmanship of M. F. Vladimirskii, and later P. G. Smidovich, was responsible for 185 enterprises. It had departments covering all the main Moscow industries and sectors such as fuel, with each department headed by a collegium, and the whole council was governed by a plenum under the dual subordination of the Moscow Soviet and VSNKh.[75]

The precise relationship between the local economic councils, the soviets, and the VSNKh and its *glavki* was the source of much confusion during the civil war. Up to early 1919 the soviets were closely involved in economic management and local economic councils, like MGorSNKh, were considered their departments.[76] In line with the policies adopted by the II *Sovnarkhoz* Congress, local soviets were relieved of some of their economic responsibilities, but not without some resistance in the localities. At an extended session of the MGorSNKh plenum on 12 January 1919, there was deadlock over a motion supported by

Smidovich to deprive the Moscow Soviet of joint control over the economic council. Several leading soviet members, including E. N. Ignatov (a member of the soviet's presidium up to October 1918 and still a member of its executive committee), argued that the measure would make a mockery of the slogan 'All Power to the Soviets'.[77] As we shall see, it was at this time that the Democratic Centralists, supported by Ignatov, were condemning the encroachments of the centre in the affairs of local soviets. The 'interference' of local soviets had already provoked the NKVD (Commissariat of Internal Affairs) in November 1918 to warn them against intervening in the affairs of enterprises, and in December 1918 the Council of Defence insisted that they were not to concern themselves with the affairs of the central ministries responsible for nationalised enterprises. When in early 1919 the Moscow Soviet abrogated a VSNKh decision, Sverdlov informed them that they had the right to complain against a central institution, but were 'in no way to contravene its resolutions'. Until the appeal was adjudicated by a central institution the order was to be 'unconditionally obeyed'.[78] In February 1919 VSNKh affirmed that the local *sovnarkhozy* were purely its own executive organs.[79] Even before this the large and medium enterprises had been under the direct control of VSNKh and its ever-increasing number of *glavki*[80] and beyond the jurisdiction of the local soviets.

This move served only to further the separation of the municipal authorities from the direct control of the economy. The local economic council, and not the Moscow Soviet, managed the smaller nationalised enterprises, of which there were 174 by May 1919, with another 714 under its supervision.[81] In June 1920 the city and *guberniya* economic councils were united to form a *guberniya sovnarkhoz* (MSNKh), but it still lacked control over the major plants. Moscow's twelve major metal plants (Guzhon, List Butyrskii and List Sofiiskii, Bromlei, Grachev, Russkaya Mashina (Mikhel'son), Dobrov and Nabgol'ts, Dangauer and Kaizer, and so on) were under the direct control of VSNKh, and now employed a total of 5745 people, 1136 (20 per cent) of whom were office workers, whereas only about eighty of the smaller plants were under the metal department of MSNKh (Moskvamet) and employed less than 5000 in total.[82] On 19 June 1920 the Moscow Soviet's own economic department was abolished following the unification of the city and *guberniya* economic councils.[83] Hence a centralised economic apparatus was created, increasingly unaccountable to the local authorities or democratic control (see Chapter 3 for the trade unions). Resources were concentrated on supplying the war effort.[84] In the summer of 1920 over twenty of Moscow's factories, including Guzhon and Bromlei, were declared *udarnye* (shock-working) and given priority in the distribution of the limited supplies of food, raw materials and fuel. In mid-1920 three-quarters of the output of Moscow's clothing industry went to the front, and a similar proportion of metal output.[85] On 5 November 1920, V. M. Likhachev reported that the majority of Moscow's enterprises were working for *glavki* at the centre and not for local needs.[86] The economy was transformed into a war economy where not only management but also output was separated from local control and local needs. The stress on economic centralisation, prompted by both practical and theoretical considerations, saw the bifurcation of the state into economic and civilian parts.

The nationalisation of small enterprises was not part of the 28 June nationalisation decree nor of the revolutionary programme in general. However, the length of the civil war, the dislocation of the financial system, raw material and supply shortages, the necessity of mobilising small industry to work for the army, the attempt to eliminate the free market, and the ideological motive of extirpating all capitalist and commodity relations, all led to the extension of nationalisation. In August–November 1920 small industrial and commercial interests were expropriated, culminating in the 29 November 1920 decree on the general nationalisation of small concerns, including craft industries.[87] Already by December 1919 MGorSNKh had 'registered' (*na uchet*) 4990 handicraft enterprises[88] and it can be assumed that their 'nationalisation' affected their juridicial status rather more than their actual working practices. Since April 1919 craft supplies and marketing had begun to be integrated into the state economy. No corner of economic life, however small, was to remain independent of the state. But although by late 1920 economic control had been extended to the furthest reaches of Moscow's economic life the problem still remained of how to manage this flood of state property, a problem never resolved during war communism and one which remains on the agenda to this day. This general nationalisation and the abolition of the Moscow Soviet's economic department marked the high point of centralisation and of the war communist offensive against private economic activity.

By November 1920 MSNKh had 1138 enterprises under its control,[89] while the largest plants remained under the direct control of VSNKh. The lack of coherence in the relationships between the various economic bodies was criticised throughout the period. Already in September 1918, Al'perovich complained about the poor organisation of MOSNKh, especially the lack of competent personnel, but above all he criticised the chaotic relations between enterprises, local and higher economic bodies, which he characterised as a form of 'bagmanism' (*meshochnichestvo*, the term used for petty market trading in grain) and marked by excessive petty interference of higher bodies in local affairs, and the lack of initiative from below.[90] By the time of the IX Party Congress in March 1920 attempts were made to instil coherence in the economy by the acceptance of Trotsky's call for a comprehensive national plan. The unlikely event of this succeeding when even partial local plans had come to nothing indicates the excess of faith in ideology over economic reality typical of war communism. The first attempts at planning for individual enterprises in Moscow proved utter failures. In the case of the garment industry in 1920 only about a quarter of the plan was fulfilled, and not only were unpredictable factors such as the supply of fuel and raw materials not taken into consideration, but even basic factors were ignored, leading to wildly optimistic targets.[91] As during the First Five-Year Plan (1928–32) this was not so much planning as using targets as a way of encouraging output. At the II *Guberniya* Soviet Congress (15–17 December 1920) V. M. Likhachev, head of MSNKh and therefore in a position to know, described the economic chaos: the economic apparatus creaked, VSNKh had too many units and it was too large, and no general plan could be drawn up for Moscow because of the enormous number of overlapping *glavki* and economic bodies and because of the friction between VSNKh and MSNKh.[92] The only solution, he suggested, was a massive dose of decentralisation with MSNKh to take over all of Moscow's industry with the exception of some trusts.[93] Such measures had to await the NEP, and in the meantime the 'bureaucratic unreality' noted by Chamberlin reigned supreme.

However, its reign was not unchallenged, and even within the terms of war communism alternatives were sought which could combine the perceived advantages of universally nationalised property with more rational forms of organisation. The economy was centralised and run by a bureaucracy in Moscow, and even the city's own industry was largely beyond the purview of the local soviet and economic council. Nevertheless, war communism was a more sophisticated economic system than the picture outlined above might lead us to believe. Already, for example, in late 1919 the unlimited ascription of central credit to enterprises and MGorSNKh was being replaced by attempts at more precise budget allocations.[94] Also in 1919 some municipalised enterprises were even leased out to private owners and co-operatives.[95] At the height of the nationalisation drive the Moscow Soviet's economic department was revived on 4 November 1920 with Likhachev, also head of MSNKh, as its chairman. Its duties now included the right to supervise MSNKh and the *glavki* in order to 'root out bureaucratism and rationally to organise the labour force'.[96] In other words, the civilian state was to act, within strict limits as shown by the appointment of Likhachev to head it, as a control mechanism over the economic state. Economic management still very much remained in the hands of the economic councils, but even this was challenged. In late 1920 the idea was mooted of forming *guberniya* economic conferences (*gubekoso*) to take on some of the functions of the *glavki*, though the one in Moscow was only formed in mid-1921. The broad outlines of the strategy applied during the NEP, such as cost accounting (*khozraschet*), if not self-financing, elements of decentralisation, and attempts to shake out the bureaucracy, were being tested at the end of the civil war within the framework of war communism. Only later historiography has presented the economic system of the civil war, later called war communism, as an inflexible economic system. War communism was not a fully worked-out 'ideal type' to which reality should approximate, but was seen as a viable and long-term approximation of the system required by a socialist country. War communism was made up of many elements, political, economic and social, but within the terms of universal state ownership the relationships between the elements of the economic system were flexible.

The extension of nationalisation and the growth of the institutions meant that by the end of the civil war the majority of Moscow's population were employees of the state. With the emergence of an 'economic state', as with all state bodies, the economic management bodies expanded into vast bureaucracies. By late 1918 the staff of VSNKh had swelled from its original 300 to 6000,[97] and the staff of MOSNKh had increased from 460 at the end of July 1918[98] to 1200 in MGorSNKh in March 1919, 230 of whom were 'specialists',[99] and 4200 in MSNKh in December 1920. Few of the latter were party members, and those who were, it was reported, rarely attended cell meetings.[100] Of the original 460, only twenty-five had been communists, and of the 383 technical personnel at that time, 180 had previously worked for bourgeois economic bodies.[101] Below the level of the top leadership the economy (like the secret police) largely functioned without direct party interference, and hence one should be wary of using the term 'party-state monolith'. Economic organisation largely had a dynamic of its own, and this was to be reiterated by the limits placed on the party cells in enterprises. The economic state rivalled the civilian state in the localities, but at the same time at the local level even the party was marginalised. Its control was political rather than through the supervision of economic affairs by cells or factions. P. G. Smidovich, chairman of MGorSNKh for most of the period, was at no stage a member of the Moscow party committee, and Likhachev himself only joined as a candidate member in November 1920 (see Table 4.1). The party was responsible for providing an environment in which state industry could function. This 'relative autonomy' of the economy as it emerged during war communism was a vital ingredient in the Soviet system of Bolshevism in power.

The Co-operatives

While the nationalisation of production was a standard socialist demand, the role of distribution co-operatives under the socialist system was less clear. In this section we will restrict ourselves to a brief discussion of their history in Moscow during the civil war to illustrate the relationship between the regime and civil society. The importance of the Russian consumer co-operative movement arose not only from the high degree of its development, especially during the First World War, with 47 000 societies and 11.5 million members in Russia in 1918,[102] but also from its dual character. A distinctive workers' co-operative movement had emerged alongside the general development of independent consumers' societies. By late 1918 the 700 workers' co-operatives had a membership of about 2 million.[103] The Moscow Union of Consumer Societies (renamed Tsentrosoyuz in 1917) acted as an umbrella organisation for hundreds of societies throughout the country. In the city alone the largest society was the Moscow Central Workers' Co-operative (MTsRK), founded in mid-1917,[104] which by mid-1918 had 150 000 shareholders, which with families served about 400 000 people. Its founding articles went beyond retailing but were also designed to meet the educational and political needs of the population.[105] The workers' co-operatives thought of themselves as a 'third form of the workers' movement', together with political parties and trade unions.[106] The Russian workers' co-operative movement stood somewhere between the populist idea of co-operatives as an alternative path to socialism which avoids capitalism, and the Western idea of them as an alternative marketing agency, that is, between idealism and practicality.

Quite apart from any ideological confusion among Bolsheviks after October 1917 as to the role of the co-operatives, their problems were compounded by the fact that the majority were dominated by political opponents, above all the Mensheviks, who since 1905 had actively worked in this legal form of activity while the Bolsheviks had remained sceptical,[107] though had been willing to use them as a refuge during periods of repression. Contrary to the Soviet view,[108] the co-operatives were not immune from Tsarist harassment,[109] and indeed the I All-Russian Congress of Workers' Co-operatives in August 1917, dominated by the Mensheviks, denounced the idea of class peace.[110] The congress, however, insisted that the co-operatives were to maintain party neutrality: in other words, their political commitment to socialism was combined with loyalty to the idea of the 'third form of the workers' movement'. The Bolsheviks had no time for 'neutrality' or middle paths, but their policy on coming to power towards the co-operatives was determined, as Peter Garvi, one of the leading co-operative activists, puts it, 'on the one hand by their theoretical views on cooperation and, on the other, by the necessity of adapting to reality. In this, ideology was often subjected to extremely unceremonious changes of interpretation in order to justify purely utilitarian actions adopted above all to preserve the party dictatorship and to conduct the utopian experiment of planting socialism in a backward country'.[111] This formulation serves also in other areas of Bolshevik policy. Lenin himself during war communism took a dim view of co-operatives, considering them a backward social form imbued with bourgeois cultural values, a 'stall' (*lavochka*),[112] and he dealt with the question not as 'a form of the workers' movement but as an . . . administrative problem'.[113] Why use co-operative mechanisms when under the socialism of war communism the state could perform their functions equally well?

In late December 1917 Lenin's ideas on co-operation were expressed in his draft plan on consumer communes calling for universal compulsory membership in nationalised co-operative organisations.[114] The plan was opposed bitterly by both the national and local workers' co-operatives, especially in Moscow,[115] as extinguishing their voluntary character[116] and the end of the 'third path'. Bolshevik economic policies in general and co-operative policy in particular were denounced at the emergency second congress of the workers' co-operative movement (30 March–1 April 1918), though the door was left open for agreement.[117] A compromise solution was contained in the 11 April 1918 VTsIK decree on co-operatives calling for the concentration of supply in each district to serve the whole population in no more than two co-operatives (national and worker). There was no question of an independent co-operative movement and the central and Moscow authorities ensured close supervision over them. The Moscow Bolshevik committee (MK) sent activists to the workers' co-operative and Goskontrol' audited their accounts.[118] In May 1918 Bukharin still insisted that the Bolshevik programme called for the compulsory association of the entire population in consumer communes.[119] In Moscow, all the workers' co-operatives were merged with MTsRK, whose membership increased from 130 000 in June 1918 to 300 000 after unification in November 1918. National co-operatives were united under the 'Kooperatsiya' society whose membership increased to 230 000.[120]

A heavy blow was dealt to the financial independence of the co-operative movement by the nationalisation of the Moscow Narodnyi Bank on 2 December 1918 in the wake of the German and Austrian revolutions and the intensification of war communist measures at the end of 1918.[121] Many Moscow Bolsheviks, such as Moscow Soviet presidium member K. G. Maksimov, still saw the co-operative movement as 'anti-Soviet',[122] perhaps not surprisingly in view of the large numbers of Mensheviks involved, their ideas on 'neutrality', and the great number of non-communist specialists employed by such bodies as Tsentrosoyuz.[123] Lenin himself considered the April agreement both a political and economic 'compromise'.[124] In late 1918 the policy of supervision over the co-operatives by the local *sovnarkhozy* turned into one of direct control. At the III Congress of Workers' Co-operatives (7–11 December 1918) the Bolsheviks found themselves with a slight majority, allegedly due to electoral malpractice,[125] and therefore gained a majority of places (10 out of 15) on the council of workers' co-operatives.[126] A split was engineered in Tsentrosoyuz, with the Bolsheviks forming Tsentrosektsiya, a huge bureaucratic co-operative apparatus.[127] A decree of 16 March 1919 finally put paid to compromise and the workers' co-operative movement was eliminated as the whole population was now forced to join supply communes.[128] Political opposition was undermined and economic centralisation achieved.[129] In effect, the co-operatives were fused with the soviet supply apparatus.[130] In July 1919 the MPO (the Moscow Supply Society – the word commune had been dropped) was formed out of the unification of the Central Workers' Co-operative and Kooperatsiya with the Moscow Soviet's supply bodies.[131]

The co-operatives, unlike the trade unions, were brought under direct state control. Nevertheless, a certain ambivalence in Bolshevik policy was evident in the compromise of April 1918, and there were further debates about policy towards the co-operatives at the IX Party Congress in 1920.[132] Later, Lenin himself returned to the question in his pamphlet *On Co-operation* (1923) and insisted, contrary to the views of some of his colleagues, that co-operatives had a role to play in the socialist society of NEP. With state power and the economy in Bolshevik hands, he argued, they could be used as a means of educating the masses, above all the peasants. His caveats themselves prevented the co-operatives fulfilling this role as they remained part of the bureaucratic distribution apparatus. Ultimately the NEP, like war communism, had no room for 'third paths'.

Supply and Distribution

The characteristic feature of war communism was the attempt to destroy the market both in production and distribution. The party programme adopted in March 1919 called for the replacement of trade by the 'planned distribution of products organised on the state level'.[133] In a period of war and scarcity the policy had a clear logic, as the German war economy had discovered, but its implementation had major deficiencies. By 1918 the delivery of supplies to Moscow had become very irregular as war and dislocation separated the city from the grain producing regions. The city was already on the verge of starvation in the early months of the year. In response to the crisis what came to be known as the supply dictatorship was imposed on 9 May 1918 whereby the grain monopoly, introduced by the Provisional Government in March 1917, was strengthened, supplies were concentrated in the hands of the state, and peasants were required to give up surpluses. The Moscow Soviet's Executive Committee (EC) was informed on 28 May 1918 that grain arrivals in Moscow had almost ceased, with some of the grain designated for the city diverted to feed the near-starving Petrograd.[134] If up to May 1918 hundreds of Moscow workers had been sent out to the countryside to exchange manufactured goods for food,[135] now a city party conference on 28 May spoke of sending thousands of the best workers on a 'revolutionary crusade' to 'obtain' grain from the producing regions.[136] The problem of grain resources was increasingly seen as a technical one of transporting the available supplies to the cities[137] and not of exchange between town and country. Lenin called these requisitions a 'loan' from the peasantry to the workers.[138]

To this end workers' detachments were formed both to aid the requisitioning programme and to conduct class war in the countryside. Committees of poor peasants (*kombedy*) were formed in early June to intensify the class war against the *kulaks* and served as part of the non-economic methods of extracting the surplus from the countryside typical of war communism. On 4 June 1918 the MK confirmed proposals for the formation of supply detachments under party and trade union control.[139] In fact, while the party insisted on its influence over them, and in its instructions of 11 June the MK called on every *raion* party organisation to donate 5 per cent of its membership,[140] officially they were subordinate to the soviet supply bodies.[141] The 'revolutionary crusade', working with the *kombedy*, often used violence and sometimes turned into simple looting. At the IV Moscow Trade Union and Factory Committee Conference Lenin admitted that the supply detachments 'often stray from the right path and turn into criminals'.[142] Concern over the behaviour of the detachments prompted the 13 August 1918 Sovnarkom decree shifting responsibility for them from the soviets to the trade unions. Nevertheless, the worries were not allayed, and at the 9 September 1918 inter-*raion* party conference, by which time Moscow had sent 1500 people, I. A. Zelenskii urged that the city should cease participating in them.[143] His motion was rejected but the meeting urged that participants should be strictly screened by the unions.[144] In February 1919 the MK formed a special commission to oversee the formation of the units, and in that month alone sent 300 communists on them.[145] By 1920 detachments were being formed less frequently, with less than a third sent out than in 1919.[146]

While the supply detachments supplied some grain, they did not end the shortages. At various times during the civil war the government and the Moscow Soviet were induced to ease the grain monopoly by legalising the so-called *meshochniki* (bagmen), a system whereby people were allowed to bring grain into the city, usually with an upper limit of 1.5 poods (24kg). The case of these *polutorapudniki* (one-and-a-half-poodniks) illustrates the problems besetting the soviet in its attempts to feed the city: on the one hand, the central authorities were loath to legalise the bagmen; and on the other, the enthusiasm of the local party activists considered any relaxation of the supply dictatorship a breach in the bulwarks of socialism. When on 24 August 1918 the soviet for the first time announced the legalisation of the bagmen,[147] the majority of the *raion* party organisations, with the notable exception of Zamoskvore-ch'e, criticised the measure, and their opposition was led by the radical *guberniya* party committee (MGK) meeting in Moscow on 29 August.[148] In September the *polutorapudniki* brought an estimated 4.5 million poods of grain to the city,[149] representing three million journeys if the legal maximum was adhered to, and this led to congestion on the railways. The Moscow Soviet was forced to rescind permission for this activity, and at the X Moscow *Guberniya* Party Conference on 3 November 1918 I. I. Minkov argued that the MGK could take the credit for this.[150]

The government supply monopoly covered not only grain but most other foods, and all non-cooperative trade and eating establishments were under the control of the Moscow Soviet. As in industry, the state was attempting to do too much, and thousands of the municipalised cafés were forced to close. In a debate in the soviet on 21 January 1919, held against the background of near famine in the city, the head of the supply department, K. G. Maksimov, supported the idea of returning some foods to the private sphere. Supporters of a liberalisation in supply policy called for some of the cafés to be reopened, and criticised the bureaucratic organisation of supply. Particular anger was aroused by the incident where a canteen, used by thousands of workers, was closed on the ground of staff shortages even though the workers had offered to run it themselves. Other speakers, however, put their faith in the existing supply policies and called for even more vigorous action against the bagmen. In his summing up, M. F. Vladimirskii, who was chairing the session, admitted that the soviet could do little since supply policy was the responsibility of central government.[151] On this question, as in the economy, Moscow's freedom of action was severely circumscribed, though it appears that the system of pickets (*zagraditel'nye zastavy*) around the city to prevent the illegal importation of food was policed less severely than in Petrograd. Soon after, apparently, bagmanism was once again legalised in an attempt to relieve the shortages.

In June 1919 the government once again summarily terminated legal bagmanism on the ground that railway transport could be used more effectively to transport government supplies. Faced with increasing discontent and intensified shortages, the soviet at the end of the month rejected calls for the re-legalisation of bagmanism (which it could not reintroduce in any case without the centre's permission), but it did relax some of the restrictions on railway travel. The party was mobilised to explain the termination of legal bagmanism as part of the attempt to defuse the tension in the city.[152] By early July 1919 the government itself was unable to issue rations in Moscow. Kamenev reported to the soviet on 12 July 1919 that the masses were 'gripped by a mood of dissatisfaction' and that several factories had gone on strike (see 'Labour protest in Moscow', pp. 93–5).[153] In 1920, bagmanism remained illegal despite the poor harvest and the increased decrepitude of the railways, and by the end of the year there were periods when no grain at all reached the city. The government took responsibility for supplying the population with food and other items, and by 1920 three-quarters of what a worker received came to him or her free.[154] A system of rations had been developed which divided the population into three groups depending on their importance to the state,[155] and a system of nearly 500 municipal canteens (replacing thousands of cafés) had been developed.[156] Despite these measures, the inadequacy of supplies led to the opprobrium of shortages falling squarely on the government, and by early 1921 the hardships provoked a massive confrontation between the workers and the authorities.

The Illegal Economy

Soviet supply policies, as outlined above, with the concentration of scarce resources in the hands of the state, had the double aim of ensuring at least a minimum level of food for the key sectors of the population, and of eliminating commodity exchange. However, in the circumstances of the time such an ambitious attempt could only be planned but not achieved. Already in late 1918, A. Lozovskii admitted 'We are setting ourselves tasks that we cannot achieve'.[157] With the decline in the economy and the inadequacies of the supply mechanism there developed an illegal 'second' economy. An illegal market had already emerged during the First World War, but under war communism it became the only market and supplied a large, though apparently declining, proportion of food. In the first half of 1918 in Moscow, 85 per cent of workers and 77 per cent of the rest of the population used the free market to buy bread; in March–April 1919 the proportions (in both capitals) were 75 per cent and 74 per cent. By 1920 only a quarter of the workers' budget was devoted to the free market and that of the non-worker higher.[158]

The lack of an effective exchange mechanism became ever more marked with the development of war communism. New methods arose to fill the gap, the foremost of which was 'speculation', a word which represented in the economic sphere what 'counter-revolution' meant in the political. As the Menshevik David Dallin put it at the II SNKh Congress:

> Speculation has grown to such an extent as never before . . . You say that it is a small fault of the mechanism. Hurry. Shoot. That is not terrible, we've got used to it. Speculation is the surrogate that you have created for the bourgeoisie.[159]

Bagmanism was only one facet of the free market. Many enterprises requiring goods in short supply entered the free market, that is, into commodity relations, to obtain essential supplies. But the free market was above all the Sukharevka, an enormous, perpetually crowded market square to the north-east of Moscow city centre (now Kolkhoznaya).[160] The name has taken on a meaning which lasts to this day and symbolises the inextirpability of commodity and commodity capitalist relations under socialist economic systems. All goods were sold there, from aristocratic silverware to goods on which a state monopoly had been declared. The socialist economy and coercive apparatus could not eliminate this excrescence of the underground. And they were partially responsible for its existence. The natural economy, that part where goods and services such as food, housing and transport were issued free, increased in importance, and fixed low prices were declared on ever more goods to restrict the commodity economy, and yet money was still being issued by the state, above all in the form of wages, which could hardly be used in the moneyless part of the economy, and so was forced to go outside it, into the illegal economy.[161] The logical step would have been to abolish money altogether and make barter the means of exchange, but the free market itself played an important role in sustaining the population and the socialist economy.

The battle against speculation became a central concern of the authorities in Moscow. A report in late 1919 noted that speculation had reached unprecedented proportions and now encompassed the majority of the population.[162] Another correspondent in July 1920 claimed that there was a vast army of speculators 'sitting openly in the cafés'.[163] The demonology of the capitalist 'NEPman' was born in the guise of the war communist speculator. The campaign for universal labour duty was closely linked to the offensive against the speculator. In April 1920, for example, it was claimed that up to a fifth of the *guberniya's* population lived a 'parasitical existence'.[164] At the same time speculation in the contemporary sense was not restricted to individual initiative but involved co-operatives and state enterprises. A report in mid-1920 admitted that the Sukharevka market thrived despite the elimination of the bagmen, who had previously been held responsible for supplying it.[165] Most of the material sold there now came from Soviet bodies themselves. The development of Rabkrin (workers' inspection) was an attempt to plug the leakage of state goods to the market. Another was the increased role of the Moscow Cheka (MChK, secret police) in policing the economic system in the absence of effective economic mechanisms. The Cheka during the civil war became an important factor in the labour process and in general a key participant in the city's political life, and indeed its very name and founding charter stressed this aspect. The MK at its meeting of 11 January 1919, for example, called on the Cheka to establish supervision over 'bourgeois' specialists,[166] and a note from Lenin on 27 January 1920 called on the MChK to provide a 'responsible, experienced party investigator to look into the completely unsatisfactory state of labour duty in Moscow'.[167] By far the largest

effort of the MChK was devoted to the battle against speculation and
job-related offences. The commonest crimes were the theft of ration
coupons and pilfering from supply stores.[168] A decree of 21 October 1919
formed a special commission under the Cheka to fight speculation and
the Sukharevka.[169] Of the 40 000 people arrested in the city between
December 1918 and November 1920, 26 700 (67 per cent) were accused
of speculation (18 000 had been arrested by the Sukharevka department
alone) and fifty-three were shot for this.[170] Over the same period 5250 (13
per cent) were arrested for labour crimes, of whom 102 were shot (forty-
seven for taking bribes and related offences, forty-seven for labour
desertion, and eight for theft).[171] In 1920 alone the MChK arrested about
14 000 'speculators' in raids on the Sukharevka and other markets, 70
per cent of whom, allegedly, had no defined occupation. At a meeting of
the Moscow Soviet EC on 1 October 1920, S.A. Messing, the MChK
chairman, argued that the Cheka's main purpose was the battle against
speculation and 'crises at the workplace' – in other words, strikes and
other forms of worker protest.[172] The attempt to wipe out the market had
a pernicious effect on social relations in that a whole range of activities
was classified as 'speculation'. Political deviancy was similarly classified,
and this provided the milieu in which the party sought to protect itself
from what were seen as dangerous corrupting influences.

The economic debates of 1920 in the party were largely over whether
concessions could be made to the market, and thus to the consumer.
Trotsky at one pole was joined by Rykov, his opponent over militarisation, on this issue, while Lev Kamenev, chairman of the Moscow Soviet
though with many other duties, emerged as the champion of the
consumer in urging the liberalisation of supply policy and allowing some
free trade.[173] At the IX Party Congress he vividly described the slow
death of the capitals. According to him, about 80 per cent of the
economy was conducted by the illegal second economy, and he urged
immediate concessions.[174] Rykov, head of VSNKh and therefore with a
vested interest in maintaining the state-run economy, dismissed Kamenev's arguments as a capitulation to the consumer point of view, and
instead put his faith in the single economic plan to integrate the various
branches of the economy.[175] The consumer interest has never been strong
in the production-orientated Soviet economic system, and indeed Lenin
rejected concessions at the time not only on economic grounds but also
out of political considerations. For Lenin, Kamenev's ideas, if
implemented, signified quite simply the end of Soviet power.[176] It would
take the major political crisis of early 1921 to change Lenin's mind and
introduce the New Economic Policy.

The civil war saw a major demographic and social collapse in Moscow, the dispersal of a large part of its workforce and major changes in the composition of those who remained. War communism saw the attempted reintegration of state and economic society, but the economic apparatus and its bureaucracy escaped from social control or the disciplines of the market place. Industry was run as a single vast state trust in which even the local Moscow authorities had little say. It concentrated on supplying the needs of the army while the Moscow consumer lacked basic goods. The illegal economy expanded to fill the gaps in the official mechanism, but the increasingly narrow definition of legal economic activity enhanced the role of the police apparatus. It was in this context that the labour relations of war communism were developed.

3 Labour and the Socialist State

THE TRADE UNIONS

The extension of state control over industry at a time of economic collapse and war had major repercussions on the organisation and industrial relations of the nationalised sector. The broad sweep of Bolshevik policy in this sphere had already been sketched out in early 1918, with state economic bodies taking precedence over the trade unions, and the trade unions over the factory committees. In other words, the state would organise and manage socialist industry, not the workers themselves, and hence the statism of war communism was an extension of the general policy of the state capitalist period, but now without the capitalists. The labour process and the organisation of production in enterprises were determined by the imperative of max-imising production. Critiques of the pre-revolutionary labour process gave way to enthusiasm for scientific management as expounded by Frederick Taylor. During war communism management was centralised and income inequalities encouraged through various incentive schemes. Given the scarcity of effective material or financial incentives, as war communism developed increased reliance was placed on coercion by state bodies, and the trade unions became increasingly marginalised.

The role of the trade unions in the Soviet state has been analysed by several works[1] so we shall restrict ourselves to some aspects of this controversial question in Moscow. The ambivalent position of the trade unions between the party-state and the working class was reflected in the party's draft programme of February 1919 in which Lenin talked of their dual function: as active participants in economic management; and as bodies for the socialist and labour education of workers.[2] The VIII Party Congress in March 1919 spoke of the ultimate transfer of management to the unions. However, there was little scope for an 'independent' trade union movement, as demanded by the Mensheviks. Al'perovich, the new chairman of the Moscow TUs, gave an unequivocal assessment of their role in 1921 when he argued that their main task during war communism had been to support the Soviet state. This had necessitated the formation of an apparatus based on centralised authority and the creation of massive unions:

With such a backward working class it could not be allowed into the centre of decision-making. Thus centralism, the subordination of the lower to the higher, was necessary.

Unions covering whole industries, he argued, were designed to break down group or professional interests among the workers.[3] With union membership compulsory during the civil war, and the number of individual unions decreasing, they swelled into massive organisations. Yuli Martov argued that 'The compulsory registration of citizens into bureaucratic trade unions [and consumer societies] does not help their organisation but, on the contrary, perpetuates their atomisation'.[4] Mel'nichanskii admitted that:

> During the civil war the boards of the unions became isolated from the masses . . . Objective conditions did not allow the extension of the influence of the trade unions on the masses by becoming close to the workers. Trade union organs and their personnel became a minuscule and inadequately trained contingent. All [TU] workers were constantly mobilised leaving only two or three qualified people in each union. In these circumstances the conduct of general work was concentrated in the chancelleries of the unions, and it was difficult to conduct organisational work in the factories.[5]

The trade unions during war communism underwent the paradoxical process of inflated numerical growth and at the same time the loss of internal authority and a fall in their relative standing in regard to the party and the soviets.

Few unions in Moscow had survived since 1905, but the ground was prepared for a massive expansion in 1917, even though the precise figures for the early period are confused, and complicated by the unclear distinction between the city and its *guberniya*. By October 1917 the fifty-three trade unions in the city and *guberniya* encompassed about 474 000 members,[6] rising to 552 664 in sixty-one unions in mid-1918. During the civil war almost everyone in employment was automatically considered a union member, with the dues collected directly from the accounts department of the enterprise or office. As a result, membership continued to increase despite the falling population. By early 1919 the number of unions had fallen to thirty-two with 639 678 members, and by January 1921 there were 789 950 members in only twenty-two massive unions (see Table 3.1). Clearly, these figures are grossly inflated, even including the *guberniya*, and illustrate the largely formal nature of trade union membership during the war. With the decline in industry the largest growth came from offices rather than factories. Between the I

Table 3.1   Membership of Moscow city and *guberniya* trade unions, 1918–21

Union	Mid-1918[b]	Early 1919[c]	September 1919[d]	August 1920[e]	1 January 1921
Health	41 280	15 730	33 000	50 721	53 608
Water transport			6 100	6 230	5 216
Agriculture		9 195	30 000	13 000	20 000
Railways	25 000	21 866	118 000	118 000	110 837
Wood		3 280	2 800	3 528	5 078
Municipal workers		32 299	34 000	31 298	30 480
Leather workers	26 542	11 292	14 800	15 963	14 184
Metal[a]	48 830	44 820	30 000	50 000	59 745
Public catering		12 699	13 850	15 093	16 780
Communications	7 285	17 000	20 000	17 849	17 881
Printing trades	28 549	14 460	10 000	18 454	18 845
Culture/education	4 860	3 637	10 000	25 765	31 000
Art		3 321	10 000	12 000	15 000
Food processing	4 888	22 022	15 000	15 930	19 119
Soviet workers			79 000	99 461	133 782
Construction	17 747	3 154	10 500	29 000	49 012
Glass/porcelain	1 448	1 100	8 000	15 620	10 089
Tobacco		4 000	3 700	3 003	3 152
Local transport		10 400	17 000	17 348	30 026
Textiles	61 840	145 173	171 600	101 682	88 995
Chemicals	41 712	24 600	25 000	15 664	19 564
Tailors	38 525	19 028	20 000	14 158	33 007
Total	342 328	419 076	682 350	689 763	786 950
Other unions and unknown	213 336	220 602			
Total	552 664	639 678			

[a] Excludes Kolomna.
[b] The figures for the metal union are for 1 out of 2 unions, for print 3 out of 4, and culture/education 3 out of 5. The first total is for 44 unions, the second includes another 17 unions with a membership of 143 336 and about 67 000 in those unions for which information is lacking.
[c] The first total is for 22 unions (2 unions each for agriculture and culture/education), and the print total excludes allied trades. The second total is for 32 unions.
[d] There were 2 unions apiece for health, art, and soviet workers, and 3 for the municipal workers.
[e] Water and railway workers were in one union, as were the chemical, glass and porcelain workers until February 1921.

Sources: 1918: *Statistika truda*, 8–9 (1918) pp. 19–21; Ignat'ev, *Moskva v pervyi god* p. 367. Early 1919: *Dva goda diktatury proletariata*, pp. 16 and 22–3. September 1919: *Obzor deyatel'nosti MGSPS*, p. 74. August 1920: *KM*, col. 680. January 1921: *Obzor deyatel'nosti MGSPS*, p. 69.

and II *Guberniya* Trade Union Conferences (September 1919–September 1920) the proportion of office union delegates rose from 22 per cent to 33 per cent and those from industrial unions fell from 46 per cent to 38 per cent. The changed occupational structure of the city is revealed by the fact that by early 1921 the number of unionised office workers had surpassed the railway and textile workers as the single largest union.

A Central Bureau of Moscow trade unions had been formed in 1905 but in illegal circumstances it had had only an episodic existence until 1917. In February 1917 it was resurrected by F. D. Denisov (the first chairman), E. N. Ignatov and T. V. Sapronov. By November 1917 it included M. Tomskii as chairman, Mel'nichanskii as secretary, and other leading trade unionists. All boards of unions organised on an occupational rather than craft basis sent representatives to what was now called the Moscow Council of Trade Unions (MSPS), and in November 1917 representation was reorganised on the principle of proportionality dependent on the size of the union. The MSPS formed an executive committee (EC) on 3 March 1917, and its powers were extended by the plenum meeting of 1 December 1917 at which thirty-nine TUs were represented, and an EC of fifteen was elected.[8] At its first session on 4 December the EC elected a presidium of five with Mel'nichanskii as chairman.[9] This was to become the key body of the centralised Moscow TU organisation. A new Moscow *Guberniya* TU council (MGSPS), now representing the city and *guberniya*, was elected on 29 September 1919 at the I *Guberniya* TU Conference, and this in turn elected a presidium to conduct current work.[10] The MGSPS plenum consisted of representatives from individual unions proportional to the size of the union. So, for example, after the II *Guberniya* TU Conference in September 1920 the plenum consisted of 118 representatives from the twenty-two unions (plus fourteen delegates from the *uezd*s),[11] with fifteen apiece from the textile and railway unions, ten from the metal union, three from the print workers, and so on.[12] At that time the presidium consisted of nine people, but there was now an even more concentrated inner presidium of three.[13] Every presidium member was responsible for several unions but had no right to change resolutions or decisions of union bodies. The full plenum had to be consulted in cases of disagreement between them,[14] though there is no record of such a conflict in this period being discussed by the full MGSPS plenum. Union affairs were clearly concentrated in the hands of the presidium which on average met twice a week while the plenum met only once a fortnight.[15]

The caucus principle was applied to the trade unions as it was to the soviets. The MK had a representative on the MSPS (Central Bureau)

from its first meeting on 2 March 1917,[16] and on 5 May a party fraction
was formed.[17] Thereafter the TU leadership in Moscow worked closely
with the party committee, and party control was ensured through the
party fraction in the MGSPS and the individual unions where the
Bolsheviks dominated. The relationship was codified by an MK
instruction of 28 August 1919 which insisted that all major TU questions
were to be decided by the MSPS fraction only after initial consultation
with the MK. In a move designed to counter any attempts at Bolshevik
TU fraction autonomy, the instruction stressed that all Bolshevik trade
union activists were subject to the same party discipline as any other
party members. All collegia and boards were to be appointed by the
party organisation, the MSPS was to give monthly reports to the MK
bureau, and there was to be mutual representation between the party
and TU fraction bureaux.[18] These guidelines were confirmed by the
party statute adopted in December 1919 which insisted on the principle
of fraction subordination to party organisations.[19] The detailed supervision over the trade unions was stressed in the party reports of the
period.[20] In particular, at a time of severe manpower shortages, the
party's right to dispose of personnel was extremely important. The
above MK instruction insisted that all union leaders were at its disposal,
but conceded that transfers of personnel should take place with the
knowledge of the TU party fraction. Given the extremely low proportion of communists in the Moscow TU organisation, which in late 1920
stood at 2.4 per cent of total membership, party influence was
organisational rather than through a mass presence, with 6 per cent of
the communist unionists employed by the unions themselves.[21] The high
level of party supervision was in marked contrast to the much greater
autonomy of the economic bodies. This relationship was challenged by
the Workers' Oppositionists in 1920, but the effectiveness of the party's
control over the trade unions meant that in the period of the TU
discussion in late 1920 the MGSPS and its presidium, thoroughly
'bureaucratised' as it was, did not challenge the party leadership as a
group and thus the oppositionists remained isolated.

It would appear that the union movement as a whole (at least in
Moscow) was increasingly on the defensive *vis à vis* party and state
organisations. Alfred Rosmer, who was in Moscow in late 1920,
observed later that the unions 'were like poor relations' with the
available reserves of manpower and supplies going to the party.[22] The
powerful economic *glavki* in particular paid little heed to the unions. The
glavk Tsentrozhir, for instance, provoked a long drawn out conflict with
the MGSPS by unilaterally closing a food plant (Bodlo) without

consultation with any union. The MGSPS riposted that 'any measures affecting workers and employees should be carried out with the knowledge and agreement of the union concerned'.[23] Following the assault on the anarchist bakers' union (see page 75) the Moscow Soviet in October 1920 militarised all the bakeries without warning the MGSPS.[24] Shortly afterwards the MGSPS was incensed when the factory committee in a cooking oil plant (Masloboinogo zavoda No. 3) was arrested by the MChK and a new director was appointed without consulting the food union.[25] At the same time, the MGSPS insisted on its own prerogatives and argued that as a matter of principle the MK and the Moscow Soviet should deal with the MGSPS and not with the individual union.[26] The MGSPS' secretary, Briskin, admitted the weakness of the Moscow unions at the II Gubernia TU Conference on 20 September 1920. He placed some of the responsibility on the lack of personnel available to the MGSPS, with no more than two to three at any one time and only fifty-six technical personnel. The links with lower union organisations and the mass of the workers, he conceded, were tenuous.[27] Davydova, responsible for cultural work, complained that the confusion over responsibilities allowed Narkompros (Commissariat of Education) and its local body MONO to poach any club, library or school established by the unions and hence only increased the isolation of trade union centres from the working class.[28] Much union activity was devoted to distributing concert and theatre tickets on a preference basis and distributing rations. The unions were clearly losing out in the battle between competing hierarchies in the first phase of Soviet power.

Nevertheless, against the background of the trade union debate, the MGSPS began to reassert itself. With the beginning of demobilisation the MGSPS waged a vigorous campaign to obtain union activists directly from the front, albeit through the MK which had sole rights in distributing party members.[29] At the same time the MGSPS secretariat was expanded to reach 165 by April 1921.[30] Above all, the Moscow union movement tried to reassert its role in economic affairs. The high hopes for the participation of the unions in running production after the revolution were given concrete expression by the formation of an economic commission under the MSPS on 26 October 1917.[31] At the 15 November 1917 plenum, B. G. Kozelev, the chairman of the Moscow metal TU, even argued that to avoid parallelism the economic department of the Moscow Soviet should be abolished and its powers transferred to the MSPS.[32] With the development of state economic bodies this commission disappeared and instead the unions transferred a large number of their most active members to these economic organisations. In March 1919, for example, 150 out of MGorSNKh's staff of 1200 were ex-trade unionists.[33] The VIII Party Congress in March 1919 resolved that unions would ultimately take over economic management, but in the short term the economic councils consolidated their hold over the economy. While personal ties were strong, on the formal level the links between the Moscow union and economic organisations were minimal. To redress the balance, on 26 September 1920, following a decision of the II Guberniya Conference, an economic department was recreated under the MGSPS to complement its other two concerned with culture and education, and labour.[34] The MK viewed the revival of the economic department with major reservations, and the latter had an uphill struggle to establish itself.[35] The attempt to increase the economic role of the unions was boosted by the success of Rudzutak's resolution at the V All-Russian Trade Union Conference (3–7 November 1920) on union participation in economic management and planning. The MGSPS presidium on 21 December 1920 urged that a report be completed as soon as possible on various proposals for the participation of trade unions in the organisation of production,[36] but it does not appear to have reported its findings. Finally, on 19 January 1921, the MGSPS achieved permanent representation on MSNKh.[37] At the end of the month an agreement was reached between the MGSPS and the Moscow labour department on trade union personnel. Both the Workers' Opposition and the Ignatov group had demanded that the unions should have greater control over this crucial question,[38] and now the agreement stated that no elected member of a factory committee (or *mestkom*) could be fired, transferred to another enterprise or institution, or sent on assignment by management without the permission of the relevant trade union.[39] From this it is clear that while the trade union debate raged the unions were *de facto* preparing themselves for the management of the economy.

Their actions were predicated on the continuation of war communism, but there were increasing signs that the system itself was disintegrating. In response to the rising tide of worker unrest and the challenge posed by the oppositions, the MGSPS and its constituent unions attempted to forge closer links with workers by such measures as holding their meetings in factories.[40] The 5 January 1921 session of the MGSPS Presidium called for a range of factory, delegate, *raion* and inter-*raion* meetings of factory managers, trade unions, factory committees and workers to discuss economic questions.[41] In practice these democratic fora never really developed and soon faded away. The problems in both war communist society and within the trade union movement could not be solved by such cosmetic responses. Alfred Rosmer noted *à propos* the trade union debate that 'Nobody basically disputed that the unions were in a state of semi-lethargy; the only difference of opinion was on the causes and cures'.[42] As the Workers' Oppositionist Yu. Lutovinov put it, not only the party was bureaucratised but also the unions :

> The trade unions are cut off from the healthy influence of the masses . . . The old methods of education of the broad masses by way of agitation and propaganda are being replaced by circulars and orders.[43]

The opposition noted that the unions were overshadowed by the state and the party:

> The behaviour of party centres and state organs over the last two years has systematically narrowed the scope of the trade unions and has reduced the influence of the workers' unions in the Soviet state to almost nothing.[44]

As Lozovskii himself put it, 'Three years after the October revolution the Russian trade unions are further from managing production than they were in the months after the October revolution'.[45] By 1920 there was not only a general economic and social crisis, but also a specific crisis of the trade unions. The centralised management of the economy was reflected in massive centralised trade unions, but these were relatively weak in comparison to the state and the party. Both these factors were the essential background to the trade union debate of late 1920.

THE STRUGGLE AGAINST NON-BOLSHEVIK UNIONISM

During the civil war the communist party waged a campaign against non-Bolshevik unionism. The question was not so much over the form of union organisation, since the Mensheviks, for example, agreed with the principle of a single production union for each industry. While the Mensheviks favoured a more Europeanised vision of unions defending workers' economic rights, they still insisted on active political struggle. At issue was the relationship of the unions to the state and therefore by implication with their own members. The Menshevik-dominated I All-Russian Congress of the office-workers' union in June 1918, for example, urged single production unions for each industry, but in another resolution called for the unions to defend the class interests of the working class independent of the state 'guided by the principles of

the international class struggle of the proletariat'.[46] The Mensheviks
were the major adversaries of the Bolsheviks in the union movement as
befitted the alternative wing of Russian Social Democracy. To their
disagreements over party organisation were added profound differences
in the way they viewed the trade unions.

Leopold Haimson has effectively argued that the Menshevik interpretation of the union movement gained little momentum in the pre-1914
workers' movement because of a lack of intellectual and social resonance.[47]
However, paradoxical as it may appear, under conditions of Bolshevik
power their programme gained increasing support. In the early summer
of 1918 the Mensheviks had played an active part in the 'non-party
worker conferences' and 'conferences of factory and plant delegates'
(*soveshchaniya upolnomochennykh fabrik i zavodov*). The aims of the
movement were encapsulated by the resolution passed in the Bogatyr'
plant on 16 May 1918: for freedom of speech and meeting; the
restoration of the old municipal authorities; and for an end to the
shooting of citizens and workers.[48] Lenin's assertion at the IV Moscow
Factory Committee Conference on 28 June 1918 that the movement was
backed by only a very small number of workers[49] was belied by his
admission earlier in the month that 'the agitation of enemies and
"waverers" had had some influence on Moscow's workers'.[50] The high
point of the movement was the organisational meeting of 5 June 1918,
attended by about 4000 workers,[51] whose ultimate aim was the
convocation of a national conference. A conference of all socialists, to
which the Bolsheviks were invited but refused to attend, met on 20 July
in, significantly, the offices of the Moscow co-operative societies where
the reports revealed widespread disillusionment with Bolshevik rule. On
the next day the discussions were cut short by a Cheka raid and the arrest
of all the delegates.[52] By the end of the month the movement had lost its
momentum in the face of severe repression[53] and was engulfed by the
civil war. Among the railway workers, support lingered with sporadic
strikes and resolutions in favour of the Constituent Assembly, and even
in December 1918 'anti-Soviet' soviets were still being purged.[54]

Non-Bolshevik parties retained their support in several Moscow
unions throughout the civil war. The anarchists had some influence in
the bakers' union, but it was the Mensheviks who presented the greatest
challenge in the print, chemicals and office workers' unions, and on the
railways. The Menshevik strongholds were in the Bogatyr' chemical
plant in Sokol'nicheskii *raion*, where they retained their influence until
1920,[55] the Aleksandrov railway, and the Bromlei metal plant in
Zamoskvorech'e, where they dominated until December 1921.[56] The

Mensheviks and SRs retained some influence in the Vtorov money printing works in Khamovniki, the Guzhon metal plant in Rogohsko-Simonovskii *raion*, the giant Prokhorovskaya Trekhgornaya Mill in Presnenskii *raion*, and in the Miusskii tram park.[57] The factory committee in the Dukat tobacco plant in Presnenskii *raion* was controlled by the Mensheviks until late July 1918.[58] In mid-1918 the Bolsheviks were excluded from the factory committees and control commissions in several plants including Guzhon itself, and the Postavshchik and Gnom i Ron military supply plants.[59] The formation of the one-party state (*infra*) was not restricted to the expulsion of non-Bolshevik parties from the soviets but included the destruction of their organised influence in worker organisations. Victory in this ongoing civil war in the factories was only achieved after the end of the war when the Bolsheviks could concentrate their resources on this front.

The major challenge to Bolshevik hegemony over the union movement was posed by the stubborn resistance of the Mensheviks in the print workers' union. Among the reasons for Menshevik support in the union the following can be briefly mentioned: a highly developed sense of solidarity in a traditionally skilled and cohesive profession; the relative success of the Menshevik leadership in defending the interests of their members *vis à vis* the Moscow Soviet and the economic organs; a unique type of union organisation which allowed a responsive relationship between the leaders and the membership, illustrated above all by the existence of a 'council of delegates' (*sovet upolnomochennykh*); and the popularity of the Menshevik leadership in the print shops. The delegate body was clearly a model for the 1918 *upolnomochennyi* movement, and it offered an alternative form of union organisation until 1921 in the print union.

The print union offered stiff resistance to Bolshevik industrial and political policies in the first months of their power. In 1918 the Bolsheviks were split over the tactics to be pursued in ridding themselves of this nuisance: whether to contest the elections in the existing union; or to form their own, the successful tactic in the railway union. Unsure of sufficient support, the Bolsheviks attempted to win control of the existing union and fought the elections to the board in April 1918. Out of 20 000 Moscow print workers 50 per cent voted, only 4000 for the Bolsheviks who received ten out of the twenty-five seats.[60] At the end of the year the Bolsheviks called for new elections, hoping for a majority. The Menshevik refusal of 2 January 1919 led to a series of stormy meetings which came to a head at a general meeting of Moscow print workers on 9 February 1919. The Bolsheviks were vehemently denounced and accused of treachery to the duly constituted union bodies. Finding themselves in a minority they stormed out and finally decided to form a new union.[61] The move was supported by the MK meeting of 22 February 1919, when A. S. Borshchevskii, the leader of the Bolshevik print workers, and Mel'nichanskii reported on the situation. On the grounds that the print union was a 'citadel of Menshevism' they urged the MSPS to create a new unon,[62] the successful tactic in Petrograd in November 1918.[63] It was at this time that a 'red' office workers' union was formed following a mass meeting of delegates where only 300 out of 1800 were Bolsheviks. It was registered by Mel'nichanskii against Tomskii's moderate counsel.[64] The creation of the new print union advanced slowly but by August 1919 a new Bolshevik national union had been formed. Few Moscow print workers joined and the Mensheviks maintained their hold on the Moscow union. Elections to its board in December 1919 confirmed their supremacy when of the 9000 print workers who voted (of a total union membership of 12 000), 7000 supported the 'yellow' union and only 2000 the 'red'.[65] It appears that following this humiliating defeat the local Bolshevik breakaway union rejoined the main union and continued the struggle from within. The strategy was outlined at the MK meeting on 20 December 1919 when the party *raion* committees (RKs) were urged to continue the struggle and Borshchevskii was assigned to recall all Bolshevik print workers from the fronts to bolster their forces.[66] At the height of the Polish war on 18 June 1920, the board of the Moscow print union was dissolved by order of the MGSPS[67] and a purge of the union was launched.[68] A long and bitter struggle now ensued, with over twenty-five strikes in Moscow print shops[69] and the arrest by the Moscow Cheka of eleven members of the Moscow print board elected in December 1919 and a number of other Menshevik leaders.[70] From this point the story becomes increasingly complicated as the Menshevik print leaders were driven underground, but despite the repression it appears that they retained control of the union until the beginning of the NEP.[71]

The extent of support for the Mensheviks at the height of the war can be seen by the fact that over a fifth of the 765 delegates to the I Guberniya Trade Union Conference in September 1919 supported the Menshevik resolution on 'independence and unity', but the solid group of 412 Bolshevik delegates were able to denounce the idea of union independence (*nezavisimost'*) from Soviet power.[72] By July 1920 only one Menshevik remained in the MGSPS plenum of over 100 people.[73] At the same time the campaign to eliminate the organised forces of the peasant anarchist leader Nestor Makhno in the Ukraine was accompanied by repression against anarchist influence in the Moscow unions. This culminated in the mass arrest of anarchist unionists in November 1920, including the leaders of the bakers' union.[74] The board of the bakers' union was dissolved and reorganised with a Bolshevik majority.[75] The Menshevik-led Moscow chemical workers' union still remained obdurate, however, and the board was careful to maintain close links with its supporters in the chemical plants by organising fortnightly meetings with factory committee representatives and other open-door measures.[76] The means by which the Mensheviks maintained their hold over Moscow workers posed as great a threat to the Bolsheviks as the mere fact of the Menshevik dominance itself. The Menshevik leaders vigorously defended their members' interests, and wages in the chemical industry, for example, rose faster than in any other industry because of the extensive application of bonus forms of payment (see page 86 and Table 3.2, p. 82). The union elected Martov instead of Lenin as their honorary chairman on 26 March 1921.[77] With the arrest of Menshevik and SR leaders in early 1921 it was relatively easy for the Bolsheviks, supported by the central trade union leadership, to eliminate the remnants of non-Bolshevik union leadership in Moscow by the end of the year using the tactics developed during war communism.[78] At the same time the trade unions and the party cells worked together to gain control of the factory committees still in non-Bolshevik hands (see Chapter 4). The coming of peace and the NEP, and not the civil war itself, saw the final end of this breach in Bolshevik hegemony.

WORKERS' CONTROL AND ECONOMIC MANAGEMENT

Following the June 1918 nationalisation decree, the trade unions in conjunction with the *sovnarkhozy* were to participate in the formation of the new collegiate management boards of enterprises. The boards were responsible to the *sovnarkhozy* for work fulfilment and finances, while the trade unions were responsible for labour discipline, wage norming and other labour tasks. Until the introduction of wide-scale one-person management in 1920 the state management boards contained elements of workers' control, but obviously their functions changed after June 1918. The transition from workers' control, dominant until nationalisation, to state management, was as drawn-out a process as nationalisation itself. The key point, however, is that the management of enterprises was transferred neither to the unions nor to their control commissions in the plants but to the economic bodies. The relationship between workers' control (factory committees and control commissions) and the new state boards appointed by the economic councils was only established after a period of conflict and experimentation. The situation is complicated, with arguments over whether workers' control was subsumed into the economic councils or whether it continued, but under the auspices of the councils,[79] and the problem is compounded by the fact that the people involved often shifted from one structure to another and therefore the categories cannot be rigidly demarcated.

The debate over the functions of workers' control had been particularly vigorous in Moscow, with the Moscow Soviet adopting its own instruction on 25 November 1917. The instruction subordinated factory committees to the soviet and gave a more restricted definition of their functions than the national instruction adopted as one of the first acts of the Soviet government.[80] The factory committees in the first months were involved in all aspects of factory life as they desperately sought to stave off economic catastrophe. The subordination of the factory committees to the unions by the I All-Russian Trade Union Congress in January 1918 in practice meant the integration of the factory committee control commissions into the trade unions and the economic commissions which were being formed at this time.[81] The absence of a city-wide factory committee organisation in Moscow exacerbated the problem of integration and attempts to form such a co-ordinating body in early 1918 were unsuccessful. Its functions were carried out by the economic department of the Moscow Soviet and the departments of workers' control (control commissions) under the *raion* soviets. Following the nationalisation decree these departments were transformed into the local control organs of MOSNKh which formed a city control commission to co-ordinate their work.[82]

General nationalisation once again raised the question of the function of workers' control, and indeed whether it was to continue at all. A resolution adopted by the Moscow metal workers' union (VSRM) of 20 July 1918, for example, restricted the duties of factory committees to ensuring internal order and labour discipline and forbade them from 'interfering' in management: 'The organs of workers' control . . . must not carry out any administrative or economic functions'.[83] As we shall see, precisely the same restrictions were placed on the activities of party cells in the factories. The instruction in practice was to prove ambiguous. The state management of Guzhon, for example, now argued on this basis that the control commission in the plant was no longer required since both VSNKh and the management looked after the workers' interests.[84] Elsewhere in the country, as in the Sormovo-Kolomna metallurgical complex, control commissions were also being disbanded.[85] After a vigorous protest by the Guzhon control commission the union now modified its position and stated that it had not called for their abolition.[86] Disputes in the Guzhon plant, with its active control commission and Menshevik factory committee, continued at least up to the end of the year.[87]

The I Congress of Economic Councils (26 May–4 June 1918) instructed that the management of nationalised enterprises should consist of two representatives of the TUs, two from the workforce, and two from the specialists and employees, but in practice there were nearly as many variations in the management of nationalised enterprises as there were enterprises themselves. The majority of factories under MGorSNKh, for example, were managed by boards consisting of one representative of the economic council, one from the relevant union, and one from the workers of the plant.[88] In some enterprises, such as the Til'mans screw plant, factory committees elected control commissions to which MOSNKh sent its representatives, which then became the kernel of collegiate management.[89] The Bogatyr' plant had a board with two representatives from the workers, two from the technical staff, and two from VSNKh.[90] More democratic initially was the screw plant where supreme authority was vested in the control commission consisting of management and factory committee representatives: the management (it is not clear how it was constituted) was responsible for general administration while the factory committee was responsible for labour discipline and the attempts to raise labour productivity, and both were subordinate to the control commission.[91] Usually nationalisation entailed a drastic curtailment in the powers of the control commissions, as in the Alekseevskii state cable plant in Rogozhsko-Simonovskii *raion*. For a year the commission there had in effect run the plant, but following nationalisation on 30 November 1918 it 'stopped interfering in the instructions of the factory management'.[92] In the Guzhon plant, long under the aegis of government, a centralised state board dominated from the first. The majority of the new boards were made up of workers,[93] but, as we shall see, this was no guarantee against 'bureaucratism'.

A statute adopted by the VTsSPS (the national union leadership) and MSPS on 2 August 1918 defined the factory committees as the local cells of the unions and the control commissions as subordinate to the *sovnarkhozy*.[94] In this way the factory committees were fractured: the factory committees came under the unions; and their control commissions under the economic bodies. This split was a specific manifestation of the transfer of economic management to special economic agencies. The unions themselves, as noted, gradually lost any direct management functions. By April 1919, for example, the functions of the Moscow VSRM control commission had been transferred to MGorSNKh.[95] In December 1918, in recognition of the *raion* soviets' traditional workers' control role, it was decided that *raion* economic departments (REO) were to be formed under the *raion* soviets combining workers' control and state management functions.[96] The precise balance between the two functions engendered controversy for the next few months in the MGorSNKh presidium, the Moscow Soviet, and in the *raions*. One group in effect pushed for economic management in the *raions* to pass into the hands of the workers' control bodies (the *raion* control commissions under the *raion* soviets), a proposal which was rejected, and finally a solution emerged in which the REO were more strictly subordinated to MGorSNKh.[97] The political arguments of this time over the rights of the soviets and the localities (see Chapter 6) were reflected in this economic debate over the powers of the *raions*, the Moscow Soviet, and the city economic council. E. N. Ignatov, for example, a member of the MGorSNKh presidium up to 22 August 1919, was a link between the two debates in his consistent defence of greater devolution of economic and political power. The issue was whether workers' participation in managing the socialist economy would be direct or indirect, a question which applied equally to the management of the socialist administrative system.

The abolition of the *raion* trade union boards in late 1918 gave a major fillip to the centralisation of the unions described above. They had consisted of delegates from factories and paralleled the organisation in *raion* soviets of factory committee delegates. Both represented the high water mark of workers' democracy in 1917. In the second half of 1918 factory TU committees (*mestkomy*) became directly subordinate to the local union branches without the intermediary *raion* organisations. These *mestkomy* were designed to replace the factory committees, but by early 1919 the process was still far from complete.[98] By the end of the war the *mestkomy* had become the primary union organisation in the factories,[99] though the situation is confused because they often, nostalgically, still called themselves factory committees. The change in name from factory committee to *mestkom* signalled the transition from the worker participation typical of early 1918 to a more restricted union consultative role in enterprise affairs. The shift was reflected in the endemic conflicts between the factory committees and the factory managements during the civil war, with 4689 reported in the 18 months from July 1918.[100] Both the trade unions and the party RKs were involved in resolving them.[101] The summary dissolution of the factory committee at the Moscow-Kazan railway print shop in March 1919, whether because of its Menshevik allegiance or as part of the militarisation of the railways is not clear, was followed by widespread strikes and is a case in point of the expendability of the factory committees in this period.[102] Nevertheless, factory committee members remained an important group. In an industrial *raion* such as Rogozhsko-Simonovskii there were 454 factory committee members by November 1919 in the 154 enterprises (2.8 per cent of the total number of workers).[103] Attempts to incorporate factory committees (control commissions) into the system of state auditing (Goskontrol') in late 1918 were unsuccessful,[104] but their functions were increasingly limited to checking the fulfilment of management decisions and they were deprived of the right to change them.[105] The reorganisation of control by the decree of 9 April 1919 (see Chapter 6) began the process whereby factory committees were integrated as units of state control, and transformed completely by the creation of a specialised inspection ministry (Rabkrin) in February 1920. The factory committees were divided between the economic councils, the unions and the state inspection bodies and were subsumed into these different bureaucratic structures. Their functions would inevitably have changed following nationalisation, but during the civil war they lost their 'from below' character.

Collegiality, or the committee system of mangement, was the major form of popular participation in administration after October 1917. Already in his *Current Tasks of Soviet Power* in April 1918, Lenin had disparaged collegiality without immediate success,[106] and following his strictures against the 'chattering' of collegiate management and the resolutions on strengthening one-person management at the II Congress of *Sovnarkhozy* in December 1918,[107] collegiate management came under renewed pressure. The new policy was opposed by the VTsSPS[108] and the MGSPS urged caution in its implementation. Many party leaders were also wary of the move, above all in Moscow. It encountered the opposition of the Democratic Centralists and the VSNKh at the IX Party Congress in March 1920 and the MGK at the XVII *Guberniya* Party Conference (13–14 March 1920),[109] and the Moscow city party conferences in March 1920 (see Chapter 7). In his defence of collegiate management in the Moscow Soviet on 28 January 1919, a certain Il'in put his finger on the problem when he argued that it had become difficult to 'use' the working class since its most active members had been destroyed by the war.[110] The snail's pace at which one-person management was introduced in 1919 testifies to the popularity of collegiate management, and possibly to its viability also. There are few examples of the introduction of one-person management in Moscow in 1919 and in the great majority of enterprises some form of collegiate management was retained. The economic (and soviet) bodies began by limiting their own collegia, and it took time for this policy to work downwards to the enterprises managed by their departments. On 14 June 1919 MGorS-NKh, following the lead of the Moscow Soviet presidium, decided to cut back sharply on the collegia of its departments, and to abolish the collegia altogether in sub-departments. By the end of 1919 only MGorSNKh's shoe-leather department had succeeded in imposing one-person management on most of its own plants.[111] The IX Party Congress, however, against the background of militarisation policies, called for its wholesale introduction despite the opposition of the SNKh congress in January 1920 and the Moscow Party Organisation (MPO). By the end of the year only about a quarter of enterprises retained collegiate management.[112] In autumn 1920, for example, a special plenipotentiary was sent from the *glavk* Gomomez to Guzhon with extraordinary powers, though the collegiate board remained but now subordinate to him. Soon after he became the first 'red director' of Guzhon.[113] Hence the introduction of one-person management was not so much a response to the necessities of war but a strategy for peacetime economic development.

PRODUCTIVITY AND WAGES POLICY

From 1917 there was a steady and at times dramatic fall in labour productivity. In the Guzhon plant, for example, in 1917 wages rose by 3–4 times while productivity more than halved.[114] By 1920 productivity per worker in the plant had fallen to a tenth of the 1913–14 level by weight and 8 per cent by value (see Table 2.8). P. G. Smidovich, at the time chairman of the city *sovnarkhoz*, informed the Moscow Soviet EC on 19 January 1920 that in the previous year productivity had halved in Moscow, with most industries fulfilling less than half of their allotted tasks.[115] Output per worker in Moscow by 1920 had fallen to a quarter of the 1913 level.[116] The reasons for this decline include disruptions in raw material and fuel supplies, the time spent in queues, the search for fuel, trips to the countryside in search of food, inadequate rations, and so on. In these circumstances absenteeism naturally increased and was an indicator of the breakdown of the legal economy. In every plant the management issued warnings aginst taking days off without permission. One such in the Guzhon plant on 23 December 1918 called on the heads of departments to take action against absenteeism and stated that written reasons must be presented for an absence of even one day.[117] In the Til'mans plant in late 1918 a guard was placed at the factory gates to check on workers arriving late and to prevent people leaving early.[118] In the last third of 1919 absenteeism in Moscow factories reached 25 per cent (one day off to every three worked), but was lower where food supplies were better, as in the food industry itself.[119] In March 1920 absenteeism on some Moscow railway lines reached 80 per cent a week,[120] and in April in the factories absenteeism averaged 44 per cent a week. The factory committees were urged to institute severe measures to improve the situation,[121] but disciplinary actions alone were insufficient when faced with desperate food shortages. In September 1920 absenteeism remained at the 40–50 per cent level of the enrolled workers as they searched for food on the black market.[122]

Faced with such a catastrophic decline in productivity and labour discipline, the authorities turned to both the carrot and the stick. The use of coercion will be discussed in the next section, but here we will note that the use of incentives and a fairly sophisticated application of 'market' mechanisms of encouragement once again reveals that war communism was a fairly flexible and responsive economic system which could combine both incentives and coercion. Nowhere was the unions' ambiguity between their state role and their traditional one of defending the interests of the workers more sharp than in wages policy and the attempt to increase productivity. Because of the predominance of the low-wage textile industry, wages in Moscow before the war were lower than elsewhere. The average annual income of a Moscow worker in 1913 was 336 rubles,[123] with the highest wages being in the print, metal and power industries (employing the highest proportion of skilled male labour) and the lowest in the chemical and food industries. Table 3.2 shows that wages rose from an average 28 rubles a month in 1913 to 153 in 1917, thereafter rising rapidly to over 11 000 rubles a month in late 1920, a 400-fold increase over 1913 on average, and in the chemical industry nearly double that. Between 1913 and late 1920 prices increased by just under 25 000 times (see Table 3.3). On these figures, therefore, prices outstripped wages by 62 times.[124] In other words, the purchasing power of factory workers by the end of 1920 had fallen by more than 50 times in comparison with 1913. However, such a conclusion has only a purely formal significance. Beginning in 1918, and even more in 1919–20, wages were increasingly paid in kind, and rations at fixed, purely

Table 3.2   Wages in Moscow city, 1913–20 (average monthly wages in rubles)

	Av. for all industries	1913 as 100	Metal	1913 as 100	Textiles	1913 as 100	Food	1913 as 100	Chemicals	1913 as 100	Print	1913 as 100
1913	28	100	36	100	27	100	22	100	22	100	35	100
1914	28	100	36	100	25	93	23	105	22	100	36	103
1915	33	118	38	106	36	133	32	145	27	123	39	111
1916	50	179	57	158	48	178	47	214	47	214	47	134
1917	153	546	143	397	157	581	169	768	137	623	153	437
1918 (I–IV)	306	1093	296	822	246	911	335	1523	378	1718	354	1011
1918 (XII)	548	1957	608	1689	502	1859	506	2300	592	2691	606	1731
1919 (I)	504	1800	442	1228	–	–	–	–	–	–	650	1857
1919 (X)	2451	8754	2426	6732	1955	7245	–	–	–	–	–	–
1919 (XI)	2174	7764	2313	6425	1213	4493	–	–	–	–	–	–
1919 (XII)	2348	8386	2556	7100	1966	7281	–	–	–	–	–	–
1920 (I)	2197	7846	2272	6311	1705	6315	2018	9173	2011	9041	3617	10334
1920 (II)	2621	9361	2953	8203	2077	7693	2085	9477	2346	10664	3406	9731
1920 (X)	9256	33057	10902	30283	8756	32430	5096	23164	14564	66200	8743	24980
1920 (XI)	9454	33764	10902	30311	9722	36007	4504	20473	14680	66727	10376	29646
1920 (XII)	11073	39546	13837	38436	10462	38748	6234	28336	17473	79423	10559	30169
1921 (I)	7912											
1921 (II)	9914											
1921 (III)	11230											

Source: Byulleten' statistiki truda Moskovskoi gubernii, MGSPS, 5–6 (March–April 1921) pp. 4–5; 7–8 (May–June 1921) p. 1.

nominal prices became increasingly important. According to S. G. Strumilin, the role of money wages decreased from 90 per cent in 1917, 52 per cent in 1918, 23 per cent in 1919, to 7 per cent in 1920,[125] and hence the role of state supply increased correspondingly. In 1913 food expenditure amounted to 27 per cent of wages, whereas in the last four months of 1920 wages, including the nominal cost of rations at fixed prices, covered only 42–49 per cent of expenditure, so that real wages fell to only about 12 per cent of their previous level.[126]

Late 1918 saw attempts by the party leadership to stabilise the currency so that it could retain its function as a medium of exchange.[127] At the same time many of the party leaders and the rank and file in Moscow were demanding the abolition of money,[128] and the party programme of March 1919 declared the intention to eliminate money – but not immediately. This conflict over the role of money was only apparently one between pragmatism and ideology. The failure to restrain inflation, with the amount of money in circulation more than doubling every year between 1917 and 1920, and to develop an effective exchange mechanism between town and country in itself destroyed money as a means of exchange and led to the naturalisation of wages. The state gradually moved towards a system of free distribution, defined by the Sovnarkom decrees of 16 August 1920 on free travel and 11 October 1920 on free food and housing. On the eve of the NEP (3 February 1921) taxes were abolished. During war communism the payment of wages in kind was a means of distributing scarce resources on the 'living minimum' principle: if there had been sufficient goods and an effective distribution system, hard prices alone would have sufficed. The manner of supply was to play an increasingly large part in the attempt to stimulate productivity and to retain skilled workers. From 30 April 1920, ear-marked supply (*tselevoe snabzhenie*), formulated by the III Trade Union Congress earlier that month, began to be applied in Moscow. Special rations were issued depending on the state importance of the enterprise where the worker was employed (the principle of shock work or *udarnosti*) and according to the productivity of individual groups within them.[129] The aim was to forge a link between the social wage (especially rations) and the productivity of labour under conditions of an increasing division between income, either money or rations, and work performed. By 1920 the proportion of income linked to production had fallen to only 6.2 per cent.[130] In the circumstances the attempt to link rations to productivity, as in the introduction of a 'labour ration' to be issued only to those who actually worked, by the Moscow Soviet in February 1920, could achieve little.[131]

Table 3.3 Inflation in Moscow city, 1913–20
(a) Market prices (in rubles)

	Rye bread (pood)	Flour (pood)	Potatoes (pood)	Cabbage (pood)	Sugar (pood)	Butter (pood)	Beef (pood)	Herring (100)	Eggs (100)	Salt (pood)
1913	1.05	0.98	0.40	1.04	5.12	18.00	7.56	5.96	2.91	0.30
1914	1.07	1.14	0.45	1.40	5.12	18.40	7.56	5.40	2.71	0.29
1915	1.43	1.80	0.45	1.83	6.75	20.86	8.76	7.70	2.87	0.66
1916 (I–III)	1.65	2.02	0.47	1.36	7.40	33.60	11.20	11.30	2.70	0.90
1916 (VI–IX)	1.65	2.00	0.58	4.24	8.05	42.80	18.40	21.10	5.00	0.90
1917 (I)	2.50	3.12	2.04	3.84	7.80	110.40	26.00	22.23	9.50	1.20
1917 (VII)	4.80	5.60	7.32	16.90	7.80	126.12	42.00	32.70	16.14	1.20
1918 (I)	80.00	60.00	24.00	10.80	160.00	400.00	114.00	73.00	29.00	0.80
1918 (VII)	340.00	350.00	83.20	32.40	710.00	758.80	316.80	174.00	104.30	4.80
1919 (I)	540	640	200	160	2 400	3 600	1 080	1 250	350	400
1919 (VII)	1 885	2 000	720	560	8 000	8 920	2 828	4 500	1 370	1 800
1920 (I)	7 120	10 000	2 400	1 560	54 000	65 000	13 320	30 000	7 000	20 000
1920 (II)	8 000	10 400	2 880	2 200	50 000	79 000	19 000	51 000	12 500	24 000
1920 (III)	11 600	14 000	3 280	2 280	62 000	108 000	21 000	70 000	12 500	26 000
1920 (IV)	10 000	12 000	3 500	2 280	84 000	84 000	22 000	70 000	20 000	34 000
1920 (V)	10 400	14 000	5 000	2 000	108 000	82 000	24 800	80 000	13 000	34 000
1920 (VI)	16 000	19 000	4 800	1 800	180 000	108 000	46 000	95 000	16 000	42 000
1920 (VII)	19 000	22 000	7 200	2 200	180 000	120 000	44 000	95 000	15 000	48 000
1920 (VIII)	20 000	28 000	8 000	4 800	160 000	188 000	51 200	60 000	21 500	49 000
1920 (IX)	18 000	25 000	7 500	5 500	180 000	180 000	48 000	50 000	19 000	45 000
1920 (X)	20 000	20 500	7 600	4 500	200 000	230 000	64 000	85 000	20 000	48 000
1920 (XI)	16 000	24 000	8 100	6 800	250 000	250 000	44 000	100 000	26 000	52 000
1920 (XII)	16 000	28 000	8 200	6 240	270 000	290 000	110 000	225 000	39 000	52 000

Note: For 1913–15, and sometimes later, prices are given for the lower or medium quality goods as these were most commonly used by Moscow workers. The prices in 1918–20 vary greatly depending on source used since the restrictions on free exchange led to wild variation within even such a comparatively small area as Moscow.

(b) Comparative market prices (1913 = 100)

	Rye bread (pood)	Flour (pood)	Potatoes (pood)	Cabbage (pood)	Sugar (pood)	Butter (pood)	Beef (pood)	Herring (100)	Eggs (100)	Salt (pood)
1913	100	100	100	100	100	100	100	100	100	100
1914	101.9	116.3	112.5	134.6	100.0	102.2	100.0	90.6	93.1	96.6
1915	136.2	183.7	112.5	176.0	131.8	116.0	115.8	129.2	98.7	220.0
1916 (I–III)	157.1	206.5	129.0	130.8	146.4	186.7	148.2	161.7	92.8	305.0
1916 (VI–IX)	157.1	204.5	143.9	407.7	157.4	239.5	243.4	300.5	171.8	305.0
1917 (I)	238.1	319.0	506.2	369.2	152.5	617.8	343.0	318.4	326.5	406.8
1917 (VII)	457.1	572.6	1 816.4	1 625.0	152.5	705.8	555.6	467.9	554.6	–
1918 (I)	7 619	6 135	5 955	1 038	313	2 238	1 518	1 045	997	271
1918 (VII)	32 381	35 787	20 645	3 115	13 881	4 246	4 195	2 490	3 584	1 600
1919 (I)	51 427	65 306	49 628	15 385	46 921	20 145	14 021	20 973	12 027	–
1919 (VII)	179 543	204 082	178 666	53 846	156 403	49 916	374 075	64 396	47 079	610 169
1920 (I)	678 000	1 022 000	595 000	150 000	1 056 000	364 000	176 000	429 000	241 000	6 780 000
1920 (VII)	1 829 000	2 249 000	178 700	211 000	3 519 000	672 000	582 000	1 359 000	515 000	16 271 000
1920 (X)	1 905 000	2 096 000	1 886 000	432 000	3 910 000	1 287 000	847 000	1 216 000	687 000	16 271 000
1920 (XI)	1 524 000	2 454 000	2 010 000	654 000	4 888 000	1 399 000	582 000	1 431 000	893 000	17 627 000
1920 (XII)	1 524 000	2 863 000	2 035 000	600 000	5 279 000	1 623 000	1 435 000	3 220 000	1 340 000	17 627 000

Note: 1918–19 figures rounded to nearest unit, 1920 figures rounded to nearest 1000.

Source: Byulleten' statistiki truda Moskovskoi gubernii, MGSPS, 5–6 (March–April 1921) pp. 4–5.

At the same time the increased use of bonuses and piece rates was an attempt to use the other main component of wages (money) as a mechanism to increase productivity. From 1918 there had been attempts to link wages to productivity by sanctioning piece rates and norming, but at first they were not extensively applied, probably due to resistance. Calls in the Moscow Soviet in early 1919 for complete wage equality gained much support and reflected the egalitarian mood of the times.[132] The party programme adopted in March 1919 insisted, however, that income equality was excluded as an immediate aim.[133] Contrary to the common impression that war communism was a period of planned *uravnilovka* (egalitarianism or wage levelling), 1919–20 saw an opening up of differentials in Moscow by a decrease in the fifty-five union tariffs of late 1918 to twelve in early 1921.[134] By 1920 major inequalities had developed in the payment of money wages, and this was exacerbated by the introduction of *udarnye* (shock work) factories in 1920. The percentage of man hours covered by bonus systems of money payment rose from 41 per cent in January to 66 per cent in November: over the same period the percentage paid by piece rates rose from 7 per cent to 15 per cent and, correspondingly, the hours paid at basic rates fell from 53 per cent to 19 per cent. Over the year wages rose fastest where piece rates were applied, followed by bonus systems, while basic rates increased by only 2–2.5 times. The high earning piece and bonus systems were not applied equally to all industries and the lowest wages were found where basic rates predominated, such as the food industry, where in November 1920 80 per cent of person hours were on basic wages, and the highest wages where piece and bonus systems were more extensively applied, such as the chemical industry.[135] There were, therefore, great variations in wages between the various categories of labour within industries, by decreasing the number of tariffs, but also great inequalities between industries because of differential money wages. The range of money wages had almost doubled from the 1913 ratio of 1 : 1.6 to 1 : 2.8 by December 1920 (see Table 3.2).[136] Rationing, of course, made for greater equality in achieved income than these figures would suggest, but this in itself ensured that fairness in rationing became a highly emotive issue. War communism in Moscow was, therefore, accompanied not by the equalisation of money wages but by an increase in inequality. With money losing its value and a shortage of skilled and unskilled workers, economic bodies and factory managements resorted to increasing wages above the set rates in order to attract scarce labour and competent employees. The problem was not confined to industry but, as S. I. Polidorov (chairman of the Moscow *guberniya* soviet) informed the IX

Party Congress, all the commissariats and even the local party organisation in Moscow were guilty of this.[137] Government policy helped to maintain a gap between the incomes of the so-called specialists and the rest of the labour force. The payment of material incentives was hampered by the lack of supplies, but was nevertheless increasingly used. In the last three months of 1920 the number of workers receiving bonuses in kind increased from 13 000 to 107 000.[138] E. G. Gimpel'son argues that the use of incentives and the national reduction in the wage scale from 1 : 5 to 1 : 4 indicates that war communism was never fully achieved.[139] This is to take an unnecessarily limited view of war communism as a programme to be implemented rather than as an economic system capable of evolution within the parameters of the communist project. As mentioned (see page 52) war communism retained a certain flexibility in tackling economic problems, and indeed the above account indicates that coercion, considered the hallmark of war communism, was not incompatible with the application of inducements. War communism was a period of experimentation and many of its labour and wages aspects were carried over to the following period.

Aware of the dangers of unfair rationing, the MGSPS waged a vigorous campaign to ensure equality in general ration distribution which ran counter to the principle of *udarnosti* and the attempt to retain skilled workers. In particular, the MGSPS tried to limit the issue of goods of own production (for example, bread to bakers) which gave some groups an unfair advantage over others. As it was, the skilled groups of metal and print workers (the latter resisted piece rates) had slipped in the wages league. The importance of the accurate issue of rations, to avoid disturbances developing on this basis, led to the creation of a permanent commission under the MK in early 1920 to oversee ration policy in all its forms.[140] In the factories and plants a bitter struggle developed over the issue of goods produced on the premises as part of wages, especially in the food and tobacco industries.[141] Tobacco, indeed, acted as a second and more stable currency. Despite the unpopularity of its position among those who benefited, the MGSPS argued that such issue as part of wages contradicted the 'living minimum' for all principle.[142] Only with the introduction of NEP were concessions made in this field, though illegal issue clearly took place in order to retain workers and to minimise theft. By the end of 1920 disturbances did develop over the question of inequality in general and not just over the privileges of the specialists. In response the MGSPS attempted to decrease the variations in wages and numbers on special rations.[143] The MGSPS was caught on the horns of the dilemma of trying to stimulate productivity while keeping rations fair. The policy of incentives was not only ineffective but also politically dangerous. The inequality that it produced was an essential source of the social support for the Workers' Opposition.

LABOUR DISCIPLINE AND UNIVERSAL LABOUR DUTY

War communism has often been seen as serving a similar mythological role in the Soviet Union to the Long March in China in 1934–35, and as having a comparable mentality to that of the Great Leap Forward of 1958. Both analogies contain an element of truth, but in practice war communism had few heroic qualities. Just as the Great Leap Forward has been discredited, so war communism as a model was highly flawed. The war communist system was distinguished from the NEP by the idealism and enthusiasm of a few, but for the majority coercion was required. As noted, incentives such as the introduction of piece rates and the payment of bonuses were used to stimulate productivity, as were the early versions of socialist emulation. Increasingly, however, reliance was placed on imposing labour discipline from outside the labour process through the Cheka, the party committees, the local soviets, and the whole weight of the agitprop apparatus inflating the cult of labour in socialist society. The old social pyramid of inequality was swept away, but in its place, as the sociologist Peter Sorokin put it, a new pyramid of exploitation emerged which he called 'state serfdom'.[144] The initial exaltation of the role of labour in socialist society was buttressed by more practical considerations as the unemployment of early 1918 gave way to increasing labour shortages.

War communism was a hitherto almost unique experiment in abolishing unemployment, although under the NEP unemployment returned and by 1923 in Moscow it had returned to the level of early 1918. Both the full employment of war communism and that inaugurated by the Five-Year Plans were accompanied by punitive measures against those who failed to work. The disorganisation of the economy and the rundown in defence orders led to increasing unemployment from late 1917. The metal industries were particularly affected since they were less able to redeploy to peacetime production than, for example, the textile industry, and metal workers comprised one of the largest group of the unemployed, standing at 18 000 in early 1918.[145] With the onset of war and its demands on the working class, and the exodus from the city, unemployment almost completely disappeared. From a high point of 89 000 in the spring of 1918 (see Table 2.4), nearly 10 per cent of the independent population, unemployment fell sharply to reach 27 783 in December, 15 822 in June 1919,[146] and had dwindled to a few hundred in 1920. With the premium on skilled workers, unemployment at first was only significant among female textile workers unable to leave the city because of family commitments. By 1919–20 a severe shortage of skilled and unskilled workers had developed. In January 1920 for every 100 unemployed people there were 123 vacancies in the city and *guberniya*, but the demand for labour was greater than these figures suggest. In June 1920 there were 5000 unfilled places for metalworkers, 50 000 for building workers and 20 000 for unskilled workers.[147] In early September 1920 there were over 30 000 vacancies registered for workers, and in that month alone this demand increased by a third.[148] The labour shortage by November 1920 was such that Narkomtrud (Commissariat of Labour) issued a list of jobs, such as tram conductors, postpersons, doorkeepers, and so on, that were to be reserved for women.[149] Such measures were inadequate and the government increasingly resorted to compulsory labour duty.

Labour duty was a basic principle of war communism and was engraved into the Soviet constitution of 10 July 1918 and the labour code of 10 December 1918. In July 1918 Bukharin was already arguing that there would be 'bread only for toilers, and labour duty for the rich'.[150] When introduced labour duty was not restricted to the rich alone. An important step towards the social direction of labour and the first move away from free labour was the decree of 3 September 1918 abolishing the right of an unemployed worker to refuse the job offered to him or her on pain of loss of unemployment benefits. In 1919 the system of labour distribution developed in the military supply factories, transport and agriculture. A decree of 12 April 1919 prohibited the spontaneous movement of workers from one job to another in an attempt to staunch the flow to the countryside.[151] In 1918–19 labour duty was still largely an aspiration despite the partial attempts to implement it. One of the major steps on this road was the introduction of labour books as a means of keeping track of workers and eliminating 'parasitism'. The idea of labour books had been mooted as early as September 1918,[152] though their introduction moved slowly. The Moscow Soviet EC on 31 May 1919 urged their rapid introduction,[153] but the June Sovnarkom decree restricted them to Moscow and Petrograd.[154] The labour book was designed to eliminate the vast army of 'speculators' noted above, to tie skilled workers to their jobs, and in general to control the labour market. But they were more than that:

It was a record of every step one made, and without it no steps could be made. It bound its holder to his job, to the city he lived in, and to the room he occupied. It recorded one's political faith and party adherence, and the number of times he was arrested.[155]

By early 1920 every able-bodied Muscovite between the ages of 16 and 50 (40 for women) had exchanged their passport for a labour book without which it was impossible to obtain government housing, food or clothing. The person was also liable to arrest for labour desertion and a period of compulsory labour.[156] Goldman notes that 'Even some communists resented the degrading innovation'.[157]

The intensified use of existing labour resources was, Bukharin argued in December 1920, the only recourse in circumstances where the stock of worn-out machines could not be renewed by purchases from abroad.[158] It was at this time that Trotsky developed a general programme of militarisation of the economy. The IX Party Congress in March 1920 stated that:

> [it] views as one of the urgent tasks of the Soviet government and trade unions a planned, systematic, persistent, and implacable campaign against labour desertion, in particular by the publication of lists of deserters who have been punished, and the formation of punitive brigades composed of deserters, or, as a last resort, their confinement in concentration camps.[159]

In Moscow's factories 'red lists' extolling labour heroes, and 'black boards' excoriating slackers, appeared. Various commissions were established to combat labour desertion, to use the contemporary term, in various industries, such as the one for transport in Moscow in May 1920 with the brief to use both repression and agitation.[160] By early 1920 the system had developed beyond partial attempts at labour distribution into a scheme of universal compulsory labour duty effected by a central labour committee (Glavkomtrud), under the Council of Defence and local committees. The scheme had been established by a Sovnarkom decree of 29 January 1920 and confirmed by the IX Party Congress.[161] In March 1920 the Moscow city committee of labour duty (Moskomtrud) was established[162] with two main departments: mobilisation and the fight against labour desertion.[163] Its aims were 'to use the available labour' and to 'eliminate parasitism'.[164] Labour duty was obligatory for all healthy male citizens between the ages of 19 and 50 (40 for women except those with young children).[165] According to the committee there were 375 000 people in Moscow unaccounted for and living off unknown

means: 'This mass comprises a hundred thousand Sukharevkas, countless craft and domestic enterprises of a speculative character'. It
optimistically estimated that labour duty would give 100–150 000 extra
workers, as well as ridding the soviet apparatus of thousands of able-
bodied workers.[166] Though many might well have gone to ground on the
day, the city census of August 1920 identified only 60 000 non-labouring
people.[167]

Moskomtrud was subordinate to the Moscow Soviet and consisted of
three people (a troika): a representative of the military commissariat,
one from the soviet's management body, and one from the soviet's
labour department. The committee was only a directing body and all its
acts were to be implemented through existing bodies such as the labour
departments, trade unions and military bodies.[168] The absence of a union
representative once again illustrates their low status, even though the III
Trade Union Congress in April 1920 charged unions to ensure that jobs
were not changed arbitrarily and to combat absenteeism.[169] The use of
the MGSPS for labour duty further alienated workers from it. For
example, when the MGSPS in November 1920 ordered the transfer of
seventy-nine workers from the Danilovskaya to the Prokhorovskaya
mill at Moskomtrud's request, it aroused a storm of protest against
itself.[170] Troikas were formed in the *raion*s of Moscow[171] and by the time
of the II Guberniya Trade Union Conference in September 1920, every
quarter of the city and *guberniya* was covered by a network of 993 labour
commissions.[172] Attempts to form labour desertion committees in the
factories were abandoned on the grounds that they would undermine the
already weak factory committees (*mestkomy*).[173]

Between February and October 1920 Moskomtrud organised over
300 000 labour days in Moscow *guberniya*, and 165 000 in the city
(excluding cartage). The work was mainly concerned with fuel, unload-
ing, market gardening, and unskilled work on the railways and in
enterprises. The committee had also mobilised 2780 construction
workers back to work, 171 water workers, 700 metal craftsmen and 2400
tailors (the last two groups being sent to state enterprises), and 1600
people were drafted from the villages to work in the fuel body
(Moskvatop).[174] In all, by the end of the year about 8625 workers had
been mobilised in Moscow.[175] The figures, in fact, belie the work of
Moskomtrud. Its first large-scale attempt at labour mobilisation was the
campaign to return building workers from the countryside to deal with
an area of greatest labour shortage. The war department was closely
involved and therefore it was a test case for the use of the army apparatus
on the home front. In the event, between June and October only 3591

building workers were sent to Moscow, and judging from the above figures, not all arrived. The report on the campaign admitted that 'We must concede the complete failure of this labour mobilisation'.[176] Since it affected only one industry, workers took cover under another. Nevertheless, the TsK in October 1920 was still calling for the 'systematic extraction of skilled workers who have settled in the countryside'.[177] The committee was no more successful in its other major campaign, waged in conjunction with the MGSPS and Rabkrin: the attempt to shake out the offices and to return 'surplus' employees to the factories.[178] No appreciable fall in the number of office workers was registered. The attempt at labour mobilisation cannot be judged a success in terms of the objectives it had set itself and few extra workers were made available for the factories. Unemployment was eliminated – at the price of the end of free labour – but militarisation could achieve little while the countryside remained a refuge. The labour process of war communism did not eschew coercion, but in conditions of scarcity coercion proved unable to secure sufficient labour or improved productivity. The main effect of the militarisation of labour was to intensify worker alienation from continuing the war communist forced march to socialism.

Yet another method of improving labour discipline was the creation of comrade-disciplinary courts. In 1920 they developed on the basis of the Sovnarkom decree of 14 November 1919, though earlier versions had existed. The III Trade Union Congress of April 1920 approved their formation and by May 1920 they were functioning under nineteen of Moscow's twenty-two unions, with the railway and water unions excluded because of their militarisation.[179] Their main task was to ensure discipline among workers and initially technical and administrative staff were excluded from their purview.[180] As Mel'nichanskii noted, 'They were useful in getting workers to fulfil labour norms, and to enforce the labour discipline established by the trade unions'.[181] Between 1 January and 1 December 1920, for example, the court under the metal trade union heard 2151 cases, in 1341 of which there were acquittals and in 810 convictions, with the greatest number concerning absenteeism, followed by sabotage and indiscipline.[182] The punishments included extra work, firing, docking of wages, or non-issue of rations. In January 1921, 346 cases were heard by all the union courts in the city and *guberniya*, in February 762, and a peak of 1112 in March 1921 at a time of maximum disturbances in the city.[183] An attempt by the official legal system (Narsud) to encroach on the prerogatives of these courts was repulsed by a conference of representatives of the disciplinary courts on 10 February 1921. The meeting insisted that all questions of a purely production character were to be decided only in the factories. In keeping with the anti-specialist mood of the times the conference extended the jurisdiction of the courts to administrative and technical personnel,[184] which may in part account for the increased number of cases brought in March. The latter democratic measure was clearly part of the response to the growing wave of protest in the city directed partially against the harsh discipline in the factories. Another response was the formation of disciplinary courts independent of the unions to judge not only labour desertion but also 'bureaucracy'. One of the first of these was formed in Rogozhsko-Simonovskii *raion* in early 1921 by the party RK.[185]

The measures described above indicate some of the first responses to the perennial problem of ensuring labour discipline and productivity under a state-run economy. In keeping with the general authoritarian tenor of war communism these measures included a large degree of coercion, but as we have noted in the previous section these were balanced by the use of incentives. Nevertheless, neither the carrot nor the stick approach could do much to halt the industrial decline.

LABOUR PROTEST IN MOSCOW

Throughout the civil war there was an underlying current of labour militancy in Moscow, and this was not restricted to the disputes within the plants discussed above. As Charles E. Ziegler put it:

> The first decade of Soviet labour history witnessed the gradual incorporation of the radicalised Russian workers into the Party-state structure. The Bolsheviks exercised little semblance of control over the working class until the end of the war communism period.[186]

The actual level of control may be debated, but both the introduction and the phasing out of war communism were marked by particularly active periods of labour unrest. Throughout, the authorities treated them as arising from supply shortages and the lack of 'consciousness'. In response to the disturbances in early summer 1918 mentioned above, for example, the metal trade union wrote:

> The VSRM *oblast* committee holds that the partial elemental disturbances by certain groups of metal workers that took place in a period of particularly severe food shortages was a manifestation of the insufficient consciousness of these groups. They were provoked by the criminal demagogy of people who are setting the masses on the path of the liquidation of their power, the power of the workers, and the restoration of the former social and economic relations.[187]

The passage clearly shows the themes of the protest movement and the official response: the danger of the restoration of capitalism, the alleged role of counter-revolutionaries, and the need for greater party consciousness to combat them. A lack of identification with the Bolshevik party was treated as the absence of political consciousness altogether. In practice, the party consciousness as it had developed in 1917 (the viewing of political problems through the prism of party identification)[188] was reversed and a general consciousness of workers' needs was restored. The protest movement attests to the erosion of the political basis of war communism as the contradiction between its economic principles and the realities of worker life was closed by coercion.

It is impossible to say what proportion of workers were involved in the various disturbances, though following the lull after the defeat of the workers' conference movement of 1918 each wave of unrest was more powerful than the last, culminating in the mass movement from late 1920 (see Chapter 8). Both in 1917 and during the civil war the pattern of worker protest in Moscow was unlike that of Petrograd. This was a reflection not only of the different social composition of Moscow, or of its cultural and political traditions, but also a facet of the urban and industrial geography of the city. In Moscow there was no Vyborg side with massive plants isolated from the rest of the city, and the closest Moscow came to having a Putilov was the Guzhon plant, less than a tenth of its size. Here no *raion* can be singled out for its special militancy, and the Moscow River was not such a barrier as to allow separate traditions to develop in Zamoskvorech'e on the south side. Instead, the concentric and radial pattern of the city focused the whole of life on the administrative centre and on the Kremlin itself.

There are few details about the sporadic disturbances during the civil war. At the Moscow Soviet plenum of 13 January 1919 several references were made to recent disorders among Moscow workers, and Vladimirskii barely restrained the communist deputies from taking on summary powers to deal with them.[189] In February 1919 a report noted the increased activity of the LSRs (supporters of Maria Spiridonova) in the Guzhon plant.[190] S. P. Mel'gunov notes that from March 'Refusals to work [swept] over Russia like a tidal wave'.[191] On 15 July Kamenev admitted that the mood of the workers had become significantly more hostile over the past few months. Several concessions were announced to the soviet, including the mentioned relaxation of supply policies permitting the bagmen to bring grain (though this was not to be reported in the press) and a relaxation of travel restrictions from the city.[190] At the end of June a Moscow committee of defence (KOM) was formed to deal with the rising tide of disturbances provoked, in part at least, by the desperate food shortages. The MK, the Moscow Soviet, and the Cheka were represented on this body, and in every *raion* a troika (sometimes called a political bureau) was formed. Party members were now given the right to arrest people accused of 'counter-revolutionary' agitation. Workers in some enterprises in Sokol'nicheskii and Lefortovo *raion*s ran up the white flag as a sign of protest.[193] KOM concentrated emergency powers in its hands, overriding the Moscow Soviet, and demanding obedience from the population.[194] The disturbances died down under the pressure of repression and, as the first of the new harvest was brought in to ease the food shortages, KOM was temporarily disbanded.

At the end of 1919 the non-party conferences (see Chapter 6) were the scene of bitter attacks against the Bolsheviks, and from early 1920 there was a wave of strikes against militarisation.[195] In late March 1920 there were strikes in some factories, and in the Sokol'nicheskii tram park. The immediate demands apparently centred on food shortages.[196] A non-party conference of 550 female workers in late March 1920 in Khamovnicheskii *raion* was the scene of bitter protest.[197] At the height of the Polish war the protests and strikes, usually provoked by economic issues but not restricted to them, became particularly frequent. As usual, they were ascribed to Menshevik and SR agitation.[198] Communists were urged by the MK to be the 'eyes and ears' of the authorities in the localities and to report on malfeasants.[199] The assault on non-Bolshevik trade unionism launched at this time was probably associated with the wave of unrest since there was a clear danger that they would provide a focus for opposition. Unfortunately, no more details are available of Mel'nichanskii's major report on the disturbances to the Moscow Soviet on 2 June 1920 other than his claim that they were provoked by supply shortages. The resolution vigorously condemned certain groups as taking advantage of the difficulties. This was obviously directed against the Mensheviks, and they demonstratively left the hall led by Theodore Dan.[200] The accusation indicates that while the disturbances might have begun as protests against supply difficulties, political demands followed. By the end of the summer of 1920 these demands became explicit and could no longer be ignored by the government, as the very foundations not only of war communism but of the regime itself were threatened.

4 Party Organisation

IDEOLOGY AND ORGANISATION

Following the October revolution, and especially in the first half of 1918, the party devoted its resources and attention to consolidating Soviet power and to the major political crisis associated with the peace of Brest–Litovsk. Committed activists and workers who disagreed with the terms of the peace enthusiastically joined the so-called revolutionary detachments,[1] whose formation was the basis of the Left Communists' enthusiasm for a revolutionary war fought by partisan methods. The MK (Moscow Committee of the Bolsheviks) itself forwarded communist volunteers to the German front,[2] and by April 1918 about 2000 Moscow communists had already joined the Red Army.[3] Although the party remained the source of authority, in organisational terms it was in danger of 'withering away'. A party meeting in the Dinamo plant on 1 April 1918, for example, discovered that party activity in the plant had almost ceased because all its members were involved in work elsewhere.[4] At the same time the economic crisis and mass redundancies reduced the numbers of the working class. The departure of workers and communists left hitherto large party cells, such as the one in the Guzhon plant, with only a few members.[5] A report on the Khamovnicheskii party organisation noted that its active members had left for the fronts or to work in offices, enterprises had closed and the workers departed for the countryside, and the remaining rank and file party members were passive and waited for leadership from the centre. Above all, the decline of the party had affected the workers, who had become less 'Bolshevik-minded . . . wavering',[6] a reference to the non-party workers' movement of the time.

Central to the alleged shift in Lenin's thought in the spring of 1918 from commune to dictatorship of the proletariat forms was the enhanced administrative role of the party as the only force cohesive enough in the transitional period to ensure the execution of the socialist programme. According to Neil Harding, by mid-1918 Lenin realised that the working class as a whole had proved itself incapable of managing the country on its own.[7] The role of the communist party in the Soviet state was reappraised and as part of .this process its organisation was improved and its leading role in the state affirmed. This argument probably exaggerates the change since both in the soviets and in economic management the embryo of centralised and bureaucratic state forms had already emerged by mid-1918. The commune state and the dictatorship of the proletariat models are not as radically opposed as Harding suggests (see page 12).

Moreover, while there was a change of emphasis in the spring of 1918, the shift towards improving party organisation had been maturing even while the dominance of state work and the discussions over the Brest peace and economic policies had relegated party organisation itself to the background. A letter from the party secretariat on 20 January 1918 stated that the party had 'bled out' its best forces and argued that this could only be remedied by increased attention to organisational questions.[8] At the VII Congress in March 1918 Ya. M. Sverdlov took this a stage further when he argued, in the light of the near split in the party over the Brest peace, that 'the interests of the party as a whole are higher than the interests of the individual party member'. A new approach was required, he argued, in which both internal party organisation and the party's integrity *vis à vis* mass organisations such as the soviets had to be improved.[9]

The turning point in the re-evaluation of the role of the party in the new state came with the TsK (Central Committee of the Bolsheviks) resolution of 18 May 1918, passed at Sverdlov's prompting. It required that 'the centre of gravity of our work should be shifted somewhat towards party building', and stated, *inter alia*:

> All party members irrespective of their employment or their functions must participate directly in party organisations and must not deviate from party instructions issued by the relevant party centre.[10]

In other words, all party members including those staffing the new state structures were to be primarily subordinate to the party and not to the organisation in which they worked. The resolution for the first time in a party document incorporated the main concerns of the civil war period: on the purity of membership and the need for periodic purging; the organisation of local party groupings; and the question of party education as a way of inculcating the party's values in the new member. In stressing the need for quality in a cadre party and opposing its dilution into a mass party, the resolution marks the end of the whole period from February 1917. On the threshold of the civil war some of the features of the party in underground conditions were revived. At the same time, the stress on the party as a body distinct from the state apparatus was an attempt to prevent the absorption of the party into the pervasive bureaucratism.[11]

M. M. Helgesen has characterised the resolution and the two follow-up letters of 22 and 29 May as a 'May programme' for the revival of the party.[12] With justification, he argues that it was promoted not only by the Lenin–Sverdlov group but also by the Left Communists, who were apprehensive about the weakening of party influence in the soviets and the infiltration of the party by petty bourgeois careerists.[13] Already in April 1918, I. V. Mgeladze, a Left Communist who later joined the MK, insisted that communist fractions in the trade unions and the soviets should be 'absolutely subordinate' to the party committees.[14] The rationale for this was provided by V. Sorin, one of the Left Communist leaders in the *guberniya* organisation, who stressed that the party was less prone to degeneration than any other body.[15] However, the organisational revival envisaged by the May programme and that proposed by the Left Communists was very different. From the first the dual nature of reform, democratic versus authoritarian, within the Soviet system had become apparent. While agreeing that an effective party organisation was essential, the Left insisted that this should not be at the expense of limiting the party member's right to criticise policy or through the infringement of the rights of mass bodies such as the soviets or trade unions. It was at this time that they criticised Trotsky's view that the civil war should be fought in a conventional manner with comman-ders, specialists and 'iron discipline'.[16] In both respects the Left Communists censured the one-sidedness of the centre's attempts to improve the effectiveness of these organisations. As regards the party, they argued that the TsK was concerned with the formal, organisational resurrection of the party, and was not concerned with making it, as the left put it, a forum for all proletarian democracy. Instead,

the leading figures (*verkhi*) of the party are no longer interested in the autonomous thought of local organisations but try, without further discussion, to subordinate them to the TsK, and these leading figures present themselves as the carriers of party thought.[17]

The whole concept of the party and the role of its members was changing, and this was to be confirmed during the civil war. The party member was to be an activist first and a discussant of theoretical questions second, if at all. This division of roles was given organisational expression in the emergence of an inner corps of party leaders. Resistance to this process took the form of the many oppositions of the civil war period. The organisational consolidation of the party at the X Party Congress in March 1921 and the ban on factions was the logical continuation of the Leninist version of the 'May programme'. The May programme was a recognition of the limited base of the new regime, if not for national order of any sort in Russia,[18] and hence the success of the socialist revolution was identified with the domination of the communist party. The actual forms of that domination took time to establish, but its general outlines were clear in the May programme. In language remarkably similar to that of the X Party Congress resolutions banning factions in the party, the May programme argued:

> Without a firmly united party, acting as one person, we will not be able to cope with the tasks facing us. [We require] a powerful core, permeated with a single will and a single aspiration.[19]

The heart of Leninism was the correspondence between the theoretical appreciation of the nature of the revolution and the organisational forms in which it was expressed. As Georg Lukács put it in a 1922 essay, written as he later admitted under the influence of the 'Messianic Utopianism' of the civil war, organisation was 'the form of mediation between theory and practice'.[20] More than a defensive reaction to the developing civil war, a programme was outlined for the new period which defined both the type of new party required and its central role in the new society.

THE PARTY COMMITTEES: FIRST PHASE, 1918–19

Even though the Moscow party organisation (MPO) lay in the shadow of the central committee and was linked to it by close personal and organisational ties, the Moscow party and its committee developed both in interaction with the centre, but more importantly in this period, as a reflection of the social and political traditions of the city itself. In 1920 the secretary of the MK, A. F. Myasnikov, was still proud of the independent traditions of the city organisation:

> The Moscow party organisation is unique in the Russian Communist Party, not like that of Petrograd or any other organisation . . . because of its specific features, the intake of workers and its strong traditions, whose reasons have to be sought in the composition of the Moscow proletariat and the structure of Moscow industry.[21]

The May programme had called for a centralised, disciplined and united party in which all members were subordinate to their territorial committees. In Moscow this entailed the creation of a city party committee sufficiently distinct from the party organisation as a whole in order to impose its will. As the party as a whole stood to mass organisations and the administrative apparatus, so the new committees were to stand in relation to the mass of party membership. However, the MK did not become the supreme political arbiter in the *raion*s until after the end of the civil war, in early 1921, and for the greater part of the period its authority was balanced by that of the *raion*s. In the first phase of Soviet power the MK existed more as a general political co-ordinating body than the organisational centre of the party in the city.

As a result of frequent arrests, the MK had survived only for short periods prior to February 1917 and the emphasis had been on fairly autonomous *raion* party organisations. A major anomaly of the MPO was the practice of direct delegation to the MK from the *raion*s and not by election at a city party conference. The first city party conference after the overthrow of the autocracy on 3–4 April 1917 had elected a committee, but once the *raion* party organisations (RPO) had established themselves the role of the conference, beginning with the third city party conference on 10 May 1917, was restricted to confirming the delegates from the *raion*s to the MK. This system remained in operation, with modifications, until May 1920. The RPOs had a variable number of delegates depending on their size, with one delegate for every 250 members.[22] Thus the railway RPO had between two and five representatives on the MK throughout the period,[23] Basmannyi had four in February 1919, and a large organisation such as Gorodskoi had eight in March 1920.[24] These representatives were elected at a local party conference, the highest body in the *raion*s in the early period, and later at delegate meetings. The terms of representation changed, and in August 1919 the MK bureau decided 'Not to set a period of authority, since the *raion*s have the right to re-elect them at every delegate meeting'.[25] This flexible system is reflected in the incomplete information on the membership, and indeed in the size (30–70 people) of the MK between 1918 and March 1920 as delegates were recalled or sent to other work (see Table 4.1). Direct delegation and the right of recall allowed the RPOs to exert an immediate influence over the MK and suggest that within the MPO some of the elements of the commune state were being practised. In late 1920 Myasnikov wrote that this system was not democratic centralism, but federalism, and indeed for the first part of the war the MPO consisted of allied but largely autonomous *raion* party organisations. Therefore, he argued, 'The MK did not lead the work of the raions either politically or organisationally'.[26] Unification with the *guberniya* provoked a major debate on the role and manner of electing the MK (see page 112 below).

Local party organisations were governed in their internal affairs by their own statutes, while their relationships with other bodies were regulated by the general party statutes adopted by the VI Party Congress in August 1917 and by the VIII Party Conference in December 1919. The Moscow statute adopted by the 30 July 1918 city party conference reflected both the desire for a more ordered city organisation following the May circulars, and the attempt to enshrine the rights of the lower party organisations, above all the RPOs. The statute stated that the city party conference was to be elected by general *raion* party assemblies and to meet monthly, and that it was the highest body in the city. The MK delegated by the *raion*s was 'To guide all the political and organisational work of all the *raion* party organisations and all communist fractions of the various institutions in Moscow'.[27] In practice, however, for most of the period it was in no position to exert significant supervision over the *raion*s for lack of its own apparatus and staff. Even though the 'withering away' of the party refers to the weakening of organisational control over a declining membership, the committees themselves worked on an *ad hoc* basis. In the early period, the organisation of the party in the localities was marked by diversity and often by extreme informality. In many of Moscow's committees, and especially in the *raion*s, all offices were elected and rotated among the members. Posts were not strictly appointed and often no one was responsible for carrying out any particular policy or job. In late 1918 the MK's own five commissions, later called departments, were still barely functioning.[28] From the first, because of its size, the MK selected a bureau (variously called a presidium, executive committee or commission) to conduct day-to-day work. It initially consisted of about five people, but by 1920–21 it had expanded to about 10 (see Table 4.1). It prepared the agendas for meetings and also had the important right of distributing party activists. On 26 July 1918 the MK formed a three-man secretariat of V. M. Zagorskii, B. A. Breslav, and D. I. Efremov as first secretary (replaced by Zagorskii in September), meeting about three times a week, and which acted as the main motor of the MK. At that time the whole staff of the MK apparat consisted of between sixteen and twenty people. Zagorskii's role in the MK was similar to that of Sverdlov in the TsK until the latter's death in March 1919, with membership statistics and personnel notes restricted to what his briefcase could contain. Sverdlov and Zagorskii were old friends from Nizhnii-Novgorod, and it was Sverdlov who recalled Zagorskii to Moscow in mid-1918, even though he had had no contact with the MPO for four years.[29] In February 1919, at a time of debate over the MK's alleged lack of leadership, the MK bureau

Table 4.1   Membership of Moscow party committee, 1917–March 1921

1A.   Members of the MK elected at the I Moscow city party conference (3–4 April 1917): A. A. Andreev, Angarskii, R. I. Berzin, Bobrov, G. K. Golenko, Konstantinov (Orekhov), K. G. Maksimov, M. S. Ol'minskii, Petin, I. A. Pyatnitskii, Rostovshchikov, R. S. Samoilova (Zemlyachka), Shternberg, A. A. Sol'ts, M. F. Vladimirskii, A. Zakharov, V. Zakharov, I. A. Zelenskii, A. A. Znamenskii and Zubkov (*Sotsial-demokrat*, 13 April 1917).

1B.   On 6 April 1917 the MK elected an executive committee of five: Angarskii, Konstantinov, Samoilova, Sol'ts and Znamenskii (*Sotsial-demokrat*, 13 April 1917).

2.   The 10 May 1917 city party conference ratified a committee of 25 members, two each from the nine *raions*, and seven elected at the conference. The seven were: Inessa Armand, Nikolai Bukharin, N. M. Lukin (Antonov), M. S. Ol'minskii, T. I. Popov, A. A. Sol'ts and R. S. Samoilova.

3.   MK members in mid-1918 (incomplete): Al'perovich, Bogov, Bukharin, Il'ya, I. E. Fradkin (B. M. Volin), Lomov, Lukin, Pokrovskii, Pronskii, Samoilova, Steklov, Radek, Skvortsov-Stepanov and Smirnov (*P*, 13 April; 7, 18, 23 July; and 2 August 1918). Six members of the MK left for the front in early August 1918: Fradkin, Ivanov, Razshchikov, Ribe, Shillert and Znamenskii (*P*, 8 August 1918). The MK bureau on 30 August 1918 consisted of B. A. Breslav, D. I. Efremov, T. F. Lyudvinskaya, A. F. Myasnikov, M. S. Ol'minskii, A. A. Sol'ts, V. M. Zagorskii and R. S. Zemlyachka (Dumova, *Sekretar', MK*, p. 97).

4.   By late 1918 the MK included the following: Belen'kii, Chernyak, Dubinin, Dzenis, Efremov, Gerasimov, Godel', Kakhiani, Kasatkin, Khmel'nitskii, Kollontai, Kozlov, Kukuev, Lipitskii, Lomskii, Lyudvinskaya, Mitskevich, Mosolov, Osipov, Petrov, Poznanskii, Radek, Reinbakh, Rivlin, Rutman, Samarin, Savel'ev, Shevkov, Solov'ev, Svobodin, Titov, Tsivtsivadze, Ukhanov, Vladimirskii and Zagorskii (*P*, 1, 5, 15 October 1918).

5.   The 25 March 1920 city party conference confirmed the 36 nominations from twelve *raion*s to the MK: Amosov, Batyshev, Bel'yanov, Filler, Ivanov, Korochkin, Kotov, Kozlov, Latsis, Lisitsyn, Moroz, Pyatnitskii, Rivlin, Rusakov, Sadovskii, Safronov, Shkiryatov, Skobeinikov, Smirnov, Sokolov, Starosvetskii, Ter, Tsikhon, Ukhanov, Vasil'ev, Yurenev and Zimin. Myasnikov and Tsivtsivadze were co-opted on to the committee (*KT*, 26 March 1920; *P*, 26 March 1920).

6A.   The 21 May 1920 I Moscow *guberniya* conference elected a joint MK of 31 members for the city and *guberniya*: Alekseev, Belen'kii, Bubnov, Bunksh, Drozhzhin, Ivanov, Kamenev, Karpukhin, Kotov, Latsis, Lidak, Lisitsyn, Loginov, Minkov, Moroz, Myasnikov, Myshkin, Ostrovitinov, Polidorov, Pyatnitskii, Shkiryatov, Sokol'nikov, Sokolov, Sorin, Sorokin, Tsivtsivadze, Ukhanov, Uryaev, Vyatkin, Zelenskii and Zimin (*KT*, 22 May 1920).

6B.   The new MK met the same day (21 May) and elected a bureau of 7: Myasnikov (unanimously elected secretary), Zelenskii (20 votes), Ivanov (18), Minkov (18), Sorin (18), Pyatnitskii (17) and Bubnov (13) (*KT*, 22 May 1920).

6C.   Zelenskii acted as secretary during Myasnikov's absence on the Polish front, and Belen'kii (12) was an MK member during his absence (*KT*, 27 May 1920).

6D. An emergency session of the MK on 11 August 1920, attended by 30 people, considered a replacement for Zelenskii who had been appointed by the TsK to work in Narkomprod. Instead of electing a single secretary a secretariat of two was created, Minkov and Pyatnitskii. Because so many members of the bureau had been sent on duties to other parts of the country new elections were held: Belen'kii, Bubnov, Ivanov, Minkov, Pyatnitskii, Sorin and Zimin (*KT*, 12 August 1920).

7A. An MK of 39 members and 20 candidates was elected at the IV Moscow guberniya party conference (20–22 November 1920): Alekseev, Antselovich, Artem (Sergeev), Belen'kii, Boguslavskii, Bunksh, Detslenko, Dorofeev, Drozhzhin, Fonshenko, Giber, Ignatov, Kamenev, Korzinov, Kol'tsov, Kotov, Krinitskii, Lavrov, Loginov, Lyudvinskaya, Marchenko, Markin, Messing, Minkov, Novikov, Podbel'skii, Rastopchin, Sadovskii, Sakharov, Sapronov, Shkiryatov, Sokolov, Sorin, Sorokin, Uryvaev, Yakovleva, Zakharov, Zamorenov, Zelenskii. The candidates included Likhachev, S. N. Smidovich, Rafail (*KT*, 23 November 1920).

7B. The MK met on 24 November 1920 and elected a bureau of nine: Artem (secretary), Belen'kii, Dorofeev, Ignatov, Kamenev, Minkov, Rastopchin, Sapronov and Sorin (*KT*, 25 November 1920).

7C. At the end of December 1920 Artem was sent to work in the metalworkers' union TsK by the party TsK and V. N. Yakovleva was elected secretary to replace him.

7D. New elections were held to the MK bureau on 25 January 1921 to reflect the changes over the trade union question: Belen'kii, Ignatov, Kamenev, Krinitskii, Rastopchin, Sapronov, Uryvaev, Yakovleva, Zelenskii (*Otchet MK za yanvar' 1921g.*, Moscow, 1921, p. 5).

8A. An MK of 32 members and 10 candidates was elected at the V Moscow guberniya party conference (19–21 February 1921): Alekseev, Belen'kii, Boguslavskii, Bushber, Dorofeev, Kamenev, Kol'tsov, Kotov, Krinitskii, Kulikov, Loginov, Lozovskii, Marchenkov, Maslov, Messing, Minkov, Rastopchin, Rostovshchikov, Skobeinikov, Smirnov, Sokolov, Sorin, Sorokin, Tseitlin, Tsikhon, Tulyakov, Uryvaev, Yakovleva, Yudzevich, Zelenskii. The candidates were: Bessonov, Borisov, Mikhailov, Murav'ev, Rozenberg, Safronov, Pashentsev, Sevenov, Zamorenov, Zheltov (*V Mosk. gubpartkonf*, Moscow, 1921, pp. 41–2).

8B. The MK session of 22 February 1921 elected a bureau of nine members and three candidates: Kamenev, Kol'tsov, Krinitskii, Lozovskii, Maslov, Smirnov, Sorin, Tulyakov, Yakovleva: and three candidates: Rastopchin, Zelenskii and Zheltov (*KT*, 24 February 1921).

---

was reorganised. The seven-person bureau and the RKs were now obliged to report on their activities to the full MK, which was to meet weekly. The bureau was to select two assistants for the MK secretary who were to act as an organisation committee.[30] In this way there was a gradual improvement in the technical efficiency of the MK, but up to early 1920 it was clearly fairly weak organisationally.

All attempts at improving party organisation were undermined by the heavy demands of the civil war. Communists could either be sent to the front or to some other duty via personal mobilisation by order of the central military authorities (the Bureau of Military Commissars and then by the Political Administration of the Council of Defence – *Politicheskoe upravlenie revvoensoveta*) (PUR RVSR)), or as part of the mass mobilisations in response to critical developments at the fronts. The latter were ordered by the TsK and ratified by a city party conference, and then implemented by the *raion* party organisations down to the cells. The first mass mobilisations took place in the Urals in late May 1918 in response to the revolt of the Czech Legion. In 1918 there were four major party mobilisations in Moscow, and in 1919–20, five. Following reverses in July 1918 the TsK decided that communist drafts were essential to stiffen the resistance of the Red Army.[31] On 30 July 1918 the city party conference decided that within a week one-fifth of all MPO members, including all those with military experience, were to be placed at the disposal of the military commissariat and all party organisations were placed on a war footing.[32] This first mobilisation sent 700 communists to the front, including many of the more experienced members.[33] A second MPO mobilisation took place after the 29 August 1918 city party conference. It is from this period that the beginning of the special communist detachments (ChON) can be dated (see page 130 below).[34] With the military situation deteriorating in the early autumn of 1918 the 15 October city party conference sent another draft of communists to the front,[35] and a fourth city mobilisation was ordered by the MK on 19 November which included a quarter of all sympathisers. According to incomplete figures, the city sent about 2000 communists, over a tenth of its membership, to the Eastern front alone in 1918.[36] This pattern of frequent mobilisations continued throughout the civil war and had a disastrous effect on the local party organisations. The 248 communists mobilised between October 1918 and March 1919 from the small Blagushe-Lefortovo *raion*, for example, represented half its total membership. In June 1919 alone, sixty-nine communists were taken, most of whom on this occasion were sent to defend Petrograd from General G. Yudenich's advance.[37] Between 1918 and 1921 nearly 70 per cent of all Moscow's communists served in the Red Army,[38] and, even in 1922, 66 per cent of Moscow's 32 000 communists had served at the front.[39] The 1920 reregistration revealed that only a third (8000 out of 25 000) members were exempt from military service, while over half of the total had been or were in front-line units.[40] This, together with the non-military mobilisations for grain, fuel, transport or (from 1920) work on the land, emphasised the party's key role in providing its own membership as a mobilising force.

Owing to the clandestine forms of party activity before February 1917 and the nature of the revolutionary struggle in that year, a large degree of autonomy was vested in the *raion* party organisations. They were the arbiters of local recruitment, they controlled the cells, and they were the scene of the debates over the most important political questions. *Raion* committees (RK) were initially elected at general meetings of the *raion* party organisations, and from mid-1918 at delegate meetings. During the withering away of the party period they had barely functioned. Gorodskoi *raion*, for example, did not have a single full-time party organiser up to August 1918, and only in that month was a secretariat of three formed.[41] The Alekseevsko-Rostokinskii RK not only lacked a permanent secretary up to mid-July, it also had no full-time activists at its disposal,[42] and this was the case in most *raion*s. The onset of the war and the mass mobilisations weakened the cells, and party work became increasingly concentrated in the hands of the committees. A major response to the party crisis on the eve of the VIII Party Congress in March 1919 was to strengthen the party apparatus itself by ensuring a corps of people devoted to party work alone. At the MK meeting of 11 January 1919, Zagorskii demanded the strict enforcement of an earlier MK resolution on the return from the front of one responsible official for each *raion*.[43] In February 1919 the Rogozhsko-Simonovskii RK complained that its greatest handicap was the lack of activists. In the two preceding months the *raion* had lost six of its leading members and the December 1918 mobilisation had ruptured the committee's links with many of the factories in the *raion*.[44] Lefortovskii RK reported that after the same mobilisation work in the cells had collapsed because of the lack of organisers.[45] The lack of activists was to be one of the main reasons why the May programme was not fulfilled in its entirety during the civil war but had to await the coming of peace. Nevertheless, despite the difficulties, the party committees began to consolidate themselves. The Sokol'nicheskii RK report for July–November 1918 illustrates the improvement: functions had been specialised and departments had been created to carry out specific duties, such as agitprop; in June 1918 the RK had occupied a single room and had employed only one secretary, with all the work being carried out by an RK of eleven to thirteen people; by November 1918 the RK occupied a whole floor of a fairly large building, and instead of a single secretary there was a whole secretariat. Following a reregistration (see Chapter 5) membership had increased sharply by the end of the year, and the number of cells increased from twenty in July to forty-five in November and were to be found in over half of the enterprises in the *raion*.[46]

The war inevitably promoted centralisation and authoritarianism in local organisations, but the responsibility of running the whole state apparatus weighed equally heavily. In February 1919 the TsK vividly described the concentration of party life in the committees:

> The organisational disintegration suffered by our party with the departure of the best forces to soviet work has now been replaced by the development of a strongly centralised party apparatus. We have marched a long way on this path, but the process can in no way be considered complete.[47]

There was a tendency for the RKs themselves to decrease in size as personnel became scarcer and functions were centralised. At the end of July 1918, for example, the Khamovnicheskii RK decreased from nine to six members and the RK bureau was abolished and its functions were transferred to a secretariat.[48] A general meeting of Butyrskii RPO on 3 August 1918 even went so far as to propose giving the RK dictatorial powers.[49] In Basmannyi *raion* work was concentrated in the RK bureau. The RK itself, elected in November 1918, had only met twice in plenary session by February 1919. There was even an attempt at a delegate meeting on 5–6 February 1919 to abolish the RK and concentrate work in the bureau, a clear breach of democratic centralism. Instead, the RK was decreased from fifteen to seven members and the bureau was abolished.[50] Elsewhere work was also concentrated in the hands of a small group of *raion* activists. In Zamoskvorech'e, the RK bureau was abolished in July 1919, and the work of the *raion* soviet was similarly consolidated.[51] In a large *raion* such as Gorodskoi the RK consisted of fifteen to twenty people, with current work being carried out by a bureau elected by the RK.[52] In each *raion* there was a revisional commission, first established in 1917 and elected at a general meeting, to oversee the financial affairs of the *raion*.[53] Concern over the chronic organisational fluidity in the *raions* prompted an extension of their functions, codified by an MK instruction of 7 June 1919. This established that they were to be composed of three MK members, and their duties included the supervision of the RKs and the condition of the party in the *raion*s.[54] They were the precursors of the control commissions established by the IX Party Conference in September 1920.

The July 1918 MPO statute had stated that the highest body in the *raion* was the general meeting, which could elect an RK of whatever size it felt necessary,[55] but it provided little guidance on the relationships between the various bodies. In early December 1918 the Sokol'nicheskii RPO, the liveliest organisation at the time, adopted a *reglament* (standing orders) which attempted to provide a more detailed definition of the functions of the cells; the delegate meetings, which were now elevated as the highest body in the *raion*s for organisational questions; the general meetings, which were to deal with general political questions only; and the RK, with a bureau to conduct current work.[56] This *reglament* was adopted by the MK on 25 December[57] and was generalised with the force of a party statute for the whole organisation by the city party conference on 18 January 1919.[58] It registered the centrality of the RPOs in the Moscow organisation and of the delegate meetings in them. On the eve of the VIII Congress the MK argued that the *reglament* would help encourage the 'self-activity and collective creativity' of the party and its members.[59] While party work was being concentrated in the *raion*s, no corresponding movement was yet taking place between the RPOs and the MK. In this sense Myasnikov in late 1920 was justified in stating that both the *reglament* and the 1918 statute reflected a 'lack of centralism or ordered system'.[60] Nevertheless, important organisational principles were emerging which defined the operation of democratic centralism within the ruling party. An example of this was when the MK in January 1919 severely censured the practice of holding private inter-*raion* meetings of party members without the sanction of either the RKs or the MK, the sin of horizontalism which could lead on to factionalism. It declared that such meetings infringed the statute and that their organisers would be strictly reprimanded.[61] Meetings of party members for whatever purpose could only take place within the given structures, and it was over this principle that the later oppositions stumbled. At the same time it ensured that the 'self-activity' of the party masses would be channelled within the course established by higher party bodies. And yet, as in the economy, war communism mainly saw the definition of aims rather than the implementation of the programme.

REFORM PROPOSALS

On the eve of the VIII Party Congress of March 1919 a major debate developed over the 'crisis' in the party. Against the background of concern over recruitment and the emergence of a party elite (*verkhi*) (see Chapter 5) the question of the nature and level of guidance to be obtained from the TsK and MK for lower party bodies was raised. At

issue was the question of how to establish effective central leadership
without undermining local authority, a question of equal relevance for
the soviets (see Chapter 6). Three main positions emerged in the pre-
congress discussion. The first is represented by those whom R. Service
calls the 'Strict Centralists', otherwise called by M. M. Helgesen the
apparatchiki, whose views were articulated by Sverdlov in the TsK and
whose main strength was concentrated in the Nizhnii-Novgorod party
organisation. Lazar Kaganovich, a member of that organisation, called
for a 'sleek hierarchy of uniformly organised party committees'[62]
working under the guidance of an improved central party apparatus.
Already a significant step had been taken in that direction by the
abolition of the Moscow *Oblast* Bureau (Committee) in January 1919,
an intermediary body which represented the regional interests of the
whole Central Industrial Region. At the other extreme were a group
based in Moscow *guberniya* and known as the Democratic Centralists
(DCs). Joined by E. N. Ignatov and other representatives of Moscow's
*raion*s, they agreed with the 'strict' group that the TsK displayed a lack
of 'planned leadership' and provided insufficient detailed guidance for
the local party organisations, but, like the Left Communists, they
stressed the need for democracy and accountability.[63] In the run-up to
the congress these two groups tended to form an unholy alliance in their
criticisms of the party centre.[64] The third view was presented by the
traditionally moderate MK. The very manner of its organisation, as a
body of delegates from the *raion*s, in itself retarded the development of
an *apparatchik* mentality. By no stretch of the imagination could the
organisational structure of the MPO be called a 'sleek hierarchy' of
uniformly organised committees. The MK claimed to steer a course
midway between separatism on the one hand, and 'bureaucratic
centralism' on the other. The now customary calls for strict party
discipline, especially over party fractions, were balanced by a range of
proposals aimed at increasing participation through delegate meetings,
party conferences and greater guidance from the centre through
circulars, and indeed a more efficient centre by the creation of a three-
person secretariat[65] (formed in April 1919 to complement the Orgburo
and Politburo which were formed in March 1919). At the congress the
MK's moderate line on the question of party reform was the dominant
one. Zinoviev's keynote speech on the question, however, conceded too
little to satisfy either extreme and the question remained on the agenda.[66]

Following the VIII congress, little attention was paid to organisational reform as the pressing needs of the war and current campaigns
took priority. The Blagushe-Lefortovo RK report for May 1919, for

example, admitted that not one of the four RK and two bureau sessions that month had discussed organisational work, or even the general condition of the party organisation. The MK and the city party conference were equally inattentive as Denikin's threat to Moscow and Yudenich's to Petrograd took precedence over organisational reform.[67] The implications of the war were driven home by Trotsky at the 24 September 1919 city party conference. Martial law had been declared in the city on 6 September, and now at his behest the MPO itself was placed under martial law: all communists were to be removed from 'civilian and undoubtedly necessary posts and transferred to military work'; all institutions were to devote themselves to the needs of the garrison; and the intensity of labour in all enterprises serving the army was to be raised.[68] This was total war, and indeed a series of plots were discovered in Moscow itself, including the plan by the monarchist National Centre to seize the city. On 25 September an explosion at the MK headquarters (organised by the LSR Donata Cherepanova working with the so-called Anarchist Underground) during a meeting attended by over 120 party activists killed twelve of the MPO's leading members, including the MK secretary V. M. Zagorskii, and wounded fifty-five more including M. S. Ol'minskii.[69].

For most of 1919, party work developed in response to immediate emergencies and the available resources. Awareness of the ramshackle condition of the organisation, however, in July 1919 prompted a review of all aspects of the work of the MPO, from the MK's own departments to the *raion* organisations, and a plan was drawn up recommending a thorough reform. Pressure of current work prevented the implementation of the plan at the time.[70] With the breathing space of early 1920 the MK returned to the issue and convened a conference of RK representatives on 9 January to discuss the reform of the MPO on the basis of the earlier plan. Myasnikov presented the main report and launched a scathing attack on all aspects of the party organisation: there was no single model or system in the work of the party committees; delegate and general assemblies did not meet uniformly, and in some places did not meet at all; the Komsomol organisations 'dragged out a miserable existence'; the party schools were 'moribund'; party registers were inadequate; there were too many plants without cells; and the soviets had to be revived.[71] Myasnikov's speech did not so much reveal the inadequacies of the organisation, though this it did vividly enough, as present a vision of the future organisation. The discussion, however, to his great annoyance, centred on the MK's own inadequacies. One speaker called for greater guidance by the MK over the *raion*s; another for the MK to be elected at a city conference; yet another criticised the tendency of the bureau to take on the full functions of the full MK, and so on. G. Ya. Belen'kii, the representative of Presnenskii RK and MK member, argued that electing the MK at a conference would isolate it from the *raion*s, while Myasnikov, who was later to change his mind, argued that the existing method of constituting the MK was 'the most democratic and allows the committee to be closely linked to the *raion*s'.[72] A commission was appointed to draft a plan on the basis of the discussion at the meeting, and its recommendations were adopted by the MK on 21 January 1920. A new statute was to be adopted to incorporate the reform proposals, the *raion*s were to be united and divided into wards (*uchastki*), a reorganisation of the MK secretariat was envisaged, and enhanced party control over Komsomol and the trade unions was planned.[73] The conference shows that calls for greater guidance, voiced before the VIII Party Congress and now, must be understood in context. They were not a wholesale acceptance of the 'strict centralist' programme, since they retained a strong commitment to the existing distribution of power, but represented a demand for the greater efficiency of the existing system. The calls for a delineation of functions, with the powers and responsibilities of the MK clearly established, was a way of preventing central encroachments on local prerogatives and arbitrary administrative actions. If the MK worked better it would 'interfere' less, and the same argument went for the centre. But at the same time the ideological framework in which they operated, of the party's leading role over the trade unions and other bodies, made the long-term viability of such a reform programme doubtful. It would be difficult to maintain the mid-path between centralism and democracy in the party.

The new draft statute was adopted by the city party conference on 18 March 1920. The city party conference became the highest juridicial and guiding body in the MPO. Hitherto, according to Myasnikov, it had been a 'ceremonial' body with large numbers from the *raion*s and the centre attending to hear 'fancy reports' and 'triumphal voting'.[74] The statute continued the system of *raion* delegation to the MK, though a term of six months was now introduced. The city conference was now not only to confirm the MK members but the MK was made responsible to it, whereas previously the individual MK member had been responsible only to his or her *raion*. Nevertheless, the manner of forming the MK still contravened the terms of the party statute (articles 33–34) adopted by the VIII Party Conference in December 1919, which stipulated that a conference should elect its committee.[75] The role of the *raion*s was enhanced and their decisions were made obligatory for the RKs. They did, however, lose the decisive role in accepting or expelling members, a right which passed to the MK.[76] General meetings lost any effective role and they were to meet only once every three months to hear general reports.[77] At the same time the city was divided into about fifty wards as part of the attempt to increase participation and to make the party more responsive to local needs.[78] This statute was the last to reflect the opinion of the city alone and marked a transitional stage to the incorporation of the Moscow organisation into a national system. This took place on unification with the *guberniya* a few months later.

THE PARTY COMMITTEES: SECOND PHASE, 1920–21

The end of the civil war in 1920 was marked by the implementation of projects for party reorganisation drafted at the height of the battles. Lack of activists and organisational heterogeneity had already prompted several plans to unite the *raion*s in 1919.[79] The proposals had been shelved in the heat of the war, but with the breathing space of early 1920 the thirteen *raion*s were reduced to seven in March (see map on p. xv).[80] The new RKs now had standard departments covering the key areas of its activities. The MK justified the move on the grounds that it would save on personnel and would facilitate the fulfilment of orders from the centre.[81] The same reasons were given for the unification of the city and *guberniya*. At the VIII Party Conference Kaganovich, the strict centralist, had called for the abolition of autonomous city committees (though he excluded those in the capitals) in favour of a uniform system of *guberniya* committees.[82] In Moscow the idea of unification had been raised by the *gubkom* in August 1919 but had been rejected by an MK jealous of its independence. While agreeing that there should be greater co-operation, the MK argued that unification was unlikely to lead to savings on personnel, the main justification for the move.[83] With the stress on economic tasks in 1920 and the pressure for standardised party organisations the question of unification was once again raised. At the IX Congress Kamenev now called for a uniform system of *gubkomy* and departments.[84] In March 1920 the TsK laid down the guidelines for the new committees[85] and Moscow was forced to adapt to this model. On 21 April 1920 the MK agreed to the unification of the two regions[86] and the 15 May 1920 city party conference, the last to be held until the revival of the city organisation in February 1931, adopted the unification plan.[87] The justification for the measure included arguments that it would save on manpower, reduce duplication, increase party influence in the countryside now that the greater resources of the city were available, and that it would be easier to implement the policies of the centre.[88] Unification, as in the *raion*s, permitted the creation of standardised departments.

Unification posed the controversial question of how to constitute the MK. The MK bureau meeting of 18 May 1920 decided that the existing MK and MGK would draw up a list of thirty-one candidates to be elected at a joint conference (which duly took place), with current work to be conducted by a bureau of seven.[89] At a stroke, direct *raion* control over the MK was abolished and its selection was now concentrated in the hands of a small coterie whose choices were usually rubber-stamped at a conference. The change marked an important step in the development in the MPO of greater MK control over the *raion*s and greater integration into the national party organisation with the loss of Moscow's autonomy. The change was precipitated both by the ideology of democratic centralism and by the perceived organisational necessities of the time, even though the war was all but over. The transformation was marked by the adoption of a new statute for the joint organisation. The *guberniya* conference became the highest body in the region, meeting every six months, and electing the MK. Already the March 1920 statute had changed the status of the MK bureau from a purely technical body into one with decision-making powers between conferences.[90] On unification with the *guberniya* in May 1920 the bureau's independence was further enhanced as it now only had to report on the more important topics.[91] The delegate meetings in the *raion*s were confirmed as the highest local body, but were now to meet only once every three months to hear reports and elect the RK.[92] These measures, adopted at the height of the militarisation of the economy, weakened direct membership control over the party's executive bodies, and the possibilities of rank-and-file discussion were curtailed. The statute stressed, for example, that the delegate meetings could only discuss political organisational questions with the permission of the RK.[93] The statute marked the apogee of centralisation in the MPO during the civil war. With the debate over party democracy from late 1920 the V Moscow *Guberniya* Party Conference (19–21 February 1921) made delegate meetings monthly and dropped the stipulation that they could only discuss questions of principle with the agreement of the RK, which had in any case been ignored during the debates of 1920.[94]

The new model MK now had direct responsibility for the work of the whole MPO, the soviets, the trade unions and other social organisations, which it exercised through the fractions.[95] Myasnikov commented on this in late 1920:

> If previously the highest practical organ of the Moscow organisation, the bureau . . . had only been a 'staff between the raions' it now became a real general headquarters of the MPO. The MK itself, from a 'high gathering' became a controlling centre.[96]

The MK secretariat had at its disposal the 540 party members (see Table 4.2) who were devoted purely to party work and probably expanded in line with the twenty-fold increase in the staff of the central secretariat from 1919, which reached 600 by early 1921.[97] The old federative principle had been replaced by strong democratic centralism with the subordination of the lower to the higher organ up to the MK and beyond. This was a crucial step in the 'internal metamorphosis' of the MPO as the RPOs became integrated into a hierarchical structure and thus lost the independence of the 'federalist' period. And, it should be noted, this was a response not to the war but to what appeared at the time as the tasks of peacetime. The price of the professionalisation, or bureaucratisation, of the MPO was the emergence of an apparatus which brought the formally democratic procedures in the organisation within its own ambit, and thereby largely freed itself from the control of the rank-and-file membership. The change in the election procedure in the MPO allowed the emergence of a new generation of Bolshevik leaders, dubbed by W. E. Mosse the 'New Bolsheviks',[98] who owed their positions less to their popularity within the party organisation and more to their standing with the central apparatus. While Moscow was no exception to the national phenomenon of *guberniya* and city committees being led by active party workers of pre-revolutionary vintage, this standing at 75 per cent in late 1919,[99] the actual composition of the MK over the period had been marked by a high degree of flux. Only one person (Zelenskii) who had been elected to the first MK in May 1917 was elected to the last in our period in February 1921, and only Belen'kii sat on every committee elected between September 1918 and early 1921 (see Table 4.1). With the election of the MK at *guberniya* party conferences the increased weight of the party's bureaucratic apparatus itself. By that time the corps of key activists devoted exclusively to party work consisted of 664 members of the MPO (1.9 per cent), a lower proportion than in the party as a whole, illustrating that the development of the apparatus in the localities imposed a proportionally greater strain on these organisations than in the relatively proletarian Moscow. Here a total of 1930 members were involved in party work as well as some other

Table 4.2　Occupation of MPO members in August 1920

	City		Guberniya		Total	
	No.	Per-centage	No.	Per-centage	No.	Per-centage
Industrial enterprises:						
responsible workers	161	0.5	43	0.8	204	0.6
of whom from workers	82	51.0	22	51.2	104	51.0
office/accounts	187	0.6	135	2.5	322	0.9
junior employees	22	0.1	7	0.1	29	0.1
workers	5 994	20.1	1 522	2.8	7 516	21.3
Total	6 364	21.3	1 707	31.6	8 071	22.9
Artisan and craft industry	423	1.4	93	1.7	516	1.5
Agriculture	739	2.5	270	5.0	1 009	2.9
Transport						
responsible workers	225	0.7	4	0.1	229	0.6
of whom from workers	92	40.9	2	50.0	94	41.0
office/accounts	202	0.7	28	0.5	230	0.7
junior employees/workers	1 152	3.9	95	1.8	1 247	3.5
Total	1 579	5.3	127	2.3	1 706	4.8
Soviet institutions:						
Responsible workers	2 629	8.8	719	13.3	3 346	9.5
of whom from workers	309	11.7	281	39.1	590	18.0
office/accounts	3 108	10.4	530	9.8	3 638	10.3
junior employees	2 427	8.1	271	5.0	2 698	7.6
Total	8 164	27.4	1 520	28.1	9 684	27.4
Red Army:						
political leaders	118	0.4	15	0.3	133	0.4
higher staff officers	90	0.3	14	0.3	104	0.3
other staff officers	1 126	3.8	208	3.8	1 334	3.8
admin. and medical	899	3.0	191	3.5	1 090	3.1
cadets	1 247	4.2	41	0.7	1 288	3.6
soldiers – line units	1 782	6.0	337	6.2	2 119	6.0
non-line units	313	1.0	60	1.1	373	1.1
Total	5 575	18.7	866	16.0	6 441	18.3
Party organisation:						
total in party work	1 461	4.9	469	8.7	1 930	5.4
of whom in party work only	540	1.8	124	2.3	664	1.9
Trade unions:						
responsible workers	288	1.0	122	2.2	410	1.2
of whom from workers	152	52.8	71	58.2	223	54.0
FZK members	363	1.2	233	4.3	596	1.2

	City		Guberniya		Total	
	No.	Per-centage	No.	Per-centage	No.	Per-centage
office/accounts/juniors	27	0.1	9	0.2	36	0.1
Total	678	2.8	364	6.7	1 042	2.5
House workers	14	0.1	4	0.1	18	0.1
Not working	264	0.9	29	0.5	293	0.8
No information	5 480	18.4	302	5.9	5 782	16.4
Total	29 820	100	5 406	100	35 226	100

Source: Materialy po statistike, pp. 42–7 and 90–3.

duties, 5.4 per cent of the total membership, of whom 34 per cent were full-time activists (see Table 4.2). However, before these tendencies or the bureaucracy could become established, the MPO had to undergo a bitter period of discussion as the centralisers and reformers clashed in the party and trade union debates.

THE PARTY CELL

During the civil war the party cell became the basic unit for party membership. The party committees tried to ensure that all communists belonged to ensure a modicum of control over them and to maintain links with the factory or office in which the cell was located. The changing role of the cell reflected the broader social and political changes taking place within the party and the debate over the cell paralleled that over the role of workers' control in the factories. The statute adopted by the VI Party Congress in 1917 had defined the *raion* or *oblast* grouping as the basic unit in the party and the cell was eclipsed by the general meeting of communists of a given area as the key organisational unit. With the decline in the organisational coherence of the party in early 1918 many cells simply dissolved and the communist's links with the party, in so far as it existed, was through a party fraction or general meeting. As in so many other respects, it was the May 1918 TsK initiatives which signalled a resurgence of the cells, but it was to take the greater part of the war for their role to be defined.

The emphasis on staffing command structures weakened the party's rank and file base in the army and industry. In August 1920 less than a

Table 4.3   Type and distribution of cells in August 1920[a]

| | Factory | | Transport | | Military | | Office | | |
	No.	Per-centage	No.	Per-centage	No.	Per-centage	No.	Per-centage	Total
Baum	127	76.0	0	–	30	18.3	7	4.3	164
Gor	14	6.3	5	2.2	69	31.1	134	60.4	222
Kras-Pres	35	30.4	12	10.4	18	15.6	50	43.5	115
Rog-Sim	40	59.7	7	10.4	18	26.9	2	3.0	67
Sok	15	11.4	52	39.7	35	26.7	29	22.1	131
Kham	8	10.4	20	30.0	29	37.7	20	30.0	77
Total	239	30.8	96	12.4	199	25.6	242	31.2	776

[a] No breakdown is available for the 133 cells in Zamoskvorech'e.
Source: Otchet MK za sentyabr' 1920g. (Moscow, 1920) p. 9.

third of the cells were in factories and they were to be found in under half the active enterprises (see Table 4.3). At this time the party layer in the industrial working class was only 7 per cent, but this, as in the army, exaggerates the number of communists actually at the bench. About a quarter of the cells in the city throughout the war were in the army. The Moscow garrison increased from about 100 000 men in 178 units in June 1919 to over 150 000 in 265 units in June 1920. The number of military communists correspondingly increased from 7250 and 149 candidates to 9792 and 2513 candidates.[100] Most units had a cell which in 1920 averaged forty-six members.[101] The party layer in the army during the volunteer period in early 1918 had been very high at about 20 per cent,[102] but with the mass mobilisations this had fallen to 4.6 per cent in early 1919 and thereafter the intensified induction of communists raised it to 8 per cent from mid-1919 to the end of the war.[103] Less than half of these, however, were line soldiers; the majority of members served in various administrative or political capacities (see Table 4.2).

The party membership in even the largest plants numbered at most a few dozen. The cell in the Bogatyr' resin plant in Sokol'nicheskii *raion* had only twenty-six members out of a workforce of about 5000 in January 1919,[104] and the cell in the Russkabel' cable and metal plant never represented more than a handful of the workforce.[105] The enterprise cells were the first reserve for recruitment to the army and offices and hence by mid-1921 the average had only fourteen to fifteen members, whereas the average membership of an office cell was sixty.[106] By mid-1919, for example, in Blagushe-Lefortovo the cells were in a miserable condition, with the majority of their members on assignments or in the army. The cells met infrequently and were mainly concerned, it was reported, with petty issues.[107] A questionnaire circulated by the RK in June 1919 revealed that the twenty-two cells (sixteen factory, five office, one military) had a membership of ninety-two, with 214 sympathisers, out of 3735 workers in the *raion*. When asked whether their cell enjoyed any prestige and authority, five gave a definite negative answer, the majority were doubtful, and only a few answered in the affirmative. All the cells reported that the workers were mainly concerned with 'economic or selfish issues' and noted that the cells were making little impact on the mass of the workforce.[108] In other *raion*s the situation was comparable. In Khamovnicheskii *raion* in May 1919 only five of the forty-five cells were in factories, the rest in offices and the army. Most of the major plants in the *raion*, dominated by the textile industry, had closed and the party organisation was faced with the remnants of the proletariat in half-closed factories, and a mass of office and craft workers in institutions and smaller enterprises and workshops.[109] In the Guzhon plant (in Rogozhsko-Simonovskii *raion*) membership had declined from seventy-five in a workforce of over 3000 in October 1917 to fifty-one out of 460 in March 1921.[110] At that time in the Guzhon ward there were only 301 communists (1.8 per cent) out of a total of 8500 industrial and transport workers and 8000 soldiers.[111] The situation was better in the proletarian Basmannyi *raion* where in April 1919 twenty-six of the forty-two cells were industrial;[112] by April 1920 the total had increased to eighty-one but only thirty-two were in factories, and these often only contained two or three members.[113] In the non-industrial Gorodskoi *raion*, however, the situation was very different. Here were concentrated the government offices and it had few large enterprises but a mass of small workshops employing 25–100 workers with, reportedly, 'no clear class consciousness'.[114] The *raion* party organisation was the largest in the city with 1017 members in May 1918[115] and 5085 in September 1920.[116] As early as mid-1918 the majority of these were not workers. By July 1919 75 per cent were '*chinovniki*' (a derogatory term for white collar workers, collectively known as *chinovnichestvo*) in the various offices where the great majority of the cells were to be found.[117] During the civil war the factory cells were denuded of membership and maintained a tenuous existence while those in the army and in offices prospered. This, as much as any changes in social composition of the party, was of critical importance in the party's development.

Throughout the war the party authorities encouraged the formation of cells in enterprises, but the very pressure of the war hindered these attempts, and even in early 1921 in some *raion*s the majority of factories

were without a cell.[118] Nevertheless, during the war the number of cells in
the city doubled from 563 in March 1918 to 1035 in March 1921.[119] The
1920 reregistration for the first time gave detailed figures on the cells in
six out of the seven *raion*s (see Table 4.3). The dominance of the military
and office cells is clear. With the approach of peace, efforts were made to
redeploy communists from offices to factories, but as Zelenskii admitted
at the XI Congress in 1922 the attempts to strengthen the party base in
this way had proved a failure.[120] The priority at first was to strengthen
the cells in the 'shock' factories, which tended to weaken the cells in other
enterprises. In September 1920 the TsK relieved party members
employed in metal plants from further mobilisations[121] as part of this
programme; this may well have been a response to the increasing strike
wave in these plants. At the same time more party activists were freed
from other duties and assigned (*prikreplennye*) to cells and wards.[122]

The formation of communist cells was as much part of the attempt to
combat non-Bolshevik influence as it was to control its own membership. The aim was to ensure party dominance on the key committees in
plants, especially the factory committees. A report from Gorodskoi
raion in 1918, for example, noted that thirty major plants had already
been 'seized' by the Bolsheviks.[123] In factories where the SRs had been
strong the Bolshevik cells became the legatees of their declining support
by October 1917, as in the Dinamo plant in Simonovskii *raion*. But
during the civil war the SRs staged a minor comeback in the Guzhon
plant and elsewhere. Even in the Dinamo plant Bolshevik dominance
was organisational, through control of the factory committee, rather
than numerical, and throughout the civil war the cell numbered no more
than about a dozen members out of about 400 workers.[124] The Bolshevik
task was more difficult in plants that were or had been Menshevik, and
above all in the print shops. The struggle against the print union at the
city level was paralleled by a policy of gradual pressure on the shopfloor.
At the ex-Kushner works in Krasnopresnenskii *raion*, for example, a cell
of three had been founded after the October 1919 party week (see p. 149
below) and by January 1920 numbered thirteen out of 565 workers. The
group waged a sustained struggle to obtain control of the union
mestkom as part of the strategy to 'seize' the print union as outlined by
Pravda in early 1920.[125] In this plant the *mestkom* was led by a wily and
popular Menshevik and he ensured that the Mensheviks remained in
control until 1922.[126] In general, the major task of the cell was to achieve
the 'communisation' of the union committee by securing a communist
majority. The party's weakness in the factories and its isolation from the
mass of the workers was one factor in the disturbances from late 1920.

The role and organisation of cells underwent major changes during the civil war. The extent to which they could be involved in the management of an enterprise, institution or military unit remained controversial. Before nationalisation the enterprise cells, often in conjunction with Bolshevik factory committees, were encouraged to play an active role in the plants, but with the introduction of state management their role became more problematic. As at the beginning of the first Five-Year Plan, initial cell involvement in a high degree of supervision over management gradually gave way to a more restricted definition of their functions.[127] Increasingly they were limited to the organisation and training of party members, providing information on local affairs to higher bodies, and conducting the ideological and organisational struggle against non-Bolshevik forces. The cells were given a variety of responsibilities but no real power. The change illustrates how in practice the transition took place from concepts of direct participation to the practice of the dictatorship of the proletariat. The increasing powerlessness of the *nizy* (rank and file) within the party was matched by increasing powerlessness in their place of work. Both the working class and the party activists in the factories were disengaged from the direct management of industrial affairs.

The army led the way in this process. The creation of a traditionally organised Red Army marked a major compromise, as the Left Communists pointed out, since the adoption of traditional military command structures entailed the curtailment of soldier control over officers, typical of 1917, and its replacement by party supervision through commissars over what were now called the military specialists (the old Tsarist officers). The party took over the responsibilities of political control previously vested in the popular movement; however the party represented not by the military cell but by its own hierarchical command structures. Although the Red Army was a child of the party, the sustained military emergency gave it a degree of independence, and therefore the issue of the role of the cells in the army is closely linked to the question of the relationship between the party and the military in general. The high percentage of communists in the army in 1918 has been noted. All decisions concerning their units, including recruitment, supply and political education were concentrated in this party group. With the introduction of conscription in 1918 the party layer decreased and at the same time the creation of a traditional army restricted their rights. The role of the military commissars, as supervisors both over the military specialists and also over the party cells, increased. Inevitably, frequent conflicts between the cells, used to having control of their units, and the commissars, developed. At the same time political departments were formed under armies, and then for individual regiments. They were initially concerned with agitprop, but by late 1918 claimed tutelage over communists in the army.[128] In Moscow views were divided over the rights of army cells. The instruction adopted by the conference of soldier communists in April 1918 had given cells extensive powers over the units and thus steered them on a collision course with the commissars.[129] Over the summer, opinion divided evenly over whether the cells were to be subordinate to the military commissariats and commissars, or to retain their earlier powers.[130] Some cells were still appointing commissars through the RKs, though all were ultimately checked by the national Bureau of Military Commissars.[131] In late August the TsK warned the local party organisations against interfering in the work of the political departments, especially in the appointment of commissars.[132] The ability of the cells to control the units and the commissars was further restricted by the TsK decree of 25 October 1918 which envisaged the cells as mainly agitational bodies. The decree forbade the formation of any party organisations, committees, groups, or any independent party institutions in the army.[133] In this way party committees as such were abolished in the army and the cells in the rear were integrated into the local party organisation. The precise rights of the local organisations still remained undefined, and the MK on 11 November 1918 called for a general instruction on the rights of cells in the army. In response, in early January 1919 the TsK issued an instruction which finally subordinated the cells to the commissars and restricted their functions to agitprop and implementing the party line. Party affairs were to be conducted by the political departments at the front and the local party organisations in the rear.[134] The development of autonomous party organisations, dubbed 'army syndicalism' by Trotsky, was prevented.

Such a major revision to the aspirations of the October revolution did not go unchallenged. On the eve of the VIII Party Congress opposition gathered to the use of specialists, the elimination of electability, and the overbearing behaviour of commissars. A general meeting of communists in Basmannyi *raion* on 16 December 1918 protested against the repression of cell activists at the front and criticised the emergence of 'boss-like relations' (*nachal'nichestvo*).[135] A meeting in Gorodskoi *raion* on 19 December criticised the use of specialists,[136] and the *guberniya* organisation protested in sharp tones against 'repression against communists'.[137] The MK itself had grave reservations about the changes and called for the rapid deployment of 'red commanders' to replace the bourgeois specialists,[138] a typical example of the specialists acting as scapegoats for systemic problems. The opposition to the use of military specialists and authoritarian methods of organising the Red Army was expressed by a resolution of the 14 March city party conference, which urged the rapid transition to a militia system to ensure the 'class character' of the army.[139] The militia army was proposed as a way of integrating military and civilian authority. The opposition came to a head at the congress. A grouping led by such ex-Left Communists as E. M. Yaroslavskii, T. V. Sapronov and V. M. Smirnov coalesced in a 'military opposition' whose ranks included Myasnikov, the future MK secretary, and the veteran Moscow communist R. S. Zemlyachka, with Stalin playing a shady role motivated by hostility to Trotsky. The opposition criticised the use of the specialists and called for greater collegiality. Smirnov attacked the development of the political departments and argued for greater autonomy for communist commissars.[140] In calling for greater powers for both the commissars and the cells (and thus for the local party organisations) the opposition argument was contradictory. In the event, Lenin's calls for a centralised conventional army using specialists won the day – but only just.[141] The party programme adopted by the congress rejected the idea of a militia army in the short term. N. Osinskii, ready to compromise, summed up the mood of the congress by conceding that 'military-command forms of the proletarian dictatorship' would have to be applied for a long time.[142] The relationship between the developments in the military sphere and in civilian life was clear to all.

With the subordination of the rear military cells to the local party organisations, the role of the MK, previously confined to temporary agitational campaigns, increased. In late April 1919 a permanent military department was formed under the MK, headed at first by Myasnikov.[143] At the 3 May city party conference, which also defeated a resolution proposed by supporters of the military opposition,[144] Myasnikov defined its aims as the raising of the political level of the army by the strict subordination of the unit cells to the RKs.[145] Nevertheless, lines of military and party discipline remained confused. Conflicts between the commissars (behind the shoulders of the '*spetsy*' – specialists), and the responsible party workers and the cells themselves, arose in nearly every unit of the Moscow garrison. For Trotsky, undoubtedly, the army commissar was senior to the others, though not always to the specialist, while the MK insisted that even the commissars were units of the party hierarchy and therefore subordinate to it.[146] At a conference of army cell representatives on 17 August 1919, the MK military department reiterated that all Red Army party members were subordinate to the

MPO irrespective of the post that they might hold. Thus the MK hoped to extend its authority over the political commissars.[147] The instruction adopted by the conference emphasised that there could be no 'privileged members' in the communist party and this applied equally to commissars and rank-and-file members: 'Among many of the administrators there are many examples of laxity and complete disregard for party work'. The commissar was to regard the cell as the key to improving the effectiveness of the Red Army, and any conflict between a cell and commissar was to be taken to a higher party body and not to administrative authorities.[148] The cell, now integrated in the party hierarchy, was defined as the agent of the party committee in the army. With the extension of the political department model to transport, the local party organisations fought hard to retain control over all communists in their locality. In October 1920, the MK once again stressed that any conflicts between the commissars and the cells were to be dealt with by the party and not the political departments: 'The commissar must above all be a communist and not stand over the cell, but guide and lead it as a senior comrade among equals'.[149] In January 1921 the MK military department was abolished and the military cells were fully integrated into the *raion* party organisations.[150] By the end of the war the army communist was subordinate to both the military and the local party authorities, and a complex relationship had developed between the two. The conflict between the commissars and the party organisations, however, was ultimately insoluble since they represented opposed visions of not only military but also civilian organisation.

In the civilian sphere the restricted definition of the cell emerged only slowly. The July 1918 statute only briefly mentioned the cells[151] and the main focus of party life was, as noted, the *raion* party organisation as a whole. In its first major statement on the role of cells following nationalisation the MK, meeting with leading managers in nationalised industry on 16 August 1918, resolved that every decision of heads of nationalisation, the MK, meeting with leading managers in nationalised industry on 16 August 1918, resolved that every decision of heads of The managers were to report on their work to the weekly cell meeting, and the cell was to be an integral part of collegiate management.[152] In other words, not only the 'specialists' but the state managers as well were to be kept under strict party control by the communist factory workers themselves, a view which veered towards the 'party' syndicalist. By all accounts this resolution encouraging cell interventionism encountered a hostile reception on the part of the managers and gave rise to a mass of conflicts. Its provisions concerning offices were dramatically reversed by the MK in a resolution of 2 October 1918 which insisted:

> The [communist] fraction in a commissariat does not have the right to interfere in the directives of the people's commissariats and their collegia. They do not have the right to demand reports from the latter. They should only concern themselves with party work among the commissariat's employees and with ensuring the correct course of work within the commissariats.[153]

It was at this time that a city-wide co-ordinating body for all communist office workers was abolished (see Chapter 6). While the tide had turned against the 'syndicalist' cell in the offices, in the factories the process took longer. A report from Lefortovo *raion* in late 1918 even applauded the cells for taking over the management of factories and considered it a 'healthy sign' of cell activity.[154] The December 1918 *reglament* provided no definition of the role of the cells and thus the field was left open for the controversy over their role to continue. Within the factories the endemic conflicts between the factory committees (*mestkomy*) and factory managements have been noted, and since the majority of the committees were composed of communists the cells were inevitably drawn into these disputes. Where the factory committee was not made up of communists, as in the notable examples of the Bogatyr' and Guzhon plants, the communist cells were placed in an ambiguous position. In many cases the cells and the factory committees merged. A report from Khamovni-cheskii *raion* noted that the cells were gradually taking on the functions of the trade unions, such as trying to regulate conditions. The 'low political level' of the cells was attributed to their involvement in the day-to-day affairs of plants at the expense of the general propagandist and political functions of the party.[155]

The more active of the cells hoped to play in the civilian sphere an equivalent role to that attempted by the army cells, described by G. Ya. Sokol'nikov at the VIII Congress as 'party syndicalism'.[156] And, as in the army, cell functions began to be limited, and so an important stage in undermining the initiative of rank-and-file communists was reached. However, while the distinction between the army or the state, on the one hand, and the party on the other, was readily drawn, the traditions and ideology of Bolshevism made it particularly difficult to resolve the proper role of the party in the nationalised factories. There has been no definitive resolution of this problem to this day.

Here the conflict between competing hierarchies was particularly intense. An MK instruction of March 1919 issued guidelines on the role of cells and insisted that they were primarily to conduct party work, while the soviet collegia and factory boards were to run their respective organisations. The cells' supervisory functions, however, were not altogether denied, as they had been in the 2 October 1918 instruction on commissariat cells. The cells were to be kept informed and to participate in the more important decisions; but they had no absolute rights over factory managements.[157] By mid-1919 the position had become clearer. An article in *Pravda* insisted that the cells were not to become part of the administrative structures but were to restrict themselves to a supervisory role, though what this was to mean in practice was not defined. Above all, they were to conduct agitprop work among the mass of workers who, the article stated, were far from being influenced by the party.[158] In the same issue Bukharin insisted that the cells were to find a path midway between detailed local involvement and abstract political sloganeering. This view was codified by the Presnenskii RK in July 1919 in one of the first attempts to provide a general definition. The cells were to concentrate on ensuring the accurate fulfilment of party duties by cell members, but above all they were to ensure that communists had a 'normal' relationship with the mass of the workers and had no 'privileges', which in this context meant the powers of administrative organs. They were, however, to report on any counter-revolutionary behaviour, which meant that the 'normal' relationship was a somewhat strained one. The ambiguity in their role is illustrated by the insistence that the cells were on no condition to 'interfere in the economic affairs of the factory committee' but were at the same time to maintain constant supervision over them.[159] Direct communist participation in management was considered a 'privilege' that would set the communist above the mass of the workers. Soon afterwards, Myasnikov provided a more detailed exposition of the cell's functions. For him they were recruiting, educational and supervisory bodies, but the last aspect was on no account to include settling major questions of principle. He criticised the vast majority of cells for interfering in technical, economic and political questions, thus evoking disputes. Above all the cells were to be concerned with the affairs of their enterprise.[160] Hence a two-fold restriction was placed on the cells: not to interfere in management; and to limit political discussion on abstract questions. Nevertheless, even at this time of military emergency, Myasnikov was adamant that the cells were not to have chairpersons but were to be run collectively by the cell bureaux with a secretary whose functions at this stage were largely technical. In other words, at least within the cells, the principle of collegiality was retained for the time being.

It was only with the adoption of the party statute at the VIII Party Conference that a general definition of the role of the cell was advanced. For the first time it was stressed that the cell and not any larger territorial area was the basic unit in the party. The party was to be based on the 'production' principle, that is, the individual factory and institution. The statute outlined the fourfold functions of the cells: agitprop; recruiting new members; supporting the factory committee; and active participation, as a party organ, in the economic and political life of the country.[161] This formulation gave no definition of what the last point was to mean in practice and still left the field open to conflicts. The March 1920 MPO statute combined Myasnikov's detailed provisions with the general statute's definition of their role.[162] The IX Party Congress refined the limited role of the cells, stressing that its members were to act as a moral example to other workers in their devotion to labour, to have no advantages over other workers, and 'in no circumstances to interfere in management' but only to ensure that the latter's decisions were fulfilled.[163] Nearly a third of the Moscow statute for the joint *guberniya*– city organisation (May 1920) was now devoted to the cells. Communists were to be redistributed so that a cell could be formed in every enterprise. They were 'to fulfil all decisions of higher party organs', to wage a 'merciless struggle against infringements of labour discipline', and among many other tasks were to ensure that the plant was managed in 'strict accordance with the principles of the RKP'. Once again it was stressed that conflicts between cells and factory managements were to be arbitrated by a higher party body[164] and not an economic body as in the 1930s. The adoption of this statute codified the cells as the focus of party life but gave them little scope for initiative. By contrast the December 1918 statute adopted by the Moscow *guberniya* party organisation, dominated by the Democratic Centralists, placed no restrictions on the cell's ability to discuss all decrees, resolutions, and instructions from soviet and party centres'.[165] By 1920 a time limit was placed on the period of discussion, and once a decision had been taken the cell's functions shifted towards implementation. This limited definition was the one applied to the cells at this time in the universal labour duty campaign.[166] As part of the change, the MK bureau on 2 March 1920 ruled that cells, and not fractions, were to be formed in offices or military institutions. Fractions were to be formed only in elected representative organisations such as the soviets and the trade unions and at conferences.[167] Whereas cells had a restricted role, the formation of a fraction implied a directing role, which was encouraged in such bodies as soviets but was henceforth to be discouraged in offices. At the same time, the bureau decided that cell secretaries were to be responsible party workers,[168] and in effect they were upgraded to act as chairpersons in all but name. This measure was facilitated by the merger of weaker cells with stronger ones on the division of the *raion*s into wards. The changed definition of the cells and the decline of party syndicalism was yet another element in the 'internal metamorphosis' of the party.

In this case the ideological shift preceded developments on the ground. Cell membership appears to have become a formal commitment lacking enthusiasm on the part of communists. In May 1920 the MK admitted that there was little life in the cells and that they limited themselves to fulfilling directives from above and getting meetings over quickly:[169] members arrived late and left early.[170] The cells were hampered by the lack of communists at their disposal, their poor organisation, the repetitive nature of meetings and the general apathy of party members. At a meeting of cell secretaries of Khamovnicheskii *raion* in March 1920 only half turned up,[171] and in July in that *raion* only a handful of communists attended a general meeting.[172] Attendance was particularly poor in the office cells. In May 1920, among the many examples reported in the press, only three members turned up for the meeting of the Narkompros cell which officially numbered 130 communists.[173] It was at this time that the first attempts were made to shift communists from offices to factories. Changes in the role of the cell were now accompanied by reforms in their internal organisation. The May 1920 MPO statute allowed disciplinary measures to be taken by a cell against its own members with the permission of the RK, and the MK in June stressed that in cases of indiscipline the party court should be used.[174] Nevertheless, the war still prevented a concentration of resources on the cells. A report in Gorodskoi *raion* in June noted that they were still too involved in local 'economic' issues and disputes with management at the expense of general party work,[175] and yet a few days later a list of cell members was distributed by the RK for mobilisation to the Polish front, prefaced by the warning that recalcitrance would be treated as desertion.[176] The major debate on party organisation in 1920 was accompanied by vigorous attempts at reviving the cells (see Chapter 7). But increasingly, the party member – to whom we now turn – became an executor of policy decided far from the workplace.

THE PARTY MEMBER

With the exodus of party members into state posts after the revolution and the decline in the cells, the link between individual communists and the party organisation to which they nominally belonged often became extremely tenuous. A survey in Moscow in late May 1918 discovered, in the words of the TsK, that 'it is clear that many communists are so only in name since they are not involved in any party work'.[177] From summer 1918 the attempt began, if not to halt the flood into the state apparatus, at least to reassert the member's affiliation with the organisation. As the 22 May TsK letter put it:

> All party members, whatever work they are doing, must pay serious attention to building up the party. We must raise the discipline of the party. Resolutions and decisions of party centres must be binding on all and must be undeviatingly implemented by every party member. From the moment a decision is taken discussion ends and the time for action alone arrives.[178]

This party discipline was to be applied both in the physical sense of making demands on the individual party member such as attending party meetings in order to prevent the emergence of a 'passive' group of members, and also in the ideological sense to ensure their subordination to central decisions and to avoid the development of a new elite based on an ideology of state service. The attempt was now made to effect Sverdlov's words at the VII Party Congress that the interests of the party were higher than those of the individual party member. The main outcome of several meetings devoted to ensuring that every communist became more involved was the reservation of Fridays for party work. Party leaders and those in state posts were to address factory meetings as a way of involving them in some party work. This type of measure was resisted as demeaning by certain leaders. The Left Communist G. I. Lomov, for example, at the time working in VSNKh, answered the MK's request not to organise office meetings on Fridays by writing: 'Comrades, I am not a child and you are not infants. I therefore ask that you do not make such requests'.[179] The demand became less formalised later with the simple exhortation that responsible workers should speak at least once a week at workers' meetings,[180] and this remained in force for the rest of the war. The 28 May 1918 city party conference called on all MPO members to join a cell and 'to unite around party organisations'.[181] In a measure designed to conserve cadres and keep track of communists, the Zamoskvorech'e party committee and soviet on 13 June insisted that no party members could leave their post without the sanction of the committee.[182] At the same time the MK urged all members to attend a party meeting at least once a week.[183] These various measures were systematised by the 30 July city party conference special decree on the party duties of communists. All were to be attached to an organisation and were to participate in party work in a disciplined way, and in tune with the increasingly strident military tone it was now stated that, irrespective of family circumstances, in case of necessity every party member was at the complete disposal of the party organisation.[184] The military note was sounded again a few days later when the MK decided that communists employed by soviet offices could only take leave with the permission of the RK or MK.[185]

With the great numbers working in offices it was only natural that the party committees concentrated on ensuring a modicum of party discipline over them, considered at the time as a way of preventing their 'bureaucratisation'. The MK meeting of 14–15 September 1918 emphasised the need for what it called 'party duty'. All RKs were to have accurate registers of party members and were to ensure that every member was drawn into party work irrespective of their post.[186] As part of this campaign in late 1918 the TsK called on all organisations to conduct a census of party members working in offices, a measure which also had military implications.[187] On the eve of the VIII Congress the TsK and the MK intensified the campaign to involve all party members in their organisations.[188] On 7 February 1919 the MK insisted that they registered with the RPOs and were obliged 'once a week, on the day designated by the RK, to carry out party work . . . in the evenings'.[189] In all spheres of party and soviet activity the committees were trying to establish a sense of party discipline. These measures, designed to avert the formation of a soviet bureaucratic caste, strengthened the role of the committees and thus ironically stimulated the formation of a party bureaucracy. In December 1918 the MK issued a list of desiderata (*nakaz*) for every communist. Any free time not spent on study was to be devoted to party work, and all were to read the party press.[190] The VIII Party Congress went further when Kaganovich, the strict centralist, took up the notion of 'party duty' (analogous to labour duty) to be established, whereby every communist was to be registered and 'correctly' used.[191] The idea was greeted favourably, with Osinskii only asking that in party duty a certain proportion of members were to be devoted to party work itself. While Osinskii devoted most of his attention to the deficiencies of the TsK, he noted that in both the centre and the localities the committees were the main beneficiaries of internal party developments in the first phase of the civil war.[192]

The problem was that the party itself had turned into a giant transmission belt extracting workers from factories and transferring them to offices or the army under the label of 'communist'. However, the recruits to the party were no longer what they had been. At the congress

Osinskii noted that at the grass roots the party was 'filling up with rubbish', with party cards in hand but without the necessary 'mental baggage'.[193] V. P. Nogin concurred that the party had 'gone to pieces', and that the behaviour of communists was bad enough to 'make your hair stand on end', and he argued that this was due to the fact that the majority of senior party members were no longer active in party work.[194] Sapronov agreed that the party's only salvation was the reinforcement of the hegemony of the party activists over the rest of the party, and, further, the logic of his position was that this corps was to consist mainly of the 'old guard'.[195] It was left to Ignatov to identify the real problem: the bureaucratisation of the party and its isolation from the working class. He gave the example of the cell in the Prokhorovskaya mill which was 'isolated from the masses as if by a wall'. The priority should be party work, he argued, and not soviet work.[196] Despite all the agitational and organisational measures, it appears that the ordinary party members remained apathetic to the party's exhortations. The Guzhon cell on 1 February 1919, for example, noted that the majority of members failed to attend,[197] and the passive response of those who did was increasingly highlighted. A report in April 1919 noted that the Friday meetings no longer interested workers, and that their wavering could only be overcome if all party members devoted at least half their spare time to the party.[198] The passivity of party members was illustrated by the 27 April 1920 Gorodskoi delegate meeting when the RK's report for the previous six months passed with almost no discussion.[199] This passivity was balanced by the activity of the RK, which had met regularly every week, and by the bureau, which had met twice weekly.[200] It was this situation which Ignatov and his supporters hoped to rectify in their reform campaign in this *raion* from April 1920 (see Chapter 7).

The MK's status was enhanced by its role in enforcing the mobilisations and in general it asserted that it alone was responsible for the distribution of communists in the city.[201] The MK insisted that refusal to be mobilised meant expulsion from the party,[202] and there were cases of this in the 1920 reregistration (see Chapter 5). The mobilisations themselves tended to reinforce the distinction between party activists and ordinary party members.[203] Once a party member was in the army, the distinction between the communist commander and the rank-and-file communist was intensified by the declining role of the cell. While the inculcation of military values took a traditional path in the army, in the rear the militarisation was no less intense. The TsK urged all communists to have an 'interest in and love for military matters'.[204] The specific instrument for this was the special communist detachments (*chasti osobogo naznacheniya* – ChON, known by various other names up to April 1919), the irregular territorial militia organisation of communists and Komsomol members. The ChON grew out of the voluntary detachments of communists formed in the months after October 1917, and lasted up to 1924. While the Red Guard was a more fissiparous organisation with limited tasks and a weak organisational stucture, the precursors of the ChON, initially not composed entirely of communists, from the first played the role of the armed force of the party and acted as a solid reserve for the Red Army. They were the first forces sent to oppose the Germans in March 1918, and at the same time the MK organised forces for combating 'counter-revolution' in Moscow by arming all party members, and established compulsory patrols in the *raion*s.[205] The process began whereby the party became not only the abstract source of authority but also its physical manifestation through the militarisation of party members in the communist detachments. As part of the same process, political opponents were rendered not only outcasts in the political sphere but also criminals.

A TsK directive of 8 May 1918 called for the compulsory military training of all communists,[206] but at first the units were organised haphazardly in response to specific crises. Following the débâcle of the LSR uprising of early July 1918, in which the main military force against the LSRs was a group of Latvian soldiers,[207] the MK launched a plan to improve its military capabilities. All *raion*s were to compile lists of communists able to fight, both experienced soldiers and raw candidates.[208] In July the Lefortovo RK issued a decree calling for the immediate registration of communists in armed detachments, which were to be under the strict control of the party committees and not the military authorities. Failure to register meant expulsion from the party.[209] The 30 July 1918 city party conference, which authorised the first party mobilisations for the fronts, also emphasised the suppression of counter-revolution in the rear. A headquarters for the Moscow units was formed, headed by a political commission consisting of Zagorskii, Myasnikov, and I. A. Pyatnitskii.[210] In the autumn of 1918 some of these units were launched *en masse* to the fronts, but following protests by Zagorskii and the MK bureau over high losses, their members were either spread through the Red Army or given a role at the rear.[211] The ChON, officially founded on 17 April 1919 by the TsK,[212] were to be formed on a militia territorial basis, composed entirely of party members, and were to be under direct party control. They were formed under factory, *raion* and city party committees, and in July 1919 the TsK stated that all party members capable of carrying a gun were to enlist.[213] Each *raion* was to form a ChON battalion of not less than 216 men, directly subordinate to the head of the Moscow ChON, with four hours a week of training.[214] By mid-1919 there were twelve ChON detachments in the city, with 7814 members, about half of total party membership. By the summer of that year 3700 of these were considered capable of carrying out military tasks.[215] At the VIII Party Conference in December 1919, Bukharin insisted on participation in the ChON and noted that the party itself was becoming more of a military organisation.[216] The structure of the Bolshevik party was particularly suited to the waging of war, and this was reflected in the development of the ChON. They played a major role in 'the militarisation of the party and its organisational transformation'.[217] The idea was to have a totally dependable force that could be relied on in any crisis – a political fire brigade. The role of the ChON was enhanced by the 19 December 1918 Sovnarkom decree allowing only communists to keep arms at home.[218] The units were assigned to such tasks as the protection of soviets, the RKs and other key points. On disturbed days they patrolled the streets, conducted raids (*oblavy*), searches, and arrests of 'speculators and counter-revolutionaries'.[219] The disastrous military situation in mid-1919 forced their wholesale use against Denikin and Yudenich, and at a critical moment 500 *chonovtsy* (ChON members) were despatched to the North to defend Petrograd.[220] Nevertheless, the ChON themselves were not immune from certain elements of corruption. Time spent for training was used as a way of avoiding work, and so in May 1919 the initial instructions were strengthened by the provision that training should take place only in free time and that ChON membership could not serve as an excuse to avoid being drafted to the army.[221] Their organisational coherence was further weakened for a period in early 1920 following their assimilation into the general system of universal military training (*vseobuch*) and the inadequacies of the ChON were often criticised.[222]

Against the background of disturbances in the city from late 1920 more attention was devoted to them. The 1920 reregistration had shown that in some places up to 60 per cent did not participate in the units. In late September 1920 the MK insisted that all communists and candidates were to be divided into companies for training[223] and on 10 October the MK announced that military training would be compulsory.[224] Their political significance increased further in late 1920 when they were sent to repress the peasant uprisings in Tambov and elsewhere, and the disorders in the city. The potential division of loyalties within rank-and-file communists between the party and their workmates was particularly acute when the call went out for communists to act as the 'eyes and ears'

of the authorities, as in mid-1920. The tension was countered by the
endless exhortations for communists to participate in the various party
ventures, and when exhortations failed stricter measures were proposed.
The disciplinarian V. A. Kotov in Sokol'nicheskii *raion*, for example, on
8 September 1919 attacked the poor attitude of party members to their
duties and insisted that this was to be remedied by 'barracks discipline'.[225] An MK circular of March 1920 on party discipline pointed out
that the MPO still had a long way to go to reach the required level,[226] a
contention borne out by the August 1920 reregistration. One problem
was the sheer burden of activities placed on each member. In December
1920, for example, an average communist in one month had to attend
the party school eight times, cell meetings four times, two *subbotniks*
(unpaid labour sessions), two ChON training sessions, one general party
meeting, two factory meetings and one ChON patrol, quite apart from
other special meetings and having a full-time job.[227] Breaches of party
discipline and lapses in Bolshevik moral probity were dealt with by the
court of honour (*sud chesti*) under the MK. In early 1918 the court was
an elective body but was later made up by direct appointments by the
MK.[228] It dealt with such cases as returning from the front without
permission, not fulfilling party directives on employment, drunkenness,
and so on. In 1920 it was increasingly used to ensure active participation
in party work.[229] Its usual punishment was censure, but it could order
expulsion.

The early Moscow statutes had barely mentioned the individual party
member. While the general party statute of December 1919 specifically
mentioned the members' right to free discussion of issues up to the time
that decisions were taken,[230] the May 1920 Moscow statute, which for
the first time had a large section on the individual, omitted all mention of
this right and instead listed members' duties as 'ardent executors' of
party policy.[231] This was a measure of the change that had taken place
since 1917. Party members were no longer governed by commitment and
comradely relations alone but by a whole battery of regulations which
ensured their subordination to the organisation and, ultimately, to the
official ideological line. The changed definition of the individual party
member illustrates the changes that had taken place during the civil war.
The MK had become the supreme political arbiter in the locality, elected
by a conference and no longer delegated, and the *raion* committees
increasingly acted as its local administrative departments when the
federalist period gave way to the unitary democratic centralist system.
The cell had been deprived of direct management functions and instead
was concerned with fulfilling party directives. The party's base in the

factories had been radically undermined, and when it was recreated it was no longer an organic growth from the factory itself but a directed process 'from above'. Passivity had become an offence, but political passivity as defined by Lukács (see page 164) was the counterpart of the organisational changes. The party's political functions were the prerogative no longer of each and every party member but primarily of the party leadership and its new model committees. The change had begun from below by the gradual 'depoliticisation' of the individual party members in the cell as they increasingly became a tool in the hands of the party committees, and by the division of responsibilities within the enterprises as the cell took on agitational functions and became separated from management. These organisational changes were consolidated by the recruitment policies of the civil war years.

5 Recruitment and Purge in the Moscow Party Organisation

THE PATTERN OF RECRUITMENT AND MEMBERSHIP

Recruitment policy and the nature of the changes in the social composition and occupational structure of party membership were a central concern and cause of controversy throughout the civil war. With the growth in bureaucracy, attempts were made to ensure a flow of party members to occupy the key posts, and so their training and political education became an important issue. The principles governing the vetting of party recruits and the expulsion of various categories of undesirables had an important role to play in the political debates and organisational developments in this period.

Until the reregistration of August 1920 the figures given for membership of the MPO, as of the party as a whole, are often contradictory and invariably exaggerated. This problem is especially marked in Moscow because of the large numbers leaving on various assignments or coming to the city for training or on secondment. The general pattern of membership can, however, be established (see Table 5.1). From the high point of 17 306 members in October 1917 (including army communists) numbers had halved to under 8000 by mid-1918. After the revolution, organisations were drained of their most active members and they atrophied as functioning party units. The party cells in factories donated the bulk of their membership to the state apparatus and many were disbanded. Sverdlov's estimate of 20 000 members in the city in March 1918 was clearly exaggerated.[1] With the onset of mass mobilisations the membership figures become even more difficult to establish. At the VIII Party Congress in March 1919, L. S. Sosnovskii cited the low membership figure in the MPO to challenge Zinoviev's inflated claims on the growth of party membership since October 1917.[2] Despite the mobilisations, membership had indeed risen to nearly 15 000 by late 1918, though less than Zinoviev's claim, and remained at this level up to the mass recruitment of the party week in October 1919, when membership doubled to over 32 000. The figures available for the following period vary considerably, allegedly peaking at over 40 000 members and 9000

Table 5.1 Membership of the Moscow party organisation, 1917–21

	City			Guber-niya	Joint organisation		
	Members	Candidates	Total	Total	Members	Candidates	Total
1917							
Feb[a]	600	–	600	200			
Apr[b]	6 000	–	6 000	8 554			
Jul[c]	15 000	–	15 000				
Oct[d]	17 306	–	17 306	–			
Dec[e]	–	–	–	10 000			
1918							
Mar[e]	20 000	–	20 000	15 000			
Jun[f]	7 300	–	7 300	–			
Nov[g]	14 694	–	14 694	2 881[h]			
1919							
Mar[i]	17 000	–	17 000	5 000			
Aug[j]	15 834	4 818	20 652				
Oct[j]	32 600	4 818	37 418				
1920							
Mar[k]	34 015	3 767	37 782	6 488			
May[k]	35 044	4 463	39 507	6 819	41 683	–	–
Jun[l]	–	–	–	–	39 854	8 936	48 790
Jul[m]	38 061	–	–	5 528	42 697	9 557	52 264[l]
Sep[m]	23 069	2 900	25 969	4 572	–	–	27 641
1921							
Jan[n]	–	–	–	–	36 720	9 280	46 000
Jun[k]	32 475	7 886	40 361	7 809	40 284	10 552	50 836
Sep[o]	26 565	4 240	30 805	7 926	34 491	6 726	40 767

Sources: [a] Ocherki istorii Moskovskoi organizatsii KPSS, 1883–1965 (Moscow, 1966) p. 214; [b] VII (aprel'skaya) vserossiiskaya konferentsiya RSDRP (b): protokoly (Moscow, 1958) pp. 152 and 154; [c] VI s''ezd RSDRP (b), avgust 1917 goda: protokoly (Moscow, 1958) p. 204. [d] Perepiska, vol. VII (Moscow, 1972) p. 438; [e] VII s''ezd RKP, pp. 4, 115, 116; [f] D. A. Chugaev (ed.), Rabochii klass sovetskoi Rossii v pervyi god diktatury proletariata (Moscow, 1964) p. 76; [g] Perepiska, vol. III, p. 197; [h] P, 25 January 1919; [i] VIII s''ezd RKP (b), mart 1918g.: protokoly (Moscow, 1959) p. 471; [j] Moskovskaya organizat-siya RKP (b) v tsifrakh, issue 1 (Moscow, 1925) p. 3; [k] Moskovskaya gorodskaya i Moskovskaya oblastnaya organizatsii KPSS v tsifrakh (Moscow, 1972) pp. 27–8; [l] Otchet MK za iyul' 1920g. (Moscow, 1920) p. 7; [m] Otchet MK za sentyabr' 1920g. (Moscow, 1920) p. 6; [n] V Moskovskaya gubernskaya partiinaya konferentsiya (RKP), 19–21 fevralya 1921g.: kratkii ocherk i rezolyutsii (Moscow, 1921) p.3;[o]Ot-chet o deyatel'nosti MK-ta RKP(b) za iyul' avgust, i sentyabr' 1921g. (Moscow, 1921) p. 22.

candidates in July 1920 for the joint city and *guberniya* organisation. This rapid increase was reversed by the August 1920 reregistration which saw a massive drop to only 23 000 members and 2900 candidates in the city in October 1920. There was a slow rise in membership up to March 1921 as soldiers returned from the fronts and recruitment continued, but this growth was halted by the party purge of 1921.

The pattern of recruitment is therefore marked by a rapid rise to October 1917, a slow fall to March 1918, a precipitous decline to mid-1918, and thereafter large increases as mobilisations were compensated by more effective recruitment. The worker communists were the first to be mobilised and the new intake was predominantly from the offices. To counteract this, worker recruitment from the factories was encouraged from late 1918, but still the proportion of office workers rose. The party week in October 1919 led to a massive rise in numbers and partially restored the balance of workers 'at the bench'. Such a recruitment pattern meant that most communists by 1921 had joined during the war (see Table 5.2). Just over a quarter (27 per cent) of the city membership of 17 306 in October 1917 remained in August 1920. Only 21 per cent had joined before October 1917, of which 5 per cent had been members in the

Table 5.2   Length of party membership (*stazh*) on 1 September 1920

	City	Gub.	Total No.	Per- centage	Per- centage for 36 gubernii (excluding Moscow and Peters- burg)	Per- centage for 38 gubernii (including Moscow and Peters- burg)
pre-1905	497	30	527	2	—	1
1905–1907	415	48	463	1	1	1
1908–1916	684	39	723	2	1	1
1917 Jan–Oct	3 117	527	3 644	10	7	7
1917 Nov–Dec, 1918	5 807	1 187	6 994	20	21	20
1919 Jan–Aug	3 729	603	4 332	12	12	12
1919 Sep–Dec	8 084	1 326	9 410	27	31	29
1920	6 999	1 580	8 579	24	26	27
Not known	488	66	554	2	1	1
Total	29 820	5 406	35 226	100	100	100

Source: Materialy po statistike lichnogo sostava RKP (b) (Moscow, 1921) pp. 62–3.

underground. A substantial majority of the MPO (84 per cent) had joined after October 1917.[3] As the seat of government the Moscow organisation had a greater concentration of pre-1917 party members than any other, and indeed their numbers exceeded the whole membership of the MPO of 600 in February 1917. Such a concentration suggests that the MPO retained pre-revolutionary traditions somewhat longer than elsewhere. It was not only the political but also the intellectual centre of the party. In general, however, membership was extremely fluid and the retention rate between 1917–20 averaged 26 per cent per annum, compared to 31 per cent nationally.[4] During the civil war the MPO had not simply doubled in size but had to a large degree renewed itself and the massive recruitment of the civil war overshadowed the original membership of 1917.

This recruitment had major repercussions not only on the composition of the party but also on its political practice. The party lost some of its exclusive character as the proportion of those who had undergone repression for their beliefs declined. By August 1920 only 3474 (11.6 per cent) out of 29 820 in the city fell into this category, a higher proportion than in the party as a whole (8 per cent), reflecting the concentration of dedicated revolutionaries.[5] The great majority of the Moscow party by the end of the civil war had not been seasoned by Tsarist repression and this was yet another factor reinforcing the gulf between the 'old guard' and the newer recruits. By 1920 the party was no longer a group of determined revolutionaries working for a future revolution but was forced to adapt itself to the enormous task of managing the country. The group of about 5000 in Moscow who had been members before the October revolution became the kernel of the party in power and tended to occupy the key posts. On the one hand there was a group of communists who had undergone the trials of being party members during the Tsarist period or under the Provisional Government and on the other hand a shifting group, a large proportion of whom were soon expelled or left the party for one reason or another, often passive in relation to party duties and marked by a high degree of political illiteracy. This was the basis of the split in the party between the 'old guard' and the mass of the membership, the *verkhi* and the *nizy*.

REREGISTRATION AND RECRUITMENT: 1918–19

During the civil war, checks on party membership took the form of reregistrations, later called *chistki* (cleansings or purges). There were three main reregistration periods: (1) from the spring of 1918 to March

1919; (2) the first all-Russian reregistration between May and September 1919 ordered by the VIII Party Congress because of increasing concern about 'unhealthy' elements joining the party; and (3) July–December 1920, instituted by the IX Party Congress in March 1920. In 1921 the party underwent the first purge known by that name, but in effect the MPO underwent a major purge in every year of the civil war, and for over half the period was in the grip of such a campaign. The first series of reregistrations took place haphazardly and on the initiative of the local organisations. They began in Moscow in the spring of 1918 and were intensified following concern at the VII Congress about 'careerists' joining the party. During a reregistration all members effectively had to rejoin their organisation and thus once again their credentials for membership were judged. Contrary to the common view that reregistrations only began in 1919[6] the first, in Moscow at least, were launched on the morrow of the revolution and indicate that one of the first tasks of the revolutionary party in power is to check its own membership.

There are not many details on the first reregistrations but the one conducted in Basmannyi *raion* in February–March 1918 illustrates the pattern. Here membership had risen from about 1800 in October 1917[7] to about 2000 in January 1918. According to the RK secretary's report the controversy over the Brest peace had revealed that the organisation was 'not at the required level' and so a reregistration had been declared, leaving only 400 members.[8] These figures, however inflated by poor accounting, indicate both the small number of 'October communists', those joining the victorious party for careerist reasons, and the massive drop-out rate and expulsions of 'unsuitable' people. In this *raion* the number of cells fell from forty-eight to fifteen between January and June 1918.[9] The figures can be taken as a measure of the tremendous 'withering away of the party' in the first half of 1918. As part of the 'May programme' of organisational renewal recruitment procedures were tightened up. The VI Congress (August 1917) decision, incorporated in the party statute, that recruits had to be recommended by two party members and endorsed (or expelled) by a general meeting of party members in the given organisation, was to be more strictly applied. The TsK circular of 29 May (which together with a circular of 22 May amplified the themes of the 18 May TsK resolution) argued that many 'alien elements' had entered the party who baulked at 'proletarian discipline'.[10] The TsK urged that the MK put its own house in order, and at Sverdlov's insistence the 28 May 1918 city party conference was dominated by organisational questions. At the conference he severely criticised infringements of party discipline by communists. The resolution noted that the 'all-party point of view had receded into the background behind the local, professional, group view'. Communists working in soviet and other institutions were to form fractions or cells and ensure that the TsK or MK line was fulfilled, 'purging the party of all elements of decay and degeneration'. The party, the resolution concluded, was to be built on the basis of unswerving devotion to the principles of democratic centralism.[11] There are some indications that the reregistrations at this early stage were deployed against the Left Communists. The 22 May TsK circular had suggested that the Left Communist movement was a result not only of the organisational weakness of the party, but also of changes in its composition through the influx of new members,[12] an argument used to explain the emergence of the Workers' Opposition in 1920. The 10 June 1918 MK meeting noted that 'the raions are increasingly interested in purging the party', and Pyatnitskii made the point explicitly when he said of the Left Communists: 'If they do not want to bear responsibility for the general line of the party, they can leave it. We do not need honorary party members'.[13] The 'May programme', apparently, was not only a response to the organisational anaemia of the party but also a specific reaction to the opposition of the left. Unfortunately, the extent to which the 1918 reregistrations were used to discipline the Left Communists is as unfathomable as is the extent to which the 1921 purge was used against the Workers' Opposition.

From late May 1918 the programme began to be implemented. In Khamovnicheskii *raion* the screening procedure for applicants was strengthened by the provision that the candidate and their recommendees had not only to attend a general meeting but also a preliminary interview by the RK bureau. Failure to attend either meeting by any of those concerned meant that an application automatically lapsed.[14] In Sokol'nicheskii *raion* membership since the end of 1917 had fallen from 1500 to under a thousand in May 1918, and following a reregistration in early summer fell by a further two-thirds.[15] The RK insisted that all party members had to undertake some party work, to pay dues regularly and to attend meetings. Against the background of the civil war the RK called for the arming of all party members[16] as the attempt to establish some sort of party discipline coincided with the need to instil military discipline. All party members were to be 'tied' (*prikreplennye*) to a cell, and party members employed in offices were to participate in party life.[17] The reregistrations continued over the summer of 1918[18] and a general reregistration was announced for the whole city in September 1918. In Basmannyi *raion* membership had increased to 816 since the earlier reregistration, and in this reregistration it fell to 550. A third reregistration in early 1919 halved the numbers from 1180 to 600.[19] In the three reregistrations in the *raion* about 2250 had left or been expelled, more than the membership itself. What happened to these people is not known, but it can be assumed that much of this sizeable 'party of the expelled' (Jacques Rupnik) harboured a grudge against the Bolshevik party. The scale of the reregistrations indicates that the attempt to achieve a stricter enforcement of recruitment procedures after the May 1918 TsK initiatives was not very effective in achieving the aim of screening 'undesirable elements'. The problem was that throughout this period recruitment took precedence over screening.

From mid-1918 the fluidity of MPO membership increased dramatically. Every day trains left Moscow bearing communists to the fronts, on grain requisitioning detachments and to act as the organisers of Soviet power throughout the country. The solution to the problem of shortage of personnel was found in the organisation of sympathisers' groups. The earliest were established in spring 1918[20] and the IV Moscow *Oblast* Party Conference on 15 May 1918 called on all party organisations to form them.[21] The MK first discussed the question on 9 August when Zagorskii called for their formation as schools of communist education. No decisions were taken until 16 August, when Lenin spoke in favour of 'widening the sphere of our influence' by 'showing greater faith in the worker masses and drawing on them for forces'.[22] The groups were intended to give workers a political education and to act as a testing ground and as a reservoir for entrance into the party. The former functions were later fulfilled by the trade unions, women's and youth organisations, acting as the famous 'transmission belts' between the party and the masses.[23] Their recruitment functions were transferred to the system of candidature with the difference that while the sympathisers' groups were part of a continuing recruitment campaign, candidature was a way of screening new members and reflected increased concern about the quality of recruits.

The statute adopted by the 31 August city party conference stated that 'anyone who supports the RKP(b) in its struggle for the liberation of the proletariat and the whole labouring people from political and economic exploitation' could join the sympathisers' groups.[24] Recruitment was to take place on the recommendation of one party member or one sympathiser, subject to the agreement of the party cell. The statute gave sympathisers fairly wide powers up to voting rights in the cell or local committee, but they were banned from closed party meetings. They existed as groups around the kernel of a party cell. In view of the concern about the quality of party membership, the *raion*s were reluctant simultaneously to conduct both a purge and a recruitment campaign. The MK call for their formation met with considerable opposition and the general meeting of Gorodskoi *raion* on 22 August 1918, for example, rejected their formation by a majority of 72 to 22 with 10 abstentions. The argument that quality and not quantity was the priority was supported in several *raion*s.[25] Success depended on the initial strength of a party cell since they were founded not on the initiative of the sympathisers themselves but on that of the local party organisations. The best results were in Rogozhsko-Simonovskii *raion* which contained half of the total number of sympathisers by late September 1918.[26] They did act as the stimulant for the creation of new cells, and in some factories there were more sympathisers than there were party members. By mid-1919 there were about 5000 officially registered sympathisers, and they helped to maintain numbers in the MPO with the departure of communists to the fronts. Sympathisers were subject to the reregistrations, like any full party member, and no latitude was allowed in their views or behaviour. They were also subject to party mobilisations. In November 1918, for example, 600 sympathisers were sent to the fronts from Moscow with the communist levy, and over 1500 participated in the supply detachments.[27] They acted as communist auxiliaries under party control and were not permitted any organisational autonomy.

The period up to the VIII Party Congress in March 1919 was marked by mounting alarm over the condition of the MPO. On the eve of a reregistration in Butyrskii *raion* in summer 1918, for example, concern was expressed over the extreme passivity of the majority of its 600 members. A meeting of party activists at the end of July 1918 noted that all the most conscious members were occupied in soviet work and devoted no time to party affairs.[28] A major article in *Pravda* in August 1918 argued that since the revolution there had been both a quantitative and qualitative decline in party membership, alien elements had infiltrated, and that the party was permeated with corruption.[29] These general alarms about the condition of the party became a common feature of the party press and meetings at this time, usually focusing on the passivity of party members, the lack of party discipline, and the intake of 'alien' elements.[30] A. Lisitsyn, a member of the Butyrskii RK, inveighed in October 1918 against passive party members and insisted that all were to be active in one way or another.[31] Towards the end of October 1918 Bergman described the case of the recruit in Moscow who insisted on party membership 'tonight, in order to get a job tomorrow'. Recommendations were being given by friends (*po znakomstvu*) to help one another. The party was not 'widening', he argued: it was degenerating.[32] There is a mass of anecdotal evidence to support his charges of the abuse of entrance procedures.[33] The rapidly changing physiognomy of party membership was noted in Zamoskvorech'e in late November 1918. At the time there were 1650 communists in forty-five cells. Even though the *raion* had just completed its third mobilisation numbers were still rising, but, as one correspondent noted, the atmosphere at general meetings (as in the factories) had changed radically. Few of the old comrades were to be found and the atmosphere at meetings was 'philistine' (*obyvatel'skii*). There was no particular revolutionary mood.[34] An article in *Pravda* a few weeks later argued that it was clear to all communists that the party was 'sick' with petty bourgeois philistinism. The party was filling up with peasants and careerists, the article argued, and the main symptoms of the sickness were endless personal squabbles and quitting the party on the eve of mobilisations.[35]

It would appear that the concern was justified and there was a steady stream of expulsions from the party alongside the reregistrations. For example, Butyrskii RPO expelled six communists in August 1918 for reasons which included 'behaviour unbecoming to a communist', refusal to go to the front, and not attending *raion* meetings.[36] Membership in this *raion* had fallen from 600 in August 1918 to 380 in January 1919.[37] Earlier, a major 'squabble' had erupted in Sushchevsko-Mar'inskii *raion* where it was allegedly discovered that some responsible party leaders 'only pretended to be Bolsheviks'. Following an investigation they were barred from holding responsible posts and the case was transferred to the MK court of honour for final judgement.[38] On 11 January 1919 the MK called on all *raion*s which had not conducted a reregistration to do so immediately. The MK bureau was called on to draw up a list of demands to be made of all party members during the check.[39] Gradually the limited aims of the first reregistrations, to clear the party of 'careerist and unworthy elements', gave way to the specific policy of improving the social composition by increasing the intake of workers and minimising the recruitment of non-workers. Economic decline, deurbanisation, the growth of the bureaucratic apparatus and the pervasive influence of the illegal economy provided the milieu for the debates over the corruption threatening to engulf the party. The response was to stress the role of the old guard and at the same time to develop the party as an exclusive organisation and to intensify the controls over party members.

With the emergence of the Bolsheviks as the ruling party, internal decay became the greatest danger as new members joined to take advantage of the patronage it offered. Internal campaigns in the form of

Table 5.3 Social pattern of recruitment in Moscow and Petrograd (percentages)

	Workers	Peasants	Craftworkers	Intelligentsia	Office staff	Other	Not known	Total
Moscow								
pre-1917	43	2	2	22	18	8	5	100
1917	55	3	2	8	18	8	6	100
1918	47	5	3	8	23	8	6	100
1919	47	9	4	5	20	7	8	100
1920	44	11	4	5	20	7	9	100
Petrograd								
pre-1917	68	1	1	11	14	5	–	100
1917	71	3	2	4	15	5	–	100
1918	60	7	3	5	21	4	–	100
1919	59	9	3	3	19	6	1	100
1920	55	11	5	3	20	6	–	100

The table shows the social composition of each intake group as it stood after the August 1920 reregistration. It therefore shows the situation only after the reregistrations, mobilisations, and so on, had altered the picture, but it does serve as a general guide to the changes in the social composition of recruitment. According to official statistics the class composition of the party as a whole changed as follows (percentages) (Rigby, *Communist Party Membership*, p. 85):

	Workers	Peasants	Office staff, etc.
1917	60.2	7.5	32.2
1918	56.9	14.5	28.6
1919	47.8	21.8	30.4
1920	43.8	25.1	31.1
1921	41.0	28.2	30.8

Source: Materialy po statistike lichnogo sostava RKP (b) (Moscow, 1921) p. xii.

reregistrations to expel the undesirables did not prevent a major crisis over recruitment at the time of the VIII Party Congress in March 1919, when general concern was voiced over the changing composition of the party. In the party as a whole 65 per cent of recruitment in 1917 had been designated 'worker' but by 1920 this had fallen to 35 per cent, with the greatest decline in 1918 and early 1919.[40] The trend was the same but slightly less pronounced in Moscow. Only in 1917 was the intake of workers over half the total, and the percentage declined thereafter (see Table 5.3), as the social composition of the city itself changed. With its vast bureaucratic apparatuses serving the whole country, the high intake of office staff – the rising bureaucratic corps of secretaries, functionaries, clerks, and so on – was a pronounced feature of recruitment in Moscow. From a peak in 1918 the recruitment of office workers in 1919–20 remained remarkably stable at 20 per cent despite all the attempts to give preference to workers. In Moscow the recruitment of workers was a lower proportion than in Petrograd (but higher than in the party as a whole) and the fact that they were in a minority was the basis for the crisis over recruitment policy. There was indeed a tendency for 'local communists to merge with soviet officialdom in a new privileged stratum'.[41] The rather nebulous idea of a 'party maximum' (partmax) whereby those in leadership positions were not to receive more than a skilled workman's wages became meaningless with the devaluation of money and the increased importance of access to various services, special rations, and to the jobs themselves. Middle level leaders not in the Kremlin itself lived in the Lux, National', and Metropol' hotels and were served with above average food and rations.

The months preceding the VIII Party Congress were marked by calls from the Democratic Centralists and others in the *raion*s of Moscow to eliminate bureaucracy and to overcome the split in the party between the activists and the rank and file, a breach perceived as one between the *verkhi* and the *nizy*. While the rank-and-file membership had been successively purged and mobilised, the factory cells weakened and in many cases disbanded, the only stable core to the organisations had become the party committees themselves, though their own personnel were not immune to mobilisation. The Rogozhsko-Simonovskii RK report for December 1918–January 1919, for example, highlighted the changed social composition of its membership and complained that at general meetings of its 600 members the few communists from the factories were overshadowed by the great number of commissars and soviet employees. The animosity between the two groups was admitted, and over divisive issues such as supply policy they split into two camps.[42] The TsK at this time was still calling for increased recruitment to avoid a renewed 'emptying' of the party by the mobilisations. Any deficiencies in the quality of recruitment could be compensated by improved training and better organisation.[43] On the eve of the congress calls for a thorough cleansing of the party grew in intensity. On 3 February 1919, I. V. Mgeladze's motion calling for a party purged of unhealthy elements was passed by the MK.[44] The word 'purge' (*chistka*) was already current and it was seen as an organisational catharsis. Just as the connection was drawn in 1918 between the emergence of the Left Communists and recruitment, the MK stressed the link between purging the party and the enforcement of party discipline.[45] The implication was that a party cleared of 'hangers on' and composed only of those who participated in party life would be able to overcome the breach between full-time party activists and its members in state posts or on the factory floor. However, as in 1918, the link between purge and party discipline did not go unchallenged. When Mgeladze once again called for a purge and strict party discipline at a general meeting of 254 communists in Rogozhsko-Simonovskii *raion* on 13 February 1919, a counter-resolution insisted that all issues to be discussed at the congress should first be debated at all party meetings, and in general argued that the TsK should permit more discussion in the party.[46] The resolution thus gave voice to rank-and-file party members who increasingly felt that decisions of cardinal importance were no longer being discussed by the party as a whole. This unease was once again evident at a delegate meeting in the railway *raion* at the end of February 1919 where the motion, while agreeing on the need for a purge, stressed that all groups in the party, including the *nizy*, should be allowed to participate in a businesslike (*delovoi*) way. The party itself, the motion argued, should be at the centre of attention.[47] The MK returned to the question on 15 February and its resolution was largely devoted to the 'adventuristic' elements who had worked their way into the party to pursue their own ends. Their shameful behaviour, it stressed, had lowered the prestige of the party in the eyes of the masses and provided fertile ground for counter-revolutionary agitation. The MK called for a thorough purge of the party to be initiated by the forthcoming congress.[48]

The hopes that the congress would be able to reintegrate the groups in the party were disappointed. It stressed the need to attract new cadres, and thus once again, as with the sympathisers' groups, the MPO was forced to absorb a new intake before it had digested the old. The party itself was to act as a massive transmission belt for the recruitment and training of thousands of new cadres to staff the state apparatus.[49] The sympathisers' groups themselves were increasingly seen as a back entrance into the party, justifying the earlier suspicions.[50] Following the congress they were abolished in several large party organisations, including Petrograd's. In Moscow, criticism centred on their role in allowing employees from soviet institutions, who were predominantly recruited from the petty bourgeoisie, to inveigle their way into the party. When in mid-1919, for example, the situation at the front became perilous with Denikin's advance, the cell under the Rogozhsko-Simonovskii *raion* soviet, two-thirds of whose members were sympathisers, simply dissolved and the 'soviet *baryshni*' (ladies, usually employed in secretarial duties), it was reported, pleaded to be expelled on grounds of health in order to avoid the mobilisation.[51] By mid-1919 restrictions were introduced on the formation of sympathisers' groups in soviet offices.[52] Following the XV *Guberniya* Party Conference (27–29 July 1919), where calls were made for their abolition on the ground that the groups were allowing bourgeois elements to join the party,[53] they were abolished in the *guberniya* on 28 August 1919, and some of their more suitable members joined the party.[54] The groups were dropped from the party statute adopted in December 1919. Zinoviev argued that the party now disposed of more effective means to attract new members, above all the non-party conferences and party weeks.[55] When in early 1922 the idea was raised to form support (*sodeistviya*) groups for the party the restrictive organisational structure of the sympathisers' groups, with a statute and the insistence that members carry out various party duties, was explicitly avoided, and a much looser form adopted.[56]

The system of candidature took over as the testing period for potential members. In late 1918 certain Moscow *raion*s, like Butyrskii, had adopted the practice of placing recruits on a probationary period of 2–3 months. The system was instituted in the *guberniya* at the time and gradually became formalised for the city as a whole. Applicants could be accepted on the recommendation of two communists whose own party standing was over six months and they then had to be accepted by a general meeting of the organisation. They had the right to attend open party meetings, but could not vote. The candidature period for workers was not less than a month, for peasants three months, and for others not less than six months. Acceptance even then was not automatic, but only if the candidate had shown 'that they were devoted to the party'.[57] The practice was generalised for the rest of the party on the basis of Moscow's example by the party statute of December 1919.[58] Candidature in principle was a more effective vetting procedure than the sympathisers' groups, but from the evidence of continuing concern over the quality of recruitment to the party it was not a particularly effective screen.

The VIII Congress had decided that in the light of the changing social composition there should be a general all-Russian reregistration of party membership. It should have been completed by 1 June, but in many organisations, including Moscow, it continued to September. Special attention was to be paid to the 'October communists' and recruitment was halted for the duration. Each member was obliged to complete a personal questionnaire and present the recommendations of two well-known communists who had been in the party for over six months. Non-fulfilment of these conditions meant relegation to sympathiser or candidate status, or expulsion. Many simply failed to comply with these conditions and were automatically dropped from party membership.[59] The large number in this category is partially explained by the fact that many of those who had been mobilised had not been taken off the registers. In the *raion*s reregistration commissions were established. In Rogozhsko-Simonovskii *raion*, for example, a five-person commission composed of A. Sokolov from the TsK, Myasnikov from the MK, and three members of the RK reviewed each member, aided by representatives of the cells. Committee members themselves were not obliged to reregister.[60] The commission worked from 11 May to 13 June and reduced the membership in the *raion* from 934 to 360, a fall of over 60 per cent.[61] No global figures are available for the reregistration as a whole in the city, though T. H. Rigby estimates that in urban organisations there was an average drop of 10–15 per cent, and J. R. Adelman suggests a fall of 47 per cent for the party as a whole.[62] The above example suggests that the second figure was closer to the truth, but between the VIII Congress and the party week in October membership in the city fell from 17 000 to 15 834, a fall of only 6.7 per cent, but this includes any recruitment that may have taken place.[63] The figures are further confused by the large-scale mobilisations of this period which, as Lenin pointed out, in themselves acted as a purge mechanism of 'cowards and malcontents'.[64] The reregistration had been designed to clear the party of the 'unhealthy' elements who had joined the party since the revolution, above all the urban petty bourgeoisie and the intelligentsia. No sooner was it completed, however, than the door was opened to a massive influx of workers and peasants.

MASS MOBILISATION AND MASS RECRUITMENT

By the autumn of 1919 party membership had fallen to the lowest level of the civil war. With the party weeks in autumn 1919 the history of party recruitment entered a qualitatively new phase. They were designed to fulfil several functions: to improve the social composition of the party by a massive intake of workers (and poor peasants); to give the party a new reserve of manpower (with the petering out of the sympathisers' groups); and also for political reasons, as a way of reestablishing the party's mass presence in society. This aspect in particular was pointed out by Lenin in assessing the weeks when he stressed that the voluntary enlistment of workers into the party at a time of grave military danger was a great moral victory.[65] This was indeed a desperate period for the Soviet government. In spring 1919 massive mobilisations had been declared to counter the renewed threat from Admiral Kolchak. Sushchevsko-Mar'inskii and Butyrskii *raion*s, for example, sent 60 per cent of their membership, and in Sokol'nicheskii *raion* only thirty-four out of fifty-four cells remained.[66] The pressure for communists to leave was so intense that even the sick and the aged were caught in the trawl.[67] At the city party conference on 3 May 1919 I. T. Smilga demanded that offices gave up their staff even if this meant that they could no longer function. Yaroslavskii pointed out, however, that even communist heads of department were hindering the release of their employees on the ground that they were irreplaceable. The conference called for a survey to be conducted of all office workers, for male labour to be replaced by women, and for the campaign against desertion to be intensified.[68] With Yudenich's advance on Petrograd in May 1919 the TsK called for yet further mobilisations of party, trade union and office personnel,[69] and in a quixotic gesture of solidarity with Petrograd Kamenev suggested that half of the Moscow Soviet's deputies go to the defence of the old capital (in fact only forty-four went).[70] A party circular of 18 June 1919 stressed that communist mobilisations had not only a military but also a political significance. It insisted that communists were to be taken from responsible posts even if departments collapsed without them.[71] These desperate measures were confirmed by the TsK on 19 July 1919 when it insisted that communists in offices, except those involved in the most politically sensitive posts, were to be replaced by trustworthy non-party people.[72]

In mid-1919 Soviet forces registered successes against Kolchak, but the main danger shifted to the south. Denikin's Moscow directive of 3 July was the signal for an attack spearheaded by General Mamontov's cavalry to reach Moscow via Kursk, Orel and Tula.[73] The party was squeezed ever harder to fill the quotas, but the quality of the recruits was falling. As Zagorskii had told an MK meeting earlier, 'All the best communists have gone'.[74] The TsK itself noted that there were many cases of communists either leaving the front of their own accord or refusing to obey orders, and drew the conclusion that despite the reregistration there were still many communists unworthy of the name.[75] The TsK still called for nine-tenths of the party to be allocated to the army, 'the sword of the working class'.[76] When a mobilisation of communists was announced at a delegate meeting in Zamoskvorech'e on 1 October 1919, perhaps in recognition that some might try to avoid the draft by going into the countryside, the order was imposed that no communist was to leave the city without permission.[77] N. Krestinskii admitted the problem at the VIII Party Conference when he reported that mass party mobilisations had ceased since 8 July 1919 because of their poor quality and instead there had been personal mobilisations for specific tasks.[78] The main burden, however, still fell on Moscow which donated, for example, two-thirds of the 5427 communists drafted in October 1919.[79]

It was against this background, and drawing on the experience of a rapid recruitment campaign in Petrograd in August 1919, that the TsK plenum of 26 September decided on a rapid intake of workers and peasants into the party, though stressed that the aim of a membership of a million was not to be at the expense of quality.[80] As we shall see, while successful in doubling party membership by an intake of about 160 000,[81] the mass recruitment of the party weeks' only aggravated the split in the party between an inner core of activists and the mass of the party. The Moscow *guberniya* party organisation carried out its week from 21–28 September 1919 but succeeded in attracting only 1254 new members.[82] It was a trial run for the city party week in which the entrance requirements were the same as those for candidates.[83] Learning from the *guberniya*'s disappointing experience, the MK decided that the entrance requirements during the city's week, which was held between 8–15 October, would be relaxed further. The need for two written recommendations was dropped, and the candidate stage was waived. The only check was to ask the prospective member's fellow communist workers to vouch for the entrant, and in many cases even this elementary requirement was dropped.[84] The number of new entrants is usually given as 14 581,[85] but with the addition of the figures for some cells in Sushchevsko-Mar'inskii and Basmannyi *raion*s this must be increased to 16 102.[86] Over half this intake was of soldiers, and hence the large peasant group represented in Table 5.3. A third of the worker intake was of women, a far higher proportion than their average in the MPO. The number of cells increased significantly during the week.[87] In most *raion*s membership doubled in the space of the week, with the 1075 communists in July 1919 in Sokol'nicheskii *raion*[88] now being joined by another 900. The most spectacular increase, however, was in the administrative Gorodskoi *raion*. Here membership had risen from approximately 1000 in June 1918 to 1540 members and 2000 sympathisers on the eve of the week.[89] During the week, numbers increased by over 400 per cent to 6381. The greatest rise was in Red Army membership (2052), but a surprising result in view of the aim of the week was that over a quarter more office than industrial workers joined.[90] Once again, despite the stated social and occupational preferences of the party leadership, the sheer pressure of the social and structural changes in the city could not be withstood.

The mass intake of new members accentuated the split in the party between the party activists and the rank and file. The weeks fuelled the controversy over party democracy in 1920. The very nature of the week as a sharp assault on the recruitment problem reflected the campaign mentality of these years. A great mass of raw party members were inducted with, in many cases (as later became clear), little understanding of the party that they were joining. The mass intake, justified on the grounds of the need to strengthen the proletarian base of the party, sacrificed the idea of the party as a whole acting as the elite vanguard in favour of a two-tier party in which the leadership of the party activists was accentuated and the position of the rank-and-file member undermined. It was from this point that the debate developed over what was called a 'narrow' party, restricted only to fully conscious members who could play an active part in decision-making, and a 'wide' party, with the greatest possible number of workers and peasants who would inevitably come under greater central direction. Echoes of this debate remain in the tension between concepts of cadre versus mass parties.

Following the weeks there was a general consensus that recruitment would have to cease for a time. At the VIII Party Conference in December, Lenin argued that the party 'gates' were now to be locked and great care taken in further recruitment.[91] Bukharin posed the issue more starkly: until the new members had been processed a temporary halt should be called to recruitment.[92] Nevertheless, membership of the MPO rose rapidly in 1920, punctuated only by the August reregistration. There were calls for a new party week following the reregistration, but in practice not only was such mass recruitment rejected but in its place in 1921 a purge was launched. As *Pravda* put it, a united and strong party was more important than mere numbers.[93] Obviously, the fear at this stage was that any large-scale increase in membership would only exacerbate the divisions within the party revealed by the party and trade union debate. At the same time the paper admitted that the great mass of party members lacked any theoretical grounding in Marxism but had joined the party out of 'instinct'.[94] This theme was taken up by Lenin in March 1922 when he severely criticised the level of the majority of the party's 3–400 000 members and stated:

> If we do not close our eyes to reality we must admit that at the present time the proletarian policy of the party is not determined by the character of its membership, but by the enormous undivided prestige enjoyed by the small group which might be called the old guard of the party.[95]

Trotsky in *The New Course* in 1923 characterised the relations between the old and the new generations (pre- and post-October 1917). He claimed that after October there was a 'rapid, even abnormal, growth of the party'. The abnormality consisted in the influx both of inexperienced workers with low consciousness and of some alien elements, hangers-on and functionaries. The party preserved its character by relying on the 'internal dictatorship of the old guard':

> The party was living, as it were, on two storeys: the upper storey, where things are decided, and the lower storey, where all you do is learn of the decisions.[96]

The rapid recruitment of the party weeks therefore provided the sociological basis for analyses of the 'old course' of the civil war which divided the party into 'a few thousand comrades, who form the leading cadres', and 'the rest of the mass whom they look upon only as an object of action'.[97] As Michael Farbman put it at the time:

> It is only fair, however, to state that the inclination of the 'Old Guard' to favour the absolutism of the CC was not the chief reason for the development of the party on centralised lines. This must be attributed largely to the heterogeneity and to the unassimilable character of the great mass of the new adherents.[98]

From this point of view there is a clear connection between the dramatic settling of the question of a 'wide' or 'narrow' party by the Lenin Enrolment of 1924 and the rise of Stalin to power on the back of the bureaucracy.[99]

The debate over a 'wide' or 'narrow' party raised questions of fundamental importance on the nature and role of the party. The implications of a 'wide' party on internal organisational development have been suggested, but at the same time the 'narrow' version had consequences of its own. The VIII Party Congress marked the transition from the generalised reregistrations of 1918 to more normative ones, where social and political criteria were varied depending on the current preoccupation of the leaders. It was no longer left to the 'market' to regulate entrance to anyone who supported the party and its aims. Now social background was elevated as a cardinal consideration in selecting members, a position stressed later by the Workers' Opposition. While understandably concerned about the falling proportion of worker recruitment, though this does not seem to have fallen by as much as was feared (see Table 5.3), and the clear evidence that many joined for opportunist reasons, this reinforced selective policy changed the party's relationship not only to non-proletarian sections of society, but also to the working class membership itself. The party leadership strengthened its prerogatives over recruitment through purges and checks: the mass of the party became increasingly malleable in the hands of the leadership as communists became exposed to the threat of expulsion, firstly for social reasons, and then for political ones.

RECRUITMENT AND REREGISTRATION: 1920–21

The party week starkly posed the question of the educational and political level of the mass of party membership. At the VIII Conference, soon after the week, V. Sorin asserted:

> It is no secret that the ideological level of our party, especially in the provinces, is not very high. A significant proportion of the party membership, probably the majority, are politically semi-literate.[100]

Nevertheless, Zinoviev argued at the conference that the new members were to be 'used' immediately by involvement in party work,[101] and it was this view which was adopted: they were to be actively employed 'in the construction of the new communist society'.[102] In other words, they were to join the state bureaucracy and the army. As Rigby puts it, 'the party leadership was proceding to expose the new crop of communists to precisely those influences which had led to the "corruption" and "careerism" of so many of their predecessors'.[103] The emphasis on the managerial functions of the party was a contributory factor to the crisis in the party in 1920. On the eve of the unification of the city and *guberniya* party organisations in May 1920, a certain Korolev argued that mass recruitment was destroying party organisation in the localities and he estimated that 90 per cent of communists were insufficiently educated to be party members.[104] Other speakers supported his argument and their fears over the quality of the new recruits were to be confirmed by the August 1920 reregistration, which in addition discovered that ignorance of the basic ideas of the party programme was not confined to those who had recently joined.[105] Within a few months at least half of those who had been recruited during the party week in Moscow were to leave or be expelled.[106]

Despite the calls for the 'door to be locked' and for the new members to be processed following the party week, recruitment in Moscow continued at a fast rate. In March 1920 alone the city organisation gained 1792 new members, but there was a net increase in membership of only about 500 since the party week of October 1919 because of the high degree of flux, with a turnover of 8 per cent in March alone.[107] Such instability encouraged the inflated membership figures revealed during the reregistration later in the year. The March 1920 Moscow statute tightened up the recruitment procedure. In most *raions* acceptance into the party had previously been ratified at delegate meetings, and it was now admitted that this had often consisted of a purely formal recitation of names. Acceptance became the responsibility of the RK and only then was the case referred to the members for confirmation.[108] Once again, functions were being transferred to committees from general meetings of communists. Expulsions continued throughout the period and 6745 cases were reported between 1918 and 1920 from the city and *guberniya* organisations.[109] The typical reasons, as in late 1918, included infractions of party discipline, not attending meetings, ignoring the orders of the cell, personal requests due to age or health, drunkenness, playing cards, misuse of factory stores, and desertion from the 'labour front'.[110] There appears to have been an increase in expulsions in 1920, with fifty from Sokol'nicheskii organisation alone between May and August 1920, just under 3 per cent of its total membership.[111] Clearly the party was not filled with a new breed of selfless revolutionary of the Rakhmetov type described in N. G. Chernyshevskii's novel *'What is to be Done?'* and epitomised by Lenin himself. This was not surprising given the scale of recruitment and the great fluidity in membership. Over the same period in the Sokol'nicheskii organisation, for example, membership increased by 400 with another 230 candidates, and the number of cells increased from 116 to 140.[112] In the two months of June and July 1920 alone total membership of the joint organisation increased, according to contemporary estimates, by over 7 per cent (2843 members and 619 candidates) and the number of cells by thirty-nine to make a total of 1328.[113]

Once again fears over the composition of the party prompted the IX Congress in March 1920 to call for a second all-Russian reregistration. This time, however, there were broader objectives. A new standard party card was to replace those issued by the local organisations for the more accurate accounting of party members. The move had an economic rationale in this period of compulsory labour duty and assignment in that the profession of members could be established and thus directed to where those skills were required. What had been achieved previously on the local level or in the army was now extended to the party nationally. I. A. Pyatnitskii proposed a three-fold categorisation of members which explicitly gave priority to those who had joined before October 1917.[114] The aim once again was to identify reserves of trustworthy cadres to replace those who had been mobilised. Its effect, however, was to reinforce the division in the party based on length of membership. For the first time the public nature of the purge was stressed, whereas previous ones had been carried out largely as internal disciplinary measures. Great play was made of public participation in later purges.[115] The open nature of this reregistration was designed to emphasise the party's close links with the masses, but in fact reflected concern precisely over the gulf between the party and the working class. The MK appealed to the public for any information on misdemeanours by communists either in the present or the past. All those unmasked, the MK promised, would be expelled. All information was to be factual and signed,[116] and the MK was at pains to stress that all information would be treated with discretion to allay fears that informants would suffer in any way.[117]

The reregistration began in Moscow on 1 August with recruitment halted from 15 July. In each *raion* a reregistration commision was formed with two representatives from the MK and one from the RK.[118] For the party as a whole the fall in numbers was less than in the 1919 reregistration at just under 30 per cent,[119] but in Moscow there was a 39.4 per cent fall in membership (see Table 5.4). However, only 1.2 per cent were actually expelled and 1.8 per cent demoted to candidature, a total of 3 per cent in some way disciplined. There were great variations between *raions*, with the lowest proportion by far in Gorodskoi *raion*. A highly significant figure is the massive 35.2 per cent who for one reason or another failed to attend the reregistration. Part of the explanation for this large number is, as Soviet sources stress, poor accounting which failed to register communists who entered and left the city. Furthermore, a third of the organisation consisted of soldiers (39.3 per cent of male membership in six *raion*s excluding Baumanskii in August 1920)[120] which made accounting even more difficult. At the same time, Rigby suggests that a large proportion of communists took the opportunity to leave the party, an indication that 'unworthy' elements were still able to join. Further, as Rigby points out in connection with Kronstadt where a quarter of the party organisation dropped out, this large category takes on a political significance in the light of later opposition to party policies.[121] The reregistration revealed serious deficiencies, including the fact that there were many communists in the city who did not even know the name of the chairman of the Moscow Soviet (Kamenev).[122] The majority of those demoted to candidacy,[123] most of whom had joined during the party week,[124] were charged with political illiteracy. An MK circular soon after admitted that the problem was not restricted to the party week cohort but included those who had joined much earlier. All

Table 5.4 The August 1920 reregistration

	Before	After					Members			
	Members	Members	Candidates	Total	Increase	Decrease	Expelled	Reduced to candidate	Not present	On missions
Baumanskii	5 048	3 422	304	3 726	–	1 626	69	–	1 557	–
Gorodskii	9 787	5 749	1 338	7 087	–	4 038	19	19	4 000	–
Zamoskvoretskii	4 784	2 867	541	3 408	–	1 897	27	460	1 310	100
Kras-Presnenskii	12 251	6 728	–	–	–	5 527	112	74	5 337	–
Rog-Simonovskii	1 709	1 229	76	1 305	–	480	19	85	259	121
Sokol'nicheskii	2 681	1 870	326	2 196	–	811	154	33	624	–
Khamovnicheskii	1 821	1 204	315	1 519	–	517	73	31	300	213
TOTAL City	38 061	23 069	2 900	25 969	–	14 992	473	702	13 383	434
TOTAL Guberniya	5 328	4 572	–	–	157	913	140	198	456	119
TOTAL	43 389	27 641	–	–	157	15 905	613	900	13 838	553

Source: Otchet MK za sentyabr' 1920g., p. 6.

party members and not just recruits were to attend the party schools.[125] As Bukharin put it, the party had not succeeded in 'digesting' the new members.[126]

The political illiteracy revealed by the reregistration was compounded by a low general level of education. There was a marked contrast in the city between those with higher education (3.2 per cent) and those with only a basic primary education (67.9 per cent),[127] and this pattern only reinforced the gulf between the communist and the specialist. The greater attention devoted to the political education of communists was reflected in the growth in the network of party schools from eight in September 1920 to sixty-three in February 1921.[128] For the mass of the membership, learning via the process of participation in party work was to be supplemented by regular lessons in party ideology, but this was to be a simplified version to motivate rather than to educate the communist. As the editors of the Moscow journal for propagandists put it earlier:

> We have no time at present to work out a 'complete world view' out of the inexhaustible treasure house of Marxism. We must receive precisely that ration of learning that is necessary for today's struggle, and no more. The worker, because of the lack of supplies, receives from the state a portion of bread not in those quantities that a man in general needs, but as much as he requires so that he can work and not collapse from exhaustion; it is the same with Marxism: it must be released in such doses as are necessary so that each of us can be a fighting political force. Anything more, and academism begins, knowledge for the sake of knowledge, refusal of practical work with the excuse of deepening one's understanding of the world.[129]

Such assertions marked the passage of Marxism from scientific method to dogma. Despite the concern over the quality of the recruits the reregistration was followed by calls for a repetition of the party weeks to strengthen links with the workers.[130] The idea was not taken up, though a vigorous discussion took place at the time. Instead, piecemeal mechanisms were introduced. Reflecting the usual concern over social composition, the IX Party Conference in September 1920 decided to make it easier for workers and peasants and harder for others to join. There are conflicting claims over the pattern of recruitment in the autumn of 1920 and up to the X Party Congress in March 1921. At the congress Bukharin argued that there had been a great increase since March 1920,[131] while the Workers' Opposition insisted that there had been a mass exodus of workers, above all during the debates following the reregistration.[132] In Moscow numbers did increase significantly, with a rise of nearly a fifth in September alone,[133] possibly due to the backlog created by the ban on recruitment during the check. Recruitment slowed in October with only 335 new members (in five *raions*), while 455 left the city and 329 arrived, giving a net increase of only 1.2 per cent.[134] The high level of turnover was exacerbated by the high proportion of military communists who were prone to fairly rapid redeployment. As the organisation was gripped by political debate in late 1920, membership increased faster. In the proletarian Baumanskii *raion*, the main support of the Workers' Opposition, in the three months from November 1920 there was an increase of 1067, nearly a third over the September level. In December alone membership increased by 712.[135] Part of the increase can be attributed to the movement of demobilised communists and others to the city, but significant recruitment still took place. By January 1921 membership of the joint organisation had increased by nearly a third (32.8 per cent) since the registration,[136] but what proportion were new members is not known. Therefore the Workers' Opposition claim that workers were leaving the party must remain unproved, while Bukharin's assertion on increased membership was justified.

The major purge ordered by the X Party Congress lies beyond the scope of this work but some comments are in order. First, the fairly anodyne term 'registration' was dropped in favour of the more sinister 'purge' (*chistka*) (which itself has now been replaced by the original term). Second, the level of actual expulsions increased quite dramatically in comparison with the 1920 registration. While the party as a whole lost a quarter of its total membership,[137] the city lost 18.2 per cent through direct expulsions.[138] Third, the political aspect of the purge was much more marked than in previous registrations, though there had been hints of this in 1918. R. Service has recently confirmed that it was used to punish oppositionists,[139] and this was facilitated by the fact that for the first time the purge commissions were independent of the local organisations.[140] There is no direct evidence that the purge was used to punish oppositionists in Moscow, but of the 7270 expelled from the joint organisation a high proportion were accused of insubordination, a charge that could well cover oppositional activity, and a full 12 per cent left of their own accord (46 per cent of these were workers) which indicates a certain level of dissatisfaction with party policies.[141] Fourth, as in 1920, great stress was placed on uncovering former members of other parties in a search for scapegoats for the political crisis in the party. In Moscow 11.4 per cent of those joining the party in 1918 fell into this category, [142] and by August 1920 they made up 8 per cent (2416 out of 29 822) of the communists in the city.[143] Allegedly, by March 1921, 7 per cent of communists nationally had passed through another party,[144] but in Moscow this had decreased to 4.5 per cent in the joint organisation (1523),[145] though the fall could be explained by members dissembling as their past affiliations became more dangerous. There was a clear trend for the proportion to decline, however, and the concentration on this issue in the 1921 purge[146] was unjustified. The expulsion of 583 former members of other parties[147] reflected the increasing siege mentality within the party. Finally, as in the 1920 reregistration, information from non-party people was encouraged.[148] The experience of the reregistrations during the civil war provided the organisational and political experience required to conduct the new model purges as they developed into major political events in their own right.

MOSCOW PARTY MEMBERSHIP, 1918–21

The reregistration and debates over the recruitment policy reflected the party's theoretical and practical role as the vanguard in society and state organisation. The Moscow party organisation, and the party as a whole, however, never represented more than a very small proportion of the population during the civil war. In mid-1918 the party as a whole comprised less than one per cent of the total population of the city and 1.6 per cent of the independent population. By September 1920 these proportions had increased to just under 3 per cent and 4.6 per cent. In 1918 there was one communist for every sixty-two of the independent population, and by September 1920 this had increased to one communist for every twenty-two. In the *guberniya* the party was an even tinier group set amidst the peasant population. At the same time the above proportions are misleading in that they were not spread evenly over the city's population but were concentrated in certain sectors. The party was overwhelmingly made up of men in their twenties and the youthfulness of the organisation might well account for some of its grass-roots radicalism. Female participation in party bodies was low, making up only 13 per cent of the joint party organisation in August 1920 (see Table 5.5). The proportion of women declined towards the end of the year to reach 9 per cent in November.[149] In Sokol'nicheskii *raion* the fall was from 11 per cent in August to 8.7 per cent in December 1920.[150] The very concept of the activist party member outlined by Lenin militated against the active participation of women. By 1920, 63 per cent of the joint organisation was under the age of 30, and 90 per cent under 40, with the single largest group in their late twenties. Party saturation in each age

Table 5.5 Age and sex structure of the MPO in August 1920

Age	City						Joint MPO					
	Men	Per-centage	Women	Per-centage	Total	Per-centage	Men	Per-centage	Women	Per-centage	Total	Per-centage
Up to 18	206	1	44	1	250	1	279	1	53	1	322	1
18–19	1 731	7	316	8	2 047	7	2 022	6	386	8	2 408	7
20–23	5 802	22	1 089	28	6 891	23	6 476	21	1 260	28	7 738	22
24–29	8 829	34	1 232	31	10 061	34	10 093	33	1 413	31	11 506	33
30–39	6 818	26	839	21	7 657	26	8 450	28	962	21	9 412	27
40 +	2 168	9	301	8	2 469	8	2 968	10	349	9	3 317	9
Not known	313	1	132	3	445	1	365	1	150	3	515	1
Percentage	87		13		100		87		13		100	
Total	25 867	100	3 953	100	29 820	100	30 653	100	4 573	100	35 226	100

Source: *Materialy po statistike*, pp. 22–7.

group showed a marked disparity between a fairly high saturation for the 18–24 age group, of whom communists represented 6.4 per cent; even higher saturation in the 25–29 group at 7.1 per cent; and thereafter decreasing sharply to 4.3 per cent for the 30–39 group; and falling to the minuscule representation of 0.9 per cent for those over 40 years old.[151] Recruitment in 1917 and later was overwhelmingly from among young people: those over 40 were a 'lost generation' as far as the party was concerned.

Given the party's vanguard role the relative smallness of the MPO is not surprising, but at the same time the party in the city was a small proportion of the working class. In late 1920 the city party had about 6000 of its members employed in industrial enterprises (see Table 4.2, p. 114), or just under 7 per cent of the total industrial workforce of 87 000. A large part of the working class was either not willing to join the party or was prevented from doing so by the general rules governing entrance. The 1920 reregistration for the first time gave details of the organisation's social composition (see Table 5.6). Office workers were concentrated in the two inner *raions* of Gorodskoi and Khamovnicheskii, whose spirit was dominated by the commissariats and the local government offices. The proportion of workers was higher in the outlying industrial *raions*. Comparison of Table 5.6(b) with the social pattern of recruitment shown in Table 5.3 shows that the designation as worker of 55 per cent of the city organisation by profession is an exaggeration. Even if we accept this figure, it illustrates that the party week in Moscow, when nearly 7000 workers joined, had no more than restored the balance for the percentage of workers in the city organisation. Table 5.6(a) is probably more accurate and shows that the percentage of workers in Moscow was higher than in the party as a whole, where the proportion fell from 56.9 per cent in 1918 to 44 per cent in early 1921.[152] This pattern is reflected in the distribution of cells. In September 1920 less than a third (30 per cent) of the 776 cells in six *raions* were in enterprises, while the largest number were those in offices (31 per cent), with the rest in the army (26 per cent) and in transport (see Table 4.3).[153] Out of the 1537 cells in the joint organisation in April 1921, 515 (33.5 per cent) were factory and transport, 470 (30.5 per cent) soviet, 119 (7.7 per cent) rural, and 433 (28.2 per cent) military.[154] Membership of a factory cell, however, did not necessarily entail employment in a manual task, as Zelenskii, by then secretary of the MK, pointed out at the XI Party Congress in March 1922.[155]

Whatever the precise figures, the proportion of workers by origin,

Table 5.6   Social composition of MPO in August 1920 (by profession)

(a) For the city and guberniya

	City		Guberniya		Total		Percentage in 36 gubs excl.
	No.	Per-centage	No.	Per-centage	No.	Per-centage	M. + P.
Workers	14 496	49	2 803	52	17 299	49	40
Employees	6 047	20	1 026	19	7 073	20	21
Peasants	2 188	7	437	8	2 625	8	22
Intelligentsia	1 999	7	181	3	2 180	6	5
Craftsmen	905	3	205	4	1 110	3	7
Others	2 676	9	572	11	3 248	9	4
Unknown	1 509	5	182	3	1 691	5	1
Total	29 820	100	5 406	100	35 226	100	100

(b) By raion

	Workers		Peasants		Employees		Intelligentsia		
	No.	Per-cent-age	No.	Per-cent-age	No.	Per-cent-age	No.	Per-cent-age	Total
Baum	1 722	54.0	402	12.6	727	22.8	337	10.6	3 188
Gor	2 596	51.5	338	6.7	1 266	23.2	935	18.6	5 035
Zam	1 664	59.6	286	10.2	591	21.2	251	9.0	2 792
Kras-Pres	4 012	54.0	1 130	15.2	1 530	20.6	754	10.2	7 426
Rog-Sim	630	65.7	114	11.9	168	17.5	47	4.9	959
Sok	1 228	63.0	163	8.4	454	23.3	104	5.3	1 949
Kham	743	46.4	216	13.5	371	23.1	271	17.0	1 601
City TOT	12 595	54.9	2 649	11.5	5 007	21.8	2 699	11.8	22 940
Gub TOT	2 960	59.6	700	14.1	1 089	21.9	217	4.4	4 966
MPO TOT	15 555	55.8	3 349	12.0	6 096	21.8	2 916	10.4	27 906
RKP TOT	96 611	45.2	40 534	19.0	48 814	22.8	10 302	4.8	213 669

Sources: KM, col. 676; *Otchet MK za sentyabr' 1920g.*, p. 18. *Materialy po statistike*, pp. 22–3 and 80–1. Figures for the 38 *gubernii* from *Lichnyi sostav RKP (b) v 1920 god* (Moscow, 1921) p. 23. Nationally there were also 12 581 craftsmen and 5 327 others. Table 5.6(b) probably exaggerates the proportion of workers and intelligentsia, cf. Table 5.6 (a).

profession and occupation had declined to less than half during the civil war. By August 1920 in the city, 9791 (33 per cent) of communists were in a production trade union, 5712 (19 per cent) in other trade unions, with no information on 14 317 (48 per cent) out of 29 820. Ten per cent of the joint organisation's members were in the metal union, 7 per cent in transport, 10 per cent in the office workers' trade union, and 6 per cent in the textile union. The single largest profession of MPO members was metalworking, reflecting Lenin's idea of the advanced consciousness associated with that profession. Less satisfactory from Lenin's point of view was the second largest group, that of office workers (see Table 5.7). A national sample of party members in October 1919 revealed that only 11 per cent of party membership were actually working in factories. More than 60 per cent were employed in state and party posts, and another quarter were in the Red Army, often occupying the key posts. Less than a quarter of the party was in its rank and file[156] as party members moved from the factory to non-manual or military work. By 1920 in Moscow the single largest occupational group was in the various institutions (27.4 per cent), followed by industrial enterprises, including management positions (22.9 per cent), and the Red Army (18.3 per cent) (see Table 4.2 on page 114). The corresponding figures for the party as a whole of 213 69 members in thirty-eight *gubernii* are 34.7 per cent, 14.1 per cent, and 20.7 per cent, and in thirty-six *gubernii* (excluding Moscow and Petrograd) with 156 751 members, 36.5 per cent, 11.8 per cent, and 20 per cent. The managerial functions of the party were more marked in the party as a whole, and especially in Petrograd, than in Moscow where the party was larger and the weight of industry more pronounced. Nevertheless, over a quarter of the Moscow party was involved in office work. Comparing the MPO by class composition and occupation shows that while about half claimed to be worker by class, only just over a fifth (21.3 per cent) were employed in a manual profession. Another fifth were soldiers at that time. Agriculture represented an insignificant proportion at 2.9 per cent of the joint organisation, indicating the minimal presence of the party among the peasantry of Moscow *guberniya*. In the party as a whole, 7.7 per cent were employed in agriculture, and, excluding the two capitals, 9.5 per cent. From the above it is clear that during the civil war the party tended to become not so much one in the working class or peasantry, in whose name the revolution had been made, but one concerned with management and the army.

Recruitment policy provided the basis for the emergence of an 'old

Table 5.7   Profession and trade union membership of MPO members in August 1920

	Profession		Trade union membership	
	No.	Per-centage	No.	Per-centage
Miners	161	0.4	109	0.3
Woodworkers	1 082	2.9	236	0.7
Metalworkers – technicians	918	2.4	3 549	10.0
– others	6 107	16.3		
Printers	970	2.6	754	2.1
Stationers	42	0.1	38	0.1
Foodworkers	630	1.7	429	1.2
Leatherworkers	908	2.4	464	1.3
Agriculture/forestry – agronomists	132	0.3	178	0.5
– others	3 159	8.4		
Construction workers	1 134	3.0	325	0.9
Transport – drivers, mates	190	0.5	2 555	7.2
– other railway jobs	542	1.4		
– waterworkers	223	0.6		
– local transport	713	1.9		
Chemical workers	464	1.2	516	1.5
Clothing workers	1 202	3.2	544	1.5
Tobacco workers	40	0.1	94	0.3
Textile workers	1 546	4.1	2 209	6.3
Unskilled workers	1 865	5.0	–	–
Municipal workers	420	1.1	1 108	3.1
Public catering, hostels	230	0.6	166	0.5
Medical – doctors, midwives, vets	194	0.5	725	2.1
– others	563	1.5		
Office workers – statisticians, etc.	555	1.5	3 395	9.6
– others	5 771	15.4		
Communications workers	768	2.0	407	1.1
Education – teachers	746	2.0	629	1.8
– others	493	1.3		
Cultural workers	383	1.0	129	0.4
Military specialists	546	1.4	–	–
Without profession	2 568	6.8	–	–
Not known	2 249	6.0	–	–
Not belonging to trade unions or not known	–	–	16 667	47.3
Total	37 514	100	35 226	100

Source: Materialy po statistike, pp. 28–9 and 52–3.

guard'. A new two-tier party emerged as recruitment and expulsion policy served instrumental ends – to improve the percentage of workers or to staff the new bureaucracy – whose timing and extent was determined by the leadership. The low educational level of the new recruits, the military emergency and the mobilisations, the concept of party duty, and the many other factors described above emphasised the dominance of the old Leninist leadership. Organisational practice during the civil war tended to consolidate this group as the rapid numerical growth was accompanied by the stifling of self-activity through 'extreme centralisation and the system of military orders'.[157] A small, active group emerged in the party, a bureaucracy, which dominated a passive group which was 'only occasionally brought into play and then only at the behest of the former'.[158] Before this process could be consolidated the party had yet to undergo the trial of the great debates of 1920.

6 Soviets, Bureaucracy and Participation

THE MOSCOW SOVIETS AND THE FORMATION OF THE ONE-PARTY STATE

The distinctive feature of the first period of Soviet power was the lack of integration both in theory and practice between its constituent elements. A powerful new state emerged but internally it was divided into sub-systems made up of an economic state (the economic apparatus), a political state (the party), and a civilian state centred on the soviets. A police and military state can also be identified, while the 'workers' state' as a system of direct workers' management remained a residual category, undefined yet exerting a powerful hold on the imaginations of the players in the great drama of the civil war. The relations between these elements provoked the constant debates within the party, and indeed the debates were a crucial element in the ideological restructuring required to maintain the organisational changes. It is misleading to talk in terms of a single 'monolith' developing in this period: a series of monoliths emerged, each relatively sovereign in its own domain. The Leninist programme called for the smashing of the bourgeois state, and this was achieved with relative ease in the first months after the revolution, but in each sphere the new states rapidly escaped from the control of popular forces. And within each domain their own type of bureaucratism emerged as politics was transformed into expanded administration. It is difficult to talk of the creation of the one-party state, with its persecution of non-Bolshevik parties and controlled elections, without analysing at the same time the enhanced powers of the police apparatus.

The soviets represented the transcending of parliamentarianism by 'the conversion of representative institutions from talking shops into "working bodies"'. In Lenin's theory they were the political form of the commune state designed to combine the political and economic demands of the workers' movement and act as the means of popular control over the various elements of the dictatorship of the proletariat. In practice the soviets suffered from a three-fold handicap: the existence of a separate political apparatus where real political power lay; the emergence of a military–economic system designed both to fight the civil war and to serve the developmental needs of the country; and an organisational incoherence, derived from flaws in the theory of the commune state, which fractured the relationship both between the soviets as a whole and their electorate, and between the soviet plenum and its executive bodies. The Moscow Soviet up to October 1917 did not play an independent political role since it was very much in second place to the Petrograd Soviet where the important decisions were taken. After October it became the scene of intense political debate between the parties, especially between the Bolsheviks and the Mensheviks,[2] and up to mid-1918 it remained to some extent a 'popular parliament'. Even though the Bolsheviks came to power in their name in October 1917, the relationship between the party and the soviets remained ambiguous. Throughout war communism the debate over their relationship continued, focusing on such issues as the powers of the localities, the role of the soviet executive committees, and the relationship of party members working in the soviets and local party organisations. As with so many other questions, these issues were resolved by the end of war communism as part of the package of solutions marking the transition to the NEP.

Even before becoming the constitutional organ of power the soviets had acquired a distinctive organisational character. Once constituted as the unique form of state power their internal organisation developed rapidly as their functions extended to cover all aspects of local life. Power moved away from the plenum to ever smaller groups at the apex of the soviet's structure. Medvedev has commented on this in the following terms:

> The combination of legislative and executive powers within one institution leads over a period of time to the disproportionate growth of the executive, thus turning representative bodies into empty appendages, providing an opening for a regime of personal dictatorship, and creating a favourable atmosphere for the development of bureaucracy and abuse of power.[3]

The city workers' soviet was united with the soldiers' soviet on 14 November 1917, and a new body, a presidium, was created in addition to the already existing executive committee (EC or *ispolkom*), and both initially were to be elected by the full plenum.[4] The presidium, which the Mensheviks refused to join on the grounds that it would take power away from the plenum,[5] rapidly accrued massive powers as it took on the extraordinary powers of the Military Revolutionary Committee, which restricted itself to security matters and at some unknown date in late

1917 disappeared. From the first the forms in which Bolshevik power was achieved, by a military operation, were institutionalised in the structure of the soviet. The new joint soviet used the existing structure of the workers' soviet, but the departments were now subordinated to the presidium and required its approval before taking even the most minor of decisions. The presidium was in almost continuous session, meeting 123 times between November 1917 and March 1918,[6] and 30 times alone in the last two weeks of November 1917.[7] At the EC session of 27 November 1917 an attempt was made to limit the presidium's functions, with political questions to be decided by the EC which was to meet twice a week.[8] The same meeting restructured the work of the soviet by forming collegia and commissions at the head of each department controlled by a commissar. Participatory forms were therefore introduced in parallel with a centralised practice, and they coexisted until the civil war and Bolshevik policies undermined the collegia system. Bureaucratism, in the sense of power moving from the floor of the elected bodies to executive organs, a process which Marc Ferro claims had begun already in mid-1917,[9] was a spectre raised by the very nature of the soviets as both executive and legislative bodies.

The slogan 'all power to the soviets' meant in practice the elimination of all previous forms of local government, the city *duma* and the *raion dumas*, which in Moscow was achieved by April 1918. The soviets became the unique form of state organisation, but at the same time they gradually became the preserve of the Bolsheviks alone as opposition was harried and ultimately outlawed as the one-party state became established. A somewhat artificial debate has taken place in the Soviet literature about the date at which the one-party state could be said to have been formed in the Soviet republic: 1920–22, 1924 or even 1930. The one-party state was the practical consequence of the theory of the commune state. Lenin's idea of the symbiotic relationship between the party and the working class was applied directly to the relationship between other parties and other classes: 'The Cadet Central Committee is the political headquarters of the bourgeois class'.[10] Lenin considered that the 'petty bourgeois' parties after October were political superstructures erected on the basis of the remnants of capitalism and petty commodity production.[11] Gimpel'son has argued that the one-party state was finally introduced in 1920–21 with the break up of the Menshevik and SR parties,[12] and that it was only introduced as a result of the implacable behaviour of the other parties during the civil war.[13] One would have to look to 1922–23 for the consolidation of the one-party system if one accepts his argument, with the final destruction of the non-Bolshevik parties and the elimination of their representation in the soviets. The mere presence of non-Bolshevik deputies in the Moscow Soviet, which lingered on up to 1923, does not indicate the existence of a multi-party system since they in no way threatened the dominating role of the Bolsheviks, and they had not done so from mid-1918.

Following the demonstration against the dissolution of the Constituent Assembly on 5 January 1918, the Moscow Soviet EC on 29 January 1918 deprived the Right SRs of the ability to participate in the soviet's executive bodies.[14] Bolshevik dominance was further strengthened by their gains in the elections to the Moscow Soviet, held in an atmosphere of bitter recriminations between the parties, in April 1918 (see Table 6.1). In these first post-revolutionary elections to the Moscow Soviet the Mensheviks already accused the Bolsheviks of electoral malpractice.[15] In contrast to Moscow, the Mensheviks won the elections to the city soviets in all the provincial capitals of the Central Industrial Region in spring 1918.[16] Following their expulsion from the central soviet body (VTsIK), the major Menshevik leaders headed by Martov joined the Moscow Soviet and used it as a forum from which to criticise Bolshevik policies. Already in mid-1918 they condemned the merging of executive and legislative powers: 'The organs of power themselves make laws, they themselves implement it, and they control themselves, while the soviet is powerless'.[17] At that time the repression against the Mensheviks was intensified, and in a declaration to the Moscow Soviet EC they complained that the Cheka was even infringing the norms laid down by the soviet itself.[18] It was at this time that the *sobraniya upolnomochennykh* emerged to counter the discredited soviets, though not to replace them (see page 72 above). According to M. S. Bernshtam, the delegate movement was a sign of popular resistance to communism and casts doubt on the 'triumphal march' of Soviet power in the first months. From this perspective, the civil war began with the Bolsheviks coming to power.[19]

The practice of the Bolshevik leaders and Lenin during the civil war swung between the complete dictatorship of the party and the theory of 'proletarian freedom'.[20] As part of the response to the delegate movement and the civil war, on 14 June 1918 VTsIK decided to exclude the Mensheviks and SRs from the central soviets, and recommended that local soviets follow suit. The same decree ordered the dissolution of the workers' conferences, and at that session Martov complained about the mass arrest of Moscow workers the previous day.[21] The MK on 17 June condemned both parties and resolved on their expulsion from the soviet, a move confirmed by the city party conference on 22 June.[22]

Table 6.1 The Moscow Soviet plenum, 1917–21

	June 1917 No.	Percentage	May 1918 No.	Percentage	December 1918 No.	Percentage	February 1920 No.	Percentage	April 1921 No.	Percentage
Total	700	100	869	100	662	100	1532	100	2115	100
Sex										
Male	677	96.7	830	95.5	634	95.8	1399	91.3	2031	96.0
Female	23	3.3	39	4.5	28	4.2	133	8.7	84	4.0
Party										
Bolshevik	230	32.8	491	56.5	430	64.9	1270	82.9	1543	72.9
Bol. symp.	–	–	114	13.1	96	14.5	50	3.3	–	–
Menshevik	221	31.6	86	9.9	19	2.9	40	2.6	12	0.6
(L) SR	132	18.9	31	3.6	8	1.2	–	–	6	0.3
Others	63	9.0	65	7.5	11	1.7	6	0.4	10	0.5
Non-party	54	7.7	73	8.4	42	6.3	166	10.8	533	25.2
Not known	–	–	9	1.0	56	8.5	–	–	11	0.5
Profession										
Manual worker	–	–	670	71.3	437	66.0	1146	74.8	–	–
Employee	–	–	63	7.3	51	7.7	250	16.3	–	–
Brain worker	–	–	142	16.3	97	14.6	136	8.9	–	–
Red Army	–	–	2	0.2	–	–	149	9.7	–	–
Not known	–	–	44	5.1	77	11.6	–	–	–	–
Occupation										
Manual worker	–	–	356	40.8	218	32.9	488	31.8	–	–
Employee	–	–	35	4.0	23	3.5	–	–	–	–
Brain worker	–	–	364	41.9	316	47.7	895	58.4	–	–
Red Army	–	–	–	–	–	–	149	9.7	–	–
Not known	–	–	114	13.1	105	15.9	–	–	–	–

Source: Moskovskii sovet za desyat' let raboty (Moscow, 1927) pp. 78–9; *KM*, cols 39–48.

At this time the Menshevik organisation in the city consisted of no more than 600 members.[23] However, it appears that the Bolshevik leaders wavered, and the counsel of the more moderate leaders, such as Kamenev, meant that at the Moscow Soviet meeting of 18 June the SRs were expelled altogether from the soviet, but the Mensheviks only from the soviet's executive bodies, though the chairman Smidovich threatened to unleash a Jacobin terror.[24] The soviet plenum of 18 June deprived the Menshevik fraction, led by I. A. Isuv and B. Kibrik, and the SRs of the rights of 'soviet parties' and expelled their representatives from the executive bodies of the soviet, and the Right and Centre SRs were expelled from the soviet altogether.[25] They were also expelled from the *raion* soviets. The Mensheviks were thus able to use the soviet's plenary meeting of 25 June to denounce the suppression of the worker protest.[26] The LSRs had resigned from the government following the Brest peace in March 1918, and following their abortive uprising in Moscow in early July the Moscow Soviet plenum on 23 July expelled the majority from the soviet, and in new elections all the other parties (except one LSR) were eliminated from its executive bodies. From this point the SRs of whatever colour played no significant part in the soviet. The beginning of the civil war therefore coincided with the establishment of a *de facto* one-party system in Moscow.

The further history of Menshevik participation in the soviet went through several phases but was marked by bitter splits within the Menshevik party itself. In Moscow, O. E. Ermanskii fought for dialogue with the Bolsheviks from the point of view of 'Marxist realism'.[27] Martov's internationalist view influenced the 14 November 1918 Menshevik decision, taken under the impact of the German revolution, to withdraw support from the anti-Bolshevik struggle and to agitate 'within the framework of soviet forms and the constitution' for the democratisation and softening of the harshest features of war communism.[28] The decision to lift the restrictions on the Mensheviks on 30 November 1918 aroused a heated discussion in the MK but the opponents gathered only five votes.[29] The readmission of the Mensheviks to the soviets was welcomed by Lenin at a time when few allies could be found during the war,[30] but did not signify that they had a continuing role to play in the new system of government. In the *raion*s, however, the local activists, perfectly logically from their point of view, greeted the change with hostility, which was not surprising considering the passion unleashed by the red terror at that time. It was only after three meetings of the Sokol'nicheskii party organisation that a majority could be coaxed in favour of the change.[31] In 1919 the Moscow Mensheviks, despite reservations, 'preferred the utopian revolution rather than join the counter-revolution'.[32]

The security apparatus (Cheka) was to play an important part in establishing the one-party state, aided in the first instance by the LSRs themselves who were among the most enthusiastic Chekists in early 1918. According to M. N. Pokrovskii, the formation of the Vecheka on 20 December 1917 'flowed out of the very nature of the October Revolution'.[33] Its justice was class justice. As Zinoviev put it later, 'The Cheka is the pride and joy of the Communist Party'.[34] The Moscow

Revolutionary Tribunal, formed on 21 December 1917, and its local branches, even though not the courts of popular justice elected by workers of a given *raion* as demanded by party activists up to mid-1918,[35] were at least accountable to the Moscow Soviet (and the Commissariat of Justice), whereas from the first the Cheka had a dizzying propensity towards independence. This factor proved highly unpopular in Moscow. In early March 1918 a Moscow Cheka was formed by the Moscow Soviet EC under M. Latsis,[36] and in principle it carried out the police tasks previously carried out by the MRC. With the removal of the central government to Moscow on 10 March 1918, and with it the Vecheka, the two bodies were united on 19 March, and the staff of the MChK joined the larger body. In principle the Vecheka was now subordinate not only to Sovnarkom but also to the Moscow Soviet EC.[37] The assault on the anarchists on the night of 11–12 April 1918 revealed the disparity between the attitudes of the Muscovites and the party activists newly arrived from Petrograd. As Ya. Kh. Peters wrote in 1924: 'In Moscow in general at that time there was a peaceful mood, and the Moscow military commissariat even issued arms to the anarchist headquarters'; he added that 'The Muscovites basically did not welcome the Cheka'.[38] The animosity was heightened by the fact that the Vecheka shot many of the anarchists without consulting the Moscow Soviet. As Latsis commented later:

> Nowadays this seems amazing, but at that time there were not a few comrades . . . for whom the principle of the inviolability of the individual was placed higher than the interests of the revolution.[39]

While reporting to the Moscow Soviet in the early summer of 1918, Peters was greeted by shouts of *okhrannik* (an employee of the Tsarist police).[40]

Following the LSR uprising in July 1918 the mood became less compromising. The assassinations of Volodarskii, Uritskii, and Zalevskii, and the attempted assassination of Lenin by the SR Fanny Kaplan outside the Mikhel'son plant in Moscow on 30 August 1918, led to widespread calls for a red terror. Militant resolutions were passed in most *raion*s, and the city party conference on 31 August called for the mass suppression of the bourgeoisie and its agents.[41] The MK tried to restrain some of the more violent proposals for retribution and supported the comparatively mild ideas adopted by a general meeting in Basmannyi *raion* on 5 September. These argued for action to be taken against bourgeois property, for the bourgeoisie to be expelled from Moscow, and for the formation of concentration camps, and so on,

stopping short of physical liquidation. These proposals were implemen
ted immediately. Within a few days 'non-labouring elements' were
expelled from the city, allegedly with few 'excesses', and the house
'purged' of the bourgeoisie were transferred to workers and their
families.[42] Such a scene is described by Boris Pasternak in *Docto
Zhivago*.

However, the initiative in the red terror moved from the party and
soviet organisations to the *raion* Chekas and took on a more bloody
aspect. The formation of the local Chekas had begun in August 1918
but now the process was accelerated[43] and a special *raion* Cheka
supervisory body was set up after the assassinations headed by Ya. M
Yurovskii. In Moscow the red terror had been envisaged as a furthe
stage in the economic expropriation of the bourgeoise but it became a
campaign for their physical liquidation as well, with executions taking
place on the Khodynka Field. The aim, as Latsis put it on 1 November
was 'to destroy the bourgeoisie as a class'.[44] Earlier doubts about th
Cheka now stimulated a movement for its restraint. A general meeting o
Gorodskoi RPO on 19 September 1918 noted the lack of party direction
over the *raion* Chekas and urged that more party members should join to
ensure control, and that the local Chekas should give frequent reports to
party meetings.[45] The *raion* Chekas, on the other hand, were keen fo
communists to join them but only in an auxiliary capacity, as th
Zamoskvorech'e *raion* Cheka implied when it asked the RK to forr
communist detachments to assist in raids and searches.[46] The MK
session on 5 October insisted that the *raion* Chekas were to be strictl
controlled by the RKs and every RK was to form a control commission
to ensure that arrests were carried out correctly.[47] By November 1918 th
Moscow Soviet felt that the city needed its own Cheka if only to
maintain control over the local Chekas, and in early December 1918 a
city Cheka (MChK) began its work headed by F. E. Dzerzhinskii and a
collegium with B. A. Breslav, Yurovskii, V. N. Mantsev (the deput
head of the Vecheka) and S. A. Messing.[48] The Vecheka became a
controlling body over the local Chekas, though it still handled the mos
important cases. In the pages of Moscow's evening paper the Cheka wa
lambasted for the enthusiasm with which it imposed the death penalty.[4
The Cheka was criticised for attempting to put itself above the loca
soviets and state organs, especially the NKVD and the Commissariat o
Justice.[50] The profound misgivings were expressed by Bukharin and M
S. Ol'minskii in *Pravda* in late 1918. They sought to restrain the Cheka
and to restore some form of legality under the party and the soviets.[51] I
Moscow one of the first results in January 1919 was the abolition of th

raion Chekas, which had distinguished themselves by the ferocity with which they had prosecuted the red terror.[52] The MK and Kamenev, chairman of the Moscow Soviet since August 1918, were in the forefront of this campaign and proposed greater powers for the revolutionary tribunals. An MK resolution of 27 January called for sentencing to be removed from the Cheka and transferred to the tribunals which were to be strengthened by inducting more party members. The Cheka was to be left with criminal investigation alone.[53] The MK's recommendations restricting the rights of the Cheka were implemented by a decree of 21 February 1919 with sentencing rights transferred to the tribunals.[54] Speaking to the Moscow Soviet in late February, Peters claimed that in the fifteen months of its existence the Cheka nationally had shot 3200 people for all offences and he explained that the drive against counter-revolution would now be led by the revolutionary tribunals, while the Cheka would tackle the main problem facing Soviet power – the battle against banditry and enemies in institutions, bribery, and other economic crimes.[55] For a brief period this division of responsibilities held and the MChK concentrated on criminal offences (the VChK dealt with the major political cases), though the city Cheka was reluctant to transfer cases to the revolutionary tribunal.[56] Despite its increased political role, economic crimes still dominated its work. Between 10 March and 15 September 1919, thirty-three of the 243 cases (sixty-six out of 638 people) involved counter-revolution, four of whom were shot, but the largest number of people sentenced to death was for theft on the railways (sixteen) which was the single largest category of offences (108 people). A total of eighty people were reported shot in this period,[57] and another 189 were shot on its orders in 1920.[58]

No general elections were held to the Moscow Soviet between April 1918 and February 1920, whereas even at the height of the civil war they were held every six months in Petrograd.[59] Instead, the principle of recall operated whereby factories and institutions could at any time change their deputy, a right guaranteed by the 1918 constitution. Under the soviet system, deputies were very much delegates rather than representatives. The use of the imperative mandate (*nakaz*) meant that the deputy was delegated to represent the interests of the workers who sent him or her and not to represent a 'universal interest'. In practice this often degenerated into a manoeuvre to eliminate non-Bolshevik deputies. Between May and December 1918, 423 deputies were recalled, an average of 53 a month and in 1919, 411, about 34 a month. In the two years a total of 834 deputies were changed, and about 99 per cent of their replacements were communists.[60] Kamenev, speaking to Bertrand

Russell in 1920, stated that the main reasons for recall were drunkenness, departure for the front, a change of politics on the part of the electorate, and failure to report back to constituents once a fortnight, obligatory for all deputies.[61] A reregistration of the plenum in December 1918 discovered that the number of Menshevik deputies had fallen from 86 to 19 through recall since April 1918. The total number of deputies had fallen from 869 to 662, indicating that a quarter had left for one reason or another, and a survey of Moscow's enterprises in February 1919 found that about 300, or two-fifths of the census enterprises, lacked a deputy in the soviet.[62]

With the onset of war communism the Moscow Soviet plenum became increasingly ineffective. The majority of its forty-two sessions in 1918 were held in the first half of the year. The plenum met only twenty-eight times in 1919, and fifteen times in the first eight months of 1920.[63] It gathered mainly for ceremonial occasions and to hear reports from one or another Soviet leader. The plenary session of 13 January 1919, for example, highlighted some of the problems amid complaints from the floor that the soviet met very rarely in plenary session. The chairman of the session, Vladimirskii, complained that deputies showed their lack of respect by leaving in the middle of proceedings, and many of those elected to responsible positions, including EC members, failed to attend at all. He called for more frequent reports to the plenum by officials, and on the basis of his proposals attendance at plenary sessions was made obligatory for all members of the EC and presidium.[64] At that time Arthur Ransome noted that the public no longer flocked to the gallery during meetings of the soviet: the excitement of 1917 had ebbed.[65]

Concurrent with the decline in the plenum the work of the soviet was streamlined. On 8 October 1918 the powers of the presidium were once again substantially increased and its membership was drastically reduced to five. At the same time it was no longer to be elected by the plenum but by the EC.[66] These moves were ostensibly balanced by the plenum decision of 16 October 1918 to make the EC more responsible to itself by demanding more frequent reports on its activities. Nevertheless the powers of the EC were enhanced and it was now permitted to issue orders in its own name.[67] The party programme adopted by the VIII Party Congress tackled the problem of bureaucracy by insisting that all soviet members were to participate in some administrative work, and called for all offices to be rotated and for more people to be drawn into administration.[68] The congress resolution called for measures against the development of a bureaucratic caste and for increased 'links with the masses'.[69] The only specific response of the Moscow Soviet was to hold new elections to the executive bodies on 27 May 1919. The EC was slightly increased in size from the forty-one elected on 23 July 1918 to forty-four members, but more significantly over half were changed as twenty-six new people joined. The presidium was doubled from the five elected on 16 October 1918 to ten members.[70] Such measures were little more than palliatives and were out-balanced by the countervailing centralising tendency. At the height of the civil war Kamenev argued that all resources should be concentrated on military, supply, and welfare tasks. In July 1919 the soviet reorganised its work to concentrate personnel by reducing the size of its twenty collegia, and the collegia were abolished altogether in some departments and in most *raion* soviets. The non-party conferences and not the soviets were now to act as the intermediaries between the soviet state and the population.[71] Further centralisation in the Moscow soviets was introduced in November 1919. Current work in the Moscow Soviet was to be conducted by a rather shadowy general management committee responsible only to the presidium, which retained ultimate political responsibility. Collegia were to be further reduced and departments centralised. All current work in the *raion*s was to be conducted by the chairs of the *raion* soviet ECs responsible to the presidia on matters of principle, and the ECs themselves were to be reduced to a maximum of ten members.[72] The introduction of one-person management was therefore spearheaded in civilian administration before being extended to the economy. With Denikin approaching Moscow the TsK summed up the organisational experience of the war. In the usual antinomian language of the time it called for the Soviet republic to be turned into a single armed camp: collegiality was to be restricted as the source of much bureaucratism and red tape, and discussion was to be cut to a minimum.[73]

The military forms employed at the fronts were to be extended to the rear.[74] With the intensification of the war in mid-1919 and the increased disturbances and 'plots' in the city, the MChK's involvement in political cases increased.[75] At the same time semi-military forms of state organisation were practised through the KOM (Moscow Committee of Defence, see page 94). It was revived on 5 September 1919 in response to the Denikin threat as martial law was imposed on the city. Kamenev was chairman, and the committee included Zagorskii (MK secretary) until his death on 25 September 1919, representatives of the Cheka including Peters, and members of the city and *guberniya* ECs.[76] KOM worked in close liaison with the TsK and the Council of Defence. With a general headquarters, partisan detachments were organised in the factories, and the ChON were put on alert.[77] KOM had dictatorial powers and its jurisdiction cut across the powers of all other civil bodies in Moscow. Decrees affecting all aspects of the city's life were issued either in its name or jointly with other bodies. As the military advantage turned in the republic's favour by the end of the year the Moscow Soviet EC on 25 December 1919 decided on its abolition,[78] though it was revived briefly in mid-1920.

The pressure of the war, the shortage of personnel and the concentration on urgent tasks engendered centralisation in the soviet, but at the same time its very structure hastened the same result. Circumstances and ideology forced the pace of change. The *raion* soviets suffered from the same pressures but even more so since they were under the shadow of the city soviet. By October 1917 the majority were dominated by the Bolsheviks, and their hold was consolidated by elections held soon after the revolution.[79] Further elections in April 1918, held in conjunction with those to the city soviet, gave the Bolsheviks 72 per cent of the seats.[80] By July 1920, 1209 (67 per cent) of the 1800 *raion* soviet deputies were Bolsheviks.[81] The fall in the percentage suggests that non-Bolsheviks found it easier to get elected to the *raion* soviets than to the carefully controlled city soviet. As noted, the peculiarity of Moscow's *raion* soviets was that up to mid-1918 they acted as the factory committee councils in lieu of a city-wide council of the type that existed in Petrograd. The *raion* soviets retained a fluidity in their practice that reflected their origins.[82] With the absorption of the factory committees into the trade union structure from early 1918, and the *raion* soviet control commissions into the economic councils from mid-1918, they lost their main role, though they retained certain popular control and administrative functions. During the civil war the *raion* soviets entered into a long decline as their workers' control, economic and political functions were limited, and they increasingly acted as the local agents of the city soviet. The Moscow Soviet EC meeting of 16 October 1918 formalised the relationship by decreeing that the *raion* soviets were directly subordinate to the city EC.[83] Their political weakness was exacerbated by the fact that the majority of their deputies were simultaneously members of the central soviet and therefore could not devote themselves, or indeed their loyalties, to the *raion*s. In effect, the *raion* soviets were simply the administrative agencies of the city soviet.

The *raion* soviets as much as the city soviet saw the centre of power shift from the plena to the executive bodies. Between February and September 1919, for instance, the Butyrskii *raion* soviet met in plenary session only about once a month, while the EC met twice, and the presidium over four times as frequently.[84] The *raion* soviets joined in the general chorus, complaining about the lack of activists at their disposal. By all accounts they were poorly organised and by 1920 politically moribund. On the eve of new elections in July 1920 Ignatov described the condition of the Gorodskoi *raion* soviet. In February 1920, out of the 306 members of the *raion* soviet, three-quarters – representing the larger plants and institutions – were also members of the city soviet.[85] The local soviet met rarely and only forty deputies had attended its last session. Since the last election in late 1918 the majority of deputies had lost contact with their constituencies.[86] During the civil war the *raion* soviets were undermined as political centres as part of the general pattern of the decline in *raion*-based democracy. They lost their economic and workers' control functions, power was concentrated in their executive bodies, and their links with the local working class became tenuous.

The lull in the civil war in early 1920 at last allowed general elections to be held in the Moscow Soviet. They ended on 29 February 1920 after fifteen days of voting and saw the Bolsheviks returned with an increased majority (see Table 6.1),[87] though the support for the 145 non-party deputies represented an anti-Bolshevik vote.[88] Out of a total of about 1.2 million people in the city, 20 per cent voted, 42 per cent of those eligible.[89] Clearly, despite some confusion in the figures, the turnout was low and indicates a reluctance to participate. At the first plenary session of the soviet on 6 March 1920, Kamenev, opposed only by Martov who received 31 votes, was once again elected chairman.[90] A. F. Myasnikov's list of Bolsheviks for the EC was opposed by both the Mensheviks and the non-party group but their protests were ignored and a purely Bolshevik list of forty members and twelve candidates was adopted.[91] The minority groupings, who comprised nearly 14 per cent of the plenum, were thereby deprived of any representation on the Soviet's executive bodies. At that session Dan, on behalf of the Mensheviks, insisted that the election results did not reflect the true situation in the city. He catalogued a whole series of factors inhibiting the Mensheviks: lack of newspapers, no meeting halls, freedom of speech curtailed, and the use of direct violence against them. Electoral privileges had been abused by the Bolsheviks, he claimed, as instanced by the 300 members of the MGSPS having the right to nominate 148 soviet deputies. Electoral geography had been gerrymandered in order to under-represent the Menshevik-inclined office workers, and because of the fusion of the electoral apparatus with the Communist Party fair elections were ruled out. Despite this, he stated, wherever Mensheviks had stood they had been elected. He insisted that the Mensheviks would assist in the struggle against counter-revolution, but called for the full democratisation of the soviet system so that the 'voice of the workers could once again be heard'.[90]

The Mensheviks had now accepted many Bolshevik propositions, and at a party conference in April 1920 they were enshrined in a set of 'April Theses'. These rather contradictorily accepted the necessity for a dictatorship of the proletariat but refused to acquiesce to the 'terrorist minority' (that is, the Bolsheviks) within that dictatorship.[93] On 20 April 1920 Martov announced to the Moscow Soviet that the Mensheviks had decided to break off all links with the II International.[94] On 8 May 1920 a meeting of all the leading Mensheviks in Moscow issued a unique declaration of support for the Soviet regime against the Poles.[95] The civil war, indeed, at this stage took on the guise of a national war. Despite their changed position the Mensheviks were still subject to harassment, and there is a mass of evidence to support the Menshevik accusations of electoral malpractice. The American journalist Marguerite Harrison states that voting by acclamation in factories inhibited the raising of dissident voices. Bolshevik strongholds were united for electoral purposes with places where they were weak, such as the creation of a single constituency out of the Moscow food administration (MPO) and the Cheka in February 1920.[96] Emma Goldman cites the case of an unnamed Moscow factory which returned an anarchist in those elections, but the soviet refused to register him and instead forced the commissar of health, N. A. Semashko, on them after the arrest of several workers. Chekists allegedly attended election meetings and cowed workers into voting for communist deputies.[97] N. Osinskii indirectly confirms such behaviour when he writes of a new approach tested in Tula in March 1920. After a long period of 'no discussion' (*bez prenii*) the party organisation had decided to make the election free:

> Our party organisation in this campaign set itself completely different aims from those in Moscow. We decided that a communist soviet was not essential . . . we set mass agitation as the highest priority even if this would be at the expense of several dozen seats.[98]

In the event, fifty Mensheviks were elected in Tula.[99] When the British Labour Party delegation met the Moscow printworkers on 21 May 1920, both Victor Chernov, leader of the SRs and sought by the Bolsheviks, and the Menshevik Dan inveighed against the restrictions on their activities:

> You think we have freedom, workers' power. Nothing of the sort. Our newspapers are closed, meetings are not allowed. Tell the proletariat of the West that it is now no better than it was under the autocracy.[100]

After the meeting Chernov managed to slip away, but Dan was less fortunate and was detained by the Cheka.[101] Bertrand Russell was in Moscow between 11 May and 16 June 1920, and he commented on his return that although the Bolsheviks claimed a greater democracy in the soviet, with recall and occupational constituencies, 'no conceivable system of free elections would give majorities to the communists, either in the town or in the country'.[102]

Following the disturbances of early 1921 the elections to the Moscow Soviet in April 1921 reduced the Bolshevik majority by 10 per cent to 73 per cent, while the 533 (25 per cent) non-party deputies represented an increased protest vote (see Table 6.1). The table illustrates the steady increase in the proportion of Bolsheviks in the soviet: from just over half in April 1918 to over four-fifths in February 1920. At the same time the proportion of non-communist or communist sympathiser deputies fell from nearly a third in 1918 to less than 15 per cent in 1920. The SR vote collapsed rapidly from mid-1917, while the Mensheviks were able to retain a significant presence up to 1920. With the beginning of the NEP the percentage of communist deputies fell, but at the same time the proportion of non-Bolsheviks plummeted to a minuscule 1.4 per cent, though the true level of support for them is probably revealed by the high proportion of non-party deputies elected. There was a marked tendency for the number of deputies in some sort of management job to rise. The agitation campaign of February 1920 managed to raise the proportion of 'fresh' manual workers to three-quarters of the total, but less than a third were actually employed in a manual occupation. The largest non-manual occupational groups were members and chairs of soviet collegia and committees, followed by the heads of institutions and enterprises, and finally members of commissions of one sort or another. There was a slight increase in the proportion of deputies with higher education, rising from 6.5 per cent in April 1918 to 9.5 per cent in 1920, while those with secondary education increased from 14 per cent to 18 per cent. The great majority, however, had only obtained elementary schooling.[103] By 1920 the single largest union represented in the soviet was that of soviet employees (140 deputies, or 9 per cent of the total), with the metal workers second with 121 (8 per cent) deputies, railway workers third with 116 (7.5 per cent), and then the textile workers with 72 deputies (5 per cent). In 1918 the textile and metal unions had shared first place, and the change reflects the decline in industry and the increased importance of the bureaucracy.[104] Another measure of the difference between the soviet of 1917 and that of 1920 was the disappearance of the rank and file soldier from the soviet. Of the 149 Red Army deputies in March 1920, ninety-three were instructors, eight were training to be officers, and a large proportion of the other forty-eight were militia men.[105] The abolition of the soldiers' soviet in November 1917 and of the soldiers' section in March 1918 deprived the soldiery, and hence the peasantry, of any organised participation in Moscow's political life. During the civil war the deputies to the Moscow Soviet became an even more youthful group and by 1920 nearly half were under 30.[106] The percentage of women remained low, at the 4 per cent mark, with the exception of the rise to 9 per cent in March 1920 which marked a particularly buoyant phase of the organised women's movement in Moscow. The proportion of those who had suffered repression before February 1917 fell from 64 per cent in 1918 to 54 per cent in 1920.[107]

The end of the worst phase of the civil war saw attempts to redress the balance of power away from the presidium and its general management body. Soon after the VIII Congress the idea had been proposed to divide the plenum into sections (the forerunners of today's standing commissions), corresponding to the soviet's departments, as a way of increasing the involvement of all deputies. With the breathing spell of early 1920, I. V. Tsivtsivadze, general manager of the soviet, once again raised the idea on the following ground:

> It is a secret to no-one that the plenum of the Moscow Soviet is a purely formal organ, judicial, ratifying or rejecting decisions of the *ispolkom*, occasionally listening to informational reports from one department or another.[108]

With over 1500 deputies the plenum could not discuss all questions in detail and had, therefore, become a purely voting body. Tsivtsivadze argued that the sections would act as a link between the factories and the executive bodies. However, while his proposals allowed the sections to supervise the work of the departments, they were not given the power to amend decisions or to interfere in their work. He was at pains to ensure that no hint of mass collegiality was permitted.[109] The plenary session of 23 March 1920 made membership of the sections obligatory but their ability to criticise the departments was limited by making department or collegia heads the leaders of the sections.[110] The restrictions placed on their work meant that the hopes of the sections enlivening the work of the soviet were disappointed. At the meeting of the transport department section on 21 April 1920, among many examples, only sixty out of 141 deputies attended.[111] By the end of 1920 only twelve out of the nineteen departments and five commissions in the soviet had sections attached to them.[112]

It was only with the unification of the city and *guberniya* soviets in

May 1920 that the city soviet became responsible to a general gathering other than the national soviet congresses and VTsIK. The idea of unification had been mooted several times in 1919[113] but had come to nothing, possibly owing to the city soviet's fear of losing its independence. In 1920, however, with pressure from the TsK to form a single system of party organisations, the unification of the soviets followed inexorably. At the 21 May 1920 *guberniya* party conference, Zelenskii argued that economic considerations also demanded the ending of artificial barriers between the city and its hinterland in respect to supplies, labour and economic planning.[114] The highest body was to be the *guberniya* conference of soviets elected on the basis of one deputy for every 2000 workers and one for every 10 000 peasants, to ensure a proletarian majority in the united soviet.[115] The *de facto* one-party state of the civil war is illustrated by the fact that out of a total of fifty-three people who served on the soviet's presidium in its eight compositions between 14 November 1917 and 3 January 1921 only five were non-Bolsheviks, none of whom served after July 1918. A significant feature of the 3 January elections to the joint soviet's executive bodies was the large proportion who joined for the first time, five out of eleven, and included figures such as M. E. Uryvaev and I. I. Zheltov who were to figure prominently in the 1920s.[116] A new generation of Moscow Soviet leaders was emerging.

The creation of the Soviet one-party state saw the elimination of organised opposition both in the soviets and in the working class, a process substantially completed during the civil war. The Moscow Soviet itself was undermined in a three-fold process: (1) the impact of the civil war hastening centralisation and the ruthless subordination of lower organs and the electorate; (2) the dynamics of commune-type organisation which stressed executive functions over legislative bodies; and (3) the existence of other 'states', such as the Cheka and the economic apparatus, which eroded its prerogatives. But above all, the major rival form of state organisation was the party itself.

THE PARTY AND THE SOVIETS

By arguing for the destruction of the bourgeois state and for its replacement by a system based on soviets, Lenin, notably in *State and Revolution*, was able to maintain a theoretical distinction between the workers' state and the revolutionary party. The working class would participate in the everyday running of the state through the soviets,

while the party was to act as the advanced minority guiding the
development of the workers' state. The party was not intended to
become the embryo of the new state but rather its political head. While
this distinction was maintained in theory after October 1917, in practice
the party, by taking the majority of the key posts and decisions in the
new state system, was in danger of becoming absorbed by the new state
machinery. Politically the party dominated but, as noted, after October
it was the party, and not the state, that was in danger of withering away.
The implementation of the 'May programme' prevented this occurring;
but it posed the problem of the relationship between the party and the
soviets, and between the party organisations and the Bolshevik soviet
fractions, all the more starkly. By the end of the civil war the relationship
had been defined and the leading role of the party established.

The central problem facing the new regime was the smallness of the
proletariat, and indeed the party, in a vast peasant country. Hence the
available resources had to be used to the maximum effect. As the Left
Communist V. Sorin put it in 1918:

> The party is always and everywhere superior to the soviets . . . The
> soviets represent labouring democracy in general; and its interests,
> and in particular the interests of the petty bourgeois peasantry, do not
> always coincide with the interests of the proletariat.[117]

According to the Left Communists, therefore, the party was the
custodian of an interest higher than that of the soviets. Earlier
theoretical considerations on the vanguard role of the party, developed
precisely in response to this problem, were confirmed by the circumstances of Bolshevism in power. The political dominance of the party over
the soviets became an administrative one as well. Such a development
was further encouraged by the emergence of a massive and unwieldy
bureaucratic apparatus in 1918. As a MOB letter put it in September
1918:

> The party must become the controlling, leading, and guiding force
> over the soviets to avoid a breach (*razlozhenie*) between party workers
> and the helplessness of the state apparatus.[118]

The Left Communists and the party leadership were therefore in
agreement that the absence of working class hegemony and the development of a bureaucracy, whose emergence and properties mystified them,
necessitated that the party should play a tutelary role over the soviets.

With such a formulation it proved difficult to maintain the vitality of
the soviet plenum as the soviet was controlled by a party fraction, itself

controlled by a party committee outside the soviet. The Bolshevik fractions became the *de facto* kernels of the soviets, and this division was accentuated during the civil war as the executive bodies took on the functions of the soviet as a whole. The fundamental question of the relationship between the party and the soviets as the organs of popular power was effectively solved in practice but it was left vague in theory.[119] In his polemic against Karl Kautsky, Lenin wrote:

> The soviets are the direct organisation of the toiling and exploited masses themselves, which help them to organise and administer their own state in every possible way.[120]

Lenin's storm of invective covered his failure to analyse the forms that the guiding role of the party would take, which was Kautsky's central argument:

> Despite the pretensions of being the dictatorship of the proletariat it has become from the very beginning the dictatorship of one party within the proletariat.[121]

In their *ABC of Communism* of 1919, N. Bukharin and E. Preobrazhenskii barely mentioned the communist party at all. Everything was left to the working class organised in the soviets and its state, the dictatorship of the proletariat, while the party was only discussed in relation to the seizure of power and as just one of the institutions at the base of the soviet system.[122] It is perhaps in this that the Utopianism of the work is most marked, rather than in the exciting new economic relationship described so enthusiastically. In practice, however, the relationship between the party and the soviets only emerged after much debate.

The principle of party control allowed conflicting interpretations. The initial problem was the relationship between the party fractions in the soviets and the party committees. From the first the caucus nature of the Bolshevik group in the Moscow Soviet was stressed. A resolution adopted by them and published on 22 March 1917 argued that the Bolshevik fraction should act as a group and not as a collection of individuals.[123] On 17 May 1917, MOB called for the formation of Bolshevik fractions in soviets to ensure that the party line was implemented.[124] The soviet fractions elected an executive bureau, and the work of both was governed by a statute.[125] The latent rivalry between the fractions and the party committees had already surfaced and the MOB resolution gave the fractions equal status with the committees, and proposed mutual representation as the link between them, with the fraction establishing itself as a separate organisation with its own executive bodies, secretary and finances.[126] However, in the new circumstances of government the party committees swiftly asserted their precedence. A few days after the October revolution the MK decreed that the Moscow Soviet EC had to give it a copy of the agenda of its meetings, and that all major questions to be dealt with by the plenum were to be discussed first by the EC meeting with an MK representative.[127]

By mid-1918 the problem in Moscow was no longer one of ensuring party direction over the soviets as a whole, but one of regulating the relations between the local party organisation and the party fractions themselves, and above all of ensuring party control over members working in soviet institutions. The July 1918 MPO statute insisted that all MK decisions were binding on fraction members, that all responsible postings in the central or *raion* soviets were to be made with the agreement of the relevant party committee, and that agendas were to be shown in good time to the committees.[128] In late July 1918, Boris Volin (Fradkin), one of the leaders of Bolshevik municipal politics, raised the question in the light of the resurgence of the party. It was absolutely inadmissible, he argued, for a communist to speak in a soviet as a soviet deputy rather than as a party member: 'Every party member must above all owe allegiance to the party, and only then to the fraction of one or another soviet institution'.[129] The problem was what contemporaries called localism (*mestnichestvo*), later called 'departmentalism', where communists identify with their own institution rather than the general interest as defined by the party, but Volin's formulation represented a significant theoretical shift. Rather than being envisaged as complementary units of a proletarian state, the fractions and with them their host institution were to be unequivocally subordinated to the party committees. In practice, many party members did not find it easy to choose between the soviets and the party. The divided loyalties often engendered bitter conflicts on a personal level and led to expulsions from the party.[130] The problem was exacerbated as the party revived over summer 1918. The communists working in soviet offices had formed a city-wide fraction bureau which acted not only as a centralised form of Bolshevik supervision over the general work of the soviets and institutions, but had also developed 'interests' of its own. In response, on 13 November 1918, the MK convened a general meeting of communists working in soviet institutions in the city. The meeting decided to dissolve the bureau, ostensibly because of the shortage of activists, and its functions were transferred to the MK in the centre and the RKs in the localities, who were urged to guide the work of the *raion* soviets.[131] Its abolition was in line with the increasingly restricted definition of the role of the cells. The bureau had acted as a horizontal intermediary between the soviets and the party committees, and during war communism it was precisely this sort of body which was swept away as lines of command were shortened.

The party's enhanced tutelary role over the soviets in the *raion*s was described by the Butyrskii RK's report for late 1918:

> [The RK's] enactments are now carried out by the soviet without any argument, whereas at first, after the October revolution, there was much friction between the raion [soviet] EC and the party committee. After the reorganisation of the soviet, and its unification with the raion duma, conflicts were gradually reduced.[132]

The report for the Blagushe-Lefortovo RK for May 1919 similarly stressed the control of the party committee over the *raion* soviet and noted its intervention in the affairs of a department which 'suffered from a lack of competent party workers and insufficient ideological leadership'.[133] By the end of 1919 the Basmannyi RK could claim complete control over the *raion* soviet:

> In the departments not a single appointment, not a single transfer, not a single question, passed by the *raion* committee without its sanction and approval.[134]

The MK was also proud of the degree of control it exercised over the Moscow Soviet. In July 1920, for instance, four MK members were on the soviet's presidium, and a fifth, Kamenev, was its chairman.[135] Nevertheless, the great prestige of the Moscow Soviet and the calibre of its leaders, and indeed perhaps a lingering respect for soviet autonomy, to some extent shielded it from the type of minute supervision exercised over the *raion* soviets. As a report put it in late 1920: 'In the raions full monolithic unity of work, but in the centre the Moscow Committee and the Moscow Soviet with an unclear definition of their relationship'.[136] There remained a residual appreciation that the soviets and the party were to work in tandem and not in 'monolithic unity', each with their own sphere of responsibilities and without party substitution (*podmena*) for the political functions of the soviet. Kamenev, for instance, had been chairman of the Moscow Soviet since August 1918 but he joined the MK only in May 1920. By the end of 1920, with the creation of a single MK and unified soviet executive bodies elected at conferences for fixed terms, the party emerged not only as the supreme political arbiter in the city but also as the key administrative centre. The party had unequivocably won in the struggle between the two hierarchies.

This process did not go, however, unchallenged. By late 1918 criticism of the trends in the relationship between the party committees and fractions, between the centre and the localities, and the general problem of bureaucratism, developed into a major controversy. The challenge was led by the Democratic Centralists (DCs), though it is difficult to describe them as a single movement. One group around Osinskii focused on the inadequacies of the party centre; another based on Moscow activists around Ignatov claimed that the party committees had usurped the rights of the soviet fractions; others reflected Ukrainian 'localism' or simply general dissatisfaction with the general state of affairs.[137] At this stage, however, the running was made by a group focusing on the question of the relationship between the 'centre' and the 'localities'. They were based largely in the Moscow *guberniya* soviet and party organisations. Their leading representative was T. V. Sapronov, the chairman of the *guberniya* soviet from October 1917 to the end of 1919, supported by members of the *guberniya* party committee (MGK) such as its secretary I. I. Minkov, Ivanov, and other members of these organisations. In 1917 the Bolsheviks here had enjoyed overwhelming support both among the workers and the peasantry, and since then the party and soviet organisations had worked in particularly close harmony. Within the *guberniya* soviet affairs were conducted by the EC and no presidium had been formed. It was this model of partnership between the party and soviet hierarchies that the group sought to generalise to the rest of the country, and in particular to their own city of Moscow.

The assault was launched at the XI Moscow *Guberniya* Conference (18–19 December 1918) and was pressed home at a joint session chaired by Sapronov of the MGK and the *guberniya* soviet EC on 26 December 1918. A motion was adopted criticising the 'bureaucratic centralism' and 'petty tutelage' of the centre in interfering in the current affairs of the local soviets, and calling for the rights of the localities to be respected.[138] It was at this time that the local soviets were being deprived of the bulk of their economic functions. A specially convened city party conference on 18 January 1919 was the scene of a bitter debate over the relationship between central and local soviet institutions, and between the party committees and fractions in the soviets. Ignatov introduced a motion demanding changes to the Soviet constitution, and in particular the elimination of Sovnarkom in order to enhance the authority of VTsIK, and for the increased autonomy of soviet fractions. He was supported by several members of the Moscow Soviet EC, and by a group of 'dissatisfied comrades from the raions'.[139] Ignatov was a member of the soviet's EC and he was also active in economic affairs and in the Gorodskoi *raion* party and soviet structures. The theme of his long oppositional career was the defence of the localities, which in Moscow meant above all the *raion*s, and the rights of particularities within the Soviet system, and it was from this perspective that he now supported the DCs. The essence of their argument was that the soviets were to be preserved as responsible political centres both *vis à vis* the local party organisations and in relation to central political and economic bodies. At the conference, Tsivtsivadze tried to mollify the opposition by admitting that some problems existed but blamed them only on certain 'inadequacies of the mechanism'. He insisted that the fractions were no more than party cells, but put forward some mild reform proposals aimed at rejuvenating the soviet plenum and at giving the *raion* soviets more scope in decision-making, whose limited effect we have already noted.[140] In his contribution, Lenin argued that only centralism could overcome the two great evils of bureaucracy and speculation. He accused the opposition of having discarded centralism in favour of localism.[141] The MK's resolution insisted on fraction subordination to party committees, but its conciliatory reform proposals remained a dead letter.

The weeks leading to the VIII Party Congress in March 1919 were marked by a vigorous debate over the condition of the party (see pages 107 and 144). The negative features of the state apparatus, such as bureaucratism and localism (departmentalism), were used to justify centralism in general and party control over its own membership in particular. The TsK proposed periodic redistributions of communists from party to state posts, and from region to region, as part of the struggle against the twin evils, and for an influx of fresh cadres from the party to the state apparatus.[142] This was the line taken by the MK speakers on the eve of the congress, and although the MK position was adopted everywhere advocates of reform gained significant support.[143] At the congress the DCs continued their attack. Osinskii argued that the central problem was that instead of authority being clearly delineated decisions were being taken, for example, by Lenin and Sverdlov in personal talks, and not by the full TsK.[144] This confusion prevailed at all levels of the state and party hierarchy, they argued. Osinskii insisted that a Soviet government, as such, did not exist,[145] and Ignatov warned that the party should not take on the functions of the soviets.[146] The final resolution on this question insisted on the undisputed political dominance of the party over the soviets and that the fractions were to be absolutely subordinate to the party committees.[147] The caveat that the party was to 'guide' and not to 'substitute' for the soviets 'within the terms of the Soviet constitution' was given no institutional expression and thus remained a pious expression of principle. In practice the resolution tackled none of the substantive issues raised by the opposition, and indeed exacerbated them. The DC call for a revision to the constitution to incorporate the experience of running the country since mid-1918 was an attempt to provide a legal framework for the rights of all parts of the Soviet governmental machinery. Their 'localism' reflected attempts not so much to limit the powers of the central authorities as to define them. The existing confusion above all worked to the disadvantage of the localities and local institutions. To this day Soviet governmental practice is ruled more by convention than by strict legal definition of powers.

Throughout 1919 the DCs, ensconced in Moscow *guberniya*, continued their demands for effective central leadership combined with competent local soviets. At the XVI *Guberniya* Conference (November 1919) Sapronov called for the rights and duties of all organisations to be clearly stated in a revised national constitution.[148] The new party statute adopted by the VIII Party Conference in December 1919, however, rejected their draft amendment which unequivocally stated that local party committees were not to interfere in the current work of local soviets and their party fractions.[149] According to the final draft the territorial form of democratic centralism was to be the only one: all party activists in an area were to be subordinate to its party committee.[150] To a large extent the Democratic Centralists were concerned not with the soviets as such, but with their executive committees: with administration rather than mass politics. At the VIII Conference, for example, Sapronov defended not so much the rights of the local soviets as those of their ECs, which in his view were to be the horizontal linkage at the local level (VTsIK was to perform this function in the centre) to prevent soviet power becoming 'a thousand separate pillars'.[151] He warned against the permanent constriction of the soviet collegia,[152] and urged that collegiate management in the soviets and the economy should act as the link with the masses.[153] But still Sapronov did not analyse the reasons for the decline in the effectiveness of the soviet plenums. As Mgeladze, one of the advocates of moderate reform in early 1919 in the MK, and now in Saratov, put it, the republic was becoming one of *ispolkomy* and not of soviets.[154]

By the IX Party Congress Sapronov and the Democratic Centralists as a whole had become more critical of the whole trend of civil war developments. Sapronov warned that a dictatorship of the party *chinovnichestvo* (bureaucracy) was being established as elections were replaced by appointments and transfers, and he went further: 'We cannot talk about the dictatorship of the proletariat, about the self-activity of the worker masses. There is no self-activity'. The machine would not save the revolution, he insisted.[155] The DC critique had now advanced beyond its earlier proposals on the eve of the VIII Congress, where the 'strict' centralists could have agreed with the substance of their criticisms, to a position which viewed the development of the party machine with alarm. The DCs had initially attempted to combat bureaucracy by bureaucratic means, by arguing that improving the mechanism would ensure an improved democratic centralism. By 1920 the debate on the soviet system had to begin with a debate on reform within the party, but when this took place from mid-1920 it marked the vindication of the DC arguments but also their destruction as a coherent tendency.

With the formation of the III International in 1919 the Soviet experience was projected on to the world stage and to countries with longer traditions of parliamentary democracy and stronger proletariats. The Soviet rationale for party control over social institutions was applied, nevertheless, to the rest of the world communist movement and codified at the II Congress of the III International in July 1920:

> As the organised advanced guard of the working class the Communist Party answers equally for the economic, political and spiritual needs of the working class. It must be the soul of the trade unions, the soviets, and all other proletarian organisations . . . For the soviets to fulfil their historic mission there must be a Communist Party strong enough not to 'adapt' itself to the soviets but to exercise on them a decisive influence, to force them *not to adapt themselves* to the bourgeoisie and official social democracy . . .[156]

The soviets therefore could not be left to express the interests of the working class on their own, but required a body external to them to ensure that they carried out the policies deemed correct. Here the underlying ideology of Bolshevik party/state relations was revealed as something independent of the specific circumstances in which it was applied in the Soviet republic. Political rather than social criteria were here defended, and yet in domestic debate the social need for the party's political dominance was the one most commonly applied. Within the soviets the Bolsheviks organised as a caucus and in effect decision-making was removed from their plenums to their executive bodies, and from there to the party headquarters. The party became the key integrating force between the competing hierarchies, but its supremacy was neither inevitable nor easily achieved, and, as history was to show, it was not unassailable either.

BUREAUCRACY AND PARTICIPATION

The term 'bureaucracy' is one of the most commonly employed in the discussing the Soviet regime and yet it is one that is least defined.[157] Its causes and consequences were one of the key themes of political life during the civil war as the Bolsheviks tried to grapple with a phenomenon that was as unexpected as it was ubiquitous. Instead of the simplification of state management described in *State and Revolution*, red tape and vast administrative offices typified Soviet reality. For the Bolsheviks, bureaucratism signified the escape of this bureaucracy from the will of the party as it took on a life of its own. For the majority of Western writers it was precisely the imposition of party control that signified the qualitative transformation of bureaucracy from servant to master. The bureaucracy of the administrative processes themselves can be distinguished from the bureaucratisation of the political process. As we have seen, the party combined both forms but strived to remain independent of the state (soviet) bureaucracy. At issue is the question of the nature of the new regime that was emerging in Russia. Did the attempt to extend political control over all facets of social, economic and political life necessarily entail the emergence of a bureaucracy, or was there a path, as the Menshevik M. Kefali (Kamermakher), one of the leaders of the Moscow printworkers, put it to the Labour Party delegation, of 'voluntary, self-reliant activity, self-discipline of the masses';[158] one which could combine meaningful participation in both administrative and political processes. Indeed, did the bureaucracy, in the sense of an expanded administrative system, have to be bureaucratic? How far was it the party which brought about an integrated power structure? Further, did the bureaucracy emerge as an independent social force (as later Trotskyists argued); were its interests expressed by a defined political group; or was the bureaucracy mainly a series of effects such as corruption, inefficiency, arbitrary power, red tape, and so on, but nothing else? Some of the answers can be gleaned from contemporary analyses of the problem.

At the centre of contemporary interpretations of bureaucracy lay the questions of the desired relationship between the centre and the

localities, between the soviets and the working class, and the relationships between all levels of the party and state apparatuses. The
bureaucratism of the party itself signified the use of administrative
methods and the increasingly formal nature of inner-party democracy as
the leadership made itself independent of the rank and file. The key
problem was how to reconcile the frequent Bolshevik exhortations for
participation within the framework of centralism and the discipline of
the 'military-proletarian dictatorship'. Already in early 1918 the Left
Communists provided the inspiration for later analyses of bureaucracy
in their focus on the alleged stifling of the self-activity of the working
class in the management of the new state, and their attack on the
bourgeois specialists was implicitly an attack on the principle of the
division of labour, the root of bureaucratism in Marxist theory. More
specifically, they criticised central interference in the work of the local
soviets,[159] though as we have seen they insisted on party control over
them. The Left Communists' initial dual response to the burgeoning
bureaucracy, where it was seen as both a social and a political
phenomenon, was the inspiration of later contradictory analyses.

On coming to power the Bolsheviks smashed the old state but rapidly
created their own apparatus to wage the political and economic
offensive against the bourgeoisie and capitalism. As the functions of the
state expanded, so did the bureaucracy. The First World War had
already seen the development of a mass of regulatory bodies,[160] but
following the revolution the process of institutional proliferation
reached unprecedented heights. Not only were a mass of economic
organisations created or expanded, as described above, but in the state
sphere the work of the Moscow Soviet was supplemented by a Moscow
Oblast Sovnarkom (MOSNK), formed in February 1918, which
duplicated the central Sovnarkom even down to having its own foreign
affairs commissariat. On arriving in Moscow in March 1918, accompanied by trainloads of Petrograd *chinovniki*, the government looked at
ways of reducing the state apparatus. In fact, most departments
continued to expand, especially with the merger of the newly-arrived
commissariats with those of MOSNK.[161] War communism provided
lush pastures for bureaucratic growth as the wages of office workers
became largely a matter of creative accounting and extra work for the
money presses. Moscow became dominated by a bureaucratic apparatus
serving the city and the whole country and despite the many campaigns
to reduce their numbers the proportion of office workers in the falling
population remained almost constant. The 231 000 people employed in
offices in August 1918 represented 14 per cent of the total population

and 30 per cent of the workforce.[162] Some reductions in the staff of central institutions were offset by an increase in the numbers employed by local offices, which rose from 84 000 in 1918 to 98 000 by May 1919.[163] At that time office workers constituted 16 per cent of the total population and 31 per cent of those employed. The old Moscow city council (*uprava*) had employed about 40 000 people before October 1917, but by May 1920 the same institution employed double that number serving a halved population.[164] The staffs of the *raion* soviets expanded in line with the general trend and by mid-1919 the small Butyrskii *raion* soviet, for example, employed 700 people.[165] By 1920 the general number of office workers had decreased by about 15–20 per cent over 1918, but they still represented about a third of those employed in the city.[166] In industry too, as noted, the proportion of white collar workers to manual workers increased. According to the industrial census of 31 August 1918, 4191 (3.4 per cent) of Moscow's 123 500 workers were involved in management or some sort of public organisation.[167] With the greatest concentration of workers and the largest amount of offices, Moscow's working class naturally provided the largest contingent for the new state apparatus. By mid-October 1918, for example, out of 1800 workers in the Mikhel'son plant only 350 remained, while the majority of the others had either been sent to the countryside or were employed in soviet institutions.[168] A report of 10 October 1918 claimed that out of 900 workers in the AMO plant in Rogozhskii *raion*, 100 were involved in some sort of public work and this was cited as a disclaimer to Menshevik assertions that 'a bureaucratic *chinovnik* state' had emerged.[169] In other words, the participation of workers in state structures was considered proof of the absence of bureaucratism.

However, the initial enthusiasm was soon tempered by a growing awareness that the class content approach to the question of bureaucratism was inadequate. Nearly every issue of Moscow's evening paper lambasted the bureaucratism affecting all aspects of the city's life. Among the multitude of examples was the problem of movement in and out of the city. A worker, for instance, going on holiday would have to wait two or three days in endless queues to obtain the necessary documents from the various departments of the Commission for the Evacuation of Moscow, by which time the need for rest would no doubt have been enhanced.[170] Vladimirskii admitted to the Moscow Soviet in January 1919 that bureaucracy and *chinovnichestvo* were rampant in offices.[171] Ironic references were frequently made to the official explanation that these were only 'small defects in our mechanism'.[172] Victor

Serge described his impression of the bureaucracy in Moscow in early 1919:

> Here committees were piled on top of Councils, and Managements on top of Commissions. Of this apparatus, which seemed to me to function largely in a void, wasting three-quarters of its time on unrealisable projects, I at once formed the worst possible impression.[173]

The prevalence of bureaucracy, of committees and commissions whose value decreased as their acronyms lengthened, permitted, and indeed encouraged, endless permutations of corrupt practices. These ranged from the style of living of communist functionaries to bribe-taking by officials. With the power of allocation of scarce resources, such as housing, there was an inordinate potential for corruption.[174]

The growth of bureaucracy and the threat it posed to the integrity of the Communist Party were constant themes in the party's political debates of the time. At the end of 1918 a survey of communists in Moscow's offices was attempted in order to understand the scale of the problem,[175] and shortly afterwards Ol'minskii and N. L. Meshcheryakov called for a purge of soviet employees. They reiterated that, in offices, recommendations for party membership often turned into a protection racket.[176] There was a justified fear that the bureaucracy was subverting the party. Following the VIII Party Congress the MK responded by the creation of yet another commission to combat bureaucracy in offices,[177] the forerunner of many such attempts. From mid-1919 strenuous efforts were made to decrease staff numbers and reduce duplication.[178] The battle against bureaucratism had political consequences as certain departments under the *raion* soviets were abolished and others curtailed in late 1919.[179] Lenin wrote on 2 February 1921 that 'The population of Moscow is bloated with office workers,' and urged that strict measures be taken to prevent further expansion.[180] In November 1920 a plan had been drafted to transfer 10 000 of Moscow's 200 000 office workers to Petrograd in order to ease the housing crisis[181] and to dilute the concentration of 'Moscow bureaucrats'.[182] This plan met with the usual lack of success and by July 1921 their numbers had increased to 228 000,[183] and by October 1922 to 243 000.[184] The nightmare proliferation of offices managing every corner of social life during war communism generated this vast bureaucracy and its spirit became an indelible feature of the Soviet system. Only the harsh economic climate of the NEP and the introduction of *khozraschet* (cost accounting) provided a temporary antidote to this malign growth.

In his political report to the XI Party Congress in March 1922 Lenin emphasised the battle between what he termed the two cultures, socialist and bureaucratic petty bourgeois, represented respectively by the party activists and the state bureaucracy:

> If we take Moscow with its 4700 communists in responsible positions, and if we take that huge bureaucratic machine, we must ask: who is directing whom? I doubt very much whether it can truthfully be said that the communists are directing that heap. To tell the truth, they are not directing, they are being directed.[185]

Table 4.2 on page 114 shows that of the 2629 responsible party activists in soviet offices in August 1920, only 18 per cent were from the working class and the total number of party activists represented only about 1.3 per cent of all employees. While the number of communists in offices (8164) represented barely 5 per cent of the total, they constituted over a quarter of party membership in the city. In a typical Moscow district the *raion* soviet would have a huge staff whereas at most a few dozen would be employed by the party committee. This helps explain why, despite his frequent attacks on the bureaucracy, Lenin never once spoke against the party machine.[186] In his denunciation of Kautsky, Lenin had extolled the mass participatory character of the soviet system, yet the central question inevitably became one of understanding the roots of the bureaucratic phenomenon, and on this depended effective measures to contain it. The contemporary debate over bureaucracy was simultaneously a political debate over the nature and possible strategies of the regime.

Contemporary analyses invoked a range of factors to explain the palpable prevalence of bureaucracy. The preferred Menshevik view stressed that the attempt to impose 'utopian socialism' (B. L. Dvinov) in a backward country with a small proletariat inevitably engendered an 'enormous bureaucratic mechanism'.[187] L. Kritsman took a similar line when he argued that the drive for rationality led to the multiplication of tasks which crystallised in the formation of countless commissions that all too frequently established only paper relationships between themselves.[188] The Left Communists emphasised the isolation of the Russian revolution from the more culturally advanced proletariat of the West. A major theme of contemporary analyses of bureaucracy was that it had somehow been contrabanded into the soviet apparatus by carriers of the old Tsarist capitalist ideology, the bourgeois intelligentsia and specialists, in whom there was, as Kritsman put it, a contradiction between their role in the new regime and their ideology.[189] Lenin was particularly fond of this interpretation and offered several versions, including the suggestion that the old bureaucrats even used party membership to advance their careers.[190] His underlying anxiety, it seemed, was that despite the capture and smashing of the bourgeois political state by the Bolsheviks, behind it, in a parody of Gramsci, lay the ramparts of a thoroughly bureaucratised Tsarist civil society which surreptitiously sought revenge by corrupting the new state with its noxious habits.

Other Bolsheviks admitted that there was a bureaucratisation of the personnel in the structures themselves, where the old bureaucrats were joined by the new ones from the party and the working class to create an indigenous Soviet *chinovnichestvo*.[191] In other words, they stressed political factors rather than social ones. At the VIII Party Congress, Mgeladze admitted that workers advanced by the revolution were becoming isolated from their own class and that the masses were no longer involved in running the state.[192] N. Ovsyannikov made the point explicitly soon afterwards when he talked of a divorce between factory workers and their representatives to the Moscow Soviet.[193] Mgeladze reported that in Moscow there were cases when the authorities did not dare to talk about supplies openly and avoided difficult questions at meetings, and because of this the masses were losing their faith in the party. In Moscow's factories, he stated, workers would listen to anybody except communists. There was a danger of communist power turning into a bureaucracy.[194] Ovsyannikov reported that 'provocateurs' now had free rein in the plants.[195] In other words, there was a gulf between the soviet apparatus and the working class. In keeping with his social analysis, Lenin, at the VIII Party Congress, argued that the low cultural level of the working class prevented mass involvement in management and this led to bureaucratism.[196] As Osinskii put it, the new state could only rely on a minuscule layer of workers while the rest were backward because of the low cultural level of the country.[197] Such culturalist assertions, which could neither be proved or disproved but which were politically highly effective in explaining the gulf, served to blur the political and structural causes of the problem. The working class was thus held responsible for the failings of the bureaucracy. At the end of the civil war the theme of the backwardness of the workers was given greater elaboration in Lenin's theory of the declassing of the proletariat, and it became popular to consider this as the main reason for bureaucratisation. Trotsky, in particular, later argued that the bureaucracy arose out of the exhaustion and wastage of the working class as a result of the cumulative trials of the wars.[198] From a different perspective, the Workers' Opposition took up the sociological explanation in stressing, like the Left Communists before them, the baleful effects of the intelligentsia and the use of bourgeois specialists, but in contrast to Lenin they maintained that the working class was capable of taking a more active part in running the state. The structural critique of bureaucracy as developed by the Democratic Centralists raised more painful political questions than did Lenin's explanation. In Moscow the more radical aspect of their analysis was advanced by Ignatov. He argued that the 'small defects' had grown into major ones not only because of sabotage or the vestiges of the past, but because of the inadequacies of the mechanisms themselves. Power had moved from the local soviets to the centre, and this centralism provoked conflict between commissars and soviets.[199] He confirmed that the soviets were losing contact with the masses, and suggested that this was due to insufficient initiative being allowed to the soviets as the party, through democratic centralism, tended to substitute for the soviets.[200] Support for structural/ political over sociological analyses comes from Boguslavskii's admission that during the civil war there had been a fear that more frequent elections would have removed experienced administrators and replaced them with novices who would have taken time to 'master the apparatus':

It must be said that this perfectly justified concern made it impossible to apply to any great extent rotation (*smeny*) methods and significantly encouraged the formation of a layer of so-called 'soviet bureaucracy'.[201]

The response to bureaucracy depended on the initial analysis. One solution was the intensification of party control. On the eve of the VIII Party Congress Lenin had argued that centralisation was the only way to combat bureaucratism, and the congress itself resolved that party supervision over the state and communists working in soviet offices could act as a check against its development. Hence the general awareness of the dangers of bureaucratism reinforced the party's leading role. Nevertheless, during war communism the question of mass participation as a check on 'defects' in the mechanism was an important one. The problem was, as Boguslavskii had suggested, how to integrate the smooth running of the machinery of state, which had a variety of economic and other priorities, with the effective participation of the working class. The apprehension that spontaneity and mass participation would reduce the efficiency of the apparatus was a classic bureaucratic response, and the much vaunted goal of participation was just one aim amongst many. The commune and soviet idea had promised the integration of the politics and economics of the socialist state, but the practice of the dictatorship of the proletariat stimulated the utmost development of a state apparatus as part of the 'superstructure', 'separate and distinct from society'.[202]

Administration was once again marked by the division of labour and as the preserve of the political and technical specialist; doubly so since now the Bolsheviks claimed exclusive specialisation in politics, which we have termed the abolition of politics, resulting in a depoliticised society. This in itself promoted the emergence of a political and administrative bureaucracy. Nevertheless, Lenin and the Bolsheviks put great stress on worker initiative and referred to it constantly. The party programme adopted by the VIII Congress, for example, called for 'the all-round raising of the initiative and sense of responsibility of toilers'.[203] But as P. A. Garvi put it, 'the very system of dictatorship, their party monopoly, the abolition of freedom for non-conformists, the regime of terror [were] insurmountable obstacles for any manifestation of genuine initiative by the masses'.[204] Phillip Corrigan *et al.* insist that 'bureaucracy was rooted in Bolshevism'.[205] Hence autonomous worker participation in the battle against bureaucracy ran against rather than with the grain of the new political structures.

This contention can be illustrated by the development of workers' inspection (Rabkrin) in Moscow, a form of mass control designed to supplement party and Cheka efforts to improve the operation of the state machine. The Tsarist office of State Control was reformed by the creation of a new Central Control Board in January 1918, and in May of that year it was restructured and renamed the People's Commissariat of State Control (*Goskontrol'*). The Moscow city department of state control was formed on 5 August by the Moscow Soviet presidium, supplemented by a Moscow workers' inspection restricted to auditing enterprise management through the control commissions. The *raion* soviets were the basis of the inspection system, reflecting their traditionally close links with the factory committees. The *raion* soviet workers' inspection departments conducted mass investigations of enterprises[206] and checked the supply apparatus and institutions.[207] In this early phase factory inspections were usually initiated by factory committees and trade unions after an accident, an epidemic, or complaints about poor safety standards, and so on, and developed into general investigations into conditions in the enterprise.[208] The organisation of workers' inspection was a way of combating the pervasive bureaucratism of factories and offices. However, there was inadequate integration between the soviet control departments and workers' inspection. In January 1919 Moscow's evening paper called for inspection bodies to be

elected directly by workers.[209] The Gorodskoi soviet plenum in April
1919 supported the call for *Goskontrol'* to be based on elections from
soviets and trade unions,[210] while other *raion*s went further and insisted
that inspection should be based purely on the factories in order to
integrate state inspection and workers' control.[211] In other words, there
was a debate over whether the control should be 'from above' or 'from
below', but all agreed that the existing system was inadequate. Lenin
criticised the *Goskontrol'* ministry at a special session of the Moscow
Soviet on 3 April 1919, and, typically, specifically noted the large
number of *chinovniki* in it.[212] Plans for reform were drawn up and Stalin,
the new commissar for *Goskontrol*, presented them in a decree of 9 April
1919 which envisaged greater public participation.[213] A central Moscow
workers' inspection was formed under the Moscow Soviet, and in the
*raion*s workers' inspection groups of the new type were usually elected
from the factory committees, the *raion* soviet economic departments
where they still existed, and the inspection collegia. Significantly, there
were no direct elections from the workplace.[214] The inspection groups
had the right to unimpeded access to all offices and departments of the
Moscow Soviet.[215]

The development of the inspection groups hastened the demise of the
old factory committee control commissions,[216] as the direct popular
participation of 1917 gave way to the new type of indirect participation,
checking the work of others. At the first plenum of the Moscow workers'
inspection on 20 September 1919, Fedenev, its chairman, argued that the
aim was to involve as many Moscow workers as possible in the battle
against 'inadequacies of the mechanism'.[217] By the VIII Party Conference in December 1919 he could report on the rapid growth of
workers' inspection in Moscow. Inspection cells had been formed in
about a third (261) of the active factories in the city, encompassing over
60 000 workers.[218] The rapid expansion of the inspection movement,
however, was not considered an unmitigated blessing. Fedenev openly
warned that the growth of such a mass movement, involving so many
non-Bolsheviks, could form the basis of an oppositional movement in
future soviet elections.[219] Such fears played their part in the further
reorganisation of popular inspection of 7 February 1920. The existing
control organs were integrated into a People's Commissariat of
Workers' and Peasants' Inspection (Rabkrin). The base of the system
was still the workers' inspection groups, but now they were to be merged
into the unified structure of the commissariat and elected by all those
with voting rights, with much greater union involvement, and constituted locally as a department of the Moscow Soviet.[220] Local Rabkrin

departments were to be formed under the *raion* soviets and subordinate to the soviet.[221] Its brief was to investigate all local administrative and economic bodies with the exception of the Cheka.[222] In its new guise workers' inspection enhanced the role of the delegated inspectors at the core of the Rabkrin groups, and the groups were reduced to auxiliaries as assistance (*sodeistvie*) cells. Group investigations were still used to check on enterprises and other organisations,[223] but clearly the February 1920 reform undermined worker initiative – for the majority indirect participation gave way to participation at third remove. In the October 1920 elections to Moscow Rabkrin the period of delegation was set at only a few months in order to maximise the numbers participating and to ensure that members were not torn away from production.[224] By December 1920 there were 673 cells in the city, and over 20 000 people were associated with the assistance cells.[225] In January 1921 the number of elected delegates to Moscow Rabkrin exceeded 800.[226] The majority of inspectors were workers, and Rabkrin turned out to be an effective way of winkling out yet more capable people from the factories who were then poached by state or party bodies, weakening Rabkrin.[227] Once again the battle against bureaucracy took second place to staffing that very bureaucracy. At the same time Fedenev's warning about the dangers of such a mass movement were heeded. An MK resolution of 3 May 1920 stated in no uncertain terms:

> Rabkrin can become one of the most powerful weapons of the working class in its struggle against bureaucracy only if all its work is conducted in close contact with the general tasks of the party, which is the highest body expressing the interests of the working class at every single moment.[228]

The aim of combining effective popular control within the general perspectives of the party proved insoluble. At the Zamoskvorech'e party general meeting on 29 November 1920, Lenin argued that Rabkrin had done little to prove itself as a school for the management of the state. Instead, 'The bureaucratism of the soviet apparatus could not but permeate the party apparatus, since these apparatuses are intimately linked'.[229] The emergence of Rabkrin as a bureaucratic apparatus in its own right contributed to its declining effectiveness so bitterly condemned by Lenin in his last article *Better Fewer, But Better*. The needs of administration and fear of unrestrained popular investigation strengthened the tendency for the party itself to be seen as the ultimate bulwark against the bureaucratic degeneration of the new state.

The problem of bureaucratism necessitated an understanding of the nature of bureaucracy. While the analyses described earlier made attempts to do so, the development of a *sui generis* new model of contending bureaucracies, which squeezed out popular control, was only partially understood. While in many ways the soviet apparatus cannot be considered a bureaucracy at all since it lacked the 'executive-expert character of bureaucratic power applying formal rationality to implement pre-set goals',[230] the structural organisation of the new system and its operation combined to foment bureaucratism. The party was part of the bureaucracy but at the same time animated it, and hence remained separate. In the Moscow Soviet, power moved from the plenum to the executive bodies; and at the same time the Soviet was responsible for a vast bureaucracy. The disappearance of the distinction between legislative and executive functions, between appointed and elected bodies, means that the analysis of bureaucracy cannot be part of the sociology of public administration, Weberian or otherwise, but must focus on the fusion of political and administrative criteria, the absence of provision for contestatory politics encouraging the growth of bureaucracy. Hence the attempts to rejuvenate the Moscow Soviet through sections was a failure, as were the attempts at mass popular inspection.

IDEOLOGY AND SOCIETY

Despite its division into a series of competing hierarchies, in its first phase Soviet power was able to present a substantially united face to the rest of society. The emphasis was on keeping the conflicts as far as possible within the corridors of power. The crusade against capitalism was accompanied by an onslaught against the bourgeoisie in all spheres, from art to public organisations, and instead of spontaneously generated social processes, what can be called an artificial civil society was created to fill the void between the new political structures and the necessities of the work place; to bridge the gulf noted in the previous section between the regime and the sections of society relevant to its existence. The old civil society was destroyed, but no organic socialist civil society was permitted to emerge. Lenin's aim of 'complete unity and complete agreement among the population' was to be achieved by the elimination of the independence of individuals or organisations.[231] As the British Labour Party delegation put it in the report of their visit in mid 1920: 'Elections become less frequent and more formal and the party aims by means of organised groups at controlling every depart-

ment and every institution of the national life'.[232] The Bolshevik project
during war communism of integral communism, as argued by Bukharin,
posited the abolition of structural pluralism.[233] The Bolshevik party
conquered the old society and at the same time tried to create a new one
which could 'transform power into authority'.[234] The authority was to be
one derived not simply from the creation of a socialist culture, as
advocated by Proletcult, but one subordinated more directly to the
party's own vision of this new society. The implementation of the project
took two forms: non-specific cultural reorganisation in which the party
created a powerful agitprop apparatus designed not only to propagan-
dise Bolshevik policies but also to ensure a degree of mobilisation of the
population; and, secondly, the creation of special bodies such as a youth
league to instil the party spirit (*partiinost'*) in the target group. Both
aspects reflected the fact that Bolshevism was not, as Nikolai Berdyaev
put it, strictly speaking so much a party as a new culture.[235] Marx's
insistence that the working class was the vehicle for the socialist project
was applied simplistically by the Bolsheviks during the civil war. It hid
the sophisticated and subtle reality of working class life. The Bolshevik
aim was not only to reduce social differentiation within the working
class but to infuse it with a homogeneous consciousness.

A major step in the creation of an ideological apparatus was the
creation of an MK agitation bureau on 7 May 1918 which acted as the
central headquarters for speakers and lecturers.[236] In the following
months each RK formed its own agitprop department,[237] and by 1919
these departments were organising an astounding number of agitprop
meetings of one sort or another. In the first half of 1919, for example, 440
meetings were held in Sokol'nicheskii *raion* alone.[238] In the single month
of July 1920 there were 2060 meetings in the city, an average of seventy-
six a day, attended by nearly three-quarters of a million people.[239] Party
reports were filled with copious details about the meetings and the
numbers attending, both to demonstrate their own achievements in this
field, and to prove that the concerns and slogans of the party committees
were shared by the working class. The scale of the agitprop campaign
served to compensate for the Bolshevik's sense of isolation and to
overcome the alleged cultural backwardness of the population. Many of
these meetings were held in working time and were thus assured of an
audience. When the hooter sounded in the middle of a meeting of 2000
workers in the Kursk railway workshops on 28 May 1920, for instance,
over half of the audience melted away.[240] The sheer scale of the MPO's
agitprop effort reflects the 'heroic' nature of the period, but it was clearly
difficult to maintain a high level of mobilisation for months on end. To

compensate, much agitprop took the form of shock campaigns organised in the form of 'weeks' devoted to a single theme such as 'red youth'
or 'the female peasant', or to mark an event such as the II Congress of the
III International in July 1920. The work was supplemented by the
foundation of factory and *raion* clubs by the party committees, which
were designed to be primarily educative rather than recreational. By July
1920, 193 were operating in the city.[241] As the emphasis shifted to
economic reconstruction, by late 1920 a special form of 'production
propaganda' emerged, espoused by Bukharin, and for which the MK in
September 1920 formed a special section to co-ordinate the campaign.[242]
In all this agitprop work the party press, which Lenin called 'a collective
agitator and propagandist', played a critical role and had a near
monopoly on information by 1920.

An intermediate form of agitprop were the non-party conferences
which supplemented the work of the soviets. They were first organised in
late 1918, and were widely practised in the next two years. About a dozen
were held every month in Moscow, aimed at target groups such as
workers, women or soldiers. Between April and October 1919 there were
seventy-five of these conferences,[342] and between June 1919 and August
1920 twenty-one non-party Red Army conferences, eighteen of which
were held in January and February 1920 alone.[244] The non-party
conference was designed mainly as a specific instrument of agitprop and
recruitment to the party.[245] Workplaces or army units would elect
delegates and these would then report back to their electors. Some were
very large, like the one organised by Presnenskii RK on 14–16 December
1918 with about 1400 delegates, at which Lenin gave the keynote speech
on the war.[246] Other conferences restricted themselves to a specific
group, such as the one in February 1919 which was designed to attract
'new layers of workers'.[247] They were often the scene of bitter struggles;
and the very name 'non-party' exposed the Bolsheviks to the charge that
their dominant role infringed the very concept of the conferences. At the
non-party conference in Zamoskvorech'e *raion* (18–23 September
1919), for example, the call for only genuinely non-party people to be
elected to the presidium met with strong support and the Bolsheviks
barely retained control.[248] Myasnikov both at the time and in late 1920
admitted that the conferences often began in a mood of some hostility
but insisted that by detailed preparation, and if the agenda was restricted
to one or two carefully prepared topics, majorities could be achieved:
'Step by step the conference is disciplined, pulled up, pricks up its ears,
and, finally, a complete turnaround takes place and ends with the
complete victory of our party'. But still, one had to be careful, because

'the slightest organisational slip-up spoils the whole thing'.[249] He recommended that the words 'non-party' should be dropped, and this began to be practised from late 1920. During the disturbances at that time they provided an effective platform for criticism of Bolshevik policies, and their frequency decreased. As Lenin admitted at the X Party Congress: 'When non-party meetings were held in Moscow it was clear that out of democracy and freedom they forged a slogan leading to the overthrow of Soviet power';[250] and in the draft of his pamphlet on the tax in kind he wrote that the conferences were used by counter-revolution – 'Caveat consules!' ('Let the consuls be vigilant!') was his recommendation.[251] They were discredited as a form of agitprop,[252] and were discontinued soon afterwards.

The communist *subbotniks* (unpaid Saturday work) were a more general form of agitation which linked the idea of labour and the communist system. The first *subbotnik* took place at the Sortirovochnaya station on the Moscow–Kazan line on 12 April 1919 when thirteen communists and two sympathisers continued to work into the night without wages after the end of the normal Saturday shift. The work was largely confined to transport, essential factory maintenance, and to cleaning up the city after the winter snows.[253] As the number and scale of the *subbotniks* increased, the proportion of communist participants fell from nearly two-thirds in 1919, when 402 were organised, to a quarter in 1920, when some 300 were held.[254] In 1920 the *subbotniks* developed as a mass phenomenon with over a million people involved, compared to just over 50 000 in 1919. Nearly half a million Muscovites took part in a special *subbotnik* on 1 May 1920[255] and the *subbotniks* took on a symbolic significance that was far greater than their actual economic contribution. In September 1919 the MK issued a proclamation extolling the *subbotniks* as a new kind of communist labour in which productivity was not tied to individual recompense. In exalted language it compared them to the labours of the workers in Thomas Campanella's *City of the Sun*, accompanied by music and dancing and imbued with the life-giving properties of the joy of labour.[256] Lenin's view of the *subbotnik* movement shared some of this idealism but also insisted on their practical functions. In his pamphlet issued soon after the first *subbotnik* he called them the 'beginning of communism,'[257] and at the 20 December 1919 Moscow city party conference he argued that they were the first sign of communism '. . . when unpaid work for the general good becomes universal'.[258] On the more practical side, at the VIII Party Conference in December 1919 Lenin stressed their agitprop and recruitment functions and not the glimpse that they offered of the future society.[259] At the same time they were, as Lenin put it in his earlier pamphlet, a means of 'purging the party'.[256] A. S. Bubnov took up this theme when he argued they were 'one of the most genuine means of continuously increasing the discipline, strength, steadfastness, and indissolubility of the party'.[261] The *subbotniks*, in other words, were a way of educating and disciplining the party members themselves. The *voskresniks* (unpaid Sunday work) had the added significance of striking a blow against organised religion.[262]

Even the *subbotniks*, often cited as an example of the idealism of the period, were soon integrated into a bureaucratic framework and were not allowed to develop as an autonomous movement. In May 1919 the MK formed a *subbotnik* bureau headed by MK secretary Zagorskii, and at the end of August 1919 the bureau was consolidated, with the brief to organise and keep statistics on them.[263] The MK instructions on the *subbotniks* of September 1919 insisted that it was obligatory for communists to take part.[264] Factories wishing to draw on the supply of unpaid labour had to notify the bureau about the type of work envisaged and the numbers required, and the workers were then distributed through the RKs. A factory could organise a *subbotnik* only with the permission of the RK *subbotnik* bureau.[265] Hence the party maintained clear control over them. At the end of November 1919 the MK and RK *subbotnik* bureaux were upgraded into departments, each led by an experienced activist,[266] and detailed instructions on their work were issued in December 1919.[267] Every party cell was to appoint an organiser to ensure by personal example that non-party workers would be drawn into the movement. Communists were to take part in at least two *subbotniks* a month, and failure to comply was threatened with punishment up to expulsion from the party.[268] The *subbotniks* were cited as solid evidence of the party's links with the working class and that communists were not a privileged class shut away in offices. They became an element in the struggle against bureaucratism and a lever for the party committees to exert over their members working in state posts. Exemptions from participation were difficult to obtain. Further, as the railway RK stressed in July 1919, on receiving applications from some administrators to be excused, absence from *subbotniks* would be treated as a breach of party discipline,[269] and this was pointedly emphasised in the case of some Cheka workers looking to be excused. The coercive aspect of *subbotnik* participation, especially as far as party members were concerned, increasingly negated their inspirational character. The Leninist stress on 'consciousness' in the pre-revolutionary period was perpetuated by a dread of 'spontaneity' once in power.

While the MPO's ideological work was impressive in statistical terms, its effectiveness was less demonstrable. At the VIII Party Congress Sosnovskii berated the abstract and repetitive nature of the MK's propaganda effort: 'Today [Woodrow] Wilson, tomorrow Wilson, the day after tomorrow Wilson, while the Mensheviks talk about supplies, problems in factories, etc.'.[270] The Lefortovo RK's report for April 1919 complained about the limited influence of their agitprop: 'Our work does not so much encompass new layers of the proletariat as regulates, directs, and broadens the work of already established organisations'.[271] The problem was stated in May 1919 by the Sushchevsko-Mar'inskii RK. They were dealing with 'raw human material, Red Army soldiers arriving straight from the countryside into the towns . . . unhappy with requisitioning . . . and backward workers who have had little taste of political life'. The RK insisted that more cells had to be formed to supplement the 42 existing ones to overcome this 'cultural backwardness'. In keeping with the increasing trend to define the cells as agitational bodies, the RK stated that they were to supplement the work of the mere three to four full-time agitators at their disposal.[272] At the IX Party Congress Kamenev was still calling for agitprop to become less theoretical,[273] though he could have called for it to become more efficient. There were frequent cases when speakers arrived late at meetings, or failed to turn up at all.[274] The agitprop effort in the countryside, the responsibility of the united organisation from mid-1920, appears to have been singularly inept, and concentrated on grain requisitioning, combating desertion, and from late 1920 on sowing campaigns. Urban activists flooded the countryside in shock agitation campaigns, as in July 1920,[275] but their effectiveness can be gauged by a report that during an earlier 'peasant week' the party agitators had done more harm than good because of their 'complete lack of understanding of the countryside'.[276]

The question of 'cultural backwardness' was particularly acute with respect to religious observance. In May 1918 Bukharin insisted that the task was not only the economic liberation of the working class but also its 'spiritual liberation from the church'.[277] Lenin's draft party programme of early 1919 did not limit itself to the formal separation of church and state but insisted on the 'actual liberation of the toiling masses from religious prejudice' through anti-religious propaganda.[278] Nevertheless, the widespread persistence of religious faith in the city is well-documented, and even exerted a powerful hold within the party. In 1920, Marguerite Harrison reported packed churches and generous donations for priests, who no longer received obligatory tithes.[279] In

April 1920, when about fifty people a week in the Danilovskaya mill were dying from dysentery from a water supply whose contamination had been identified the previous autumn, a religious service was attended by nearly half of the predominantly female 7000 strong labour force in an incident which aroused particularly severe censure.[280] The religious debates in the city, in which a Bolshevik luminary, often A. V. Lunacharskii, would 'dispute' with a leading cleric, attracted large audiences. At one, in September 1920, Lunacharskii confronted Bishop Antonin before a packed hall in the Polytechnical Museum, and honours were even as the vote split down the middle.[281] As the propaganda increasingly spoke of the imminence of communism, socialism in the factories appeared to recede as workers entered the illegal economy to survive, and lacked a 'conscious approach to labour'.[282] Under the pressure of the collapse of effective public life apart from that via bureaucratic channels, workers were returning to earlier forms of solidarity such as mutual self-help organisations (*kassy vzaimopomoshchi*).[283] In the party, the MGK in mid-1919 warned that any communist observing religious practices would be punished.[284] Despite such threats a meeting of *raion* secretaries and agitprop activists in mid-April 1920 noted that communists were still being married in church and their children baptised. The meeting adopted an uncompromising line on the question: either the party or the church.[285] There was a steady stream of expulsions for infringements of this rule,[286] including twenty-eight during the August 1920 reregistration. The attitude of the communist to religion became yet another test of loyalty to the party.

The super-centralising tendencies of war communism even extended to the ideological sphere. In late 1920 there were attempts to concentrate all party, state and military agitprop and educational work under a new body called Glavpolitprosvet, formed in November 1920 under Narkompros, and nominally headed by N. K. Krupskaya.[287] Its formation as the supreme *glavk* in the ideological sphere prefigured the organisational methods of the 'cultural revolution' in the early 1930s. At the IX Party Conference Myasnikov argued for the incorporation of all party agitation and schools in this body as a way of ensuring organisational cohesion and an adequate political content in cultural and educational work.[288] The state educational apparatus was to amplify the party's message. Lenin took the view that the party should retain its autonomy in this field,[289] and in Moscow the discussion over the respective roles of Glavpolitprosvet and the party agitprop departments continued into 1921.[290] The V Guberniya Party Conference in February 1921 resolved that the party ought to keep its own agitprop departments,[291] and the division between state and party agitprop remained with the formation of the Moscow Glavpolitprosvet in March 1921. The X Party Congress rejected Lunacharskii's proposal to abolish party agitprop departments and the party was able to retain control over this crucial sphere.[292]

On the level of more specific bodies the development of the Communist Youth League (Komsomol) vividly illustrates the transition of ideology into organisation, and indeed expressed the feeling that the Bolshevik revolution was one of youth against tradition, a new world against the old. Its transformation into a monolithic youth organisation structured on the lines of the party became the model for later communist youth organisations. On the practical level the importance of an organisation of youth for the Bolsheviks stemmed from the large numbers employed in industry, and its value increased as mature workers were drafted and replaced by youths (and women). Already in April 1918, when demobilisation had allowed some (male) workers to return, the census had shown that some 52 000 people under the age of twenty-five were employed in factory industry, a third of the industrial proletariat in the city. Nearly a fifth of all workers were teenagers.[293] This was reflected in the youthful age structure of the party (see page 158).

Youth associations had flourished in the ferment of 1917, with one of the most active a group in Zamoskvorech'e called 'III International'. While inspired by the Bolsheviks it appealed to all working-class youth and was not directly affiliated to the party. By the summer similar groups had been formed in all Moscow's *raions*. The MK joined the fray and in June 1917, against Krupskaya's advice,[294] formed its own Youth Union consisting solely of young Bolsheviks. The VI Party Congress in August 1917, however, rejected the MK's approach and resolved that Bolshevik influence would be more effectively advanced if the party and youth groups remained organisationally separate.[295] This formulation was to underpin later developments. On 8 October 1917, at the I Moscow city youth conference, the MK youth union dissolved itself into the much larger 'III International' organisation, now called the Union of Young Workers, which survived in name up to November 1918.[296] In reality, this body largely disintegrated during the upheaval of the Brest peace, losing a large part of its members to the voluntary military detachments, while others, in keeping with the radicalism of the organisation, resigned in opposition to the peace.[297] The MK of the union dissolved and the remnants devoted themselves to work in Proletcult.[298]

The influence of Proletcult ideas on popular culture and the

autonomy of mass organisations profoundly affected the youth organisation, and there are many parallels between the two movements. The
founding conference of the Moscow Proletcult, for instance, of 23–28
February 1918, at the height of the Brest controversy, called for the
formation of a 'special, purely mass organisation' (that is, independent
of the party). The relationship between the local party organisation and
the Moscow Proletcult was an uneasy one and marked by the latter's
resistance to party domination. Party control was only achieved with the
abolition of Proletcult autonomy by its fusion with Narkompros in
December 1920.[299] At the founding congress of the Russian Communist
League of Youth (RKSM) (29 October–4 November 1918) the question
of autonomy caused a major controversy.[300] Proletcult influence was
reflected in the key resolution insisting on the independence of the league
from the RKP, though conceded that it should work under its
'guidance'.[301] Opposed interpretations of this resolution were to lie at the
centre of a debate in the Moscow youth and party organisations which
continued into 1920. While the party stressed that Komsomol, though
independent, was a school where 'new conscious communists are
formed' and a reserve for the party,[302] a group within the Komsomol
based in Moscow stressed its internal autonomy and mass nature. Their
views were incorporated in the programme adopted by the I Congress,
insisting that youth was 'the most revolutionary part of the working
class'.[303]

Following the congress the Moscow Komsomol organisation began
to organise itself on the model of the Communist Party. The 17
November 1918 city youth conference decided that the MK RKSM
would consist of three representatives from each *raion*, whereas up to
then affairs had been run on an informal democratic basis by simple
meetings of activists in each *raion*.[304] These attempts were thwarted,
however, by the union's continuing close ties with Proletcult.[305] Certain
Komsomol leaders in Moscow, such as V. Dunaevskii, who favoured
greater autonomy, now argued that the youth league could not fulfil the
objectives set out in the programme and become a mass organisation of
working youth while it was closely tied to the RKP.[306] The debate was
conducted against the background of the military crises of 1919. It was
of this period that N. Ostrovskii, author of *How the Steel was Tempered*,
wrote that 'with the Komsomol card we received a rifle and 200 rounds
of ammunition'.[307] In the three national and many local Komsomol
mobilisations a total of nearly 25 000 members were sent to the fronts.[308]
Membership of the Moscow RKSM organisation, united with the
guberniya in June 1920, correspondingly grew slowly, with a city

membership in October 1918 of 2500, and barely 200 more a year later.[309] With the easing of the military emergency membership climbed faster, boosted in October 1919 by a 'week of red youth', the equivalent of the party weeks, which doubled membership to 5250 by February 1920,[310] and by October 1921 membership reached 9000.[311] By mid-1921 the average age of the Komsomol member had fallen from nineteen to about sixteen as not only individuals but whole factory cells were drafted, distorting not only the age profile but also the social composition of the organisation.[312]

Komsomol's activities centred on the factory clubs and on schools and colleges.[313] The latter were particularly important in view of the extraordinary increase in student numbers, which had more than doubled in the city since 1913 to reach nearly 70 000 by August 1919. Over the same period, however, the number of secondary school pupils had nearly halved to 21 000.[314] Komsomol fought against the many non-party, and even party, groups organised beyond its aegis, and indeed in a manner typical of the war communist scramble for a place in the Soviet sun (and of the cultural revolution), in its own field it tended to act as the RKP writ small. Groups such as the All-Russian Federation of Communist Youth, formed in mid-1919, and several organised by the anarchists, were extremely popular and shared a cultural orientation akin to that of Proletcult and were part of the same effervescence of cultural and non-structured political life. The groups, however, were vigorously attacked by the party and the Moscow Komsomol on the basis that they deflected youth from the class struggle. They were dissolved by fiat and by force: the former predominated where workers were a majority, and the latter where they were dominated by the 'bourgeoisie'.[315] In 1920 the party became directly involved in this campaign, and in April the MK bureau formed a special communist section to give political leadership among students.[316] It was at this time that attempts were made to bring both the Komsomol and Moscow University under stricter party control. In September 1920 the student section was upgraded into a party fraction and given the right to settle academic questions. The fraction bureau was consolidated by the appointment of three senior party members.[317] In that month a major conference of all colleges (VUZy) convened by the bureau called for the radical reform of all higher educational establishments, the creation of proletarian universities, and the intensification of party control. The conference condemned the many student revolutionary associations and stressed that there were to be 'no intermediaries between communists and non-party people'.[318] The reform of higher education was therefore designed not only to counteract bourgeois influences but also to undermine any interest aggregations between the party and the mass of students.[319]

The links between the Moscow Komsomol and party organisations took various forms. Above all, the party insisted that its members under 20 were to join the youth organisation, though judging by the frequency with which this injunction was repeated it was observed more in the breach.[320] By October 1919, 11 per cent of the RKSM nationally consisted of communists,[321] and by March 1921, 4 per cent of the RKP were under the official minimum age of party membership of eighteen, and 15 per cent were aged between nineteen and twenty.[322] All party and Komsomol committees sent representatives to each other, but whereas from the start the party representatives had voting rights and were to supervise, as the MK put it, the 'ideological and organisational work' of Komsomol,[323] the youth representatives were only granted this right in June 1920.[324] A joint TsK RKP and RKSM instruction of August 1919 firmly swung the compromise definition of party–Komsomol relations in favour of the party by insisting that the Komsomol committees were under the 'direct subordination' of the corresponding party committees. The instruction now allowed the formation of party cells or fractions in Komsomol.[325] This, apparently, was in response to the above-mentioned criticism of the inadequate mass nature of Komsomol. Since early 1919, Dunaevskii had been arguing that special mass organisations, alongside the Komsomol, of soviets of working youth and youth sections under the trade unions were to be formed to defend the interests of the 'toiling youth of Russia'. In a critique which went beyond that of the Democratic Centralists, and which in many ways prefigured that of the Workers' Opposition, he argued that the 'guiding role' of the RKP had created an elite within the party. He criticised the emergence of 'thinking kernels' (*myslyashchie yadra*) in general which stifled the self-activity of the masses. The Komsomol, he argued, should develop as an organising centre allied to but independent of the party.[326]

The debate continued despite the overwhelming rejection of Dunaevskii's ideas at the II RKSM Conference in October 1919.[327] The MK bureau on 29 December 1919 analysed the 'crisis' in the Moscow Komsomol organisation and criticised it for concentrating on cultural rather than political work. In other words, it had been too involved in Proletcult activities. The more open definition of its purpose was reflected in looser organisational structures. Measures were adopted to transform Komsomol into 'a genuine preparatory stage for entry into the RKP', but the proposal to form a party fraction in it was referred to a full MK meeting on 21 January 1920.[328] T. F. Lyudvinskaya, who had been an MK representative on the MK RKSM, insisted on a series of disciplinary measures including the formation of a fraction and called for a communist delegate to every Komsomol cell. While the MK agreed with her general conclusions, the majority baulked at her authoritarian approach and decided not to form a fraction.[329] Once again the relative liberalism of the MK was confirmed. The TsK RKP came to share this view and in March 1920 argued that such fractions were not to be formed in Komsomol organisations, as had become common, and neither were youth departments to be formed under party committees since this had led to 'misunderstandings' and substitutionalism.[330]

In mid-1920 Dunaevskii, now a member of the Komsomol Central Committee, once again raised his earlier ideas. In September 1920 the TsK issued a circular attacking the 'secret factional grouping' in the TsK RKSM and insisted that 'youth syndicalism . . . counterposed not the proletariat as a class to the bourgeois class, but young proletariat to adult proletariat'.[331] Dunaevskii was suspended from the party for six months, and his fate was an augury for future oppositionists. In Moscow the debate over autonomy for the youth organisation reached fever pitch. The majority of the MK RKSM supported Dunaevskii, and now the Moscow youth organisation 'broke its ties with the party'.[332] The crucial test was to be the II United *Guberniya* Youth Conference, which met on the eve of the III National Komsomol Congress (2–10 October 1920). Already the suggestion, reminiscent of the MK's approach of 1917, had been made at the IX Party Conference (22–25 September 1920) that Komsomol be disbanded and its functions transferred to party youth departments. Instead, N. Krestinskii's proposals for tighter party control over Komsomol were adopted.[333] The MK bureau, meeting on 27 September, decided to form a party fraction at the *guberniya* conference to direct its work. The tactic proved effective and despite rowdy sessions the fraction carried the day, and a new MK RKSM was selected more amenable to party control.[334] The Komsomol oppositionists shared many of the concerns worrying the party and trade union oppositionists of this period, such as the problem of inner-party democracy and the emergence of leading centres.[335] Bukharin put it another way at the III Congress on 2 October 1920 when he argued that the RKSM suffered from many of the same ills as the party, which he ascribed to sociological rather than political factors.[336] This view was belied by the effect that the defeat of the Komsomol dissidents, confirmed at the III Congress, had on the morale of the youth organisation. The new MK RKSM in December 1920 admitted that both rank-and-file members and activists had lost interest in the league,[337] and this marked passivity was confirmed by the national leadership.[338] The reregistration of early 1921, allied to a large fallout rate, led to an astonishing drop of over 50 per cent in national membership to under a quarter of a million in 1922.[339] Discontent over the defeat of the oppositionists and the end of Proletcult autonomy was compounded by indignation over the introduction of the NEP. Resentment against the organisational changes was compounded by ideological dissatisfaction. Komsomol had retained its organisational independence but this was vitiated by party control exercised at several levels. The Moscow Komsomol had tried to reflect the idealism of its ideology in the structure of its organisation and by participation in the creation of a new culture, but this was undermined not so much by the war as by the imposition of controls by the party. The Komsomol was unable to resist the process as effectively as it might have if it had not itself acted in an authoritarian manner with respect to the other youth groups in Moscow.

The political characteristics of the other major mass movement were very different. Since 1914 the wars had accelerated the induction of women into the labour force. By spring 1921 they had become a majority in several Moscow trade unions, with over 100 000 (70 per cent) in the *guberniya* textile union, nearly 15 000 (75 per cent) in the tailoring union, over 3000 (79 per cent) in the tobacco workers' union, 18 000 (35 per cent) in the food workers' union, 18 000 (33 per cent) in the print workers' union, and they comprised a large part of the expanding bureaucracy. About half of the 400 000 workers covered by the MGSPS were women.[340] By certain conventional criteria the standard view of Russian women workers as being marked by 'passivity and lack of consciousness'[341] is accurate. Women made up a small proportion of the party (see page 158) and comprised only 7 per cent of the Moscow soviet in November 1920.[342]

On the surface, therefore, it would appear that this group would be an obvious target for party agitprop and organisational work, and yet the situation here was more complicated than with the youth organisation. A further ambiguity is that once this work was launched it was very much a question of consciousness coming 'from outside' via certain committed Bolshevik feminists, and hence no political or ideological movement for organisational autonomy arose among the female labour force or its institutions comparable to that in the youth movement. From the outset most radical female worker political organisation was focused on the party. The post-revolutionary history of the communist

women's movement in Moscow at first centred on the journal *Zhizn'
rabotnitsy*, issued from the autumn of 1917 but based on a journal of the
same name published by MOB from June 1917. In early October 1917
the MK and MOB organised a special commission to conduct agitprop
among women whose aim was primarily to organise support for the
Bolsheviks,[343] but it appears to have disappeared after October.
Following the revolution the MOK, with Inessa Armand a frequent
member, was more active in this field than the city committee, and it was
the organisational force behind the I All-Russian Congress of Female
Workers and Female Peasants of November 1918.[344] The delegation
from Moscow was by far the largest, with 35 delegates from Basmannyi
raion alone. Lenin and Sverdlov limited their speeches to general
comments on the need to draw women into soviet and communist
construction.[345] The congress called for the formation of female worker
agitprop commissions under party committees.[346] Their formation was
co-ordinated by a female worker commission under the TsK in which
Armand, until her death in 1920, and Aleksandra Kollontai were active.

Even before the congress several *raion*s had begun to form these
commissions, and towards the end of December one was formed under
the MK.[347] However, it was only on 2 February 1919 that the MK
commission set to work and they were then formed in the remaining
*raion*s.[348] Both the central and *raion* commissions in 1919 usually
consisted of no more than a secretary and a couple of agitators each and
were mainly concerned with trying to involve women in the work of the
'soft' departments of the soviets, dealing with food and welfare.[349] As
could be expected, the development of the female worker commissions
encountered at best indifference and at worst hostility. Not all the RKs
were convinced that this sort of work was necessary, an opinion shared
by heads of soviet departments, rank-and-file workers, and even
communists.[350]

The lack of party commitment to the commissions led to calls from the
MK commission in May 1919 for it to be upgraded into a party
department, with greater help from the MK itself. The MK refused the
request at the time,[351] probably considering the war and other tasks as
more urgent than supporting the female worker movement, which in any
case posed no political threat to party hegemony. In August 1919,
however, the MK did decide to form a female worker department
(*Zhenotdel*) headed by S. N. Smidovich and called on the RKs to do
likewise, and on the cells to appoint a person to be responsible for this
work.[352] In September of that year the TsK also reorganised its
commission into a department headed initially by Armand. It had taken

a long campaign by the female worker activists to convince the party committees of the necessity of this change. On the other hand, there are indications that the conversion of the commissions into party departments was a measure designed not only to improve their effectiveness but also to ensure adequate party supervision over the organised women's movement. I. I. Minkov informed the November 1919 Moscow Guberniya Party Conference that the commissions had tended to work independently from party committees. Most of the commission members had been 'very young party members or sympathisers who did not know how to conduct active and correct work', and he called for one or two committee members to join the *Zhenotdely*.[353] Faced with a multitude of other demands, only eighty-seven cells had appointed someone responsible for female worker organisation by January 1920, but by September the figure had risen to 275, and by mid-1921 to 628.[354] The *Zhenotdely* sponsored a unique form of organisation, with delegates (*delegatki*) elected not for one meeting but for a certain term (usually three months), with one delegate representing fifty female workers at all meetings held in that period. In addition to the many *raion* conferences, five city-wide female worker delegate meetings had been held by mid-1920, in which the numbers of delegates had risen from 200 at the first in late 1919 to 3771 at the fifth in July 1920.[355] Despite the impressive growth only about 5 per cent of the city's factories had delegates by the end of the period.[356]

The Moscow female worker movement, therefore, was from the first organisationally closely allied to the party, whereas the youth movement from 1917 took on a mass character distinct from the party's youth organisation and was only later brought under party control. No such independent movement developed among female workers. Both movements suggested 'mass' rather than 'class'-based organisations, though Dunaevskii had tried to combine the two, but in the case of the female workers' movement this political suspicion, voiced by Minkov, was enhanced by traditional prejudices and the spectre of 'bourgeois feminism'. The price of party support for the *Zhenotdely* was a compromise between the general ambitions of the movement, proposing fundamental changes in social relations, and the more limited undertaking of ensuring support for Bolshevik policies. During the 1920s the compromise was for a time broadened to encompass the whole range of social conditions of life known as *byt*, yet the legacy of the civil war was a women's movement integrated into the party apparatus and vulnerable to shifts in party policies.

The party's general ideological work, and the policies towards mass movements, accented the dominance of administrative methods. 'Iron discipline' within the party stimulated military methods in relation to non-party groups, which in turn reinforced dictatorial methods within the party. A. F. Myasnikov gives a vivid description of the cycle when for a short time from mid-1920 the party and trade union debates allowed the issue to come into the open:

> The times created a long chain of the recurrence of party pressure (*nazhim*) and the dictatorship of the committees. We must not forget that pressure was brought to bear not only by the all-Russian centre but by every local centre in relation to its own periphery: the gubkom, uezd committee, and even the cell bureau. We recall (and indeed it is probably still practised) how many of our comrades, rank-and-file worker communists, at a factory or plant meeting put pressure on the non-party masses. I remember how at a meeting of one of Moscow's enterprises (Mars) I asked the factory committee, composed of communists, why the general meeting on elections to the Moscow Soviet was conducted in such a dictatorial way. The leading comrade (he is a member of the opposition now) answered me in these precise words: *One cannot deal with the masses in any other way.* And do not comrades remember the many incidents in our agitational work: the barring of factory gates so that workers could not leave meetings, and so on.[357]

From the barring of factory gates to the direct use of coercion through the Cheka, the party imposed its will on society and its own supporters. Such methods were justified at the time by the military emergency but drew their inspiration from ideological positions. The struggle for hegemony became a struggle for *partiinost'* and was waged by administrative rather than political means. The Bolshevik party became a crucial element in the uneasy coalition that made up the Soviet state and expanded to encompass all intermediary associations. Civil society was suffocated and became a casualty of the implementation of the Bolshevik project of integral communism. The integral state came later but the ideology of state–society relations acted as a powerful integrative force. The changes within the party were to a large extent a result of the way that the party defined itself in relation to society. Organisational conformity to the party was in danger of becoming ideological conformity within the party. Few Bolsheviks spoke against this process as applied to mass organisations, but when the soviets were undermined and their party fractions became executors of policy decided elsewhere, a section of the party became increasingly concerned, and it is to this debate that we now turn.

7 The Rise of the Reform Movements

THE CRISIS OF WAR COMMUNISM AND MILITARISATION

Esther Corey, an American communist, provides a vivid portrait of Moscow in 1919:

> Military men in motor cars were dashing recklessly through the streets. Limousines bearing soviet dignitaries and rickety carriages pulled by boney horses raised a clattering symphony on the cobbles . . . There was a certain amount of barter on the Sukharevka market, but this was a dangerous undertaking. Many a Russian lost his life after a Cheka raid on the market.[1]

On her arrival in Moscow in early 1920 Emma Goldman was struck by the ubiquitous presence of soldiers and Chekists. John Reed described the atmosphere in the city to her at the time:

> Moscow is a military encampment: spies everywhere, the bureaucracy most autocratic. I always feel relieved when I get out of Moscow. But then, Petrograd is a proletarian city and is permeated with the spirit of the revolution. Moscow always was more hierarchical. It is much more so now.[2]

The war and the Bolshevik system of power had reinforced each other to create a powerful political and military machine. The question was now one not only of devising effective institutional mechanisms to restrain it but also one of finding some ideological justification for doing so. The elimination of popular control and debate in the army had been extended to the rest of society and the militarisation process was threatening the party itself. Could an alternative balance of power, combining effective rule with elements of popular and rank-and-file party control, be established as the war came to an end? The next two chapters will be devoted to this question.

By early 1920 it was clear that the regime had reached an impasse. Industrial production had fallen catastrophically, labour discipline was low, the bureaucracy worked fitfully if at all, and there was a general sense that the whole apparatus needed a shake-up. The three main features of the crisis in 1920 can be characterised as:

216

Not only the breach (*otryv*) of the party *nizy* [rank and file] from the party *verkhi* [higher ups], but also the isolation of the party from the working class, and the isolation of the working class from the peasantry.[3]

The third aspect was ultimately to force a retreat from the economic rigidities of war communism, but for the present no fundamental re-evaluation of this question was undertaken. Instead, the year was devoted mainly to political issues and to plans for improving the existing system. Against the background of economic decline and labour and peasant unrest, two key controversies developed which were to accompany the slow expiry of the war communist economic system.

Oppositions were not a new feature of the party under war communism, and several have already been described. However, in 1920–21 they developed into two major debates which challenged the political system as it had developed during the war. The Democratic Centralists, now joined by various other groups, shifted their attention from earlier concern over the organisation of the state structure to the party itself. This issue, which for convenience can be dubbed the party debate, focused on the split between an increasingly politically passive membership and the leadership: the problem of privilege and inequality in the party, bureaucratism, the role of cells, the rights of party members and party democracy, and the effectiveness of party committees. The second controversy focused on the role of the trade unions and raised crucial questions about the limits of party control over its members working in such key working class organisations and on the relationship between the new state, nominally a workers' state, and the working class itself. The trade union debate, as the MK put it in a key resolution of 18 January 1921, involved 'the relationship between the leading elements of the proletariat organised in the RKP and the rest of the broad proletarian masses'.[4] The problem, as Alexander Shlyapnikov, one of the leading figures in the Workers' Opposition, put it at the X Party Congress, was not only that the party was split, but that the party itself represented a *verkh* in regard to the non-party *nizy*.[5] The problem of the lack of autonomy of the party's lower ranks, as noted, had surfaced at several points during the civil war, but the Workers' Opposition now took up the issue in a consistent way. The fundamental question was whether a more democratic party should play an absolute tutelary role in society or whether its guiding role, which no communist denied, could be carried out in tandem with the working class organised in trade unions.

Both debates were attempts to find a way out of the social and political crisis engendered by the policies of war communism. But while both offered alternatives to the political system, they offered little analysis of war communist economic structures. Discussion was restricted to party members, but the rest of the population increasingly made its presence felt on the streets of Moscow, the villages of Tambov, and finally on the battlements of the naval fortress of Kronstadt. The issues raised by the debates had long been discussed but it was precisely now, at the end of war communism, that certain responses were consolidated which were to lie at the basis of the ensuing period and which in many ways hold to this day.

The background to the oppositions with their radical solutions was Trotsky's no less radical militarisation plans. Both were predicated on the continuation of the economics of war communism, but offered diametrically opposed solutions as they took the potentialities of war communism to their respective extremes. We have noted the emergence of a Bolshevik military machine and the first attempts at universal labour service. Trotsky now proposed their fusion to deal not only with the economic crisis but also implied that these methods could be systematised and extended to the political sphere, threatening the political prerogatives of the party itself. From his analysis of the economic problem Trotsky developed a solution which could be extended to the political sphere, whereas the other oppositions extended their analysis from the requirements of the political system, as they saw them, to the economic sphere. His was a brave if politically inept attempt to address the key economic problems of the period.

For Trotsky, the militia system was to form the basis for the militarisation of labour. At the 24 September 1919 city party conference Trotsky had exhorted strict labour discipline and military methods, above all on the railways. By the end of 1919 he came to the conclusion that if war communism was to continue (and in February 1920 he put forward some tentative proposals for a tax in kind which were rejected by the TsK),[6] then general militarisation was the only solution to the most pressing economic problems. With Kolchak, Yudenich and Denikin repulsed, Trotsky outlined his plans at the XVI Guberniya Party Conference (23 November 1919):

> I believe that if we can soon end most of our fronts we will have at our disposal an apparatus of universal labour duty. In May 1918 we doubted if we could mobilise 10,000 workers. Now we can mobilise millions of workers and peasants. This is part of our general soviet

apparatus. We will liquidate the war, go over to *Vseobuch* [universal military duty], and the military apparatus will be available for the economic needs of the country . . . Victories at the front prepare the way for victories in the fields of culture, the economy and management.[7]

In the absence of the European revolution and the decimation of the working class and the old underground activists, the methods that had proved themselves in war were to be applied to the home fronts.[8] In December 1919 he put forward concrete proposals for the extension of the militia system and the militarisation of labour, which, with slight modifications, were adopted with Lenin's support by the TsK on 22 January 1920.[9] The distinction between the military and civilian spheres was to be obliterated through universal labour duty and the militia system, and the comparatively efficient machinery of the Red Army was to be harnessed for economic purposes. Labour was to come under military discipline enforced by an array of punitive organs to punish 'labour desertion' and other offences (see Chapter 3), and inevitably the trade unions would become part of the military–bureaucratic apparatus.[10] As he informed the MK on 6 January 1920, with Russia cut off from foreign aid and with a stock of worn-out machines, labour would have to be substituted for capital.[11] On this, Richard Day writes:

> The civil war brought with it a steadily widening gap between traditional socialist ideals and economic necessity. Within little more than two years a pattern of organisation emerged which in many ways provided a prototype for Stalin's five-year plans of the 1930s. Ironically the main architect of this system was Trotsky.[12]

Trotsky provided not only the organisational model for Stalin but also the theory: A 'production ideology' emerged, the economistic interpretation of Marxism noted in Chapter 1, which gave priority to the development of productive forces over the development of non-capitalist forms of production relations. The 'relative autonomy' of the Soviet labour state for the first time threatened the party itself.

Trotsky's proposals were adopted within the context of a general discussion in the run-up to the IX Party Congress over the respective roles of the trade unions, soviets and the party in the Soviet state. In late 1919 Shlyapnikov formulated a division of tasks whereby the party was to be concerned with political management, the soviets with political power, and the trade unions with economic management.[13] It was an attempt to restore the unions to a central position in the new system and out of the obscurity described in Chapter 3. In March 1920 he developed these ideas to include greater autonomy for the communist fractions in the unions, a clear challenge to the party leadership's organisational pre-eminence.[14] In his defence of the MK's position on the question at the 17–18 March 1920 city party conference, Bukharin put forward what was to become the orthodox interpretation of the unions as educators and organisers of the proletariat but not the direct managers of the economy.[15] The MK rejected Shlyapnikov's syndicalism and insisted on the subordination of communist trade union fractions and the trade unions themselves to the party but, while broadly agreeing with Trotsky's arguments, accepted Tomskii's arguments, as head of the national union organisation, that one-person management in industry should be introduced only with great care, and collegiality preferred where possible.[16] Without one-person management Trotsky's plans were meaningless. The growing opposition to militarisation was revealed by the heated discussion at the conference and by the slim majority of ten by which the MK theses were adopted.[17]

A second city party conference on 25 March turned its attention to general economic policy. Trotsky once again defended the rationale behind his plans by insisting that the 'social-compulsory' labour which he envisaged could be very effective since 'this forced labour has nothing in common with the forced labour in bourgeois economies'. Only the spiritual (*dukhovnyi*) backwardness of the population delayed its application. He insisted that economic management should be concentrated in the economic agencies while 'the interference of the trade unions in the economy must be ended'. Emergency bodies such as *Glavpolitput'*, a central political department under the Commissariat of Transport (NKPS) formed in January 1919 as part of the militarisation of the railways, were to militarise industry and raise the productivity of labour, while centrally constituted *oblast* economic and party bodies would reduce the excessive centralism of the *glavki*. His plans combined the idealism of the *subbotnik* movement with the ruthlessness of the army high command. The conference unanimously supported the TsK line, but its uneasiness was once again revealed by its reservation over one-person management.[18]

With the threat of militarisation hanging over not only the economy but also the soviets and the party, Osinskii's warnings of late 1919 against extending military culture to other spheres[19] became sharper at the IX Party Congress in March 1920. Above all, he warned against the indiscriminate application of one-person management to civilian and party apparatuses.[20] Lenin, however, supported Trotsky's plans on the ground that compulsion was the only resource available to impose unity and discipline in the absence of capital, and that the army was the source of this discipline.[21] The congress adopted the militarisation programme with its reduced role for the unions and hence for the working class.[22] The way was now clear for the vigorous application of labour duty in order to erase the distinction between the army and labour.[23] However, Trotsky's contention at the 25 March city party conference that the party itself should be militarised through 'extraordinary actions and exceptional measures'[24] found little support at the congress. Vladimirskii agreed with Trotsky,[25] but Kamenev as usual equivocated in arguing that while militarisation was to be supported in general it was not to be applied to the party,[26] while Sapronov insisted that the political departments, whose conflicts with the MPO have been mentioned, signified nothing other than the militarisation of party life.[27]

In Moscow the controversy over the extension of militarisation to civilian life came to a head over the prerogatives of the railway (*Zheleznodorozhnyi*) party organisation. It was based in Sokol'nicheskii *raion*, where four out of the eight networks had their offices, and the *raion* committee's influence stretched far up the lines.[28] In his capacity as transport commissar Trotsky was able to implement his plans, first through *Glavpolitput'*, then from August 1920 through *Tsektran* (TsK of rail and water unions. Not only was the independence of the transport trade unions undermined, but also that of the party organisations in transport. This had long engendered hostility between *Glavpolitput'* and the Moscow railway party organisation. The former had arbitrarily intervened in the work of the RK and its cells on the railways, organised parallel clubs, libraries, and so on, and had convened party meetings without consulting either the cells or the RK. Above all, it had been accused of 'overbearing behaviour'.[29] Early partisans of militarisation, such as Zimin and Vompe, were thwarted in their attempts in 1919 to have the special railway RPO abolished altogether as their opponents, such as Pyatnitskii, insisted that the political departments required political guidance from the party.[30] The TsK itself was split on the question and shelved the VIII Party Congress decision on the abolition of such non-territorial party organisations as the one for the railways.[31] This is how the matter stood when in February 1920 *Glavpolitput'*, headed by A. P. Rozengol'ts, was reorganised and its party functions extended.[32]

Glavpolitput' now pushed strongly for the abolition of the railway party organisations throughout the network.[33] While the TsK's own position was ambiguous,[34] the MK several times rejected abolition. At

its meeting on 29 March 1920, however, despite Pyatnitskii's rearguard
action which argued that the political departments were in no position to
undertake the work of party organisations, a commission of Pyatnitskii,
Myasnikov and Bubnov was appointed to report on the question.[35]
Several *raion* party general meetings supported motions in favour of the
railway *raion*.[36] The hostility in the city to militarisation encouraged the
MK on the eve of the IX Congress to give its full backing to the
campaign against the extension of *politotdel'chestvo* (Political depart-
mentism) on the railways and to other industries. Together with the
railway trade union TsK they protested against the *Glavpolitput'*
proposals to give administrative personnel the right to fine and in
general to punish workers and employees. The MK, well aware that the
party itself was under threat, tried to hold the line and counter-attacked
by calling for the political departments to be deprived of all political
functions.[37] At the congress itself Myasnikov questioned the dual role of
Glavpolitput' as a state and party organisation. On the key issue of
appointments and the distribution of party members he called for
consultation between political deparments and local party organisations,[38] while Kamenev went further and argued that primacy in this
field should lie with the RPO, though in consultation with the political
departments.[39]

The IX Party Congress decided that the political departments were to
have the dominant say in party work in transport on the grounds that the
unions were too weak to transmit party influence.[40] In the light of this the
railway organisation was dissolved in May 1920 and *Glavpolitput'*
became the sole party organiser on the railways. The victory of the
militarisers left a legacy of bitterness in the city organisation and evoked
many disputes between communists on the railways and the new
political department leaders.[41] The application of militarisation had
raised the political temperature in the city and evoked a growing distrust
of Trotsky personally. The attempt had not been so much a function of
the war as part of a strategy to deal with the country's economic
problems. At the same time, the party itself stood as an obstacle in the
way of the complete statist solution and hence itself came under attack.
It was against this background that the debate over reforms in the party
developed in the city.

THE PARTY DEBATE: FIRST PHASE

While the party and trade union debates were part of the same general
search for a way out of the economic and political impasse of war

communism, they were nevertheless distinct movements. Both sought to temper the centralism and *dirigisme* of Bolshevism as it had developed during the civil war, but they focused on different aspects of the problem. The party debate concentrated on developments within the party, both in terms of changes in its composition and its organisation. The problem was admitted by the TsK in its report to the X Party Congress in March 1921 which argued that the party weeks and general recruitment policies had weakened the integrity of the party, and that the rank-and-file party member now had more in common with the ordinary non-party worker than with the *verkhi*, the party leadership.[42] At the same time the TsK insisted that the 'ideological temper' of the party had changed because of a large intake of former members of other parties. Both arguments, stressing social factors, devalued the specific political criticisms of the oppositions. These centred on the bureaucratism and inefficiency of the leadership groups which had allegedly given rise to 'petty tutelage' over lower soviet and party organisations. While agreeing that a gulf had developed between the party and soviet leadership and the working class, which manifested itself in privileges and inequality,[43] the TsK ingenuously argued that the bureaucratism itself had led to the breach and therefore avoided analysing the factors which had given rise to the bureaucratism in the first instance.

In the spring and summer of 1920 the conflict gave rise to a series of tortuous organisational contests for dominance over the various party committees in the city (and *guberniya*). The first major incident in this growing crystallisation of positions took place in Gorodskoi *raion*. For months, as at the 9 January 1920 city party conference, there had been growing criticism directed against the alleged inefficiency and authoritarianism of the existing committees. The Gorodskoi RK itself had long been accused of not devoting enough attention to work in the *raion*.[44] At a delegate meeting on 27 April, its critics, including Ignatov, long an opponent of 'bureaucratism', S. P. Medvedev and R. I. Berezin, surged to power and took four out of the five places on the RK bureau.[45] A flurry of organisational reforms were launched designed not only at overcoming the vertical division within the party but also at raising the party's standing among the 'non-party masses'.[46] The Ignatov style democratic reforms were designed to revive the party's leading role within the framework of political hegemony rather than a depoliticised administrative dominance. They posed a threat only to the entrenched habits of the party bureaucrats. The latter's attitude was revealed by the storm of protest which greeted P. Zaslavskii's proposal at a meeting of RK secretaries on 3 May 1920 that two or three rank-and-file cell members should be invited to attend delegate meetings in order to encourage them to play a more active role. The scandalised secretaries argued that the measure would destroy the *delovoi* (businesslike) atmosphere of the meetings.[47]

A specific apparat ideology of brisk executive action, to be *delovoi*, had developed in the party, as in the army, at the expense of debate and participation. The ability to 'get things done' is one of the central features of Bolshevism in power.[48] In war and at the fronts this had been accepted as a necessary evil but as victory approached there was a growing unease at its social and political consequences – the divisions within the party and the debasement of the political process. The very classification of party members accentuated the divison. In Sokol'ni-cheskii *raion*, for example, 208 members were registered as 'responsible party workers' at this time, the *verkhi*, and the other 2300 members presumably constituted the *nizy*.[49] As the year passed it became rare for the *verkhi/nizy* division not to be raised at party meetings. Kotov, for example, an arch-disciplinarian and hence a supporter of Trotsky's plans, commented that the 30 August Sokol'nicheskii *raion* delegate meeting had been exceptional precisely because the 'usual demagogy' on the split had not dominated the meeting, and instead it had been conducted in a *delovoi* way. A new RK had been elected and 'an atmosphere of mutual respect and trust had been established between the RK and the cells'.[50]

While the tensions in the MPO accumulated, the glorious vistas opened up by the Red Army's advance on Warsaw relegated the debate to the background for a time. At the emergency Moscow *Guberniya* Conference (21–22 August 1920) the delegates were inspired by Bukharin's and Sorin's reports on the prospects for international revolution as Lenin revived the idea of a revolutionary war.[51] The Soviet victories appeared to offer a solution to the impasse and the conference called for yet more sacrifices to ensure success at the front.[52] The Polish war encouraged the continuation of wartime policies at a time when the pressure for change was approaching a critical level. At the conference itself, Zelenskii's report on the work of the MK was followed by speeches once again criticising its shortcomings. A commission was entrusted with drafting a resolution incorporating the proposals for reforming the MK.[53] Its work, however, was pre-empted by the crisis which now enveloped the MPO.

The signal for a major revolt against the old style of party work was given in the heavily proletarian Baumanskii party organisation. In spring 1920 the Baumanskii revisional commission, the majority of whose members were later to join the Workers' Opposition, issued a devastating indictment of the work of the *raion* committee for 1919 and early 1920. It accused the RK of exceeding its authority, deciding questions that should have been settled by the organisation as a whole, of stifling party cells, and so on. All this, in their view, had led to 'the death of living thought' in the *raion*. The report alleged that those bold enough to have their own opinions, including senior and long-time party members, had been removed from party work, and that cells had been suborned by pressure from the apparatus.[54] These were to become the standard complaints of the Workers' Opposition. Their analysis had a resonance far beyond the borders of their *raion* and encompassed the whole structure of power as it had developed since the revolution. Already, at the IX Party Congress, Kiselev, a leading figure in the Workers' Opposition, had complained that the party centre had a tendency to 'suffocate' thought in the localities.[55] The notion of the 'suffocation' of civil society in Eastern Europe by the authorities has become one of the central themes of observers of these countries, but here we see the concept in the context of the first sustained attempt in a Soviet-type regime to maintain, within the party at least, a political sphere independent of administrative functions where 'living thought' could breathe and challenge the leadership. This in a sense is the secret coda of the endless repetition of the charge of 'bureaucratism' heard since the foundation of war communism, and the refrain of Aleksandra Kollontai's pamphlet of early 1921 *The Workers' Opposition*.

The criticisms of the Baumanskii RK ended with a call 'for the necessary conclusions to be drawn'. The report prompted an unsuccessful 'coup' against the old RK, on the lines of the earlier takeover in Gorodskoi *raion*, at a meeting of 28 August 1920. The oppositionists roundly condemned the emergence of the *verkhi* and they elected a troika for the co-ordination of further actions, and in particular to organise an opposition presence at the forthcoming national party conference and congress. The group had breached the unwritten rule against the formation of a 'faction', and the matter was taken up by yet another commission appointed by the MK. Its conclusion, presented to the MK plenum of 20 September 1920, stated that the 28 August meeting had been conspiratorial by dint of the creation of a 'leading organ' in the form of a troika which constituted the kernel of a 'separate organisation'. The commission warned the offenders that a repetition of the incident might lead to expulsion from the party, and meanwhile severely reprimanded them and recommended their suspension from the party for six months. The MK plenum itself, however, contained several people who were in sympathy with the oppositionists' claim that they had only tried to 'identify the party's ailments' and 'to refresh party work', and the plenum now limited itself to issuing a 'severe censure' to the meeting's organisers and forbade them to hold a responsible post for three months.[56]

Splits within the party leadership in Moscow, therefore, enabled the opposition movements to survive and gain ground. They met with some success in other areas, such as Khamovnicheskii, where 'fresh' communist workers from some of the largest factories in the *raion* were elected to an enlarged RK.[57] Later this measure was to degenerate into a convenient method of packing committees with suitable voting fodder, but at this time it was a key Workers' Opposition demand. The relatively tolerant attitude of the TsK secretaries Krestinskii, Preobrazhenskii and L. P. Serebryakov[58] allowed the oppositionists to gain ground, and on the eve of the IX Conference the whole party was drawn into the controversy. The party leadership was faced with a clear challenge from sections of its own rank and file led by the oppositionists. The TsK admitted that there was indeed a gulf between the rank-and-file communists and certain leaders but ascribed it to 'incorrect relations' between them and the abuse of power and privileges. All provincial committees were to form commissions to investigate the grievances of communists.[59] Ignatov, Sapronov and some MK members were included in a party commission to look into the problem of the *verkhi* and privileges. It recommended that control commissions should be formed in the centre and in the localities, and insisted that all party members were to be involved in party work by being assigned (*prikreplennye*) to a cell.[60]

The depth of feeling was acknowleged by the MK in its report for September 1920.[61] In one of two key documents on the eve of the conference the MK argued that the two-fold split between, on the one hand, the party and mass organisations such as the unions, and, on the other, within the party engendered by the need for 'iron discipline', was inevitable up to the time that the proletariat established its hegemony. In other words, until then not only the party but its leadership in particular was the guarantor of the success of the revolution.[62] Absent from this analysis, and from the second document, the MK's theses for the IX Conference, were any but the most general proposals for the transition to 'proletarian hegemony'. The second document even insisted that 'centralised military–proletarian forms of dictatorship' would have to continue until 'the final victory of the international proletariat'.[63] The forms of party organisation were determined by the tasks the party set itself and were therefore invested with the sanctity of its ultimate aims, and an almost insuperable barrier was erected to immediate radical party reforms. The document conceded the rote nature of most party meetings, their intellectual torpidity, and that a bureaucracy had emerged isolated from the masses and with a tendency to escape from party control, but insisted that this could be remedied by ensuring that all communists fulfilled their party duties. This period was remarkable for the frankness with which the party's ills were analysed, and in general the MK provided one of the most sophisticated defences of the political regime of war communism, though avoided taking too close a look at the structural components of the problems. The proponents of reform did their case no good by insisting that 'bureaucratism' had a social base. In a series of articles A. F. Myasnikov rebutted the opposition's facile claims that the *verkhi* could be identified with the intelligentsia on the justified grounds that many of the former, especially in the *raion* party leaderships, were proletarian themselves and equally isolated from the workers.[64] He conceded that the mass of the workers had lost their enthusiasm and that the non-party conferences had turned into banal meetings to which the masses were indifferent.[65]

The improved military situation and the pressure for reform were reflected at the IX Party Conference in late September. It marked the high point of the reform movement in the party and was therefore in marked contrast to the X Party Congress held in March of the following year. In his report on the party, Zinoviev admitted a range of defects but vitiated his own reform proposals by insisting that their full implementation would have to wait for more propitious circumstances, and, in the meantime, 'iron discipline' was to be maintained.[66] Nevertheless, the majority of the concrete recommendations of the above documents, such as more open soviet and party meetings, more reports and discussions, freer criticism, and the formation of control commissions, were adopted.[67] The major achievement of the IX Conference was to establish a certain model of desired reform, even if in practice little was achieved. The great problem, however, was that these reforms were considered in isolation from the pressing economic crisis and were posited within the context of the continuation of war communism. At the X Congress a few months later this model of party reform was largely jettisoned as part of the package of reforms which were to lead to the introduction of the New Economic Policy. Not for the last time, while the criticisms of the system's inadequacies were radical, the remedies were decidedly tame.

At first it appeared that the IX Conference had irreversibly shifted the practice of power towards a more open and participatory system. The

MK took the reforms seriously and on 26 October adopted a wide-ranging instruction on democratising party life. The aim was 'to attract the masses into active participation in the most important questions of party and soviet life'. To this end all party committee meetings were to be open to the next tier down, and they were to act as fora for discussion of party, economic and soviet questions, and at these extended sessions co-rapporteurs were to be allowed. Full discussion was to be permitted on all key questions until decisions had been taken at a higher level, though the criticism was to be 'healthy' and not 'demagogic'. A uniform wage and standard rations were to be introduced for all party leaders.[68] Despite its caveats, this instruction served as a charter for the debate that now unfolded over party democracy, and allowed extended discussion in the trade union debate.

The period after the IX Conference saw the full emergence of the oppositions into, as Myasnikov put it, 'a significant and "threatening" force'.[69] The trade union controversy at this stage was restricted to the upper reaches of the party and so the issues of the party debate were still in focus. In Baumanskii *raion* the conciliatory attitude of the MK had not restored peace. The opposition launched a campaign for the full rehabilitation of those punished, and they continued their assault on the RK, which they accused of stifling criticism and of being isolated from the workers.[70] Their demands for new elections were finally crowned with success and at the 11 October *raion* delegate meeting they obtained a majority on the RK, and on 12 October at the first session of the new *raion* soviet plenum, 83 per cent of whom were Bolsheviks, they gained control of the soviet's EC.[71] In this way the Workers' Opposition took control of the party and soviet apparatus in one of Moscow's largest *raion*s. In Gorodskoi *raion* the Ignatovtsy, who styled themselves as the 'group of active workers of the *raion*s of Moscow', now moved beyond the 'constitutionalist' position of the Democratic Centralists and shifted towards the Baumanskii Workers' Opposition views on the need to revive inner-party democracy in the *raion*s. They proposed a radical critique of the 'lifeless' way that the party ran the city. Since April 1920 they had been putting their ideas into practice in their *raion*, but after the IX Conference they went even further in introducing the elements of genuine party democracy. Party structures were to be opened to the participation of all members down to the very smallest cell, and elections were to be used as genuine tests of confidence in the RK.[72]

After the IX Conference the MK itself came under increasing criticism from the various oppositionists, though the extent of co-ordination between them is unknown. The Baumanskii group argued that in the six months since its election the MK had lacked a 'single and firm general organisational line'. They claimed that among the 'most conscious and active segment' of the Moscow working class, whom they represented, there was growing a 'healthy discontent with the policies of the MK'. Under pressure, the MK acceded to opposition demands for an emergency *guberniya* party conference to be convened on 20 November, at which the MK could be re-elected.[73] At stake was control over the largest party organisation in the country, which now seemed to be within the grasp of a coalition of oppositions. In the MK itself they gained increasing support and insisted that the punishment of the Workers' Opposition in Baumanskii *raion* should be reviewed.[74] There now followed a bitter struggle for advantage in preparation for the conference. The 26 October instruction had relaxed what was apparently an unwritten convention that only MK members could give political reports, and now any communist could speak as a co-rapporteur at meetings. For six months the oppositions were granted a constitutional platform to advance their views from a position of equality with MK members.

In the run up to the conference, five out of the seven RPOs were to varying degrees critical of the MK. The resolutions expressing a lack of confidence in the MK were only rarely printed in the official Moscow party newspaper *Kommunisticheskii trud* (*Communist Labour*) but were issued by the oppositions in the form of leaflets and distributed in the *raion*s. The controversy breathed new life into the local party organisations. The discussion at a typical delegate meeting of the time in Rogozhsko-Simonovskii *raion* on 12 November went on until well into the night. On that occasion Ignatov emerged triumphant with a majority of the seventy delegates over the resolutions proposed by N. V. Lisitsyn for the RK and Minkov for the MK.[75] One of the other two *raion*s, Sokol'nicheskii, strongly endorsed the MK and urged it to take a hard line against the oppositionists 'who could weaken party members with low consciousness'.[76] In this *raion* it was Kotov, long an exponent of militarised forms in the party, who was clearly the driving force behind the condemnation of the oppositions. A fortnight before the IX Conference he had still been calling for the 'RK apparatus to be transformed on military lines',[77] and obviously the conference had not changed his hard-line Trotskyist views. (It was to be his misfortune that as an organisational hard-liner he was to fall from grace as part of the campaign against Trotskyists in 1925, even though his views were in tune with the emerging Stalinist orthodoxy). In Krasnopresnenskii *raion* in late October, Minkov's and Lisitsyn's motion supporting the MK was passed, but even here it called on the MK to strengthen its control over the Moscow Soviet and the trade unions as part of the battle against bureaucracy and *glavkocracy*.[78] Two opposed concepts of reform were at issue: one called for a more efficient party machine *tout court*; and the other for an improved party mechanism in order to preserve the elements of party democracy. In the selection of delegates to the conference both sides accused each other of insisting on proportionality when they were in minority, and of taking all the seats when in a majority. In principle, proportionality was the rule in these elections and therefore the conference accurately reflected the relative strengths of the positions.

On the eve of the *guberniya* conference the TsK became increasingly concerned about the success of the oppositions in Moscow. After preliminary discussion in the Orgburo and Politburo in early November, the TsK plenum on 9 November decided to reinforce the MK by placing two TsK members onto the new committee to be elected at the conference, and it also sent others to speak in the *raion*s on behalf of the MK.[79] Lenin himself became increasingly worried about the surplus of politics within the party and at the delegate meeting in Baumanskii *raion* on 18 November he criticised not so much the views as the activities of the Workers' Opposition. In the lively discussion following Bukharin's and Ignatov's speeches, Lenin, typically, called for more attention to be devoted to practical economic issues rather than to debate.[80] His attempts to suppress the controversy carried the dangerous implication that politics itself would become increasingly marginalised in the party. His attitude was in tune with the 'no nonsense' approach of the communists returning from the fronts. At an extended meeting of party activists in Rogozhsko-Simonovskii *raion* on 18 November, for example, Myasnikov's attack on the oppositions was vigorously supported by a group who had recently returned from the fronts. They argued that 'the party and party workers require the old party discipline, the hardness (*zakalennost*') of the army'.[81] The official line was bolstered as more and more of the military party activists returned from the fronts. Much later Trotsky identified the army communists as a definite group:

The demobilisaton of the Red Army of five million played no small role in the formation of the bureaucracy. The victorious commanders assumed leading posts in the local soviets, in economy, in education, and they persistently introduced everywhere that regime which had ensured success in the civil war. Thus on all sides the masses were pushed away from the actual participation in the leadership of the country.[82]

The root of the problem lay in the very organisation of the army on traditional lines, for which Trotsky himself had been responsible, and against which the Left Communists in 1918 had warned. Not only were the rank-and-file factory communists as a group weakened by the mobilisation but once drafted they were deprived of an effective controlling voice. The party commanders and activists imbued the military spirit while serving at the fronts and the mobilisations reinforced the spirit of 'campaignology' in the party. Faced with one threat after another the party centres consolidated their prerogatives over the party member and took on quasi-military forms. The shock style permeated all aspects of the MPO's work. Nevertheless, while the changes in the MPO were undoubtedly powerfully influenced by the war, they were not determined by it. Military methods were accepted as necessary, but as soon as the chance arose they were mitigated, as in the abolition of the emergency dictatorial body KOM. The civil war did not guarantee the victory of the centralisers over the democratisers: this was to be the legacy of these debates themselves.

The *Guberniya* Party Congress (20–22 November), with 289 voting delegates, allowed all the main groups to have their representatives on the presidium.[83] Rykov reported on the economic situation and Bukharin gave a low-key report on production propaganda. Lenin's main address on 21 November once again stressed economic reconstruction as the main task following the military victory. His speech was remarkable, however, in that for the first time it was announced publicly that the party was undergoing a crisis and that it contained opposition groupings. On the party debate he offered no initiative and instead called for 'the most rapid liquidation of the so-called opposition line'.[84] The report on the MK's work over the past six months aroused the greatest controversy. Kamenev's resolution on behalf of the MK admitted that the war had curtailed inner-party democracy, but insisted that victory 'would create the possibility and necessity to move on to a new stage in the internal organisational life of the party'. The basic premise for reforms, it argued, was the 'merciless elimination' of all intrigues and 'unprincipled little groups' and for party work to be conducted in a *delovoi* way.[85] Several concrete proposals were adopted to improve the work of the MK and to 'revive' the communist fractions in the trade unions.[86]

Ignatov's motion argued that the MK's poor organisational and political leadership had resulted in 'pettyfogging supervision' over the *raion*s. The MK lacked faith in the *raion*s' ability to manage their own affairs. Furthermore, preoccupation with the leadership of the unions and soviets had isolated the MK from the working class. A group on the

MK were accused of blocking the reforms adopted by the IX Conference. The emergence of opposition in the party was subdued by means of 'surgical operations' which encouraged passivity out of fear of reprisals. The motion insisted that such criticisms were not new but that for two and a half years the opposition had called for the application of democratic centralism.[87] The voting revealed a great degree of support for these views: Ignatov's motion obtained 124 (45 per cent of the votes cast) to Kamenev's 154.[88] Following their defeat the oppositions twice met in separate conclave and declared that they absolved themselves of further responsibility for the work of the MK. Lenin later called these meetings the policy of the 'two rooms'.[89]

Voting for the new MK took place on 22 November. There had initially been two lists but the majority at the conference withdrew its own[90] in favour of one drawn up by the Politburo and Lenin on 19 November.[91] They decided to enlarge the MK from thirty-one to thirty-nine members in order to satisfy opposition demands for greater representation of the lower levels of the party and workers (see Table 4.1 on page 103). The idea was to replace at least half of the MK to the benefit of worker communists still on the shopfloor, to take in some activists from other organisations, including F. A. Sergeev (Artem) who was elected MK secretary replacing Myasnikov, and to admit some members of the opposition, such as Sapronov and Ignatov, and thus to avoid an overt split. The broadening and 'workerising' of the MK, the attempt to deal with a political problem by social measures, prefigured Lenin's expansion of the TsK in 1922 as part of the attempt to counter the emergence of a party bureaucracy. The opposition failed to secure an MK in which membership was proportional to the strength of the groups at the conference; Lenin scorned the idea as rendering the MK *nedelovoi*.[92] The TsK list was adopted with 164 votes[93] and the oppositionists were included, as it were, on sufferance and not as of right. The oppositionists had been defeated at the conference, but the extent of their support had been registered, as had their right to exist. They had put forward alternative inner-party organisational policies to those of the leadership and were on the verge of organising separately. This opposition was indeed a 'threatening' force and in many ways the most sustained and coherent seen by the Soviet regime.

Following the conference, the party debate continued with, for example, a strong attack on bureaucratism by the Workers' Opposition at a general meeting in Zamoskvorech'e,[94] but, in general, attention was increasingly concentrated on the trade union debate. At the moment when the party opposition was on the verge of achieving real change the trade union debate emerged to undermine it. For a time the issue of party reform was lost in the welter of conflicting positions and manoeuvring associated with the second debate, and by the time the party debate once again emerged in the run-up to the X Congress the very premises on which the calls for party democracy had been founded had changed owing to the bitterness and divisiveness of the union debate and because of the tide of popular protest.

ORGANISATIONAL REFORM

The period of intense debate in late 1920 was accompanied by attempts to implement political and economic reforms. It was at this time that the Moscow trade unions launched a campaign against privileges and tried to mitigate their own 'bureaucratism' by holding meetings in factories, and other measures. The Moscow Soviet was also affected by the spirit of reform and began to hold meetings in factories and in general accepted the need to change its working practices. The situation at the fronts had improved dramatically. For the first time in three years no major armies confronted the Soviet state; the truce with Poland held; and on 16 November 1920 the Allied blockade was lifted. The 'small civil war', nevertheless, continued in the rear against peasant groups burdened by the exactions of forced requisitioning. The economic system of war communism itself was intensified as small enterprises were nationalised but at the same time some attempts were inaugurated to adjust war communism and make it more responsive to local needs as some of the smaller plants hitherto controlled by *glavki* were transferred to local economic bodies. With all its faults, war communism was seen as an evolving system which corresponded to the economic and political requirements of the period. The key question was whether the economic reforms and the attempts at democratisation and the elimination of bureaucratism were compatible with the system as it had developed since 1918. The changes of this period were two-sided as democratic reform clashed with authoritarian reform: one trend was inspired by the reforming sentiments of the IX Conference and the attempts to democratise the political structure of war communism; the other emphasised the isolation of the regime and put efficiency above democracy. Above all, the oppositionists tried to restore political control over the increasingly efficient party apparatus.

In the spirit of the IX Party Conference and the November *guberniya* conference, the MPO itself set about a programme of reform. Its key elements were the improvement of the work of the party departments and the cells, and the increased effectiveness of the agitprop apparatus, to combat the rising discontent in the city. Artem, the new MK secretary, outlined a series of reform measures to implement the November conference decisions to the MK on 1 December 1920. More general party meetings were to be organised and cell secretaries were to be involved in party work. Responsibilities to implement reforms were allocated among MK members. A. I. Krinitskii set about improving the MK apparatus, Artem himself became head of the communist fraction in the Moscow Soviet, and Ignatov was sent as MK representative to the bitterly divided Komsomol organisation.[95] Oppositionists were given posts, and in general it should be borne in mind that as the debate unfolded its contributors were usually burdened with administrative and political tasks. The democratic reformers as much as the authoritarians were responsible for the 'internal metamorphosis of the party'. For the first time since the beginning of the civil war the MK had a reserve of experienced cadres at its disposal and could devote itself to organising the party itself. The forms that this took were no longer determined, if they had ever been, by military tasks, and now the centralising practices of the war period were tempered by the reform programmes of the September and November party conferences as the two models of the postwar organisational system developed.

In January 1921 the MK set itself an ambitious programme to improve the work of the party organisation. Relations within and between departments were to be defined to avoid parallelism, cells were to be drawn closer to their higher party instance and their work improved. The MK vigorously set about implementing its policy of September 1920 that emphasised the cells as the main priority.[96] A uniform system of party committees was to be instituted at all levels and their relations with the party fractions in the soviets, trade unions and Komsomol were to be defined.[97] While much had been made of these points during the civil war, little had been achieved, and indeed the importance of the war period and its enduring legacy was that it had seen the formulation of the tasks for the succeeding period. The war had confirmed the effectiveness of Bolshevik organisational principles, but its second face, that of participation and control, had not entirely disappeared. During the war the 'shock' approach to mobilisations and party work in general through such campaigns as 'weeks' had disrupted progress towards the effective integration of all party members irrespective of their posts into a uniform party system. As the November conference had illustrated, the premium was now on effective and detailed guidance from the centre avoiding 'petty tutelage' balanced by competent lower involvement, and in this programme there was enough to satisfy all groups in the party.

The major victor of the end of the civil war was the MK. It consolidated its position as the supreme political arbiter in the city and established its control over all party members. As part of the reform programme the political departments in transport had been abolished in September 1920, restoring normal trade union practices, returning the MK's prerogatives, and vindicating its stand earlier in 1920 against party militarisation. In January 1921 the army cells were directly integrated into the RPOs by the abolition of the MK military department. The introduction of a uniform party ticket and more accurate registration of members enabled the MK to plan the disposition of communists more effectively. The MK was now redistributing party members from soviet offices to factory cells, moving members from the city to the countryside, concentrating resources in the *udarnyi* enterprises, and systematising the selection of party members from cells for more 'responsible' work.[98] The MK jealously defended its rights over the disposition of communists and warned that punitive measures would be taken by institutions that poached members demobilised from the army.[99] With widespread mobilisations continuing for various economic and administrative purposes, in January 1921 V. N. Yakovleva, who had become MK secretary in Artem's absence, insisted that all appointments had to be made through the MK and warned against *raion* organisations 'seizing' demobilised communists.[100] The consolidation of the apparatus's ability to deploy party members as it saw fit coincided with the debates and was a factor in them. The Baumanskii oppositionists had long accused the MK of abusing the right. Kollontai protested at the IX Conference against the practice of sending inconvenient people who criticised too frankly 'to eat peaches' far away from Moscow.[101] On the eve of the November conference, Bukharin revealed the potency of this weapon when he had argued that 'we must heal the Moscow organisation' by getting rid of the most quarrelsome elements and replacing them with new people from outside Moscow, though he stressed that even the most extreme people were not to be expelled from the party.[102]

One of the critical issues which tested the MK's ability to organise the mass of membership at this time was participation in the *subbotniks*. There had long been criticism over the irregular participation of communists[103] and non-attendance was considered a breach of party discipline.[104] An MK circular of September 1920 admitted that up to 90 per cent of communists evaded the work on one pretext or another, including almost all the responsible and most middle-level party workers. The MK threatened that in the light of the IX Conference decisions against privileges, such a massive avoidance of party duties would be countered by a range of punitive measures up to expulsion. The *subbotnik* departments were strengthened by the addition of full-time activists.[105] A movement that had begun with some idealism had, as far as many communists were concerned, degenerated into an irrational waste of time and labour. At the X Congress Ignatov called them a 'burden' and declared that they had become a purely formal exercise.[106] Rafail argued that the soul of the 'great beginning' (*velikii pochin*) had been destroyed by the payment of extra rations as a reward for attendance, the obligatory nature of participation twice a month, and punishment for non-attendance.[107] They were defended by G. Korzinov, head of the MK *subbotnik* department, on the grounds that they made up for labour shortages and insisted that they still acted as a model of revolutionary labour.[108] In spite of the MK's strictures, attendance by communists and non-communists alike continued to decline into early 1921.[109] Despite their unpopularity an MK commission on the *subbotniks* in January 1921 insisted that the active participation of communists could transform them from 'barracks type compulsion', similar to 'forced labour', to 'schools of communist labour', and reduced attendance to once a month.[110] With the introduction of NEP the *subbotniks* continued as an inspirational movement but were organised much more rarely. The unlimited right of party committees to deploy party members was an important development, but the resistance revealed by the *subbotnik* movement's decline illustrated both the limitations of mobilisational endeavour and the general vacuity of war communist enthusiasm.

The fate of the control commissions further illustrates the ambiguity of reform implementation at this time. Prior to their establishment at the IX Conference a special MK commission had been established to investigate responsible soviet and party workers with the aim of eliminating *komissarstvo* (domineering behaviour) and bureaucratism,[111] and the oppositionists hoped that this would be institutionalised by the creation of control commissions. However, their functions were defined soon after as less to scourge bureaucratism than to overcome factionalism in the party by clearing it of 'petty bourgeois elements',[112] and they were now allowed to investigate not only misdemeanours on the part of communists but also to combat the alleged unhealthy tendencies in party organisations.[113] In this way the oppositions themselves became the object of scrutiny. Such a development forcefully illustrates the opposed concepts of reform in the *post bellum* period. These commissions were elected in the *raion*s at the same meetings which elected delegates to the November *guberniya* conference, and at the conference the Moscow *guberniya* control commission (MKK) was elected. The commissions can be likened to the workers' inspection movement (Rabkrin). Both suffered from the distrust of higher officials for grass-roots or mass-based control mechanisms. The commissions played no significant role in the politics of the city up to March 1921 and thereafter fused with the party hierarchy[114] and became yet another weapon in the armoury of control over party members.

The Moscow Soviet itself was not immune from the reforming mood in late 1920. In a set of theses presented to the II Moscow Guberniya Conference of Soviets (15–17 December 1920) Kamenev admitted that the soviets were moribund, bureaucratic, and the plenums devoid of political debate. Soviet affairs were conducted by a small group of about twenty people who, he argued, against their will became bureaucratic irrespective of how much they might inveigh against bureaucratism. Such an admission of the structural sources of bureaucratism was Democratic Centralist in tone, and indeed in spirit also the range of radical reforms which he proposed went far beyond the conventional denunciations of the evils of bureaucratism by the exponents of 'workers' democracy' such as Zinoviev (see page 254). The powers of the soviet sections were to be increased, the plenary sessions rejuvenated, closer links established between deputies and factories, and open sessions of the soviet held. In resounding terms he insisted that the political and economic powers of the soviets in the centre and in the localities and of their executive bodies (VTsIK in the centre) should be extended as part of the transition to peaceful conditions.[115] These proposals indicated the broad support for practical reform at this time within the Bolshevik leadership. However, as Dvinov comments:

> The problem for Kamenev, and some of the other Bolsheviks who at this stage wavered in favour of 'proletarian freedom', was how to preserve the soviets as meaningful political institutions given the fact that decisions were taken elsewhere. How could serious debate take place without opposition and with the soviet simply a party fraction. Hence Kamenev's attempts to breathe some life into the soviet by creating sections, the idea of non-party deputies, and the closer links with the factories.[116]

The soviet conference itself met in an optimistic mood.[117] Ignatov and Sapronov shared the presidium with mainstream representatives such as Kamenev, Lisitsyn and Uryvaev. To counter the social analysis of bureaucratism put forward by the oppositionists, Kamenev argued that even if all the bourgeois specialists were sacked, bureaucracy would still not disappear. Instead of such a superficial view, he insisted, the real reasons for bureaucracy lay in the poverty and backwardness of the country and in the creation of an extremely complex system of state management without the basic elements available to support such a structure.[118] The time was ripe, he argued, for the working class itself to learn state management and for the drift of power to the centre to be reversed.[119] His speech, so positive in tone and content, had no time for superficial analyses such as the 'declassing of the proletariat'. A reform resolution was passed on the basis of his proposals, and even Trotsky no longer argued for more centralisation but restricted his muted comments to noting that the debate was between centralisers and decentralisers.[120]

We do not know what pressure was brought to bear on the malleable Kamenev, but at the VIII Congress of Soviets (22-29 December 1920) his tone had changed and he no longer spoke of reform but concentrated on the economic reconstruction programme, the theme of the congress which saw the adoption of the GOELRO programme for the electrification of Russia. Political reforms which could threaten the status quo, accepted by Kamenev at the Moscow conference, it now seemed were being deliberately upstaged by grandiose economic plans. The measures adopted to revive the soviets were little more than cosmetic, including the recommendation that ECs were to meet as often as possible in factories.[121] The momentum for soviet reform was lost, and on 4 March 1921 an instruction on the Moscow Soviet was adopted which stressed only the need to make it more efficient, and to this end power was further concentrated by the creation of an inner *ispolkom* and inner presidium. In July of that year the soviet's collegia were 'workerised'; and the percentage of workers 'from the bench' rose from between ten and fifteen to sixty.[122] Now formal workerisation was to substitute for genuine reform: social responses for structural analyses.

A foretaste of the type of changes that would take place with the transition to NEP can be seen from the work of the Sokol'nicheskii RK in the last four months of 1920. In this *raion*, as we have seen, the reform movement gained little support, and indeed, it was vigorously opposed by the disciplinarian Kotov. The RK argued that the 'organisational crisis' in the party evoked by the transition from military to economic priorities could only be overcome if the activity of the party masses was channelled into an organisational course:

> We must always remember that the struggle on the economic front demands no less a centralised party apparatus, no less discipline, than the military front.[123]

Hence even before Lenin's argument at the XI Party Congress that a retreat required greater discipline than an advance, this *raion* had formulated a programme which justified the increased power of the party apparatus in time of peace because of the nature of the economic tasks facing the country. A strategy had been developed in which reform came to signify only the improved effectiveness of the committees themselves, and the other half of the reform proposals, the democratisation of party and soviet structures and the restoration of their competencies, was lost. The democratic reforms were deeply flawed because the structural roots of the problem were barely understood, and the reformers themselves were deeply compromised. Ignatov himself, for example, supervised the aftermath of the destruction of Komsomol autonomy. Nevertheless, while the profundity of the reform proposals must not be exaggerated, they had gained significant support and achieved some successes. Bolshevik ideology, like war communism itself, permitted some flexibility within the overall pattern of authority. The end of the war and not the war itself permitted the consolidation of the powers of the committees over their own organisations and as the general manager of the social bodies in their localities. However, before this strategy could be implemented the party was to witness the most bitter round in the inner-party controversy, the trade union debate.

8 The Defeat of the Reform Movements

THE CRISIS OF THE REGIME

From the summer of 1920 the economic crisis gradually developed into a political crisis of the regime. Strife within the party was paralleled by peasant uprisings and worker protest culminating in the Kronstadt events of March 1921. The atmosphere, an observer noted, was 'steeped in the spirit of protest'.[1] It was at this time that Bertrand Russell asserted that free elections would have swept the Bolsheviks from power. Food shortages were compounded by disorganisation on the railways, and a drought not only spoilt much of the harvest but also made drinking water unsafe in Moscow. Fires in the peat workings and forests reduced fuel supplies and smothered the city in a pall of smoke for several weeks, much to the inconvenience of the delegates to the II Congress of the III International in July. In September, cold weather set in earlier than usual. To compound the difficulties there were rumours that the government was planning to close the markets and stamp out the vestiges of free trade.[2] In short, the period was marked by the collapse of the war communist economy.[3] Manifestations of discontent were made easier by the fact that the immediate threat of a White restoration had been lifted, while hopes for an imminent socialist revolution on a world scale had declined and with it the prospects of assistance from the outside to halt the all too obvious spiral of decline in industry.

Disturbances in the city were often provoked by food and other shortages, and these were exacerbated by the emphasis on supplying the needs of the army. The army itself at the close of war communism appeared less reliable. It had changed from being a predominantly working-class body to one in which peasants comprised two-thirds of the soldiers in 1919 and over three-quarters in August 1920.[4] The majority of army communists themselves were peasant youths, 'village types, not conscious, less influenced by the spirit of communism than the proletarian masses'.[5] A quarter of the MPO consisted of soldiers, with the largest influx of nearly 8000 during the party week in October 1919. With the creation of the MK military department there had been a sustained attempt to mould the political consciousness of the military communists, with more meetings, lectures and non-party Red Army

240

conferences.[6] Despite this, the conferences in the city from late 1919 saw acrimonious criticism of the government, and this probably explains the steep decline in the number held in mid-1920. At the end of the year they were revived, as Myasnikov had recommended earlier, simply as Red Army conferences. But by mid-1920 the signs of discontent in the Moscow garrison were clear. In August 1920 an alleged 'mutiny' took place in the city's barracks when bast shoes (*lapti*) were issued instead of boots.[7] In September the MK admitted that conditions were very hard, with a lack of warm clothing and food, and conceded that this was used by 'counter-revolutionary propaganda', but claimed that the communists still retained their dominance and that the grumbling was not 'tainted with counter-revolution'.[8] This would appear to be an over-optimistic assessment. The six Red Army (non-party) conferences in October 1920 revealed that the soldiers were 'dissatisfied with military and civil "bureaucratism" and the arbitrariness of the local authorities'.[9] The authorities were worried enough to organise a series of emergency meetings of commissars, political organisers, and cell secretaries, and drafted more activists into the MK military department.[10] According to S. P. Mel'gunov, about 2–300 soldiers of the Moscow garrison were shot during the disturbances from late 1920.[11] Desperate attempts were made to improve conditions by increasing supplies for the army, and the working day in the city was extended to ten hours, with priority in the clothing and leather industries.[12] These measures, together with the punitive ones, were sufficient to contain the crisis. The unreliability of the army in the capital, somewhat reminiscent of 1917, was undoubtedly a factor in the termination of the economic policies of war communism soon after. At the same time, the concentration of the meagre resources on the army and the lengthened working day only increased the hardships of the civilian population.

From the summer of 1920 the supply shortages became steadily worse, much to the alarm of the party authorities.[13] From 21 January 1921 only thirty-three wagons of grain a day were arriving instead of the minimum of forty-four required to feed the city. On 22 January the bread issue in the heartlands of the regime, Moscow, Petrograd, Kronstadt and Ivanovo-Voznesensk, was cut by a third. Rations were further cut on 30 January for office staff and those with light work.[14] From this point sporadic disturbances developed into a general assault on the war communist system. There are few details on the disturbances in Moscow and therefore it is not possible to analyse the structure of the protest movement, its leadership and organisation, except to suggest that while the Mensheviks and SRs did play some part in them, their

criticisms were supported by a broad stratum of workers disillusioned
with the current policies. As Marcel Liebman put it, the Mensheviks
became 'the political voice of a *working class* reality'.[15] The pattern of the
movement, however, is fairly clear. Meetings in factories and plants
gathered and criticised government policies, beginning with supply and
developing into general political criticism. Complaints against the food
shortages were now joined by demands for free trade, free labour, and
the easing of repression. There are only very general indications of inter-
plant contacts, usually confined to synchronising street demonstrations,
and even less of attempts to form a national movement comparable
to the workers' conferences of 1918. However, by insisting that the
disturbances were no more than supply riots, manipulated by Menshevik and SR counter-revolutionaries, the government imputed to the
participants a pre-industrial level of consciousness. When communists
at meetings, however, suggested that the discontent was associated
purely with 'stomachs' the comment usually aroused a storm of
protest.[16] Food shortages were the catalyst that brought out the
underlying dissatisfaction of the workers. Industry and society were no
longer governed by capitalist social relations but by new patterns of
authority which Trotsky and Bukharin insisted required a high degree of
coercion. It was against this physical and political coercion that the
protests were directed, and therefore by implication against the
Bolshevik regime itself. The working class had been severely weakened
and changed during the war, and yet, in a paradoxical inversion of
Marxism, while it may no longer have been a class 'in itself' it was still a
class 'for itself'. The authorities ascribed to the movement no more than
what Leninists called a trade union consciousness, but even the best of
the party thinkers of the time were unable to develop a satisfactory
general theory of the relationship between the working class and the new
state. The movement itself could only articulate the first demands, often
couched in traditional language, of the as yet not entirely depoliticised
labour force against the socialist state.

The first response of the civil authorities to the disturbances was
increased repression, but the Cheka's heavy-handedness itself was a
cause of the disturbances. Between December 1918 and November 1920
the MChK admitted to shooting 578 people and arresting just under
40 000, nearly 6 per cent of the adult population.[17] According to
Mel'gunov, 345 people were shot in Moscow during the period that the
death penalty was officially abolished from 18 January to 24 May 1920.[18]
On the eve of the abolition the MChK was alleged to have summarily
executed about 2–3000 prisoners in Moscow and thus presented the

government with a *fait accompli*.[19] Of those arrested about two-thirds were released. For example, of the 17 426 arrested in the first six months of 1920, 11 344 (65 per cent) were freed.[20] The sole inspection by Rabkrin of thirty-eight places of detention in Moscow in April 1920 recommended the release of 3074 prisoners, 42 per cent of the number incarcerated.[21] The conditions under which the large number of juveniles were imprisoned, many on suspicion alone or for stealing food, was particularly scandalous.[22] Still, the Cheka was especially active in late 1920. In November, for example, the MChK sent three people to prison for five years apiece for 'spreading provocative rumours subverting the authority of Soviet power'. The MChK vowed that it would 'deal mercilessly' with all counter-revolutionaries who spread panic and rumours which could be used by enemies of the republic.[23] At the same time, as a prophylactic measure in view of the widespread rumours of an impending uprising in the city, the Cheka called for all privately held arms in the city to be handed in, and allowed an amnesty if this was done before 15 January 1921.[24] (The holding of arms at home by non-communists had been made illegal in December 1918.) As the number of striking factories increased some concessions were introduced. In a series of emergency meetings between the MK, the MGSPS, the Moscow Soviet and district party activists, attempts were made to develop a unified response to what was called 'the supply crisis and wage misunderstandings'.[25] The party and trade union commission, formed in November 1920, to improve the living conditions (*byt*) of workers was strengthened by the addition of Cheka representatives in January 1921.[26] Particular attention was paid to the developing crisis in the metal plants, and on 27 January 1921 the MGSPS, now in a more assertive mood, censured the local metalworkers' trade union for not having reported on the situation, and insisted to MSNKh that no economic body in Moscow had the right to close a factory without consultation. Lozovskii was urgently assigned to form a commission to investigate the 'abnormalities' at certain plants and to take the necessary measures. The practice of holding meetings in factories and the other measures mentioned earlier were born out of this crisis atmosphere. At the same time the MGSPS urged the Cheka not to take further repressive measures and for the already announced factory closures to be rescinded.[27]

As in 1917 it was the metalworkers who led the way. Against the crisis background the I Moscow *Guberniya* Metalworkers' Union Conference met in Moscow from 2–4 February. How many of the thousand delegates were communists is not known since no registration appears to have taken place.[28] The first speakers called for the personal safety of the delegates to be guaranteed, a demand accepted by the conference chairman, Smidovich. There then followed, according to one *émigré* source, a flood of passionate denunciations of Bolshevik power. Crimes against the country and workers were listed and individual communists singled out as criminals and liars. A resolution was passed calling for free trade and the replacement of forced requisitioning by a fixed tax in kind.[29] As the report in *Pravda* noted: 'There was a complete break between the party and the masses, and between the masses and the trade unions'.[30] On the last day of the conference Lenin conceded that the relation between the working class and the peasantry could now be reviewed. In other words, his thoughts were now turning to the idea that requisitioning might be replaced by a tax in kind, and indeed he reported that in thirteen *gubernii* requisitioning had been halted.[31] A few days later (8 February 1921) Lenin penned his draft theses on replacing requisitioning by the tax.[32] The conference passed a motion against 'privileged' rations (*spetsstavki*), which were issued to about 10 000 top party leaders, just under 2000 scholars in Moscow, and about 50 000 office-based soldiers in the rear, and against the issue of goods produced in an enterprise as part of wages, especially in the food industry.[33] In his speech Kamenev was correct to claim that they were being reduced.[34] Aware of the unpopularity of these privileges the MGSPS since December 1920 had tried to reduce the numbers receiving them.[35] Opposition to special payments in money or in kind reflected the powerful anti-specialist current prevalent at the time, noted by the chairman of MSNKh at the II Guberniya Soviet Congress in December 1920,[36] and tapped by the Workers' Opposition and the Ignatovtsy. Traditional hostility to the intelligentsia and contemporary loyalty to socialist egalitarianism were intensified by the general scarcity. Kamenev informed the Moscow Soviet plenum on 15 February 1921 that he had proposed the abolition of privileged rations to the TsK because of the metalworkers' resolution, and he called for a campaign against the issue of goods of own production.[37]

The disturbances came to a head in February 1921. The month was marked by severe frosts and in several factories white flags had once again been run up as a traditional mark of protest. In early February a resolution was delivered to the chairman of VTsIK (M. I. Kalinin) by a special delegation of workers from Khamovnicheskii *raion* with three demands: the restoration of free trade; the convocation of a legislative assembly; and an immediate change in economic policy 'which would stop provoking the hostility of other powers' – reflecting the popular belief that the Bolsheviks had brought the civil war on themselves.[38] The Moscow street demonstrations began, significantly enough in the light of Krestinskii's comments on the money printing press as a 'machine gun' against the bourgeois financial system, with a strike at the Vtorov money printing works in Khamovniki on 20 or 21 February. The military units called in refused to open fire, and they were replaced by the armed communist detachments (ChON) who shot at the striking workers, killing and injuring several of them. That evening mass protest meetings were held at the university, on the railways, and at the women's higher education institute. The following day several factories went on strike. About 1500 people took part in a demonstration in Khamovniki and they tried to call out the soldiers. The units in the *raion* barracks, however, were disarmed and locked in as a precaution. All Moscow's communists were now mobilised and organised in armed detachments. There was sporadic shooting as these detachments came across groups of protesters in the streets.[39]

The movement climaxed with a major street demonstration on 23 February in which about 10 000 workers took part. The Bolsheviks and their policies were severely criticised by the speakers. On that day Moscow was placed under martial law with a 24-hour watch on factories by the communist detachments and trustworthy army units. Over the next days leading Soviet personalities such as Kalinin, V. Kuibyshev and Krupskaya were mobilised by the MK to speak in the districts, and on 1 March the Moscow Soviet issued a proclamation calling for calm,[40] for workers not to go on strike, and for soldiers not to give in to 'provocation which, in the guise of solidarity with working people, in fact weakens unity'.[41] Kamenev later admitted that the disturbances were accompanied by a widespread go-slow (*volynka* or *zaderzhka*),[42] an early example of the 'Italian strike' where workers turn up but do not work. In the plants a movement developed for the recall of Bolshevik deputies to the Moscow and district soviets and to replace them, one report claimed, by Mensheviks standing as non-party candidates. Other plants instead of recalling their Bolshevik deputies, sought to bind them with a Menshevik or anarchist mandate (*nakaz*). The Sal'mson plant elected a 'non-party' Menshevik, the Avtoremont plant adopted a Menshevik *nakaz*, and the Manometr plant elected a Menshevik.[43] At the same time wide-scale arrests deprived the movement of its leadership. On 25 February nearly all the activists in the Moscow Menshevik organisation, about 160 people, were arrested[44] and held in Butyrskii gaol (the infamous Butyrka), though some were released after the Kronstadt events and the restoration of order.[45] Those who remained were among the 300 socialists beaten by the Cheka on the night of 25–26 April.[46] Sporadic agitation continued into March. There were disturbances at the Menshevik-dominated Bromlei works on 5 March, the fifth of the year, resulting in the now customary arrest of workers.[47] A general meeting at the plant on 25 March called for new elections to the Moscow Soviet. The management dispersed the meeting but the workers called on other plants to support the calls for new elections. As usual, the ringleaders were arrested. The Moscow Soviet itself initially agreed to hold elections but the TsK had decided to postpone them so that calm could be restored.[48] After a delay of several weeks the elections were, in fact, held in April 1921, accompanied by a bitter campaign and the usual Menshevik allegations of electoral malpractice.[49] The results were remarkable in that the protest vote returned over a quarter of the total as non-party deputies (see Table 6.1 on p. 169). Only half of those eligible voted, and many factories, including some of the largest, did not return communist deputies.[50]

The demands of the Moscow protest movement for the three freedoms – labour, trade and political – and for a freeing of the soviets from party control were echoed in other conferences and cities.[51] But in Kronstadt on 28 February, on the eve of the X Party Congress, the demands provoked an insurrection which was brutally suppressed. The Moscow disturbances gradually subsided because of the lack of practical support from the soldiers and the actions of the Cheka and armed communists, supplemented by a blanket on press coverage and timely concessions in the form of emergency food supplies and goods. Even the most anti-Bolshevik of observers conceded that the movement was not opposed to socialism (that is, supported the state ownership of industry).[52] The movement's major weaknesses lay in the absence of any coherent theoretical or organisational programme. While the anti-autocracy movement in February 1917 had a long tradition of struggle and social self-defence organisations to call on and was institutionalised by the soviets, the trade unions and the parties, the novel experience of opposition under a communist regime, culminating in Moscow in the February 1921 days, found these forms of organisational practice colonised by its adversary. It lacked a coherent philosophy of opposition which could have justified and inspired the emergence of new forms. Nevertheless, the movement seemed to justify the Ignatov group in their opinion that the working class retained an awareness of its own interests.[53]

No significant splits appeared within the communist party, a unity symbolised by the participation of Workers' Oppositionists in suppressing the Kronstadt movement. They were included in the TsK list of activists sent to calm the workers in the districts, and in one case Kiselev and Kollontai joined Lunacharskii and Nogin in trying to pacify Baumanskii *raion*, the stronghold of opposition support,[54] In Kronstadt many communists joined the insurgents but little information is available about the feelings of the rank-and-file party member in Moscow. There are indications that some sympathised with the calls for a change in economic policy. The cell in the Aviapribor plant, for example, complained about the burdens imposed by Soviet power, of the near starvation, and spoke of the anger of communists.[55] Nevertheless, the party essentially maintained a united front during the disturbances, and the political controversies remained confined to its ranks. Despite this, Lenin waged an increasingly vigorous struggle against the continuation of the debates and asserted at a meeting of Moscow activists on 24 Februrary that 'Moscow has broken all records in the discussion'. Ominously, he warned that 'we can no longer tolerate such things'.[56]

THE TRADE UNION DEBATE

While the party debate allowed concrete reform proposals to emerge, some of which became official policy at the IX Party Conference, the trade union debate was bitterly divisive and appeared 'artificial and almost unreal'.[57] At a time of the collapse of the state-run war communist economy, and of worker and peasant unrest, at opposite poles Trotsky and the Workers' Opposition demanded an almost revolutionary alteration in the pattern of authority established since October 1917, and this at a time not of revolutionary *élan* but after nearly three years of exhausting civil war. Trotsky proposed transferring yet more functions to the state and the intensification of war communist policies, no longer as a temporary expedient necessitated by the war, but as a general strategy for development predicated on Russia's continued isolation and the need for sustained internal coercion. Militarisation of the economy had already been developing, but in late 1920 he tried to reverse the basic programme outlined at the VIII Party Congress for the ultimate transfer of the management of the economy to the trade unions, and instead called for the merger of the trade unions with the state. At the V All-Russian Trade Union Conference on 3 November 1920 he argued that the trade unions were suffering from a 'profound internal crisis' and that the only way to revive them was through a 'shake-up' (*peretryakhivanie*) and their 'statification', that is, their militarisation. The screws of war communism were to be tightened. His motion was rejected by the communist delegation at the conference and by the TsK plenum of 8–9 November by a majority of 10 to 4 led by Lenin, but ten members remained neutral and later formed the so-called buffer group led by Bukharin. A five-man commission under Zinoviev, hardly the best choice for a peace-maker, was appointed to look into the question in an attempt to limit discussion.[58] The interdiction on public debate was ineffective and was repealed by the TsK plenum on 24 December, and the issues on the agenda of the X Party Congress were delcared open to debate. That day Trotsky aired his views at the former Zimin theatre, and the next day his pamphlet 'The Role and Tasks of the Trade Unions' was published. The mass trade unions debate had begun.

The Workers' Opposition main demands centred on giving the unions a greater role in managing the economy through an all-Russian congress of producers. The party was to remain the political head of the working class, but the state's economic role would be transferred to the working class itself. Many of their views were similar to those of the Left Communists' in 1918, as in their criticisms of centralisation, the use of bourgeois specialists, the bureaucratisation of the state apparatus and their distrust of the peasantry. Their position reflected a profound anxiety about the role of the 'intellectuals', and hence insisted on the 'workerisation' of the state and the party.[59] The unions were to manage their own affairs and hence the party's monopoly over appointments was challenged. Their programme represented a major breach in the whole structure of the political process as it had developed during war communism, and therefore aroused Lenin's ire. On the other hand, the union movement itself had become 'bureaucratised', and it was hardly a paragon of proletarian solidarity as witnessed in its approach to non-Bolshevik unions, and in particular the Menshevik print union. The Workers' Opposition critique contained too many unresolved theoretical and practical questions to mount an effective challenge to the war communist labour system, let alone to its political system.

Between the Trotsky and Workers' Opposition positions there emerged a host of differing platforms. The Democratic Centralists were in favour of the obligatory candidature by the trade unions to economic bodies, a demand supported by the buffer group who foresaw a gradual merging of the state and the unions.[60] V. N. Yakovleva, briefly MK secretary in early 1921, was the major exponent of this position in Moscow. The Ignatov group largely shared the analysis of the Workers' Opposition on this issue and agreed that the unions, through some form of national congress, were to manage the economy, but they were more realistic in conceding that this elected body was to be confirmed by VTsIK and thus ultimate responsibility would still lie with the party and the state. The group saw the unions not only as tools for the inculcation of communism in the working class, as in Lenin's position, but stressed that the unions themselves were the crucial expression of the hegemony of the proletariat. Therefore the unions were to be strengthened and made genuinely democratic, and given greater powers in running the economy, broadly supervised by the party. No economic or union cadre was to be transferred without the agreement of the unions, a point conceded at this time. Eight of the leading second-rank party leaders in Moscow, including S. Smirnov, joined Ignatov on this platform[61] which represented perhaps the most practical of all the contributions in the trade union debate. Up to February 1921 they maintained an independent platform, though sharing many Democratic Centralist ideas, and they tended to vote with Lenin on union issues, but in that month they created a sensation by joining with the Workers' Opposition.

Lenin, quite rightly, argued that these positions would undermine 'the leading role of the party',[62] and when taken together with the attempts of trade union communist groups to act more independently of such bodies as the MGSPS,[63] it was clear that the whole edifice of democratic centralism was under threat. All the oppositions united in objecting to the 'petty supervision' of the party over the unions and, as Shlyapnikov put it, insisted that the party should have more faith in the collective experience of the unions.[64] By January 1921 even Trotsky was no longer calling for a shake-up of the unions from above but for greater economic powers to be transferred to them as they stood. As Kamenev, a signatory of Lenin's platform, pointed out, all the oppositions were promising more for the unions than Lenin's Platform of the Ten, and therefore a loose bloc began to coalesce against Lenin's group.[65] Lenin's initial encouragement of Trotsky's views on the militarisation of labour had by November 1920 given way to deep misgivings. His political instincts warned him, especially after the September 1920 party conference, that a struggle similar to the one over the Brest peace would have to be waged to implement them. His doubts were deepened by the course of the party debate in Moscow, culminating in the 'two rooms' at the November Moscow conference. Once again the spectre of a split in the party was raised. Lenin now emerged in the unusual guise of the arch-conciliator: against the harshness of Trotsky's position; but opposed to the radicalism of the Workers' Opposition. He now accepted that the unions should represent the workers' interest even in the workers' state (a term which he regarded as 'an abstraction'), since it had a peasant majority and was ensnared in bureaucratic distortions.[66] The unions were to act as the link between the vanguard party and the masses,[67] and this was the basis of his famous definition of the unions as 'transmission belts', a term he used in his speech to the MGSPS on 30 December 1920, and as schools of communism, the basis of the Platform of the Ten.[68] More and more, Lenin's arguments stressed the danger of a split in the party, and the actual content of the debates was relegated to the background. On several occasions in late 1920 and the first weeks of 1921 he had recognised the legitimacy of group struggle and ideological debate in the run-up to a party congress,[69] but as the debates continued and, perhaps, as his position became the dominant one, a change took place. The issue increasingly became the debate itself and not the various arguments, which he insisted had a tendency towards the demagogic.[70] By late January the theme of the dangers of factional struggle became dominant: 'Any disagreement, even the most petty, can become politically dangerous if there is the chance of it developing into a split'.[71] Indeed, at the February 1921 Moscow party conference Minkov characterised the MK in this period as composed of 'several small groups, and over every question we were forced to talk more than act'.[72]

The MK first fractured on the shoals of the trade union debate at its meeting of 1 January 1921 when the Ten emerged with a clear majority over the combined oppositions.[73] The MK hoped to use this vote to damp down the controversy in Moscow, but at the 3 January meeting the Ignatovtsy supported Sapronov's argument that 'there is no need to shield the party member' and insisted on unlimited debate. The Ignatov group also opposed limits to the numbers of co-rapporteurs. Despite these objections the MK adopted a plan whereby debate would only be permitted after a city party conference on 10 January where the speakers would be chosen by the MK and a Moscow view adopted.[74] The hopes for such an ordered debate were shattered by the Petrograd party organisation's 'Address to the Party'. The Petrograd organisation under Zinoviev was one of the first to rally to Lenin's trade union platform, and on 6 January a city conference adopted the Address which condemned Trotsky's 'mistaken theses' which could 'provoke a breach between the party and the trade unions'.[75] The Address aroused a storm of protest in Moscow, and at the 10 January MK session the oppositions, united on little else, joined together to condemn it. The meeting, held with eleven MK members absent, decided to forbid the printing of the Address in the Moscow press and *Pravda* on the grounds that it would pre-empt the discussion in Moscow. That evening the designated conference of party activists took place at which Trotsky criticised the Leninist position, Bukharin presented his own ideas, and the new chairman of the MGSPS, Lozovskii, supported the Leninist position of the trade unions as educators of the masses.[76] At special meetings the next day of the MK and its bureau, the oppositions again joined forces to censure the Address. Trotsky and Zinoviev took part in the lively debate in the bureau, and at the MK meeting the Democratic Centralists urged that the debate should begin in the districts and only then move to the MK, and not vice versa. This argument was rejected by the majority who felt that the depth of the disagreement should be concealed from the mass of the population and abroad, and were unwilling to unleash an uncontrolled debate which could threaten the very functioning of the party. The TsK should control the course of the debate, and not the Petrograd organisation, the dangerous implication of the Address.[77] The Petrograd organisation had indeed hoped to circumvent the paralysed TsK and impose its own views on the party. Such an attempt was bound to arouse Moscow's anger in which political considerations were reinforced by the traditional rivalry between the two cities. A full MK plenum meeting that evening was once again devoted not to the trade union debate but to the Address. A bloc formed, with the exception of Ignatov's group which argued, independent as usual, that the Petrograd organisation had every right to propose ideas for the conduct of the debate, and a motion was passed by a majority of one censuring the Petrograd Address and by implication the Leninist position that it supported.[78]

The next day (12 January) the TsK plenum sharply criticised the MK for its decision and called it an 'unprincipled and brazen bureaucratic perversion of democratic centralism'.[79] On his return to Moscow on 13 January, Artem, a signatory of the Platform of the Ten, absolved himself from all responsibility and accused the majority of having steamrollered the resolution through without waiting to consult the eleven missing MK members.[80] Nevertheless, that evening Trotsky and the buffer group succeeded by one vote in defeating a motion in the MK bureau to support the TsK resolution.[81] The TsK's response to the MK's resolution aggravated the already tense relations in the bureau and provoked yet another bout of infighting.[82] The MK finally determined its position on the trade union question at a two-day expanded meeting with activists on 17–18 January. The debate in Moscow can be seen as the fulcrum of the discussion in the country, and at this meeting eight platforms were represented. A series of votes narrowed the field and gave Lenin a victory of 62–18 over Trotsky.[83] The resolution of 11 January was reversed and the MK now called on the Moscow party to support the Leninist platform. It allowed free discussion but insisted that the unity of the party was to remain 'inviolable'.[84] To ensure a clear Leninist majority a new MK bureau was elected at the MK plenum of 25 January 1921 in which the old guard of fractious individuals such as

Minkov and Sorin gave way to the new generation of Krinitskii, Uryvaev and Zelenskii (see Table 4.1 on p. 103).

The debate had already spread to the districts. In Baumanskii *raion*, which counted a large number of students among its 1740 members and 465 candidates,[85] the Leninists led by Kulikov, later a member of the Stalinist Central Committee, tried to use the trade union debate to wrest control from the Workers' Opposition. In so doing they were as guilty of Fractionalism as the opposition had been in August of the previous year. The oppositionist RK survived a vote of no confidence on 5 February, but failed to carry the *raion* with it on the union issue a fortnight later.[86] In sharp contrast to the solid support for an opposition programme in the party debate, the RK almost unanimously supported the Leninist union platform.[87] In Gorodskoi *raion* the Ignatov group were more successful and their union line, supported by the RK, was adopted by the party organisation on 11 January.[88] In two other *raion*s, Zamoskvorech'e and Sokol'nicheskii, the Trotsky line was adopted.[89] The latter *raion*, with 3000 party members, was the main stronghold of Trotsky's position. Already in late November 1920 the RK had supported Trotsky's union platform with only one dissenting voice (Lyudvinskaya),[90] and his support was confirmed on 15 January.[91] The transport workers in the wagon repair plant, the huge tram park and the railway workshops had become familiar with his presence during the Tsektran experiment, and no doubt Trotsky had been able to place his own supporters in key positions. This *raion* had proved to be one of the staunchest supporters of the official line in the party debate, with Kotov the scourge of the oppositions, but now with the advent of the union debate it became an 'opposition' centre itself: but this was an authoritarian opposition rather than a democratic one. However, the Leninists launched a counter-attack, and Lenin personally called in the leading oppositionists to the Kremlin to persuade them.[92] Under such pressure the 22 January delegate meeting, despite Trotsky's oratory, finally voted in favour of Lenin's platform. This defeat, coming on the heels of the general city discussion meeting on 21 January which saw Trotsky's platform receive barely a fifth of the total votes,[93] may well have prompted Trotsky to modify his position. By late January, forty-three of the ninety-three RK members in the city had supported one opposition platform or another, but fifty supported Lenin.[94] By the eve of the February *Guberniya* Party Conference the Leninists had achieved majorities in all the RPOs on the union question, but only after a severe struggle.

The arcana of the controversy seemed far removed from the bureaucratic realities of the union movement. The MGSPS in late

January supported Lozovskii's Leninist union platform, but insisted on real reforms within the terms of this approach in production and management.[95] The metalworkers' union, not surprisingly, supported their long-standing leader Shlyapnikov.[96] At the metalworkers conference of 2–4 February, which was the scene of the bitter protest described above, the discussion following Lozovskii's speech on the question characterised the unions as 'worth little', weak and isolated from the masses. Speakers were unanimous that the unions had to reform themselves and set about the task of organising production.[97] The motion called for strictly observed democratic elections to all union organs, with freedom of speech and meeting guaranteed; greater elected control over factory management and no representatives to be sent to them by any organisation (including the party) with voting powers unless they had been elected by a general meeting of workers and then confirmed by the union. The resolution insisted on the free movement of labour from one factory to another.[98] The mood of the conference was in many respects even more radical than Shlyapnikov's programme, and reflected the strong resentment among the Moscow working class against the degeneration of the union movement under war communism.

The *Guberniya* Party Conference (19–21 February 1921) reviewed the course of the debate in Moscow. Discussion was curtailed on the grounds that all were aware, if not heartily sick of the main arguments. Short speeches were made by Kamenev for the Leninist position, Kiselev for the Workers' Opposition, and a long speech by Bukharin who insisted that the new joint programme with Trotsky differed significantly from the first variants of their programme. The idea of obligatory union candidature to economic bodies remained part of the new programme. Ignatov caused the greatest shock when he announced that his group, hitherto leaning towards Lenin, now agreed with the Workers' Opposition. In the voting, 217 out of 367 delegates voted for the Ten, 52 for the Trotsky-Bukharin platform, 45 for the Workers' Opposition, and only 13 for the Democratic Centralists.[99] This was to be the last Moscow party conference in which the oppositionists were able to muster significant support.

THE PARTY DEBATE: SECOND PHASE

Following the November *Guberniya* Conference the party debate receded into the background as attention turned to organisational questions and the union debate. In early 1921, however, the issue of party reform re-emerged with full force as the various tendencies presented their platforms and sought support in the run-up to the X Party Congress. All groups realised that fundamental decisions would be taken at the congress, and that Moscow's position would be decided and the delegates chosen at the February *Guberniya* Party Conference. Yet this second phase of the debate took place in very different circumstances from the first. The protests in the streets of Moscow alerted the leadership to the precariousness of the regime and tended to rally support for the existing party committees. The organisational reforms since late 1920 had consolidated the position of the party leadership and gave them greater leverage over movements within the party. And the trade union controversy had embittered the atmosphere and seemed to make the luxury of debate all the more superfluous. At the same time, the issue of party reform was none too subtly co-opted by certain leaders as a useful weapon against the militarisers. Leonard Schapiro suggests that the trade union debate was deliberately used to defuse the pressure for reform within the party. In addition, Zinoviev had a personal score to settle with Trotsky.[100] Zinoviev's earlier indifference to party reform, which had a pedigree dating back to the VIII Party Congress and had only recently been evident at the IX Conference, had changed into enthusiastic support for more power to the *nizy* and he had become, in Myasnikov's words, 'a fantastic prophet of "workers' democracy"'. Myasnikov, for one, was not taken in, and in early 1921 he launched a virulent attack on Zinoviev's opportunism.[101]

As in the union debate, the MK plenum of 11 January tried to contain the debate within the terms of an agreed set of theses to be drafted by Kamenev, Sapronov and Yakovleva.[102] It was hoped that by including representatives of the three major tendencies (excluding the Workers' Oppositionists) the theses would be acceptable to a broad range of opinion. And indeed, the theses, while still predicated on the assumption that the basic aspects of war communism were to continue and therefore 'all methods of party work are always subordinate to the demands of revolutionary expediency', remained in the spirit of the reforming IX Party Conference in analysing the party's ills and in proposing the application of 'workers' democracy'. Lack of faith in the party (or syndicalism) had developed, they argued, because of the bureaucratisation of the party leadership and hence the gulf with the *nizy*. The theme of improving the quality of the existing membership rather than continued expansion was one taken up by the X Party Congress resolution on the party [103] and resulted in the 1921 purge. The cells, according to the MK, were to act primarily as educational bodies and not to take on the functions of the organs of power, which alienated them from the masses; the petty party tutelage over the unions and soviets was to be 'decisively' ended; and the regular transfer of party members between soviet and party work would ensure a decrease in bureaucratism.[104] While reforming, the theses allowed little scope for the independence of party members, and by insisting on a limited role for the cells saw them more as transmission belts rather than the nuclei of working-class self-management. The division between an active and politically passive membership was once again apparent.

The other groups also formulated their positions in the form of theses for the X Congress. Foremost among these were those of the 'active workers of Moscow's *raions*', the Ignatovtsy. Stimulated by their developing alliance with the Workers' Opposition they provided a powerful critique of current practices in the party.[105] They concentrated on the role of the rank-and-file party member (the *nizy*) and insisted that with the ending of the war the old military methods in the party, soviets and unions should be ended to allow the active participation of the party masses. The theses insisted that the party *nizy* were dissatisfied with the small role that they had been assigned, and the growth in their consciousness now demanded changes which had been blocked – despite the reforming resolutions of the past few months – by the bureaucratic habits of the leading party workers in all apparatuses:

> The stagnation of the development of the organisational forms of party building towards their greater democratisation has led to what we call the party crisis. In essence this is the disparity between outmoded party forms with the demands, dictated by class instinct and growing consciousness, of the proletariat and the party masses in their desire to create new forms of communist society.

While Lenin and his supporters saw only a 'declassed' proletariat (and it was probably not accidental that it was at this time that they made great play of the issue), the Ignatovtsy saw a proletariat, though ravaged by war, growing in consciousness and able to take hold of its own destiny. In this analysis we encounter for the first time a phenomenon that Rudolf Bahro was later to call 'surplus consciousness'.[106] This is essentially the contradiction between frozen organisational forms (bureaucratism), and the striving of groups and individuals for a more active and responsible participation in the party and political processes. This comes up against the opposition of the entrenched cadres, the Ignatovtsy stated. They proposed a wide range of measures designed to advance workers, broaden decision-making, guarantee free discussion for all opinions in the party, and above all to increase the role of the cells, and in contrast to the MK insisted that these reforms were to be implemented irrespective of whether 'the domestic or external situation deteriorates'.[107] The Ignatov group had therefore moved from a position broadly in line with the Democratic Centralist critique of party structures and the Platform of the Ten's emphasis on the educational role of the unions, to one where rank-and-file party members and ordinary workers were to play an active and autonomous role in political life. Hence their switch at the February conference to support the Workers' Opposition. However, the group now adopted some of the 'workerist' positions of their allies such as a ban on all non-worker recruitment to the party and an obligatory two-thirds worker representation on all party committees. By insisting that the split in the party between the *verkhi* and *nizy* was also a social one between workers and intelligentsia the Ignatovtsy exposed themselves to the charge of Makhaevism, the idea that the intelligentsia through their specialised knowledge exploited the workers, and indeed were accused of this on the eve of the February conference.[108]

Shlyapnikov's own criticisms of the party centres were very similar, and he acknowledged his debt to the Moscow district activists in providing the substance of his critique published in the first issue of the discussion paper promised by the IX Party Conference.[109] He argued that the IX Conference had not tackled the roots of the party crisis but that the party had only 'mechanically' tried to gloss over difficulties by holding open meetings and suchlike. To solve the crisis, he insisted, every party member should be allowed to 'find his tongue, as they say in the *raion*s', and participate in the debate. Instead, he argued, 'comradely' relations had been replaced by 'orders and obedience' (*prikazanie i poslushanie*):

> The party, as the managing and creative collective, has become a sordid bureaucratic machine. The party work of the masses has been reduced to the fulfilment of a few very basic duties such as subbotniks, guard duty, patrols, and so on.

He supported his plea for an end to bureaucratic and coercive methods in the party, and for greater activity by rank-and-file party members, by referring to the events in the Moscow party organisation, in particular the suppression of the Baumanskii oppositionists and the interference of the TsK at the November party conference. He then made his often quoted claim of chicanery, similar to the claims of the Mensheviks but now concerned with the internal operation of the party itself:

This interference revealed itself in a whole system of pressure and struggle against comrades who were dissatisfied with the work of the MK. In those districts where the opposition was in a majority, they insisted on the distribution of delegates proportional to the number of votes received. There, where the majority were supporters of the old MK, proportionality was not allowed.[110]

At the November conference Lenin had argued that while proportionality was necessary in selecting delegates to the conference, implying that this unusual procedure had been applied by the Leninists before the conference, it was absolutely inadmissible in electing a leading body such as the MK.[111] Shlyapnikov's charges can neither be proved nor disproved, but they reveal the increasing tendency for both the Workers' Opposition and the Leninists to concentrate on the minutiae of the debate itself and not on the main issues.

The Democratic Centralists reduced the difficulties in the party to the problem of the transition from military to economic tasks. Sapronov explicitly condemned the rise to dominance of the union question when, he insisted, party and soviet issues were the key ones.[112] They called for strictly defined structures from top to bottom on the basis of democratic centralism: as they put it, pyramids instead of pillars. As opposed to the Ignatovtsy, they identified a fall in the consciousness of the masses, though concurred in noting a decline in internal party democracy, which they agreed could be halted by making the cell the focus of party life.[113] While Sapronov openly identified himself with the Moscow opposition,[114] Osinskii was more hostile. Referring to the misquotation of an earlier speech (delivered in Tula in May 1920) he launched a blunt attack on the Workers' Opposition in February 1921. All talk of the self-activity of the masses under the circumstances, he argued, was nonsense. All that could be done was to involve them in 'active work' under the guidance of the party.[115] This split between Sapronov and Osinskii marked the end of the Democratic Centralists as a coherent tendency. An aura of paternalism and not radical worker politics had long clung to their reform proposals, and the present debate forced them to choose between democratic and, if not authoritarian, then bureaucratic, reform.

On the basis of these platforms battle was now joined in the districts of Moscow in the weeks prior to the X Congress. The Ignatovtsy carried the standard for the Workers' Opposition, but were severely weakened by the independent Democratic Centralist platform. The Democratic Centralists won in Zamoskvorech'e, the MK by a narrow margin over the Ignatovtsy in Sokol'nicheskii *raion*,[116] and by a large margin in Rogozhsko-Simonovskii *raion*.[117] The highly confused situation facing the party member in voting on the various platforms is illustrated by the case of Yakovleva, who defended the MK line in this debate while supporting the Trotsky-Bukharin platform on the union question. It does show, however, that the Trotsky-Bukharin supporters on the union question were consistent opponents of radical reform in the party. Further, the divisions between various opposition platforms occasionally allowed the MK victory by default, as in two wards in Gorodskoi *raion*.[118] In that district the Ignatovtsy were losing their pre-eminence and the MK position was adopted on the eve of the February conference, and likewise in Baumanskii *raion*,[119] though the oppositionists succeeded in having delegates to the conference elected proportionally and not by the 'winners take all' system.[120] As usual, the greatest support for the MK was mustered in Krasnopresnenskii *raion* led by a strongly Leninist RK,[121] while in Sokol'nicheskii *raion* on 18 February, a week after the earlier vote, the MK crushed the Ignatov group by sixty-five votes to eight. On the same day a delegate meeting in Zamoskvorech'e saw the MK snatch a victory with forty-one votes against twenty for the Ignatov group and eighteen for the Democratic Centralists.[122] With the exception of Baumanskii *raion*, where the party issue dominated, delegates to the conference were elected proportionately to the voting on the union issue.

The Moscow *Guberniya* Party Conference (19–21 February 1921), attended by 367 delegates, met in the shadow of the collapse of the war communist system and pessimism over the prospects for the international revolution. Hence, as Karl Radek put it, they had to rely on their own resources and establish 'correct' relations with the 80 million peasants in the country.[123] Disquiet over the extension of militarisation and the fear of further wars led the conference to reject the immediate transformation of the Red Army into a militia force[124] and, later, even the limited experimentation in this field permitted by the X Party Congress was not taken up by Moscow.[125] The 'unreality' of the union issue was reflected in the little time spent on it, and by far the greatest amount of the proceedings were devoted to the crucial party debate. Three reports were presented on the issue. Kamenev for the MK once again outlined his views on workers' democracy, and ridiculed Ignatov's proposal that the party's leading bodies should consist of two-thirds workers, and at the same time he attacked the DC idea of introducing 'independent' people into the TsK.[126] Ignatov accused the party leadership of having transformed itself into a group of 'specialists', perhaps a euphemism for bureaucrats. He continued his crusade against the alleged petty bourgeois infiltration of the party by proposing that all those other than workers or peasants who had joined before 1 October 1919 should be expelled. In this demand it was clear that the initial intellectual clarity of the Ignatov group had been undermined by too close contact with the Workers' Opposition, but his group now dropped the demand for two-thirds workers representation.[127] The report by Bubnov for the Democratic Centralists stressed the continuity of the party crisis since early 1919, and he attacked both the incorrect policies of the TsK and the danger represented by the Workers' Opposition. The voting gave the MK resolution 251, Ignatov 57, and Bubnov 30.[128]

In the discussion on the MK's work since November 1920 several speakers deplored the harmful effects of the union debate on the attempts to implement organisational reform in the MPO. Yakovleva, in the main report on the question, argued that the change of three MK secretaries in as many months had been particularly detrimental.[129] Uryaev's resolution accepting the report aroused less controversy than the similar report at the November conference, and indeed the selection of a compromise composite MK in November was condemned. This resolution was adopted with 230 votes, while Ignatov and the Workers' Opposition obtained 46 (15 per cent of votes cast) and Bubnov 38 (12 per cent).[130] Elections to the MK, as at the November conference, aroused the most heated discussion. Bubnov argued that they should be postponed until after the X Congress to allow workers' democracy to be introduced. The Ignatovtsy concurred with the Leninist majority's view that the MK elected in November had been composed of conflicting groups and had therefore failed to provide leadership, and agreed that the elections should be delayed. All were of one mind that it had been a mistake to elect the MK on the basis of union platforms and not on the party issue. After two votes it was agreed to elect a new MK at the conference, whereupon the Ignatovtsy declared that they would not take part. The list prepared by the MK obtained 220 votes, 43 abstained, and 42 refused to take part in the voting. Ignatov, Sapronov and some other oppositionists lost their seats (see Table 4.1 on p. 103). The TsK report at the X Congress correctly noted the change in the relative strength of the major positions since November but underestimated opposition support at the two conferences at two-fifths and one-sixth, respectively.[131] In fact, at the first the oppositions mustered 45 per cent of the delegates, and at the second 27 per cent.

The election of delegates to the X Party Congress took place on the basis of the union platforms: the Platform of the Ten received twelve places; the Trotsky–Bukharin group and the Workers' Opposition six each; and the Democratic Centralists two.[132] The majority of the MK were once again Leninists, though the legality of the elections was contested by the oppositions who appealed to the TsK. Lenin gave their complaints short shrift at a meeting with Moscow party activists on 24 February, arguing that 'the system of two rooms can no longer be tolerated . . . What sort of democracy is it if the conference cannot elect the MK?'[133] In a declaration to all party members soon afterwards, the new MK gave notice of a new style of leadership: 'All hail to the united, powerful organisation of Moscow communists under the leadership of its renewed centre'.[134] Against the background of the disturbances the MK outlined measures to invigorate its apparatus, and to improve contacts with local party organisations and over such organisations as Komsomol. [135] All party departments in the centre and the districts were to be standardised.[136] With the transition to NEP this programme was implemented in what was called a *perestroika* (restructuring). The same issue carried denunciations of 'counter-revolutionary' agitation in Kronstadt and elsewhere, and called on all to unite around the soviets. Following the X Congress the MK launched a campaign for the 'workerising' of soviet organs[137] and under the slogan 'to the masses' argued that the 'counter-revolutionary wavering' of the non-party masses was to be countered by intensifying party unity.[138] This was to be the slogan of the NEP.

THE DEBATES IN PERSPECTIVE AND THE X PARTY CONGRESS

At the 24 February meeting of party activists Lenin had stated that 'Moscow had broken all records in the discussions'. He argued that the *émigré* press was taking advantage of the struggles within the party, and against the background of disturbances in the streets he issued the stern warning that the period of discussion was drawing to a close:

> We have given everybody a chance to speak their minds, we have carried out a discussion – and the congress will decide, and now we are at battle stations. We must unite and understand that one more step in the discussion and we will no longer be a party.[139]

The vigour of the debate in the MPO had clearly shown that while pluralism had been undermined in society at large, it had found a refuge, if only temporarily, within the party membership, and was institutionalised, for example, by the practice of having a co-rapporteur representing a different view at meetings. There was a growing body of party legislation, however, designed to enforce party discipline and to ensure the ability of *delovoi* action by higher party bodies. The transition from military to economic priorities at the end of the civil war was marked initially by a flowering of debate, indicating that the war *per se* cannot be held responsible for limiting the discussion rights of party members, but the tendency to regard economic reconstruction as a military campaign continued to undermine the 'common law' rights of discussion.

There are several reasons why the discussions were so intractable in Moscow. Here were concentrated the leading party, soviet and trade union activists and hence the debates in Moscow acted as a platform for the debate in the country. Support in the MPO, the largest and most prestigious in the republic, acted as a powerful prop to any group in its attempts to influence party policy. The sharp reaction to the attempt by the Petrograd party organisation, in its Address on the unions, to over specific questions, was seen by all sides in Moscow as a threat to the very principle of free discussion in party organisations. The objective reasons for the strength of the oppositions in Moscow were based both on conditions in the city and in the MPO itself. The working class had decreased in size and changed in composition, but the protest movement from late 1920 made clear that it was not a negligible force and that in an inchoate way it retained a vision of socialism which was not identified entirely with Bolshevik power. Hence those who had alternative ideas on the organisation of Bolshevik power took a more positive view, like the Ignatovtsy, of the capacities of the working class. Lenin's arguments on the declassing of the proletariat was more a way of avoiding this unpleasant truth than a real reflection of what remained, in Moscow at least, a substantial physical and ideological force. At the same time the political traditions of the MPO, with the emphasis on district initiative and a weak centre, and widespread acceptance that discussion was a right and not a privilege, allowed the discussion full reign. The peculiarly Moscow grouping of the Ignatovtsy bridged the two main strands of opposition activity, between the party and trade union discussions, and linked the demands for democracy within the party with those calling for greater initiative to be allowed to the working class.

The two debates allowed of separate solution but by late 1920 the issues in the party debate had become lost in those of the trade unions. The attempts to reform the party were submerged and by the time they re-emerged on the eve of the X Party Congress the very bitterness of the union debate and events such as the Kronstadt rising militated against a democratic reform solution to the party's problems. Instead, elements of their proposals were integrated into the alternative authoritarian reform solution. The question remains: what were the preconditions for greater worker self-activity? Would it not require a fundamental relaxation of party control over all of society? As Kamenev put it later, if democracy was to be granted within the party then what would prevent the unions, the working class, and so on, also asking for democracy.[140] This was the logic of their position, as Lenin realised, but the oppositionists, no liberals, drew back from this conclusion and were thus condemned to the margins of history. There is some legitimacy in Stalin's comment that there were no questions of principle at stake in the trade union debate: 'The leading role of the party fractions in the unions, and of the unions within the working class, remain undisputed truths'.[141] The very conditions that gave rise to the oppositions were also the cause of their defeat. The near Kronstadt in Moscow in February 1921 allowed the Leninist majority to claim that the existence of organised opposition allowed the 'petty bourgeois' parties, above all the Mensheviks, to threaten the very existence of Soviet power in its Bolshevik form. Kronstadt itself, and its Moscow counterpart, provided the justification for Lenin and his supporters to 'put the lid' on the opposition. The X Party Congress made explicit what had become increasingly clear: that the real issue in the trade union debate was not the unions as such, but the leading role of the party in economic and political life; and that the issue in the party debate was not whether but how the leadership would exercise its power.

At the X Congress Lenin made clear the political consequences of his concept of the declassing of the proletariat. It encouraged, in his view, the growth of 'petty bourgeois anarchist tendencies' of the type of the Workers' Opposition.[142] Referring to the Kronstadt events he argued:

> Here there appeared petty bourgeois, anarchist movements (*stikhiya*), with slogans in favour of free trade and always directed against the dictatorship of the proletariat. This mood has profoundly influenced the proletariat. It has influenced the factories in Moscow, it has influenced factories in many parts of the provinces. This petty bourgeois counter-revolution is undoubtedly more dangerous than Denikin, Yudenich and Kolchak taken together.[143]

The call for free trade was an assault against the cornerstone of war communist economic policy and this, Lenin insisted, had developed into a general attack on the dictatorship of the proletariat. In other words, in

Lenin's view the development of independent 'speculationist' relations by the general economic crisis at the end of war communism was not only an economic category but also a political one, and together they had provided a hospitable environment for the various oppositions. In this way the content of the opposition criticisms was undermined in favour of emphasising their witting and unwitting results. Just as Lenin considered the emergence of the bureaucracy a social rather than a structural phenomenon, so he ascribed a 'petty bourgeois' basis to the oppositions without analysing their political or structural basis: and the emergence of the union debate allowed him to avoid facing the implications of the issue of party reform. The trade union debate undermined the emerging democratic reform coalition and allowed the authoritarian definition of inner-party relations to emerge as the dominant one in the transition to the NEP. The implications for the relationship between the party and its own social base were similarly drawn.

Lenin expressed the conclusion that he drew from this in the words of the II Congress of the III International: 'The dictatorship of the proletariat is impossible without the communist party'. From this point of view he ridiculed Kollontai's and Shlyapnikov's arguments in favour of an all-Russian congress of producers in which the working class and its organisations would play the leading role.[144] The congress decision on the trade unions emphasised the leading role of the party in the unions, but allowed that this should be of an ideological nature and not the minute regulation typical of war communism.[145] The resolution on party building provided the true reflection of six months of debate. It outlined a broad programme of change in the party, based on the organisational practices of the war communist period, which was to provide the basis for a crucial *rassemblement* of the party: 'We must once again gather up the party which during the war was broken up into several groups'.[146] The *verkhi* and the *nizy*, the military and civilian workers, the old and new party members, were to be fused into the greater body of the party, controlled by the party centre. The two supplementary resolutions 'On the unity of the party', banning factional activity on penalty of expulsion, and 'The syndicalist and anarchist deviation in our party', which castigated the Workers' Opposition, were commentaries on this basic programme. The congress further agreed to Radek's proposal to outlaw and destroy the Menshevik and SR parties.

In contrast to the heated debates on party and trade union policy, the adoption of the first measures of what came to be known as the New Economic Policy was accepted with little debate. As Lenin put it later,

'The change that we made in the spring of 1921 . . . was necessitated by such extremely powerful and convincing circumstances that no debates or disagreements arose among us about it'.[147] It was a short step for Lenin at the congress to forge a link between economic concessions and increased party discipline:

> We require, on the one hand, the maximum unity, endurance and discipline within the proletarian party, and on the other hand, a whole range of economic . . . concessions.[148]

The introduction of the NEP altered the framework within which the debates had been conducted, but the issues raised by them remained in the forefront in the 1920s. The oppositions during the civil war were not merely ephemeral phenomena doomed to failure. The broad participation in them of large numbers of party members at all levels suggests that 'living thought' had not died out in Moscow's districts either in the party or the working class. The end of the war and the return of party members from the fronts signalled a new era in the party. An authoritarian oppositionist such as Kotov survived the transition and went on to head the Sokol'nicheskii party organisation until 1925.[149] Ignatov devoted himself to the Moscow Soviet and its history, while some of his supporters found it impossible to reconcile themselves to a period of social concessions and participated in such groups as the Panushkin Workers' and Peasants' Socialist Party, destroyed in summer 1921, G. Myasnikov's Workers' Group, inspired by the Workers' Opposition, and the Workers' Truth Group, inspired by Alexander Bogdanov and Proletcult. The oppositions were destroyed, and their failure heralded a larger failure to use the opportunity of the onset of peace to create new relationships between the party and the working class. The long-running debate during the war between authoritarian and democratic reform was settled as the war came to an end. Zinoviev-type debasement of reform programmes as part of inner-party struggles became the norm, and bureaucracy and administrative measures took the place of debate and democracy. The party and not the working class was henceforth to be the dominant force in the country, and within the party the leadership was consolidated, and it was this formulation of the dictatorship of the proletariat that was to be the enduring result of the ideological changes and political responses of the period of war communism.

Conclusions

Out of the storm of the civil war a new system of power emerged in the Russian republic, denoted by the term war communism. When the Bolsheviks came to power in October 1917 they had no detailed blueprint for the future communist society but they did have some general principles derived from the writings of Marx and from over half a century of struggle against capitalism, other socialists, and the autocracy. Bolshevism differed as much from the communist project as Russia differed from Western Europe. It was a phenomenon which blended elements of the socialist tradition with the mechanics of achieving and maintaining power. Many Bolsheviks laid down their lives during the civil war, but in Moscow, the heart of Russia and since March 1918 the heart of the revolution as well, their comrades had a unique opportunity to put their vision into practice. Their policies provoked the civil war as much as the policies themselves were evoked by military exigencies. The war acted as a catalyst for the implementation of the maximalist programme, and in two and a half years of conflict some of the details of the future society were established. By 1920 the victors, not only of the revolution but also of civil war and foreign intervention, could survey a country devastated by war, a city depopulated, its factories barely working, and its working class dissipated and to a large extent hostile. And yet, capitalism and the bourgeoisie had been driven to the margins of economic and political life, victory had been achieved in the civil war, and the principles of war communism could in the main be claimed to have been successful. But precisely at the moment of victory a number of factors ranging from economic collapse, a broadening social movement of protest against the regime, and political conflict within the party induced the relaxation in economic policy known as the New Economic Policy.

The roots of war communism stretch down into Western political theory and Russian political traditions, and its influence lasted long after its official termination in early 1921. The October revolution had been followed by the creation of what was intended to be a transitional state apparatus designed to eliminate bourgeois political power and to neutralise capitalist economic power. Against the background of developing civil war in mid-1918 the state launched a second offensive against capital, no longer limited to neutralising its economic power but aimed at its elimination. Marx's capitalist state, modified shortly before the October revolution by Lenin in his theory of imperialism, was rooted in the economic system, and Lenin's socialist state developed both to counter the old economic system and to create a new one. The casualty of the emphasis on the economic revolution, which involved the abolition of commodity exchange and private property, was the functioning of a free sphere of politics, civil society, the arena in which the battle for freedom, justice and equality is fought. Marx's communist project had sought, however contradictorily, to combine the end of economic exploitation with social emancipation, but the lack of a developed notion of civil society meant that to maintain itself the Bolshevik project threatened both. The negative evaluation of the role of civil society in Marx, the contradictory way he treated Hegel's balance between the state and social particularities, and the absence of the concept in Lenin's work was the ideological context for the emergence of the Soviet system.

In many respects war communism corresponded to the fundamental aims of the Bolshevik project in both the economic and political spheres and was more than an expedient forced by the war. War communism was a unique balance combining Utopian inspiration with pragmatism. Pragmatism was especially marked in the economic sphere, as in the use of wage differentials and the employment of specialists. But the pragmatism was a small part of the larger loyalty to the establishment of an integral socialism. It was in this period that the majority of what are now the familiar elements of Soviet-type systems were introduced. These include the emergence of a *de facto* one-party state, extreme economic centralisation, the abolition of most private economic ownership (with the partial exception of agriculture), the elimination of mediating social forces between the state and the individual, and the stress on collective action rather than individual conscience. Before it could be established, the Bolshevik project, tailored to Russian conditions, had to displace the communist project, designed for advanced industrial countries. The debates of the period were a reflection of war communism as a time of sustained organisational experimentation and ideological restructuring. A social project which threatened the political achievements of half a century of labour struggle and centuries of bourgeois democratic development was reflected in the tensions within the Bolshevik project. The contradictory legacy of the communist project – economic central-isation and political decentralisation – had to be overcome. The system of dual values – ultimate objectives versus transitional measures (see page 12) – had to be reconciled.

War communism was therefore a fundamentally unstable system both ideologically and organisationally. The maximalist ideological demands of the communist project and of Bolshevism itself, such as for the abolition of money or for the fusion of labour movement with the economic apparatus, themselves came to threaten the survival of the regime. The abolition of commodity exchange strained the economic resources of the system to the utmost. The tensions were reflected in the almost constant debates over economic and political policy in this period. Moreover, war communism contained the seeds of two radically divergent forms of development: extreme militarisation; or extensive participation through collegiality in industry and politics. Lenin's own vacillations, such as his retreat in November 1920 from the all-out militarisation advocated by Trotsky (see page 247), symbolises the lack of integration of the ideological and organisational elements of the emerging regime. Lenin's middle course was ideologically unsatisfactory and ineffective but politically expedient. The legacy of war communism was not a monolithic power system but one riven by internal contradictions, above all between its economic and political aspects. This was a period of extensive institution-building as the regime sought to consolidate its power. Rival fiefdoms – the party, the economic apparatus, the soviets, the police, and perhaps even the trade unions – competed for predominance. The institutional conflicts of the time were not so much between the centre and the locality as between competing hierarchies. The changing balance between these bodies provides much of the dynamic for change within the Soviet system. Under Lenin's leadership these various elements were kept in check, though curbing the trade unions required a vigorous struggle which came close to splitting the party. Lenin's successors were faced with the formidable task of maintaining the delicate balance between the antagonistic ideological and institutional components of his legacy. The undertaking proved impossible, in the short term at least, and was not facilitated by the impoverishment of the political processes themselves.

The economic policies of war communism were justified by ideology but often evoked by necessity. Against the background of depopulation and a major social revolution, capitalism and commodity relations were largely extirpated during war communism (see Chapter 2). In their place a centralised system managed the whole economic life of the country through a proliferation of vertically organised controls, the *glavki*. The Moscow authorities lost the direct control over their own major industries and the soviet's own economic management functions were undermined. The Moscow economic council became an executive unit of the central economic apparatus. At the same time, the organisation of the economy reveals the limits of the concept of the 'party-state monolith'. On the local level, the party organisation and the party members working in enterprises were separated from economic management (see pp. 53 and 124). The ideological radicalism of local party activists occasionally limited the freedom of action of state bodies, as in their opposition to the relaxation of the grain monopoly (see page 58). The party's functions were reduced to providing a favourable climate for the operation of the economic apparatus. Trotsky's concept of the Labour State implicitly challenged the notion of the party-state: the economic apparatus was posed against the political state. From this flowed, in November 1920, Lenin's disavowal of the militarisation of labour, which threatened the militarisation of the party and its subordination to the economic state. This breach in its hegemony led to the party's decline when the state's economic functions expanded massively at the time of the 'socialist offensive' of the first Five-Year Plan. Following October there had been no adequate integration between the Bolshevik political revolution and the new state's economic functions.

War communism as an economic system was more flexible than is sometimes assumed (see Chapter 3). The battle between collegiality, a fundamental principle of the early Bolshevik period, and one-person management was in the balance until the very end of the period. In wages policy, egalitarianism, while never abandoned as a final goal, was already in conflict with the need to improve productivity even in conditions of scarcity, and a wide variety of incentive and bonus systems were applied. The egalitarianism of war communism was one based on the obligation to work and not on equality in achieved income. It was an extension of the liberal tenet of equality before the law to the economic sphere: an equality in relation to the economic system. The conflict between the ideological legacy of the communist project and the realities of Bolshevism in power was stamped on the new state's labour relations. Both the trade unions and the working class as a whole by the end of war communism had been reduced to a subordinate role. But they were subordinate in relation both to the party and to the state. The formation of state economic councils deprived the trade unions of direct economic management functions, and the later restrictions on collegiality only confirmed their subalternity. Instead, the unions concentrated on labour and wages policy, and in enterprises the factory committees lost their control functions. The lack of integration between the socialist democratic political revolution and the state socialist economic revolution was starkly revealed to the committed workers organised in party cells when 'syndicalist' forms of participation in running enterprises were brought to an end (see Chapter 4). At the time of the trade union debate Trotsky and the Workers' Opposition proffered alternative ways to achieve the integration of the socialist state and the labour movement but the party's own political dominance prevented this occurring. The workers' movement of 1917 was consumed not only in the furnace of the civil war but also in the offices of the new state. The sustained, though ultimately futile, attempts to revive an autonomous workers' movement, especially in mid-1918 and from late 1920, failed owing to repression and because both the discourse and organisational practice of a workers' movement were colonised by the Bolsheviks. The workers' movement left the centre of the stage during war communism as other actors took its place.

Bolshevism emerged from a communist project which undermined the role of an autonomous civil society in communist society. In the Bolshevik project a massively extended role for the party was to take the place of independent social movements. The party would act not only as the organisational linchpin but also as the source of cultural dynamism. Prior to the revolution this was limited to the party's centrality in the revolutionary process: the achievement of power. After a certain hesitancy in the first months of the new regime the party in practice became the kernel of the new state. The theoretical lag was reflected by, among others, Bukharin's almost complete silence about the role of the party in the new system. The resurgence of the party after May 1918 as a body separate from the state was followed by a period in which the party consolidated its own internal organisation (see Chapter 4). Responsibilities were divided between the state, primarily concerned with the economy, and the party as the source of supreme political authority. In this system the party became the master of the political sphere, analogous to the role of the *glavki* in industry.

The internal organisational developments in the party during war communism were provoked by an amalgam of theoretical and practical considerations. Just as Marx had provided only the broadest outlines of the future society, so Lenin had established only general principles concerning internal party organisation. On this question Lenin had little specific to say during the civil war other than stressing the need for discipline. The practical development of internal organisation took place within the general theoretical constraints of the functions of the ruling party in the dictatorship of the proletariat. Robert Michels and Max Weber have provided important analyses of the internal development of bureaucratic organisations in general. But the professionalisation of the Bolshevik party during the civil war took hitherto unique form, which developed in interaction with its functions. The party displayed an extraordinary organisational vitality during the civil war, illustrated by the constant plans for reform. But equally striking was the futility of much of the reform effort (see Chapter 4). A novel type of organisation was created by a fusion of the party's democratic traditions, which led to the use of elections and the maintenance of the principle of accountability, with its growing control functions, which transformed elections and accountability into instruments of control. Party groupings beyond the auspices of the committees were discouraged and ultimately banned as the practice of democratic centralism in the ruling party was defined. The ideology of democratic centralism was used in 1920 to end 'federalist' tendencies in the Moscow party organisation (see page 112). The party's discipline began to be turned against its own membership.

Simultaneously, the recruitment policies of the party reinforced the division between a group of activists and an increasingly malleable rank-and-file membership (see Chapter 5). Concern over the social pattern of recruitment and the debate over the broad or narrow party only emphasised the dominance of the party leadership in deciding these crucial questions. The alternating pattern of purge and recruitment weakened the solidarity of the rank-and-file party membership. The social context in which recruitment took place, the changing composition of the working class and the growth of bureaucracy allowed the traditional Leninist concept of the vanguard party in the pre-revolutionary situation to be transferred and intensified in the post-revolutionary contest.

The debate on the role of ideology and pragmatism, of theory and exogenous circumstances, is focused on the role of the civil war in stimulating the changes in internal party organisation and in the consolidation of the state in general. The civil war was an ideological crusade against capitalism fought by pragmatic means. We have argued that there was a specific ideology of Bolshevism, derived partially from Marx, which had both a political and economic aspect. But the hallmark of practical Bolshevism was its flexibility within the terms of its basic project. To some extent the contradiction between ideology and pragmatism was no more than the problem of retaining power. Thus the pragmatism was ideologically charged, while the ideology was to some extent restricted to what would be useful for prosecuting the war. The manner in which the war was fought and the absence of a revolution on a world scale stimulated the emergence of authoritarian patterns. The party was able to retain control over the army, and they borrowed from each other certain organisational traits as the army was professionalised and the party militarised. But while the party managed to ward off a potential Bonapartist restoration, a new challenge arose to its hegemony for which the French Revolution offered no precedent. The absence of programmatic control over the revolutionary process, sought by Bukharin in 1917 and 1918 (see pp. 15 and 17), had its most devastating effect in the unrestrained violence launched by the Bolsheviks against their enemies, and ultimately against themselves. Much to the consternation of the Moscow Bolsheviks, party and soviet control over the internal repressive apparatus was fragile (see Chapter 6). Just as the economic apparatus developed a certain life of its own so the secret police machinery, with its arbitrary executions sometimes taking place directly contrary to party directives as in January 1920 (see page 242), emerged as an almost autonomous fiefdom despite several attempts by the Moscow party organisation and the national leadership to bring it under control. The party's failure to establish its hegemony over the secret police during the civil war exacted a heavy toll on the victors of October under Stalin.

The soviets were to act as the instruments of civilian administration and as the channel of popular participation in the socialist state. The theory of the dictatorship of the proletariat presupposed a powerful central political apparatus while the commune idea added the element of popular control. In practice it proved impossible to harmonise the two. Even at this early stage the electoral system was fused with the power system and precluded effective popular control over the soviets. The fusion of executive and legislative functions in a militarised environment endowed the executive bodies with overwhelming power. Bolshevik leaders as varied as Kamenev and Ignatov admitted that the soviets had become moribund as their caucus-based organisation stimulated bureaucratic routine to replace effective mass participation. The emphasis on the simplicity of administration in the post-revolutionary society opened the door to the emergence of an uncontested power centre beyond the control of popular forces. Despite several attempts at stimulating participation through the sections and collegiality, the executive bodies became largely autonomous of the mass of deputies. The theoretical limitations of the idea of the commune state were compounded by the practical developments after the October revolution. By the end of the war the party committee had established control not only over the soviets but also over the party fractions working in them (see pages 184–5). The real power centre lay not in the soviet but in the constitutionally undefined prerogatives of the Bolshevik party. The legacy of the civil war and Bolshevik practice was that even the most minor of issues had to be referred to the party committees for adjudication, a facet of the 'petty tutelage' against which the oppositions railed. The well-documented electoral gerrymandering, the near-suppression of non-Bolshevik political parties, and the establishment of the principle that Bolshevik deputies owed primary loyalty to their party organisation rather than to the soviet in which they sat, illustrates that internal contradictions as much as exogenous circumstances limited the development of Soviet democracy.

While the Bolsheviks established full control over the soviets there was a third area (together with the economic apparatus and the secret police) where social or institutional forces emerged with a life of their own – the bureaucracy. The bureaucracy was in part inherited from the old regime but above all it emerged from the new conditions, the civil war and the tasks that the Bolshevik project set itself. Political rather than social factors underlay the development of the bureaucracy and bureaucratism (see Chapter 6). The economic management of the country was removed from the jurisdiction of the local soviets, and the bureaucracies were freed from political control from below. Power, and with it the bureaucracy, emerged out of contending 'states', and not from the interaction of 'state' and society. The state bureaucracy controlled the whole life of the country, but the party itself felt threatened by the expanding bureaucratic apparatus. In order to avoid 'bureaucratism' the party insisted on the subordination to itself of all party members working in the state apparatus, and of the apparatuses themselves to the party as a whole, but this in itself acted as yet another spur to the power of the committees. During the civil war the party acted as the integrating force in the new bureaucracy, but even this role was lost for a time at the height of Stalinism.

By the end of the civil war all political life outside the communist party led a harried existence. All particularities were swept away, together with the political institutions of bourgeois democracy. After the revolution the Bolshevik party moved out of the arena of civil society, where parties conventionally belong, and moved into the sphere of the state, and subsumed all political life. A new type of politics emerged in which agitprop and 'transmission belts' replaced debate and contestatory social and political movements (see Chapter 6). A distinction should be drawn between the bureaucracy and bureaucratised politics. Bureaucracies are endemic to all modern (and not so modern) states, but bureaucratised politics signifies the process whereby mass participation becomes the dissemination of a new slogan and attendance at a mass meeting. The agitprop offensive kept Moscow's population and working class in a state of mobilisation, though its achievement was more to neutralise opposition than to win active support. The development of the *subbotnik* movement reveals the ambiguity of popular participation in mass movements under bureaucratised politics (see pages 203–4); and the distrust of popular control is revealed by the development of Rabkrin (see pages 197–9). The tension between genuine mass popular organisations and bureaucratised 'transmission belt' politics was revealed in the bitter debates within the Komsomol organisation (see pages 207–12). In a sense the Bolshevik project was a thoroughly bureaucratised one from the first, and hence the idea of a later degeneration must be treated with scepticism. The party organisation and its committees from the first absorbed or destroyed all intermediary aggregations between themselves and society.

Within the party not only had an organisational transformation taken place, but also an intellectual revolution. The relatively democratic internal organisation of the early period had by early 1921 given way to hierarchical command structures subordinate to committees which were increasingly independent of their own party organisations. But before this new model party could be introduced it encountered the trial of a vigorous debate. There was the genuine problem of trying to maintain discipline and cohesion in a socially heterogeneous and expanding ruling party. While most of the oppositionists were willing to countenance a great degree of centralisation, and even militarisation, during the war, the approach of peace forced the resolution of certain cardinal issues that had been shelved during the hostilities. The emergence of the oppositions themselves forced the pace of ideological restructuring and organisational consolidation. The astonishing feature of the first years of Soviet power was the extraordinary speed with which the problems emerged which await an adequate response to this day. Perhaps even more surprising is how quickly the responses to those problems became the ones of today.

The debates of 1920–early 1921 focused on three key areas (see Chapters 7 and 8). The first centred on internal party developments and sought to accompany the transition to peace with a democratisation of inner-party life. A single standardised party was developing in which the rank-and-file party member in the cells and in the *raion*s was losing the ability to influence the development of party policy. The oppositions sought to develop a relationship between the party committees and the membership which would combine effective central leadership without infringing local and individual rights. The Baumanskii oppositionists and the Ignatov group took the lead in this question. In the second debate the challenge to internal party developments was extended to the economic state which had undermined the labour movement. By focusing on the role of the trade unions the oppositions sought to establish a relationship between the state and the working class which, without denying the party's leading role, would allow greater worker participation as an organised class in the management of the economy. The major achievement of the Workers' Opposition was the challenge it posed to the 'petty tutelage' of the party over worker bodies. The problem was how to avert 'suffocation' within the party and of the elements of the dictatorship of the proletariat if the party was simultaneously 'suffocating' the rest of society. It is on this question that the Ignatovtsy came closest to providing an answer. The third key issue was a general one which underlay all the debates of the period: the problem of the intelligentsia in the revolution. The inability to achieve the organic integration of the vanguard role of the party and the masses was both cause and effect of the emergence of a centralised full-time party bureaucracy. Kautsky had defined the party as the 'confluence of socialism and the working class'.[1] The civil war saw the basis laid for the organisational supremacy of the party centres and of the 'thinking kernels', as Dunaevskii had put it (see page 210). The problem of the role of the intellectual in the revolution was raised to the level of a conscious problem by the Ignatov group and the Workers' Opposition. They attempted to merge the working class movement and the problem of ideas (consciousness) but their solution implied that the party itself was not such an effective confluence and suggested that the problem could only be solved by somewhat reducing the party's 'thinking kernel' role. Hence in three crucial respects, internal party developments, the party and the working class, and the theoretical basis of party supremacy, the Leninist concept of the party was challenged in a loose reform programme for the democratisation of the Soviet system. The Ignatov group in particular provided a sophisticated and coherent left critique of Leninist practice, somewhat reminiscent of the theoretical arguments of the coalitionists in late 1917.

The liveliness of the debates of 1920 undermines the argument that the civil war, like some terrible *deus ex machina*, cut down the intellectual vigour of the party. However, while the intellectual life of the party during the civil war can be written as the history of oppositions, the period closed with the defeat of reform proposals and the discrediting of independent thought itself. The 'Moscow Autumn' of 1920, like the Prague Spring of 1968, ended with a long period of 'normalisation'. The opposition movements were weakened by the circumstances in which they took place: international isolation, economic collapse and internal disorders. But it was not the organisational changes of the civil war in themselves which precluded the possibility of democratic reform, but the responses to the onset of peace. Social and organisational changes certainly altered the balance of forces within the party. As the leadership realised, there was indeed a social basis to the opposition, resting on the division between an active and passive membership, but it was the activists who articulated the unease. Their conflation of political and social arguments, however, ultimately weakened their case. They had the advantage neither of appealing to an identifiable social base, nor of a clearly articulated *political* alternative. But they were primarily undermined by mutual feuding and internal inconsistencies. The party and trade union debates, instead of reinforcing each other, split the movement for democratic reform and were skilfully used by the Leninists to neutralise each other (see Chapter 8). Trotsky's rather weak championing of his own cause in the trade union debate in Moscow prefigured his irresolute performance in the struggle against Stalin in the 1920s. The intellectual challenge of his position seemed to stimulate him more than its sordid defence in the political market place. Soviet-type regimes periodically go through phases when reform is on the agenda and self-criticism becomes the order of the day, but these reforms can be of two types – authoritarian or democratic, from above or from below. The trade union debate obscured the two types of reform. Its ultimate achievement, ironically, was to undermine democratic reform within the party and make authoritarian reform all the more urgent as far as the leadership was concerned.

The mutual feuding between the oppositions reflected the institutional conflicts of war communism. The Komsomol, the trade unions and the party itself all tried to become dominant in their own fields in this period of vigorous institution-building. Each spawned dissenting groups who sought greater autonomy for their own organisations and themselves. In this game of ruthless bureaucratic advancement the liberties of which they deprived others could not be retained by themselves. The debates of the 1920s over strategies for the development of the Soviet economy were, leaving aside the technical validity of the arguments themselves, as much debates over the institutional balance within the Soviet polity as with factional or social struggles. But the oppositions of 1920 were more than an internal power struggle between various sections of the new elite. They reflected the ideological tensions within war communism. The corollary of the argument that the measures taken by the Bolsheviks between 1918 and 1921 were not the

result simply of factors external to the revolution is that the oppositionists no longer appear as idealists isolated from practical realities but as
reformers offering an alternative to the Leninist synthesis of war
communist policies. The problematic of reform was first firmly placed
on the Soviet agenda in December 1918 by the Democratic Centralists in
their attempts to revive the soviets. The Workers' Opposition can be
seen as an expression of the anti-authoritarian radicalism of 1917, and
its defeat marked the triumph not of a monolithic party-state
bureaucracy but of the pattern of relations within the new polity which
had become established during the civil war. The oppositions threatened
not so much the party's leading role in the new society, as the forms
which this leading role had taken during war communism. The
oppositions from mid-1920 marked the last flare of a significant
movement in favour of genuine reform in the party and against the
bureaucratic consolidation of the state. They were not a purely
conjunctural reflection of the prevailing economic collapse and social
changes in the party but an aspect of the structural crisis of the system
which had been held in check during the civil war. The managerial vision
of authoritarian (or *dirigiste*) reform could only be implemented after
the ideological restructuring was complete. The oppositionists and the
party leadership were both all too ready to find social factors at the root
of political problems and hence the ambiguity of the entire reform
process from late 1920. It was not so much the civil war that undermined
the social base of soviet democracy as the political processes of the time.
Out of the resolution of the debates came a new stabilisation which
formed the bases for the further development of the regime. The failure
of the oppositions marked the wider failure in the transition to the NEP.

In early 1921 some of the harshest economic features of war
communism were dismantled. The broad aims of the movement were
not discarded, but only shelved, as the regime adopted a strategy of siege
rather than assault. The economic civil war was not over, only deferred.
But for the moment the principle of gradualism in the socialist economic
development of the country, dropped in mid-1918, was restored. In the
political sphere war communist practices were intensified. The economic
state and the party bureaucracy were confirmed as the twin foci of
socialist movement itself and that segment organised in the party's lower
organisations. Authoritarian reform was implemented in the party (see
pp. 238 and 260). War communism in the political sphere marked the
emergence of a permanent pattern of political authority. It signified the
shift from persuasion to coercion, from spontaneity to discipline, and
from a degree of workers' control and genuine participation to

centralised bureaucratic administration. The enthusiasm of later Bolsheviks for war communism as a heroic period was fundamentally misconceived. War communism was fraught with conflict, torn by privileges and inequality, and pervaded by arbitrariness. But in so far as it constituted a set of structures basic to communist rule in a country not so much backward as unreceptive or unready for the implementation of their programme, and able to meet the developmental needs of that country, their evaluation was correct. Lenin's genius was the ability to harness the massive potential of the modern state to the cause of socialism as defined by the Bolshevik project. Not only the civil war, but the Bolshevik definition of economic tasks, forced the concentration of economic power in the state and political power in the party. Therefore, despite the contradictory evaluations of war communism, after its close much of what had been developed during the civil war remained. If war communism was marked by the political supremacy of the party, Lenin during the NEP had no doubt that this should continue. As he put it in a speech to the Moscow Soviet on 20 November 1922: 'This little nucleus [the party] has set itself the task of remaking everything, and it will do so'.[2] As for the state apparatus, Lenin was more critical. In the same speech, and in many others of the period, he stressed the need for the party to control the state machinery, and his warnings were correct. Rapid industrialisation and collectivisation would give undue power to the economic and police apparatus and threaten not just the already enfeebled trade unions but the party itself.

Hence there are important discontinuities, and it would be a mistake to regard war communism in its entirety as a form of proto-Stalinism. The two systems, though based on an identical relationship with society, had a different balance within the state structure: Lenin's based on the dominance of the party; Stalin's on the maximum development of precisely the three areas where the party had been weak during war communism – the labour state, the secret police and the bureaucracy. While the validity of the post-Stalin 'return to Leninism' espoused by Nikita Khrushchev and his successors might be theoretically dubious, on the practical level it is an accurate reflection of the institutional shift that took place in the transition from Leninism to Stalinism. Both models had emerged in parallel during the civil war within the nexus of war communism. The struggle between the two was a reflection of two models of intra-state relations. During the civil war the rhetorical emphasis was on participation and the party survived as an independent and freely functioning organism, despite the threats from the economic state, the police and the bureaucracy, and the presence of militarisers within the party itself who would later form the kernel of the Stalinist leadership. Its congresses met regularly and it remained the ultimate political authority, and a vigorous inner-party life continued. It was the peace and economic reconstruction which saw the end of war communist ambivalences and the consolidation of authoritarian reform which was to lead on to full-blown Stalinism. The NEP for a time offered a respite to the economic inconsistencies of war communism; but the programme of authoritarian reform within the party and the political system inaugurated at the same time was no less far-reaching. In the political sphere the NEP marked the antithesis of the democratising reform programme proposed by the oppositions during war communism. Organisational reform acted as a substitute for political reform.

Was the system of war communism an early form of totalitarianism? The extension of state control over the economy, the expanding police apparatus, the destruction of intermediary groups and institutions in society, and the principle of strong leadership, all might suggest the birth of a proto-totalitarian system. However, the implication is as analytically misleading as it is descriptively accurate. While dominant, Lenin was not a dictatorial leader, and in Moscow there was no single leader at all. Given his many other duties and his character, Kamenev's chairmanship of the Moscow Soviet was largely symbolic, and the city party organisation until early 1921 was run by a fractious and collective leadership. The system was too full of tensions, society retained too many of its traditions, and there were too many unintegrated elements for it to qualify as totalitarian. This study confirms, however, the contention that war communism provided the necessary, if not sufficient, conditions for the emergence of the Stalinist version of totalitarianism; the belief in the need to remould society; the emergence of new-style party committees increasingly free from the control of the mass of the membership; the increasingly formal nature of mass participation; the confusion of economic aims with the ultimate aims of socialism; increased intolerance within the party and the end of legitimate oppositional activity; and the use of coercion to maintain an ideological line. When applied to the reality of the Soviet state after October 1917 the logic of the communist project and the theory of imperialism combined to suggest that the autonomy of civil society was both disappearing and dispensable.

War communism was a combination of economic and political practice which saw the emergence of radically new power relations. During the civil war, loyalty to a broader vision was implemented by pragmatic experimentation. But the Russian communist revolutionary movement failed to provide a detailed concept of the institutional relationships in the new society which would combine political democracy with the economic tasks of the revolution, or to provide an analysis of the role of the party in the new system. Instead the Bolsheviks maintained a credulous approach to the political culture of the new system whereby the abolition of commodity production and the other goals of the original communist project seemed to absolve them of the need to deal with the human practicalities of the Bolshevik project. These deficiencies might not have been so pronounced in a more advanced nation. But the socialist revolution was established in an isolated and industrially under-developed country, raked by the fire of civil war and foreign intervention. In this context the emerging political system became more suited for the negative task of destroying the old society than for building the new one.

The development of the party and the local state in Moscow were determined by these general factors. The sociology of the city did have some impact on the development of policies, but the paradigm relationship between party and class was transferred to those between regime and society. Aims and objectives were largely set irrespective of local conditions. The Moscow of 1921 was hardly recognisable as the one of 1917. Traditional Moscow had disappeared and nearly every institution had been transformed. The city was dominated by a pervasive bureaucracy. Control of industry had passed to the state, and society was organised as branches of the state or party. Political power in the city belonged to the party committees, and in place of the multifarious *raion*-based democracy of 1917 the city's politics were concentrated in the centre. A new type of party had come to power during the October revolution, but during war communism a new system emerged that remains the basis of the new society.

Notes and References

1 Introduction

1. Karl Marx, 'Civil War in France', in Karl Marx and Frederick Engels, *Selected Works in One Volume* (London: Lawrence and Wishart, 1968) p. 295. cf. B. Ollman, 'Marx's Vision of Communism: A Reconstruction', *Critique*, 8 (1978).
2. Radoslav Selucky, *Marxism, Socialism, Freedom: Towards a General Democratic Theory of Labor-Managed Systems* (New York: St Martin's Press, 1979) p. 73.
3. Marx and Engels, 'The Communist Manifesto', *Selected Works*, p. 53.
4. Marx, 'Civil War in France', pp. 291, 293–4.
5. Jean L. Cohen, *Class and Civil Society: The Limits of Marxian Critical Theory* (Amherst: University of Massachusetts Press, 1982) p. 23.
6. Robert C. Tucker, 'Marx as a Political Theorist', in Shlomo Avineri (ed.), *Marx's Socialism* (New York: Lieber–Atherton, 1973) p. 146 ff.
7. Alvin Gouldner, *The Two Marxisms: Contradictions and Anomalies in the Development of Theory* (London: Macmillan, 1980) p. 357.
8. Gouldner, *The Two Marxisms*, p. 357.
9. Tucker in Avineri, *Marx's Socialism*, p. 129.
10. Shlomo Avineri, 'The Hegelian Origins of Marx's Political Thought', in Avineri, *Marx's Socialism*, pp. 12–13.
11. Gouldner, *The Two Marxisms*, pp. 348–51. For an extended discussion of Lenin's 'State and Revolution' see A. J. Polan, *Lenin and the End of Politics* (London: Methuen, 1984).
12. Marx, 'Civil War in France', p. 293.
13. Ferenc Feher, 'The French Revolutions as Models for Marx's Conception of Politics', *Thesis Eleven*, 8 (January 1984) p. 73.
14. Polan, *Lenin and the End of Politics*, p. 6.
15. K. Marx, 'Critique of the Gotha Programme', *Selected Works*, p. 331.
16. Tucker in Avineri, *Marx's Socialism*, p. 149.
17. Cohen, *Class and Civil Society*, p. xiii.
18. Gouldner, *The Two Marxisms*, pp. 324–33.
19. G. Konrad and I. Szelenyi, *The Intellectuals on the Road to Class Power* (Brighton: Harvester Press, 1979) ch. 9.
20. Gouldner, *The Two Marxisms*, p. 340.
21. Ibid., p. 341.
22. J. Cohen, *Class and Civil Society*, p. 197.
23. Gouldner, *The Two Marxisms*, p. 345.
24. *Loc. cit.*
25. Neil Harding (ed.), *The State in Socialist Society* (London: Macmillan, 1984) pp. 27 and 32.
26. José Casanova, review of Jean L. Cohen, *Class and Civil Society* in *Telos*, 59 (1984) p. 194.
27. Cohen, *Class and Civil Society*, p. 25.

28. Casanova, *Telos*, p. 190.
29. Feher, *Thesis Eleven*, pp. 68–9.
30. Robert Eugene Johnson, *Peasant and Proletarian: The Working Class of Moscow in the Late Nineteenth Century* (Leicester: Leicester University Press) 1979, p. 14.
31. Victoria Bonnell, *Roots of Rebellion: Workers' Politics and Organisations in St Petersburg and Moscow, 1900–1914* (Berkeley, CA: University of California Press, 1983) chs 2 and 10.
32. For example, in Lenin's 1920 article 'Left Wing Communism an Infantile Disorder' and in 1922 in his tenth anniversary of *Pravda* speech, see E. H. Carr, *The Bolshevik Revolution, 1917–1923* (Harmondsworth: Pelican, 1966) vol. 1, p. 19.
33. Philip Corrigan, *et al.*, *Socialist Construction and Marxist Theory: Bolshevism and its Critique* (London: Macmillan, 1978) p. 26.
34. John Molyneaux, *Marxism and the Party* (London: Pluto Press, 1978) p. 15, from K. Marx, 'The Poverty of Philosophy' (Moscow, 1966) p. 150.
35. Mihaly Vajda, *The State and Socialism: Political Essays* (London, Alison and Busby, 1981) p. 95. The term 'integral politics' is used by Konrad and Szelenyi, *The Intellectuals*, p. 73.
36. C. A. Linden, *The Soviet Party-State: The Politics of Ideocratic Despotism* (New York: Praeger, 1983) pp. 25 and 53.
37. Merle Fainsod, *How Russia is Ruled* (London: Oxford University Press, 1963) p. 45.
38. A. I. Arenshtein, *Rannim Moskovskim utrom* (Moscow, 1967) p. 129.
39. Arenshtein, *Rannim*, p. 155.
40. Carr, *Bolshevik Revolution*, 1, pp. 25–6.
41. These were the major arguments of the Moscow printworkers in their journal *Pechatnik* between October 1917 and late 1918.
42. For a classic statement of the issue see Joseph A. Schumpeter, *Capitalism and Democracy* (New York: Harper Brothers, 1950) pp. 235–49 and *passim*. For the USSR see Carmen Sirianni, *Workers' Control and Socialist Democracy: The Soviet Experience* (London: New Left Books, 1982).
43. Feher, *Thesis Eleven*, p. 59.
44. Albert L. Weeks, *The First Bolshevik: A Political Biography of Peter Tkachev* (London, 1968).
45. Michael Lowy, *Georg Lukács: From Romanticism to Bolshevism* (London: New Left Books, 1979) pp. 132 and 136.
46. Chantal Mouffe (ed.), *Gramsci and Marxist Theory* (London: Routledge & Kegan Paul, 1979) p. 264.
47. Timothy W. Luke, *Ideology and Soviet Industrialisation* (London: Greenwood Press, 1985).
48. N. Bukharin, *Imperialism and World Economy* (London: Merlin Press, 1972) pp. 128, 157 and 159.
49. V. I. Lenin, *Ocherednye zadachi Sovetskoi vlasti* ('Current Tasks of Soviet Power') April 1918, *Polnoe sobranie sochinenii* (henceforth *PSS*), 36, pp. 167–208. For an extended analysis of the primacy of development over socialist solidarity in the Bolshevik project see Thomas. F. Remington, *Building Socialism in Bolshevik Russia: Ideology and Industrial Organisation, 1917–1921* (Pittsburgh, Pa: University of Pittsburgh Press, 1984).

50. N. Bukharin, *The Politics and Economics of the Transition Period*, K. J. Tarbuck (ed.) (London: Routledge & Kegan Paul, 1979) p. 41; Leon Trotsky, *Terrorism and Communism* (London: New Park Publications, 1975) p. 55.
51. Polan, *Lenin and the End of Politics*, p. 14 and *passim*.
52. Engels in the 1891 preface to the 'Civil War in France'.
53. Feher, *Thesis Eleven*, p. 73.
54. Tucker in Avineri, *Marx's Socialism*, p. 145.
55. David W. Lovell, *From Marx to Lenin: An Evaluation of Marx's Responsibility for Soviet Authoritarianism* (Cambridge: Cambridge University Press, 1984) pp. 191–2.
56. Ibid., p. 192.
57. Marc Raeff, *Comprendre l'ancien régime Russe: état et société en Russie impériale. Essai d'interprétation* (Paris: Editions du Seuil, 1982) ch. 7, pp. 178–89 and 224.
58. Richard Pipes, *Russia Under the Old Regime* (London: Peregrine Books, 1977).
59. For example, Manfred Hagen, *Die Entfaltung politischer Offentlichkeit in Russland, 1906–1914* (Wiesbaden, 1982).
60. N. Berdyaev, *The Origin of Russian Communism* (London, 1937) p. 145.
61. Theodore Dan, *The Origins of Bolshevism* (London: Secker and Warburg, 1964) p. 11.
62. Linden, *The Soviet Party-State*, pp. 1–5.
63. Zygmunt Bauman, 'Review-Symposium on Soviet-Type Societies', *Telos*, 60 (Summer 1984) p. 178.
64. N. N. Bazhenov, 'La Revolution Russe', *Pages actuelles*, 1914–19 (Paris, 1919) p. 49.
65. Antonio Gramsci, *Selections From the Prison Notebooks* (London: Lawrence and Wishart, 1971) p. 238.
66. Wladyslaw Bienkowski, *Theory and Reality: The Development of Social Systems* (London: Alison and Busby, 1981) p. 162.
67. R. M. Savitskaya, 'O rabote V. I. Lenina nad vtoroi programmoi partii', *VI KPSS*, 4 (1984) p. 22.
68. Boris L. Dvinov, *Moskovskii sovet rabochikh deputatov, 1917–1922: vospominaniya* (New York, 1961) pp. 58–9.
69. Vajda, *State and Socialism*, p. 95.
70. *The Bolsheviks and the October Revolution: Central Committee Minutes of the Russian Social-Democratic Labour Party (Bolsheviks), August 1917–February 1918* (London: Pluto Press, 1974) pp. 140–2.
71. *Materialy po peresmotru partiinoi programmy* (Moscow: Moscow Oblast Bureau, 1917) pp. 23–34.
72. William G. Rosenberg, 'Russian Labor and Bolshevik Power after October', *Slavic Review* (Summer 1985) pp. 213–38; David Mandel, *The Petrograd Workers and the Soviet Seizure of Power: From the July Days to July 1918* (London: Macmillan, 1984).
73. Lenin, *PSS*, 36, p. 71.
74. O. N. Znamenskii, *Vserossiiskoe uchreditel'noe sobranie* (Leningrad, 1976) p. 357.
75. Lenin, *PSS*, 35, pp. 162–6.

76. Lenin, *PSS*, 36, p. 66.
77. Lenin, *PSS*, 34, p. 161.
78. Vajda, *State and Socialism*, p. 87.
79. N. Bukharin, *Programma kommunistov (bol'shevikov)* (Moscow, 1918) pp. 11–12, 14, 36, 43 and 45.
80. W. H. Chamberlin, *The Russian Revolution, 1917–1921*, vol. 2 (London, 1938) p. 96.
81. Paul C. Roberts, ' "War Communism": A Re-Examination', *Slavic Review* (June 1970) pp. 238–61.
82. Maurice Dobb, *Soviet Economic Development Since 1917* (London, 1948) p. 122.
83. Lenin, *PSS*, 44, p. 151.
84. Serge Mallet, *Bureaucracy and Technocracy in the Socialist Countries* (London: Spokesman Books, 1974) p. 34.
85. Moshe Lewin, *Political Undercurrents in Soviet Economic Debates* (London: Pluto Press, 1975) p. 77.
86. Lenin, *PSS*, 43, p. 379.
87. V. D. Polikarpov, *Nachal'nyi etap grazhdanskoi voiny: istoriya izucheniya* (Moscow, 1980) pp. 10–14 and *passim*.
88. Lenin, *PSS*, 36, p. 404.
89. N. Bukharin, *Ot diktatury imperializma k diktature proletariata* (Moscow, 1918) pp. 35–6.
90. Lenin, *PSS*, 36, p. 4.
91. D. Footman, *Civil War in Russia* (New York: Praeger, 1962) p. 22.
92. Lenin *PSS*, 39, p. 406.
93. Evan Mawdsley, 'When did the Civil War Start?', Unpublished paper presented to the Soviet Industrialisation Project Seminar, Centre for Russian and East European Studies, University of Birmingham (January 1985) p. 8.
94. Lenin, *PSS*, 39, p. 406.
95. Roy Medvedev, *The October Revolution* (London: Constable, 1979) p. 178.
96. Naum Jasny, *Soviet Economists of the 1920s: Names to be Remembered* (Cambridge: Cambridge University Press, 1972) p. 7.
97. I. A. Gladkov, *Ocherki sovetskoi ekonomiki, 1917–1920gg.* (Moscow, 1956) p. 273.
98. *Loc. cit.*
99. Medvedev, *October Revolution*, pp. 117–31.
100. Laszlo Szamuely, *First Models of the Socialist Systems: Principles and Theories* (Budapest, 1974) pp. 46–62.
101. Silvana Malle, *The Economic Organisation of War Communism, 1918– 1921* (Cambridge: Cambridge University Press, 1985) p. 16. For a discussion of the economic policies in Spring 1918 see E. G. Gimpel'son, *"Voennyi kommunizm": politika, praktika, ideologiya* (Moscow, 1973) pp. 8–39.
102. Lenin, *PSS*, 39, p. 358. For Lenin's evaluation in October 1921 of the policies of Spring 1918 see Lenin *PSS*, 44, p. 199.
103. Trotsky, *Terrorism and Communism*, p. 121 and *passim*.
104. N. Bukharin, *Transition Period* in Tarbuck (ed.), pp. 36 and 48.
105. Stephen F. Cohen, *Bukharin and the Bolshevik Revolution: A Political*

Biography, 1888–1938 (New York: Vintage Books, 1975) pp. 90–5.
106. Malle, *Economic Organisation* pp. 4–6.
107. *Ibid.*, p. 5. This indeed was the classic Stalinist view, discussed by Charles Bettelheim, *Class Struggles in the USSR: First Period, 1917–1923* (Brighton: Harvester Press, 1976) pp. 20–9.
108. Corrigan *et al., Soviet Construction*, p. 60.
109. Ibid., p. 43.
110. Szamuely, *First Models*, p. 44.
111. Ibid., p. 8.
112. Lenin, *PSS*, 43, p. 220.
113. Malle, *Economic Organisation*, p. 11.
114. Lenin, *PSS*, 44, p. 204.
115. L. Kritsman, *Geroicheskii period velikoi russkoi revolyutsii: opyt analiza t.n. "voennogo kommunizma"* (Moscow/Leningrad, 1926) pp. 82–4.
116. Ibid., p. 71.
117. Gimpel'son, *"Voennyi kommunizm"*, pp. 191–2.
118. Szamuely, *First Models*, p. 65.
119. Norman Davies, 'The Missing Revolutionary War', *Soviet Studies*, XXVII, 2 (1975) p. 179.
120. Chamberlin, *The Russian Revolution*, p. 296.
121. This has been shown by Robert Service, *The Bolshevik Party in Revolution 1917–1923: A Study in Organisational Change*, (London: Macmillan, 1979) ch. 2, for the country as a whole; Alexander Rabinowich, *The Bolsheviks Come to Power: The Revolution of 1917 in Petrograd* (New York, 1976) for Petrograd; and B'Ann Bowman, *The Moscow Bolsheviks, February–November 1917*, PhD Dissertation (Indiana, 1973) for Moscow.
122. Bukharin, *Transition Period* in Tarbuck (ed.), p. 49.
123. Service, *The Bolshevik Party*, p. 3.
124. Carl J. Friedrich, 'Evolving Theory and Practice', in *Totalitarianism in Perspective: Three Views* (London: Pall Mall Press, 1969) p. 107.
125. Zygmunt Bauman, 'The Party in the System–Management Phase: Change and Continuity', in A. Janos (ed.), *Authoritarian Politics in Communist Europe* (Berkeley: University of California Press, 1976) p. 97.
126. Trotsky, *Terrorism and Communism*, pp. 122–3.
127. Carr, *Bolshevik Revolution*, 1, p. 192.
128. A. Avtorkhanov, *Proiskhozhdenie partokratii*, vol. 1, *TsK i Lenin* (Frankfurt: Posev, 1973).
129. Jonathan R. Adelman, 'The Development of the Soviet Party Apparat in the Civil War: Center, Localities and Nationality Areas', *Russian History/Histoire Russe*, 9, pt 1 (1982) p. 87. The main positions on these questions have been summarised by Service, *The Bolshevik Party*, pp. 4–7.
130. Neil Harding, *Lenin's Political Thought*, vol. 2, *Theory and Practice in the Socialist Revolution* (London: Macmillan, 1981) p. 175.
131. R. V. Daniels, *The Conscience of the Revolution: Communist Opposition in Soviet Russia* (London, 1960) pp. 117–8.
132. Leonard Schapiro, *The Origin of the Communist Autocracy: Political Opposition in the Soviet State, 1917–22* (London, 1955) p. 217.
133. Carr, *Bolshevik Revolution*, 2, p. 270.
134. Lowy, *Georg Lukács*, pp. 189 and 208.
135. Neil McInnes, 'Georg Lukács', *Survey*, 70–73 (1969) p. 128.

2 Society and Economy in Moscow

1. For an analysis of the cultural and symbolic rivalry between Moscow and St Petersburg see Richard Wortman, 'Moscow and Petersburg: The Problem of the Political Center in Tsarist Russia, 1881–1914', in Sean Wilentz (ed.), *Rites of Power: Symbolism, Ritual and Politics since the Middle Ages* (Philadelphia: University of Pennsylvania Press, 1985) pp. 244–71.
2. *Statisticheskii spravochnik g. Moskvy i Moskovskoi gubernii 1927g.* (Moscow, 1928) p. 24.
3. *Krasnaya Moskva: sbornik statei (KM)* (Moscow, 1920) cols. 52–3; *Izmeneniya sotsial'noi struktury sovetskogo obshchestva: oktyabr' 1917–1920* (Moscow, 1976) p. 248.
4. J. H. Bater and R. A. French, *Studies in Russian Historical Geography* vol. 2 (Academic Press, 1983), pp. 282 and 301.
5. *KM*, col. 170.
6. Bater and French, *Studies in Russian*, p. 285.
7. On urbanisation and municipal government, see Michael F. Hamm, 'The Breakdown of Urban Modernisation: A Prelude to the Revolutions of 1917', in M. F. Hamm (ed.), *The City in Russian History* (Kentucky, 1976) pp. 182–95; and James H. Bater, 'Some Dimensions of Urbanisation and the Response of Municipal Government: Moscow and St Petersburg', *Russian History/Histoire Russe*, 5, pt 1 (1978) pp. 46–63.
8. *Statisticheskii ezhegodnik g. Moskvy i Moskovskoi gubernii*, issue 2, 1914–1925 (Moscow, 1927) p. 9.
9. *KT*, 21 August, 22 October 1920.
10. H. G. Wells, *Russia in the Shadows* (London, 1920) p. 134; *Sunday Express*, 28 November 1920.
11. *Vechernie izvestiya Moskovskogo soveta (VIMS)*, 3 September 1919.
12. *Vechernyaya krasnaya gazeta*, 28 September 1918.
13. *O naselenii Moskvy* (Moscow, 1980) p. 29.
14. 11 days p.a. in 1917, 19.2 in 1919, *KM*, col. 186.
15. *VIMS*, 3, 31 May and 11 November 1919.
16. *KT*, 25 October 1921.
17. S. G. Wheatcroft, *Famine and Factors Affecting Mortality in the USSR: The Demographic Crises of 1914–1922 and 1930–1933*, CREES, University of Birmingham, Soviet Industrialisation Project Series), *SIPS* 20 (1981) pp. 13–14.
18. From 231 485 in 1918 to 189 811 in 1920, *KT*, 22 October 1920.
19. *KT*, 18 March 1921.
20. *KT*, 4 August 1920. On housing and other aspects of the social crisis, see William John Chase, *Moscow and its Working Class, 1918–1928: A Social Analysis*, PhD dissertation (Boston, 1979) pp. 39–47 and *passim*.
21. *Stat. spravochnik*, p. 29.
22. *Stat. ezhegodnik*, p. 171.
23. *KM*, col. 688.
24. Ya. Piletskii, *Rabochii klass i khozyaistvo Rossii v 1914–1919 godakh* (Kiev, 1919) p. 25.
25. Diane Koenker, *Moscow Workers and the 1917 Revolution* (Princeton, NJ: Princeton University Press, 1981) pp. 78–83.

26. *Statistika truda*, 6–7, 1918, p. 2.
27. *Sotsial-demokrat*, 12 September 1917.
28. *P*, 6 April 1918.
29. *KT*, 21 September 1920; *KM*, col. 686; *Bor'ba klassov*, 7–8, 1934, p. 184.
30. Medvedev, *October Revolution*, p. 155.
31. *Lenin i Moskovskie bol'sheviki* (Moscow, 1977) pp. 331–2.
32. *Ocherki istorii Moskovskoi organizatsii KPSS, 1883–1965* (Moscow, 1966) pp. 332, 334 and 339.
33. *IV Moskovskaya gubernskaya konferentsiya profsoyuzov, 14–15 sentyabr' 1921g.* (Moscow, 1921) p. 13.
34. Piletskii, *Rabochii klass*, p. 23.
35. *Pechatnik*, 3–4, 1 April 1919, p. 12.
36. Piletskii, *Rabochii klass*, p. 23.
37. Vydro, *Naselenie Moskvy*, p. 39.
38. N. M. Aleshchenko, *Moskovskii sovet v 1917–1941gg.* (Moscow, 1976) p. 222.
39. *Izvestiya Moskovskogo soyuza rabochikh i sluzhashchikh po vyrabotke pishchevykh produktov*, 2, 25 November 1918, p. 3.
40. *KM*, col. 184.
41. *VIMS*, 5 July, 3 November 1919.
42. *TsGAOR*, 7952/3/212/217.
43. *P*, 27 July 1919.
44. Vydro, *Naselenie Moskvy*, p. 47.
45. *Stenograficheskie otchety Moskovskogo soveta (Stenotchety MS)*, 2 (1920) p. 26.
46. *KT*, 15 April 1920.
47. *Trudy TsU*, vol. 26, issues 1–2 (Moscow, 1926) pp. VIII, XXI and 16.
48. *KM*, col. 167.
49. Whereas in Petrograd in 1917 82 per cent of the working class were employed in enterprises of over 500 workers (*Izmeneniya sotsial'noi struktury*, p. 131) with an average of 740 workers per enterprise, in Moscow concentration averaged 209 over 960 enterprises (*KM*, col. 169) or 176 averaged over 1064 enterprises (*Stat. ezhegodnik*, p. 198). The relative weight of Moscow's textile and metal industries in 1917 has been contested as part of the debate over Moscow's 'petty bourgeois' character. For a wealth of information on Moscow's working class in 1917 see D. Koenker, *Moscow Workers*.
50. *KM*, col. 169.
51. *KM*, cols. 169–70.
52. M. Gorky, *History of the Civil War in the USSR*, vol. 2 (London, 1974) p. 68.
53. *KT*, 22 October 1920.
54. *Stat. ezhegodnik*, p. 171.
55. *KT*, 7 November 1920.
56. *KT*, 26 March 1920.
57. *KT*, 7 November 1920.
58. N. Rodionova, *Gody napryazhennogo truda. Iz istorii Moskovskoi partiinoi organizatsii 1921–1925gg.* (Moscow, 1963) p. 4.
59. *KT*, 17 December 1920.
60. *TsGAOR*, 7952/3/210/189.

61. *Istoriya Moskvy*, vol. 6, book 1 (Moscow, 1957) p. 206.
62. Rudzutak was the first chairman, followed by Al'perovich in July 1918–, *Izvestiya MOSNKh*, 1, 1 September 1918, p. 3.
63. R. V. Kostina, 'Moskovskii gorodskoi sovnarkhoz v reshenii voprosov upravleniya promyshlennost'yu stolitsy, 1918–1920gg.', *Istoriya SSSR*, 4 (1984) p. 117.
64. This figure comes from the MREK list of 2 April 1918, in *Uprochenie sovetskoi vlasti v Moskve i Moskovskoi gubernii: dokumenty i materialy*, (Moscow, 1958) pp. 243–9, and that of VSNKh of 1 June, in *Narodnoe khozyaistvo*, 4 (1918) p. 5.
65. A. V. Strakhov, 'Natsionalizatsiya krupnoi promyshlennosti goroda Moskvy', *Uchenye zapiski MGPI im. V. I. Lenina*, 200 (1964) p. 223.
66. Ibid., p. 256.
67. Ibid., p. 257.
68. Ibid., p. 273.
69. N. M. Aleshchenko, 'Moskovskii sovet v 1918–1920gg.', *Istoricheskie zapiski*, 91 (1973) p. 90.
70. *Trudy II vserossiiskogo s''ezda sovetov narodnogo khozyaistva, 19–27 dekabrya 1918g.: stenograficheskii otchet* (Moscow, 1919) pp. 1–6.
71. Ibid., p. 18.
72. *Narodnoe khozyaistvo*, 12 (1918) p. 56; A. V. Venediktov, *Organizatsiya gosudarstvennoi promyshlennosti v SSSR*, vol. 1, 1917–1920 (Leningrad, 1957) pp. 549–50.
73. *Trudy II s''ezda SNKh*, p. 223; Venediktov, p. 550.
74. *Izvestiya MOSNKh*, 1 (1918) p. 1.
75. Aleshchenko (1973) p. 90; Kostina, 'Moskovskii gorodskoi', pp. 117–8.
76. E. G. Gimpel'son, *Velikii Oktyabr' i stanovlenie sovetskoi sistemy upravleniya narodnym khozyaistvom* (Moscow, 1977) p. 18.
77. *VIMS*, 13 January 1919; *Ekon. zhizn'*, 14 January 1919.
78. Venediktov, *Organizatsiya gosudarstvennoi* p. 565.
79. Gimpel'son (1977), p. 53.
80. In 1918 alone 42 *glavki* were formed (*II S''ezd SNKh*, p. 76) and the number mushroomed thereafter to cover ever smaller segments of industry. In early 1921 the Moscow metal and chemical industries were run by no less than 14 apiece – *Byulleten' MSNKh*, 5, 10 April 1921, p. 1.
81. *Ekon. zhizn'*, 6 May 1919; Kostina, 'Moskovskii gorodskoi', p. 123.
82. *Byulleten' MSNKh*, 14, 31 August 1921, pp. 5–6.
83. *KT*, 3 September 1920.
84. *Ist. Mosk. rab.*, p. 71.
85. *KT*, 6 November 1920.
86. N. Nikolaev, *Moskovskii rabochii i krest'yanin* (Moscow, 1921).
87. *Byulleten' MSNKh*, 1, 30 January 1921, p. 13.
88. Kostina, 'Moskovskii gorodskoi', p. 123.
89. *KT*, 18 November 1920.
90. *Izvestiya MOSNKh*, 2, 15 September 1918, p. 2.
91. *Byulleten' MSNKh*, 2, 15 December 1920, p. 2.
92. *KT*, 17 December 1920.
93. *Byulleten' MSNKh*, 1, 30 January 1921, p. 13.
94. *Ekon. zhizn'*, 13 December 1919.

95. Kostina, 'Moskovskii gorodskoi', p. 126.
96. *Byulletin' MSNKh*, 2, 15 December 1920, p. 17.
97. *VIMS*, 7 October 1918.
98. V. Z. Drobizhev, 'Obrazovanie sovetov narodnogo khozyaistva v Moskovskom promyshlennom raione (1917–1918gg.)' in *Iz istorii velikoi oktyabr'skoi sotsialisticheskoi revolyutsii* (Moscow, 1957) pp. 107–8.
99. Kostina, 'Moskovskii gorodskoi', p. 118.
100. *KT*, 6 February 1921.
101. Drobizhev (1957), pp. 107–8.
102. Peter A. Garvi, *Zapiski sotsial-demokrata, 1906–1921* (Newtonville, MA: Oriental Research Partners, 1982) p. 381. According to VSNKh figures on 1 January 1918 there were 23 000 societies with a membership of about 10 million (*Narodnoe khozyaistvo*, 3 (1918) p. 4). The numbers rose sharply in 1918.
103. Garvi, *Zapiski*, pp. 326–7.
104. Koenker, Moscow Workers, p. 248.
105. G. S. Ignat'ev, *Moskva v pervyi god proletarskoi diktatury* (Moscow, 1975) pp. 260–1.
106. Garvi, *Zapiski*, p. 300.
107. Ibid., p. 313; Carr, *Bolshevik Revolution*, 2, pp. 124–5.
108. V. V. Kabanov, 'O "neitral'nosti" kooperatsii v 1917–1920gg.' in *Bankrotstvo melkoburzhuaznykh partii Rossii, 1917–1922gg.*, pt 2 (Moscow, 1977) p. 99.
109. Garvi, *Zapiski*, p. 317.
110. Ibid., p. 323.
111. Ibid., p. 328.
112. Lenin, *PSS*, 36, p. 161; and 37, p. 409.
113. Garvi, *Zapiski*, p. 329.
114. Lenin, *PSS*, 35, pp. 206–10.
115. Ignat'ev, *Moskva v pervyi*, pp. 261–2.
116. Garvi, *Zapiski*, p. 336.
117. Ibid., p. 338; Ignat'ev, *Moskva v pervyi*, pp. 262–3.
118. Ignat'ev, *Moskva v pervyi*, pp. 265–6; Garvi, *Zapiski*, pp. 345–6.
119. *Programma kommunistov*, p. 41.
120. Ignat'ev, *Moskva v pervyi*, p. 266.
121. Lenin, *PSS*, 37, p. 348.
122. Ignat'ev, *Moskva v pervyi*, 266–7.
123. Jasny, *Soviet Economists*, p. 14.
124. Lenin, *PSS*, 37, p. 343.
125. Ignat'ev, *Moskva v pervyi*, p. 266; Garvi, *Zapiski*, p. 351.
126. Garvi, *Zapiski*, pp. 355–6.
127. Ibid., pp. 358–9.
128. Ignat'ev, *Moskva v pervyi*, pp. 267–8; Garvi, *Zapiski*, p. 359; Carr, *Bolshevik Revolution*, 2, pp. 238–9.
129. Garvi, *Zapiski*, pp. 360–1.
130. Kritsman, *Geroicheskii*, p. 65.
131. *Izvestiya VTsIK*, 17 July 1919; Kostina, 'Moskovskii gorodskoi', p. 127.
132. Garvi, *Zapiski*, pp. 366–7.
133. Lenin, *PSS*, 38, p. 99.

134. Ignat'ev, *Moskva v pervyi*, p. 248.
135. Ibid., pp. 235–8.
136. *P*, 30 May 1918.
137. *Moskovskaya gorodskaya i Moskovskaya oblastnaya organizatsii KPSS v tsifrakh* (Moscow, 1972) p. 21.
138. Lenin, *PSS*, 39, pp. 357–8; 40, pp. 109, 120 and 186. On the attempts to provide goods in exchange for grain, and on Soviet supply policies in general, see Gimpel'son *Voennyi kommunizm*, pp. 56–85.
139. *Uprochenie*, pp. 319–20.
140. Ibid., p. 325.
141. Ibid., pp. 323–4, 330–2, 337–42 and 345.
142. Lenin, *PSS*, 36, p. 448.
143. *P*, 13 September 1918.
144. *P*, 22 September 1918.
145. *Mosk. gorodskaya*, p. X.
146. *Bor'ba klassov*, 7–8 (1934) p. 184.
147. *P*, 25 August 1918.
148. *P*, 1 September 1918.
149. Kritsman, *Geroicheskii*, p. 140.
150. *P*, 12 November 1918.
151. *Stenotchety MS*, 2 (1919) pp. 17–32.
152. *P*, 25 June 1919.
153. *P*, 15 July 1919.
154. Kritsman, *Geroicheskii*, p. 130.
155. *KT*, 17 April 1920.
156. *KT*, 20 March 1920.
157. *IT s"ezd SNKh*, p. 111.
158. Kritsman, *Geroicheskii*, p. 139.
159. *IT s"ezd SNKh*, p. 26.
160. Among the most vivid descriptions of the Sukharevka and other markets are Emma Goldman, *My Disillusionment in Russia* (London, 1923) pp. 23–4; Aleksander Berkman, *The Bolshevik Myth: Diary 1920–22* (London, 1925) pp. 55–60; and Marguerite Harrison, *Marooned in Moscow* (New York, 1921) pp. 150–7.
161. Kritsman, *Geroicheskii*, p. 142.
162. *P*, 17 September 1919.
163. *VIMS*, 21 July 1919.
164. *KT*, 28 April 1920.
165. *KT*, 4 June 1920.
166. *P*, 18 January 1919.
167. Lenin, *PSS*, 54, pp. 424–5.
168. *KT*, 20 March 1920.
169. *Dekrety Sovetskoi vlasti*, vol. 6 (Moscow, 1973) pp. 217–8.
170. *KM*, col. 631.
171. *KM*, col. 632.
172. *KT*, 2 October 1920.
173. *Izvestiya TsK RKP*, 12, 4 January 1920.
174. *IX s"ezd RKP(b), mart–aprel' 1920 goda: protokoly* (Moscow, 1960) pp. 195–6.

175. *IX s"ezd*, pp. 179–80.
176. *IX s"ezd*, p. 27.

3 Labour and the Socialist State

1. On the national debate see, A. Brodersen, *The Soviet Worker: Labour and Government in Soviet Society* (New York, 1966); M. Dewar, *Labour Policy in the USSR, 1917–28* (London, 1956); Isaac Deutscher, *Soviet Trade Unions: Their Place in Soviet Labour Policy* (London, 1950); T. T. Hammond, *Lenin on Trade Unions and Revolution, 1893–1917* (New York, 1957).
2. Lenin, *PSS*, 38, p. 97.
3. S. Al'perovich, *Chetvertyi s"ezd profsoyuzov i puti Russkogo profdvizheniya* (Moscow, 1921) p. 2.
4. Quoted in Garvi, *Zapiski*, p. 333.
5. *IV Mosk. gub. konf. profsoyuzov*, p. 18.
6. Koenker, *Moscow Workers*, p. 171.
7. *Obzor deyatel'nosti MGSPS za period mezhdu II i III gubernskimi s"ezdami (sentyabr' 1920–mai 1921gg.*) (Moscow, 1921) p. 73. In Russia as a whole the percentage of union members working in production fell from 57 per cent in 1918 to 34.7 per cent in 1921. A. Aluf, *Professional'nye soyuzy v period voennogo kommunizma* (Moscow, 1925) p. 28.
8. *Moskovskii sovet professional'nykh soyuzov v 1917g.: protokoly* (Moscow, 1927) p. 135.
9. Ibid., p. 141.
10. *KM*, col. 679.
11. *Obzor deyatel'nosti MGSPS*, p. 3.
12. *Protokoly MGSPS*, 1, 26 September 1920, p. 6.
13. Ibid., p. 3.
14. *Protokoly MGSPS*, 9 (1920) pp. 36–7.
15. *Obzor deyatel'nosti MGSPS*, pp. 3 and 8.
16. *MSPS v 1917g.*, p. 5.
17. *Velikaya Oktyabr'skaya sotsialisticheskaya revolyutsiya. Dokumenty i materialy. Revolyutsionnoe dvizhenie v Rossii v aprele 1917g. Aprel'skii krizis* (Moscow, 1958) pp. 41–2.
18. *P*, 2 September 1919.
19. *VIII konferentsiya RKP(b), dekabr' 1919g.: protokoly* (Moscow, 1961) pp. 231–2.
20. For example, *Otchet MK za sentyabr' 1920g.* (Moscow, 1920) p. 4.
21. Out of a union membership in Moscow of 689 763 in September 1920 (Table 3.1) only 16 763 were communists (2.4 per cent). A total of 1042 communists (678 in the city) were employed in the movement, 664 of whom (540 in the city) were full-time union organisers (Table 4.2).
22. Alfred Rosmer, *Lenin's Moscow* (London: Pluto, 1971) p. 93.
23. *Protokoly MGSPS*, 17 (1920) p. 8; *Obzor deyatel'nosti MGSPS*, p. 22.
24. *Protokoly MGSPS*, 13 (1920) p. 50.
25. *Protokoly MGSPS*, 14 (1920) p. 5.

26. *Protokoly MGSPS*, 29 (1920) p. 13.
27. *KT*, 21 September 1920.
28. *KT*, 23 September 1920; *KM*, col. 685.
29. *Protokoly MGSPS*, 18 (1920) p. 11; 30 (1920) p. 15.
30. *Obzor deyatel'nosti MGSPS*, p. 2.
31. *MSPS v 1917g.*, p. 124.
32. *MSPS v 1917g.*, p. 131.
33. Kostina, 'Moskovskii gorodskoi', p. 118.
34. *Protokoly MGSPS*, 7 (1920) p. 30.
35. *Protokoly MGSPS*, 7 (1920) p. 30.
36. *Protokoly MGSPS*, 33 (1920) p. 21.
37. *Obzor deyatel'nosti MGSPS*, p. 5.
38. *P*, 19 January 1921.
39. *P*, 26 January 1921.
40. *Protokoly MGSPS*, 34 (1920) p. 22; 37, 1921, p. 4.
41. *Protokoly MGSPS*, 37 (1921) p. 4.
42. Rosmer, *Lenin's Moscow*, p. 117.
43. *Vestnik truda*, 11 (December 1920) pp. 11–14.
44. *Partiya i soyuzy* (Petersburg, 1921) p. 362.
45. *Partiya i soyuzy*, p. 166.
46. *I vserossiiskii s''ezd profsoyuzov sluzhashchikh (iyun' 1918g.)* (Moscow, 1918) p. 9.
47. Leopold Haimsom, 'The Problem of Social Stability in Urban Russia, 1905–1917', pt 1, *Slavic Review*, 4 (23) (1964) pp. 619–42; pt 2, 1 (24) (1965) pp. 1–22.
48. M. S. Bernshtam (ed.), *Issledovaniya noveishei Russkoi istorii*, vol. 2, *Nezavisimoe rabochee dvizhenie v 1918 godu: dokumenty i materialy* (Paris: YMCA Press, 1981) pp. 145–6.
49. Lenin, *PSS*, 37, pp. 90–1.
50. Lenin, *PSS*, 50, p. 90.
51. Bernshtam, *Issledovaniya*, p. 185.
52. Raphael R. Abramovitch, *The Russian Revolution, 1917–1939* (London: George Allen & Unwin, 1962) p. 164.
53. *Dekrety Sovetskoi vlasti*, vol. 2 (Moscow, 1959) pp. 343 and 360–2.
54. *P*, 1 December 1918. For the Mensheviks in the soviets in spring 1918 see Vladimir Brovkin, 'The Mensheviks' Political Comeback: The Elections to the Provincial City Soviets in Spring 1918', *The Russian Review*, vol. 42 (1983), pp. 1–50.
55. *Desyat' let: sbornik materialov Yu.O.K. Sokol'nicheskogo raiona – k 10-letiyu oktyabr'skoi revolyutsii* (Moscow, 1927) p. 60.
56. *KT*, 17 December 1921.
57. Shustova, p. 52; *Vechernyaya krasnaya gazeta*, 61, 28 September 1918.
58. *P*, 1 August 1918.
59. Ignat'ev, *Moskva v pervyi*, p. 150.
60. *Pechatnik*, 5, 31 May 1918, pp. 6–7.
61. *Moskovskii pechatnik*, 1, 15 January 1921, p. 6; *Pechatnik*, 1–2, 15 January 1919, p. 3.
62. *Moskovskii pechatnik*, 1, 15 January 1921, p. 7.
63. *Pechatnik*, 1–2, 25 January 1918.

64. Dvinov, *Moskovskii sovet*, p. 81.
65. *VIMS*, 25 December 1919.
66. *P*, 20 December 1919.
67. *P*, 23 June 1920.
68. *KT*, 19 June 1920.
69. *KT*, 25 June 1920.
70. *Sotsialisticheskii vestnik (SV)*, 1, 1 February 1921, p. 15; 2, 16 February 1921, p. 15.
71. *Profsoyuzy Moskvy* (Moscow, 1975) p. 156.
72. *P*, 27 September 1919.
73. *Otchet MK za iyul' 1920g.* (Moscow, 1920) p. 3.
74. Victor Serge, *Memoirs of a Revolutionary, 1901–1941* (Oxford: Oxford University Press, 1967) (trans. Peter Sedgwick) p. 122.
75. Harrison, *Marooned*, p. 73. Cf. Paul Avrich, *The Russian Anarchists* (New York, 1978) p. 223.
76. *KT*, 6 March 1921.
77. Schapiro, *Origin*, p. 203.
78. A Bolshevik breakaway chemical union, for example, was formed in late 1921, *KT*, 4, 7 October 1921.
79. E. G. Gimpel'son, 'O rabochem kontrole posle prinyatiya dekreta o natsionalizatsii promyshlennosti v SSSR', *Istoriya SSSR*, 4 (1981) p. 117.
80. *Dekrety Sovetskoi vlasti*, vol. 1 (Moscow, 1957) p. 84.
81. Venediktov, *Organizatsiya gosudarstvennoi*, p. 102.
82. *Izvestiya MOSNKh*, 1, 1 September 1918, p. 3.
83. *TsGAOR*, 7952/3/212/197–8.
84. Ibid., listy, 231–2.
85. Gimpel'son, 'O rabochem kontrole', p. 121.
86. *TsGAOR*, 1952/3/212, 228–30.
87. Gimpel'son, 'O rabochem kontrole', p. 119.
88. Kostina, 'Moskovskii gorodskoi', p. 123.
89. *Izvestiya MOSNKh*, 1, p. 23.
90. *P*, 5 January 1919.
91. *Izvestiya MOSNKh*, p. 23.
92. N. M. Laman, Yu. I. Krechetkova, *Istoriya zavoda 'Elektroprovod'* (Moscow, 1967) p. 137.
93. Gimpel'son, 'O rabochem kontrole', p. 118.
94. *Izvestiya MOSNKh*, 2, 15 September 1918; A. M. Pankratova, *Istoriya razvitiya fabzav. predstavitel'stva i fabzav. komitetov v Rossii* (Moscow, 1924) p. 89.
95. *VIMS*, 11 April 1919.
96. *Izvestiya VTsIK*, 18 December 1918.
97. *Ekon. zhizn'*, 28 January 1919; Kostina, 'Moskovskii gorodskoi', pp. 120–1.
98. *VIMS*, 11 April 1919.
99. *KM*, col. 679.
100. *KM*, col. 684.
101. *P*, 11 July 1919.
102. *Pechatnik*, 3–4, 1 April 1919.
103. *VIMS*, 3 November 1919.

104. Gimpel'son, 'O rabochem kontrole', pp. 119–21.
105. *II s"ezd SNKh*, pp. 400–402.
106. Lenin, *PSS*, 36, pp. 198–203 and *passim*.
107. *II s"ezd SNKh*, pp. 128–9.
108. Gimpel'son, *Velikii oktyabr'*, p. 39.
109. *Ocherki istorii Moskovskoi organizatsii KPSS*, vol. 2 (Moscow, 1983) p. 177.
110. *Stenotchety MS*, 3 (1919) p. 39.
111. Kostina, 'Moskovskii gorodskoi', p. 122.
112. No figures are available for Moscow but nationally the proportion of enterprises under one-person management rose from 3.4 per cent in late 1918 and 10.9 per cent in 1919 to 71.2 per cent in 1920. V. Z. Drobizhev, *Glavnyi shtab sotsialisticheskoi promyshlennosti*, (Moscow, 1966) p. 121.
113. *Bor'ba klassov*, 7–8 (1934) p. 189.
114. *VIMS*, 7 September 1918.
115. *VIMS*, 20 January 1920.
116. *Moskovskii sovet za desyat' let raboty, 1927–1927gg.* (Moscow, 1927) p. 19.
117. *TsGAOR*, 7952/3/212/274.
118. *Izvestiya MOSNKh*, 1 (1918) p. 24.
119. *KM*, col. 187.
120. *KT*, 11 May 1920.
121. *KT*, 2 April 1920.
122. Malle, *Economic Organisation*, p. 597.
123. 253 rubles according to *Byulleten' MGSPS*, 2 (15), 15 February 1922, p. 6.
124. Fifty-two times according to another source – *Byulleten' statistiki truda Moskovskoi gubernii*, MGSPS, 5–6, March–April 1921, p. 6.
125. Cited by V. Ya. Yarotskii, 'Trud v SSSR', *Entsiklopedicheskii slovar' (Granat)* 7th edn, vol. 41, pt. 2, p. 259.
126. Calculated from *Byulleten' stat. truda*, 5–6, March–April 1921, p. 11.
127. R. W. Davies, *The Development of the Soviet Budgetary System* (Cambridge: Cambridge University Press, 1958) p. 26.
128. *VIMS*, 15 October 1918.
129. *Byulleten' stat. truda*, 5–6, March–April 1921, p. 6.
130. Calculated by Strumilin, in Yarotskii, 'Trud v SSSR', p. 263.
131. *KM*, col. 12.
132. *Stenotchety MS*, 1 (1919) p. 14.
133. Lenin, *PSS*, 38, p. 98.
134. *KM*, col. 684; *Obzor deyatel'nosti MGSPS*, p. 48.
135. *Byulleten' stat. truda*, 5–6, March–April 1921, pp. 1–3.
136. Strumilin calculated that national wage differentials had fallen to 1.02:1 by early 1921: see Alexander Baykov, *The Development of the Soviet Economic System* (Cambridge, 1947) p. 43.
137. *IX s"ezd RKP*, p. 73.
138. *Obzor deyatel'nosti MGSPS*, pp. 47–8.
139. Cited in Malle, *Economic Organisation*, p. 23.
140. *Protokoly MGSPS*, 30 (1920) p. 15.
141. *Stenotchety MS*, 16 (1919) pp. 246 and 248; *KT*, 25 March 1920.
142. *Protokoly MGSPS*, 18 (1920) p. 9; 29 (1920) p. 13.

143. *Obzor deyatel'nosti MGSPS*, p. 48.
144. P. A. Sorokin, *Sovremennoe sostoyanie Rossii* (Prague, 1922) pp. 23–4.
145. *Stat. ezhegodnik*, p. 207.
146. Piletskii, *Rabochii klass*, p. 18.
147. *KT*, 24 June 1920.
148. Leites, *Recent Economic Developments*, p. 150.
149. *KT*, 9 November 1920.
150. *Vechernyaya krasnaya gazeta*, 3, 19 July 1918.
151. G. Leggett, *The Cheka: Lenin's Political Police* (Oxford: Oxford University Press, 1981) p. 241.
152. *VIMS*, 16 September 1918.
153. *VIMS*, 2 June 1919.
154. *Izvestiya VTsIK*, 28 June 1919; *Dekrety Sovetskoi vlasti*, vol. 5 (Moscow, 1971) pp. 304–6.
155. Goldman, *Disillusionment*, p. 109.
156. Harrison, *Marooned*, p. 95.
157. Goldman, *Disillusionment*, p. 109.
158. *P*, 18 December 1920.
159. *KPSS v rez. i resh.*, vol. 2, p. 192.
160. *KT*, 11 May 1920.
161. On labour duty see Leggett, *The Cheka*, p. 242; Dewar, *Labour Policy*, pp. 52–6; Carr, *Bolshevik Revolution*, 2, pp. 211–18.
162. *KT*, 20 March 1920.
163. A. M. Anikst, *Organizatsiya rabochei sily v 1920 godu* (Moscow, 1920) p. 8.
164. *Izvestiya Moskovskogo komiteta po trudovoi povinnosti*, 5, 21 June 1920.
165. Ibid., 8, 16 October 1920.
166. *KT*, 5 May 1920.
167. *KT*, 17 December 1920.
168. *Izvestiya MK po trud. pov.*, 5, 21 June 1920.
169. *KT*, 20 March 1920.
170. *Protokoly MGSPS*, 20 (1920) p. 12.
171. *KT*, 25 March 1920.
172. *KT*, 24 September 1920.
173. Anikst, *Organizatsiya rabochei*, p. 55.
174. *Izvestiya MK po trud. pov.*, 8, 16 October 1920.
175. A. Bubnov (ed.), *Grazhdanskaya voina, 1918–1921gg.* (Moscow, 1928) Appendix 11.
176. Anikst, *Organizatsiya rabochei*, pp. 32 and 34.
177. *P*, 9 October 1920.
178. *KT*, 14 September 1920; *Protokoly MGSPS*, 24 (1920) p. 20.
179. *KT*, 11 May 1920; KM, col. 685.
180. *IV Mosk. gub. konf. profsoyuzov*, p. 11.
181. Ibid., p. 16.
182. *KT*, 22 December 1920.
183. *Byulleten' MGSPS*, 1, 23 January 1921, pp. 8–9.
184. *KT*, 15 February 1921.
185. *KT*, 14 January 1921.
186. Charles E. Ziegler, 'Worker Participation and Worker Discontent in the Soviet Union', *Political Science Quarterly* (Summer 1983) p. 247.

187. *TsGAOR*, 7952/3/212/199.
188. Diane Koenker, 'The Evolution of Party Consciousness in 1917: The Case of the Moscow Workers', *Soviet Studies*, XXX, 1 (January 1978) pp. 36–62.
189. *Stenotchety MS*, 1 (1919) pp. 14–15.
190. *VIMS*, 6 February 1919.
191. S. P. Mel'gunov, *The Red Terror in Russia* (London: Dent, 1925) p. 51.
192. *Stenotchety MS*, 18 (1919) pp. 265–7.
193. N. G. Dumova, *Sekretar' MK (povest' o V. M. Zagorskom)* (Moscow, 1966) pp. 109–10. In Hungary in November 1956 the white flag was also hoisted above factories to indicate that governmental power stopped at the factory gates.
194. *P*, 27 September 1919.
195. Leites, *Recent Economic Developments*, pp. 195–7.
196. *KT*, 28 March 1920.
197. *KT*, 1 April 1920.
198. *KT*, 4 June 1920; *Iz istorii grazhdanskoi voiny v SSSR: sbornik dokumentov i materialov*, vol. 3 (Moscow, 1961) pp. 213–14.
199. *KT*, 8 June 1920.
200. *KT*, 3 June 1920.

4 Party Organisation

1. *Put' k oktyabryu*, 3 (Moscow, 1923) p. 119.
2. Yu. P. Petrov, *Partiinoe stroitel'stvo v sovetskoi armii i flote (1918–1961gg.)* (Moscow, 1964) p. 10.
3. Yu. P. Petrov, *KPSS – rukovoditel' i vospitatel' krasnoi armii (1918–1920gg.)* (Moscow, 1961) p. 101.
4. *P*, 4 April 1918.
5. *P*, 5 April 1918.
6. *P*, 7 July 1918.
7. Harding, *Lenin's Political Thought*, vol. 2, pp. 187 and 196.
8. *Perepiska*, vol. II (Moscow, 1957) p. 171.
9. *VII ekstrennyi s"ezd RKP(b), mart 1918 goda: stenograficheskii otchet* (Moscow, 1962) pp. 171–2.
10. *Perepiska*, vol. III (Moscow, 1967) p. 64; *P*, 19 May 1918.
11. The themes of this resolution were developed in two circular letters to local party organisations of 22 and 29 May 1918, *Perepiska*, vol. III, pp. 72–4 and 81–3; *P*, 22, 29 May 1918.
12. Helgesen, *Origins*, p. 196.
13. Ibid., p. 194.
14. *Otchet severnoi oblastnoi konferentsii s 3-go po 6-e aprelya: dve rechi G. Zinov'eva* (Petrograd, 1918) p. 30.
15. *Kommunist*, 4 (June 1918) p. 1.
16. For example, the Left Communist theses, *Kommunist*, 1 (April 1918) pp. 4–9.
17. *Kommunist*, 4, p. 15.
18. Theda Skocpol, *States and Social Revolutions* (Cambridge: Cambridge

University Press, 1979) p. 206.

19. 22 May TsK circular, *Perepiska*, vol. III, p. 73.
20. Georg Lukács, 'Towards a Methodology of the Problem of Organisation', in *History and Class Consciousness* (London: Merlin Press, 1971) p. 299.
21. *KM*, col. 657.
22. *Ustav Moskovskoi organizatsii RKP* (Moscow, 1918) pp. 4–5.
23. *Zheleznodorozhniki i revolyutsiya* (Moscow, 1923) p. 47.
24. *P*, 20 February 1919; *P*, 26 March 1920.
25. V. N. Tarusov, 'Deyatel'nost' Moskovskoi partiinoi organizatsii po organizatsionnomy ukrepleniyu svoikh ryadov, 1918–1922 gg.', *Sbornik trudov iz istorii Moskovskoi partiinoi organizatsii*, MOPI im. Krupskoi, 239, 2 (Moscow, 1973) p. 29.
26. *KM*, col. 658.
27. *Ustav MPO 1918*, pp. 3–4.
28. *KM*, col. 658.
29. Dumova, *Sekretar' MK*, pp. 93 and 99.
30. Tarusov, 'Deyatel'nost' Moskovskoi', p. 25.
31. 29 July 1918, *Perepiska*, vol. III, pp. 127–9.
32. *P*, 2 August 1918.
33. *Ocherki ist. MO KPSS*, p. 330; *Istoriya Moskvy*, vol. 6, bk 1, p. 161.
34. *Mosk. gorodskaya*, p. 21; I. M. Razgon, *Moskva v period inostrannoi interventsii i grazhdanskoi voiny* (Moscow, 1947) p. 13.
35. Ignat'ev, *Moskva v pervyi*, p. 210.
36. K. I. Bukov and G. A. Nagapetyan, 'Ideino-organizatsionnoe ukreplenie Moskovskoi partiinoi organizatsii v gody grazhdanskoi voiny', *VI KPSS*, 6 (1959) p. 64.
37. Manevich (ed.), *Ocherki po istorii revolyutsionnogo dvizheniya i bol'shevist-skoi organizatsii v baumanskom raione* (Moscow, 1928) pp. 169–70.
38. *Vserossiiskaya perepis' chlenov RKP 1922g.*, 4 (Moscow, 1922) p. 11.
39. *Izvestiya MK RKP*, 2, 20 June 1922, p. 9.
40. *Materialy po statistike*, pp. 10–11.
41. *P*, 31 August 1918.
42. *P*, 18 July 1918.
43. *P*, 18 January 1919.
44. *P*, 2 February 1919.
45. *P*, 30 January 1919.
46. *P*, 12 December 1918.
47. 4 February 1919 TsK circular letter, *Partiya v period inostrannoi voennoi interventsii i grazhdanskoi voiny (1918–1920gg.): dokumenty i materialy* (Moscow, 1962) p. 74.
48. *P*, 23 July 1918.
49. *P*, 15 August 1918.
50. *P*, 20 February 1919.
51. *VIMS*, 1 August 1919.
52. *P*, 8 July 1919,
53. *P*, 11 January 1919.
54. *P*, 17 June 1919.
55. *Ustav MPO 1918*, p. 6.
56. *P*, 12 December 1918.

57. *P*, 11 January 1919.
58. *P*, 1 February 1919.
59. *P*, 19 February 1919.
60. *KM*, col. 658.
61. *P*, 18 January 1919.
62. Service, *The Bolshevik Party in Revolution*, p. 106; see ibid., p. 108, Helgesen, *Origins*, p. 312.
63. 2 March 1919 Moscow *guberniya* party conference resolution, *P*, 5 March 1919.
64. Helgesen, *Origins*, p. 313.
65. 15 February 1919 resolution for the VIII congress, *P*, 19 February 1919.
66. *VIII s''ezd RKP*, pp. 284–7.
67. *P*, 11 July 1919; *Perepiska*, vol. VIII, pp. 369–70.
68. *P*, 26 September 1919.
69. L. Bychkov, *Vzryv v Leont'evskom Pereulke* (Moscow, 1934) pp. 14–22.
70. *P*, 11 January 1920; *KM*, col. 666.
71. *KM*, cols. 666–7.
72. *P*, 13 January 1920; *KM*, col. 667.
73. *P*, 28 January 1920; *KM*, col. 668.
74. A. F. Myasnikov (Myasnikyan), *Izbrannye proizvedeniya* (Erevan, 1965) p. 258.
75. *KPSS v rez. i resh.*, pp. 130–1.
76. *KT*, 21 March 1920.
77. *VIMS*, 11 March 1920.
78. *KT*, 18 March 1920.
79. *P*, 17 June, 11 July 1919.
80. Butyrskii raion was united with Sushchevsko–Mar'inskii and Presnenskii *raions* to form a massive new *raion* called Krasnopresnenskii covering a third of Moscow; Alekseevsko–Rostokinskii was joined with Sokol'nicheskii *raion*; and Basmanny was merged with Blagushe–Lefortovo to form Baumanskii *raion*.
81. *KT*, 18 March 1920.
82. *VIII konf. RKP*, p. 152.
83. *P*, 2 September 1919.
84. *IX s''ezd RKP*, p. 309.
85. *Izvestiya TsK RKP*, 14, 1920.
86. *KT*, 24 April 1920.
87. *P*, 23 May 1920.
88. *KT*, 25 April and 22 May 1920.
89. *KT*, 20 May 1920.
90. Myasnikov, *Izb. proiz.*, p. 260.
91. *Ustav Moskovskoi organizatsii RKP (b)* (Moscow, 1920) p. 5.
92. *Ustav MPO 1920*, pp. 1–7.
93. *Ustav MPO 1920*, p. 6.
94. *V Mosk. gubpartkonf.*, pp. 40–1.
95. *Ustav MPO 1920*, p. 4.
96. *KM*, col. 668.
97. *X s''ezd RKP*, p. 56.
98. W. E. Mosse, 'Makers of the Soviet Union', *Slavic and East European*

Review, XLVI, 106 (January 1968) p. 141.
99. *Izvestiya TsK RKP*, 9, 20 December 1919.
100. *Otchet MK za sentyabr' 1920 g.* (Moscow, 1920) p. 9; *Otchet o rabote voennogo otdela Moskovskogo komiteta RKP za vremya sushchestvovaniya s 15-go aprelya 1919 goda* (Moscow, 1920) p. 13 and appendix.
101. Petrov (1964), pp. 107–8.
102. Petrov (1964), p. 12.
103. *Otchet voennogo otdela*, p. 14.
104. *P*, 5 January 1919.
105. *Shest' let na revolyutsionnom puti. K yubileyu zavodskikh organizatsii 1917–23 gg. Gos. russko-kabel'nyi i metalloprokatnyi zavod 'Russkabel'* (Moscow, 1923) pp. 13 and 19.
106. *KT*, 4 November 1921.
107. *P*, 21 May 1919.
108. Manevich (ed.), *Ocherki po istorii*, p. 170; *P*, 11 July 1919.
109. *P*, 29 May 1919.
110. Table 2.8; TsGAOR, 7952/3/209/186.
111. *KT*, 5 February 1921.
112. *P*, 20 May 1919.
113. Manevich (ed.), *Ocherki po istorii*, p. 167.
114. *P*, 7 July 1918.
115. *P*, 16 July 1918.
116. *KM*, col. 676.
117. *Otchet o deyatel'nosti MK za iyul', avgust i sentyabr' 1921g.* (Moscow, 1921) p. 22.
118. *Otchet Sokol'nicheskogo RK-ta RKP za vremya s 1/IX–1920g. po 1/I–1921g.* (Moscow, 1921) p. 7.
119. *KT*, 25 April 1920; *KM*, cols. 669–70; *Mosk. gorodskaya*, pp. 148–9.
120. *XI s''ezd RKP*, pp. 444–5.
121. *Izvestiya TsK RKP*, 22, 18 September 1920, pp. 23–4.
122. *KT*, 17 November 1920.
123. *P*, 16 July 1918.
124. *Dinamo – 25 let revolyutsionnoi bor'by* (Moscow, 1923).
125. *P*, 12 February 1920.
126. *Pyat' let raboty yacheiki RKP(b) tipografii 'Krasnyi proletarii' 1919–24gg.* (Moscow, 1925) pp. 8–9 and 23.
127. P. O. Gooderham, *The Regional Party Apparatus in the First Five-Year Plan: The Case of Leningrad*, CREES, University of Birmingham, Soviet Industrialisation Project Series *SIPS* 24 (1983) pt. 2, p. 4 and *passim*.
128. Schapiro, *Origins*, p. 242; Petrov (1964), pp. 49–51.
129. John Erickson, *The Soviet High Command: A Military–Political History, 1918–1941* (London, 1962) pp. 43–4.
130. Petrov (1964), p. 60.
131. Petrov (1961), p. 51.
132. *P*, 19 August 1918.
133. *Perepiska*, IV, p. 74.
134. *P*, 10 January 1919.
135. *P*, 19 December 1918.
136. *P*, 24 December 1918.

137. *P*, 7 March 1919.
138. *VIMS*, 25 February 1919.
139. *P*, 16 March 1919.
140. *VIII s"ezd RKP*, pp. 158–9.
141. *VIII s"ezd RKP*, pp. 20 and 273.
142. *VIII s"ezd RKP*, p. 190.
143. *P*, 6 May 1919.
144. *Ocherki ist. MO KPSS*, vol. 2, p. 122.
145. *Otchet voennogo otdela*, pp. 19–20; *KM*, cols. 671–2; *P*, 6 May 1919.
146. *Otchet voennogo otdela*, p. 9.
147. *Loc. cit.*
148. *Otchet voennogo otdela*, p. 10.
149. *Otchet MK za oktyabr' 1920g.* (Moscow, 1920) p. 35.
150. *KT*, 18 February 1921.
151. *Ustav MPO 1918*, pp. 6–7.
152. *P*, 20 August 1918.
153. *P*, 5 November 1918.
154. *P*, 4 December 1918.
155. *P*, 8 February 1919.
156. *VIII s"ezd RKP*, p. 148.
157. *P*, 4 March 1919.
158. *P*, 19 July 1919.
159. *P*, 2 August 1919; *VIMS*, 29 July, 8 August 1919.
160. *P*, 13 August 1919.
161. *VIII konf. RKP*, p. 197.
162. *VIMS*, 11 March 1920.
163. *IX s"ezd RKP*, p. 426.
164. *Ustav MPO 1920*, pp. 10–13.
165. *Ustav Moskovskoi gubernskoi organizatsii RKP(b)* (Moscow, 1919) p. 3.
166. *Izvestiya po trud. pov.*, 5, 21 June 1920.
167. *VIMS*, 6 March 1920.
168. Tarusov, 'Deyatel'nost' Moskovskoi' p. 25.
169. *KT*, 8 May 1920.
170. *KT*, 15 May 1920.
171. *KT*, 21 March 1920.
172. *KT*, 31 July 1920.
173. *KT*, 15 May 1920.
174. *KT*, 15 May 1920.
175. *KT*, 16 June 1920.
176. *KT*, 18 June 1920.
177. *Perepiska*, III, p. 121.
178. Ibid., p. 73.
179. *Lenin i Moskovskie bol'sheviki*, p. 322.
180. *P*, 20 June 1918.
181. *P*, 30 May 1918.
182. *Uprochenie*, p. 41.
183. *P*, 20 June 1918.
184. *P*, 2 August 1918.
185. *P*, 8 August 1918.

186. *P*, 15, 16 September 1918.
187. *Perepiska*, V, p. 60.
188. *P*, 8 February 1919.
189. *Lenin i Moskovskie bol'sheviki*, p. 375.
190. *Kommunar*, 56, 14 December 1918.
191. *VIII s"ezd RKP*, p. 180.
192. Ibid., pp. 183–4 and 164–6.
193. Ibid., pp. 164–6.
194. Ibid., pp. 168–9.
195. Ibid., p. 170.
196. Ibid., pp. 181–2.
197. *VIMS*, 6 February 1919.
198. *VIMS*, 5 April 1919.
199. *KT*, 4 May 1920.
200. *KT*, 5 May 1920.
201. *KT*, 26 August 1920.
202. *KT*, 18 May 1920.
203. *Otchet o deyatel'nosti MK RKP za iyul' 1920g.* (Moscow, 1920) p. 6; *KT*, 4 August 1920.
204. TsK circular letter of 14 July 1919, *Perepiska*, VIII, p. 148.
205. S. M. Tel'nov, 'Boevye kommunisticheskie otryady osobogo naznacheniya v bor'be s kontrrevolyutsiei, 1918 god', *Uch. zap. MOPI im. Krupskoi*, *Istoriya KPSS*, vol. 215, 13 (Moscow, 1968) p. 190.
206. *Iz istorii grazhdanskoi voiny*, vol. 1, p. 127.
207. Tel'nov, 'Boevye kommunisticheskie,' p. 190.
208. Ibid., p. 191.
209. *P*, 20 July 1918.
210. *P*, 2 August 1918.
211. 23 September 1918, *Perepiska*, IV, p. 273.
212. *P*, 23 April 1919; *Perepiska*, VII, pp. 40–2 and 94.
213. *Perepiska*, VIII, pp. 98–9.
214. *Ocherki ist. MO KPSS*, p. 343.
215. K. I. Bukov, *V bitve velikoi* (Moscow, 1960) p. 113.
216. *VIII konf. RKP*, p. 165.
217. L. M. Spirin, *Klassy i partii v grazhdanskoi voine v Rossii (1917–1920gg.)* (Moscow, 1968) p. 333.
218. *Dekrety Sovetskoi vlasti*, vol. 4 (Moscow, 1968) pp. 196–200.
219. Manevich (ed.), *Ocherki po istorii*, p. 171.
220. *Izvestiya TsK RKP*, 5, 20 September 1919.
221. 8 May 1919 TsK circular, *Perepiska*, VII, p. 94.
222. For example, *KT*, 25 March 1920; cf. *KM*, col. 665; V. I. Kratov, *Chonovtsy* (Moscow, 1974) p. 23.
223. *KT*, 29 September 1920.
225. *P*, 12 September 1920.
226. *VIMS*, 9 March 1920.
227. *KT*, 12 December 1920.
228. *P*, 2 September 1919.
229. *KT*, 23 April 1920.
230. *VIII konf. RKP*, pp. 197–8.
231. *Ustav MPO 1920*, p. 14.

5 Recruitment and Purge in the Moscow Party Organisation

1. *VII s"ezd RKP*, pp. 4 and 115.
2. *VIII s"ezd RKP*, p. 173.
3. *KT*, 21 September 1921.
4. MPO figure derived from Table 5.2; the national figure from Jonathan R. Adelman, 'The Development of the Soviet Party Apparat in the Civil War: Center, Localities and Nationality Areas', *Russian History/Histoire Russe*, 9, p. 1 (1982) p. 93.
5. *Materialy po statistike lichnogo sostava RKP (b)* (Moscow, 1921) p. 66.
6. Marcel Liebman, *Leninism under Lenin* (trans. Brian Pearce) (London: Merlin Press, 1980) p. 308.
7. Y. I. Baganov, *Moskovskie bol'sheviki v ogne revolyutsionnykh boev* (Moscow, 1976) p. 143.
8. D. A. Chugaev (ed.), *Rabochii klass sovetskoi rossii v pervyi god diktatury proletariata: sbornik dokumentov i materialov* (Moscow, 1964) p. 96.
9. Chugaev (ed.), *Rabochii klass*, pp. 96 and 99.
10. *P*. 29 May 1918.
11. K. I. Varlamov, N. I. Slamikhin, *Razoblachenie V. I. Leninym teorii i taktiki "levykh kommunistov" (noyabr' 1917–1918gg.)* (Moscow, 1964) p. 372; I. A. Popov, 'Deyatel'nost' Moskovskoi partiinoi organizatsii po ukrepleniyu svoikh ryadov (okt. 1917–yan. 1919gg.)', *Uch. zap. MOPI im. Krupskoi, Istoriya KPSS*, vol. 215, 13 (1968) p. 73.
12. *Perepiska*, vol. III, p. 73.
13. Varlamov and Slamikhin, *Razoblachenie*, p. 373.
14. *P*, 28 May 1918.
15. V. V. Anikeev, 'Svedeniya o bol'shevistskikh organizatsiyakh s marta po dekabr' 1917 goda', *VI KPSS*, 2 (1958) p. 147; *P*, 25 May, 18 July 1918.
16. *P*, 5 June 1918.
17. *P*, 18 July 1918.
18. *P*, 9 June, 23 July 1918; Chugaev (ed.), *Rabochii klass*, p. 76.
19. Chugaev (ed.), *Rabochii klass*, p. 96.
20. *P*, 22 February 1918.
21. Chugaev (ed.), *Rabochii klass*, p. 370, n. 33.
22. Lenin, *PSS*, 37, pp. 46–7.
23. T. H. Rigby, *Communist Party Membership in the USSR, 1917–1967* (Princeton, NJ: Princeton University Press, 1968) p. 72.
24. *P*, 3 September 1918.
25. *P*, 31 August, 4, 13 September 1918.
26. *Ocherki ist. MO KPSS*, p. 363.
27. Chugaev, *Rabochii klass*, p. 370, n. 33.
28. *P*, 1 August 1918.
29. N. Kopylev in *P*, 25 August 1918.
30. *P*, 21 September, 1 October 1918.
31. *P*, 8 October 1918.
32. *P*, 19 October 1918. This was the incident recounted by Zinoviev at the VIII Party Congress, *VIII s"ezd RKP*, p. 294.
33. Paul Dukes, *Red Dusk and the Morrow* (London, 1923) p. 267.
34. *P*, 30 November 1918.
35. *P*, 17 December 1918.

36. *P*, 15 August 1918.
37. *P*, 1 August 1918; 5 January 1919.
38. *P*, 17 August 1918.
39. *P*, 18 January 1919.
40. *Materialy po statistike*, p. XI.
41. Rigby, *Communist Party Membership*, p. 75.
42. *P*, 2 February 1919.
43. TsK circular of 4 February 1919, *Partiya v period inostrannoi voennoi interventsii*, p. 75.
44. *P*, 6 February 1919.
45. *P*, 8 February 1919.
46. *P*, 20 February 1919.
47. *P*, 28 February 1919.
48. *P*, 19 February 1919.
49. *VIII s"ezd RKP*, p. 423.
50. *P*, 5 January 1919.
51. *P*, 23 July 1919.
52. *P*, 11 July 1919.
53. *P*, 30 July 1918.
54. *P*, 7 September 1919.
55. *VIII konf. RKP*, p. 140.
56. *Izvestiya MK RKP (b)*, 1, 20 March 1922, p. 54.
57. *P*, 7 September 1919.
58. *VIII konf. RKP*, p. 227.
59. *P*, 12 June 1919.
60. Rigby, *Communist Party Membership*, p. 76.
61. *P*, 12 June 1919.
62. Rigby, *Communist Party Membership*, p. 77; Adelman, 'Development of the Soviet Party' p. 97.
63. *VIII s"ezd RKP*, pp. 471, 544 and n.78.
64. Lenin, *PSS*, 39, p. 27.
65. Lenin, 'The Results of the Party Week in Moscow and Our Tasks', *PSS*, 39, p. 234; Trotsky made the same point in *Terrorism and Communism*, p. 115.
66. *Ocherki ist. MO KPSS*, vol. 2, p. 123; *P*, 9 May 1919.
67. Manevich (ed.), *Ocherki po istorii*, p. 169.
68. *P*, 6 May 1919.
69. *Izvestiya TsK RKP*, 1, 28 May 1919.
70. *Stenotchety MS*, 15 (1919) p. 232; 17 (1919) p. 252.
71. *Perepiska*, VIII, pp. 56–7.
72. Ibid., p. 169.
73. John Bradley, *Civil War in Russia, 1917–1920* (London: Batsford, 1975) p. 123.
74. *Lenin i Moskovskie bol'sheviki*, p. 348.
75. 5 July 1919, *Perepiska*, VIII, pp. 105–6.
76. 14 July 1919, *Perepiska*, VIII, p. 146.
77. *P*, 4 October 1919.
78. *VIII konf. RKP*, p. 28.
79. *Ocherki ist. MO KPSS*, p. 331.

80. *Izvestiya TsK RKP*, 6, 30 September 1919; *VIII konf. RKP*, pp. 241–2.
81. *Izvestiya TsK RKP*, 8, 2 December 1919.
82. *P*, 6 November 1919.
83. *P*, 7 September 1919.
84. *P*, 26 October 1919.
85. *Izvestiya TsK RKP*, 15, 24 October 1919.
86. Bukov and Nagapetyan, 'Ideino-organizatsionnoe ukreplenie' p. 58.
87. Manevich (ed.), *Ocherki po istorii*, p. 170.
88. *P*, 26 July 1919.
89. Chugaev (ed). *Rabochii klass*, p. 76; *KT*, 5 May 1920.
90. *KT*, 5 May 1920.
91. *VIII konf. RKP*, p. 24.
92. Ibid., p. 166.
93. *P*, 9, 18 March 1921.
94. *P*, 30 March 1921.
95. Lenin, *PSS*, 45, pp. 18 and 20.
96. Leon Trotsky, *The New Course* (London, 1956) pp. 14–15.
97. Ibid., p. 18.
98. Michael S. Farbman, *Bolshevism in Retreat* (London, 1923) p. 165.
99. 24 622 people joined the MPO, 17 361 in the city alone (*Moskovskaya organizatsiya RKP (b) v tsifrakh*, 1 (Moscow, 1925) p. 23). Membership increased from 53 121 on 1 January 1924 (*Mosk. gorodskaya*, p. 28) to 77 743, an increase of 46 per cent. Trotsky initially welcomed the enrolment, but later changed his mind and argued that it had diluted the revolutionary vanguard and thus freed the bureaucracy from its control, Leon Trotsky, *Revolution Betrayed* (London: New Park Publications, 1973) p. 98.
100. *VIII konf. RKP*, p. 31.
101. Ibid., p. 139.
102. Ibid., pp. 200–3.
103. Rigby, *Communist Party Membership*, pp. 81–2.
104. *Vestnik propagandy*, 8, 12 July 1920, pp. 23 and 25.
105. *Pervyi bukvar' kommunista* (Moscow, 1920) p. 24.
106. *V Moskovskaya gubernskaya konferentsiya RKP(b), 19–21 fevral' 1921g,: kratki ocherk i rezolyutsii* (Moscow, 1921) p. 26.
107. *KT*, 25 April 1920.
108. *KT*, 21 March 1921.
109. *Ocherki ist. MO KPSS*, p. 366.
110. *KT*, 20 June 1920.
111. *P*, 10 September 1920.
112. *P*, 10 September 1920.
113. *Otchet MK za iyul' 1920g.*, p. 7.
114. *KT*, 28 August 1920.
115. For example, E. M. Yaroslavskii (ed.), *Kak provodit' chistku partii* (Moscow/Leningrad, 1929) pp. 23–5.
116. *KT*, 2 July 1920.
117. *KT*, 21 July 1920.
118. *KT*, 1 August 1920.
119. Adelman, 'Development of the Soviet Party', p. 97.

120. *Otchet MK RKP(b) za sentyabr' 1920g.* (Moscow, 1921) p. 10.
121. Rigby, *Communist Party Membership*, p. 84.
122. *P*, 2 September 1920.
123. *Otchet MK za sentyabr' 1920g.*, p. 8.
124. *KT*, 3, 24 September 1920.
125. *Otchet MK za sentyabr' 1920g.*, pp. 49–51.
126. *P*, 17 September 1920.
127. *Materialy po statistike*, pp. 16–17.
128. *Otchet MK za sentyabr' 1920g.*, p. 38; *Otchet MK za yanvar' 1921g.*, pp. 32–3.
129. *Vestnik propagandy*, 3, 24 September 1919, p. 4.
130. N. Meshcheryakov in *P*, 26 September 1920.
131. *X s"ezd RKP*, p. 326.
132. Ibid., pp. 236–7.
133. *Otchet MK za sentyabr' 1920g.*, p. 6; *Otchet MK za oktyabr' 1920g.*, p. 17.
134. *Otchet MK za oktyabr' 1920g.*, p. 17.
135. *KT*, 5 February 1921.
136. *V Mosk. gubpartkonf.*, p. 3.
137. Rigby, *Communist Party Membership*, p. 97.
138. *Izvestiya MK RKP (b)*, 1, 20 March 1922, pp. 14–15.
139. Service, *The Bolshevik Party*, pp. 164–5.
140. Rigby, *Communist Party Membership*, p. 96.
141. *Izvestiya MK RKP (b)*, 1, pp. 16–18; *XI s"ezd RKP*, p. 754.
142. *Vserossiiskaya perepis' chlenov RKP (b), 1922g.*, 4 (Moscow, 1923) p. 47.
143. *Materialy po statistike*, p. 66.
144. Yu. A. Shchetinov, *Krushenie melkoburzhuaznoi kontrrevolyutsii v Sovetskoi Rossii (konets 1920–1921g.)* (Moscow, 1984) p. 47.
145. *Byulleten' MK RKP (b)*, 1, 8 April 1921, p. 6.
146. Lenin, *PSS*, 44, p. 124.
147. *Izvestiya MK RKP (b)*, 1, pp. 16–18.
148. Lenin, *PSS*, 44, p. 123.
149. *KT*, 6 November 1920.
150. *Otchet Sok. RK-ta*, p. 7.
151. Calculated from Table 5.5 and *Stat. spravochnik*, p. 29.
152. Shchetinov, *Krushenie melkoburzhuaznoi*, p. 68.
153. *Otchet MK za sentyabr' 1920g.*, p. 9.
154. *VI Moskovskaya gubernskaya konferentsiya RKP, 25–28 iyunya 1921g.: doklady, kratkii otchet MK i rezolyutsii* (Moscow, 1921) p. 31.
155. *XI s"ezd RKP*, p. 443.
156. Rigby, *Communist Party Membership*, p. 81; *Izvestiya TsK RKP*, 15, 24 March 1920. The sample was of 17 312 communists.
157. *X s"ezd RKP*, p. 561.
158. Lukács, 'Towards a Methodology', p. 319.

6   Soviets, Bureaucracy and Participation

1. Lenin, 'State and Revolution', *PSS*, 33, p. 46.
2. Dvinov, *Moskovskii soviet*, p. 60.

3. Roy Medvedev, *On Socialist Democracy* (London: Spokesman Books, 1975) pp. 140–1. See also John Keep, *The Russian Revolution: A Study in Mass Mobilisation* (London: Weidenfeld & Nicolson, 1976) ch. 25.

4. *Sotsial-domokrat*, 15 November 1917; *Podgotovka i pobeda oktyabr'skoi revolyutsii v Moskve: dokumenty i materialy* (Moscow, 1957) p. 474.

5. Dvinov, *Moskovskii sovet*, p. 62.

6. *KM*, col. 32.

7. Aleshchenko (1968), p. 27.

8. *Loc. cit.*

9. Marc Ferro, 'The Birth of the Soviet Bureaucractic System', in R. Carter-Elwood (ed.), *Reconsiderations on the Russian Revolution* (Cambridge, MA: Slavica Publishers, 1976) pp. 113–20.

10. Lenin, *PSS*, 35, p. 135.

11. Lenin, *PSS*, 44, p. 352.

12. E. G. Gimpel'son, 'Iz istorii obrazovaniya odnopartiinoi sistemy v SSSR', *VI KPSS*, 11 (1965) p. 30.

13. E. G. Gimpel'son, 'Kak slozhilas, sovetskaya forma proletarskogo gosudarstva', *VI KPSS*, 9 (1967) pp. 14–15.

14. *KM*, col. 20.

15. Dvinov, *Moskovskii sovet*, p. 152.

16. Brovkin, 'The Mensheviks' Political Comeback', p. 4.

17. Dvinov, *Moskovskii sovet*, p. 152.

18. Ibid., pp. 155–6 and appendix 8.

19. Bernshtam, *Issledovaniya*, p. 50; Brovkin, 'The Mensheviks' Political Comeback', pp. 16 and 47.

20. Dvinov, *Moskovskii sovet*, pp. 64–5.

21. *Protokoly zasedanii VTsIKa 4-go sozyva: stenograficheskii otchet* (Moscow, 1920) pp. 36, 419; Dvinov, *Moskovskii sovet*, p. 65.

22. *Uprochenie*, pp. 46–7.

23. Spirin, *Klassy i partii*, pp. 157–8.

24. Dvinov, *Moskovskii sovet*, p. 67.

25. Ibid., *KM*, col. 7; *Uprochenie*, pp. 49–51.

26. Dvinov, *Moskovskii sovet*, appendix 11, pp. 159–60.

27. O. A. Ermanskii, *Iz perezhitogo* (Moscow/Leningrad, 1927) p. 188.

28. Ibid., p. 186; *P*, 19 November 1918; *VIMS*, 22 November 1918. For Martov's views see Israel Getzler, *Martov: A Political Biography* (Cambridge: Cambridge University Press, 1967) p. 173 ff.

29. Rudolf Schlesinger, *History of the Communist Party of the USSR Past and Present* (Delhi: Orient Longman, 1977) p. 145.

30. Lenin, *PSS*, 37, pp. 188–97.

31. *P*, 12 December 1918. Resolutions against admitting the Mensheviks were also passed in the Presnenskii and Basmannyi RPOs, *P*, 28 December 1918.

32. Dvinov, *Moskovskii sovet*, p. 86; cf. Spirin, *Klassy i partii*, pp. 306–7 and 392.

33. M. N. Pokrovskii, *Oktyabr'skaya revolyutsiya* (Moscow, 1929) p. 399, from *P*, 18 December 1927.

34. Mel'gunov, *Red Terror*, p. 244.

35. Pokrovskii, *Oktyabr'skaya revolyutsiya*, p. 399.

36. *MChK – iz istorii Moskovskoi cherezvychainnoi kommissii 1918–1921gg.: dokumenty* (Moscow, 1978) p. 5.

37. *MChK*, p. 5.
38. Ya. Kh. Peters, 'Vospominaniya o rabote VChK v pervyi god revolyutsii', *PR*, 10 (23) (1924) pp. 8–9. On the anarchists see Avrich, *Russian Anarchists*, p. 184.
39. M. Latsis, 'Tov. Dzerzhinskii i VChK', *PR*, 9 (56) (1926) p. 86.
40. Peters, 'Vospominaniya orabote . . .', p. 11.
41. *P*, 1 September 1918.
42. *P*, 13 September 1918.
43. *P*, 14 September 1918.
44. Quoted in Mel'gunov, *Red Terror*, p. 39.
45. *P*, 22 September 1918.
46. *P*, 27 September 1918.
47. *P*, 6 October 1918.
48. *MChK*, p. 5; *P*, 4 December 1918.
49. *VIMS*, 10, 11 October 1918.
50. *VIMS*, 14 October 1918.
51. Leggett, *The Cheka*, pp. 117–8.
52. Ibid., p. 137.
53. *P*, 30 January 1919.
54. Leggett, *The Cheka*, p. 145.
55. *P*, 26 February 1919.
56. *VIMS*, 2 June 1919.
57. *Stenotchety MS*, 21 (1919) p. 326.
58. G. P. Maximoff, *The Guillotine at Work*, vol. 1, *The Leninist Counter-Revolution* (Orkney: Cienfuegos Press, 1979) p. 142.
59. Gogolevskii, *Petrogradskii sovet*, pp. 56 and 62.
60. *VIMS*, 14 February 1920.
61. Bertrand Russell, *The Practice and Theory of Bolshevism* (London, 1920) p. 75.
62. *Stenotchety MS*, 3 (1919) p. 33.
63. *KM*, col. 5.
64. *Stenotchety MS*, 1 (1919) p. 14.
65. Ransome, *Six Weeks*, p. 46.
66. *KM*, col. 5.
67. *VIMS*, 17 October 1918.
68. *KPSS v rez. i resh.*, p. 45.
69. *VIII s"ezd RKP*, pp. 423–4; *P*, 6 May 1919.
70. *KM*, col. 35.
71. *P*, 15 July 1919; *VIMS*, 14 July, 1 August 1919.
72. *VIMS*, 13 November 1919.
73. *Vse na bor'bu s Denikinym*, 9 July 1919, *Perepiska*, VIII, pp. 114–29.
74. *VIMS*, 23 October 1919.
75. *KM*, cols. 629–30.
76. Aleshchenko (1976), p. 129.
77. *VIMS*, 30 September 1919.
78. *VIMS*, 26 December 1919.
79. No overall figures are available, but the election in Presnenskii *raion* on 23 November 1918 which gave the Bolsheviks 83 out of 94 seats can be taken as representative – *Moskovskii sovet za 10 let raboty* (Moscow, 1927) pp. 73–4.

80. A total of 467 deputies were elected: 338 Bolsheviks, 42 Mensheviks, 28 LSRs, and 59 others, D. A. Tolstikh, *Deyatel'nost' Moskovskoi partiinoi organizatsii po sozdaniyu organov Sovetskoi vlasti v Moskve (oktyabr' 1917–iyun' 1918g.)* (Moscow, 1958) p. 407.
81. *Otchet MK za iyul' 1920g.*, p. 3.
82. *P*, 20 July 1918.
83. *VIMS*, 17 October 1918.
84. *VIMS*, 12 September 1919.
85. *KM*, cols. 49–50; *KT*, 17 July 1920.
86. *KT*, 2 July 1920.
87. Various figures have been given for the results, but the following are probably the most accurate: communists 1316 (84.3 per cent); communist sympathisers 52 (3.3 per cent); non-party 145 (9.3 per cent); Mensheviks 46 (2.9 per cent); Anarchist–Maximalists 1; and the Jewish Socialist Party 1, to give a total of 1561 deputies – *VIMS*, 8 March 1920; *P*, 3 March 1920; *KM*, col. 673.
88. *KT*, 31 March 1920.
89. *Stenotchety MS*, 1 (1920) p. 1; *VIMS*, 8 March 1920.
90. *Stenotchety MS*, 1 (1920) p. 2.
91. *Stenotchety MS*, 1 (1920) p. 13, *KM*, col. 37.
92. *Stenotchety MS*, 1 (1920) pp. 12–13.
93. Ermanskii, *Iz perezhitogo*, pp. 191–4.
94. *KT*, 21 April 1920.
95. Dvinov, *Moskovskii sovet*, appendix 16, pp. 163–71.
96. Harrison, *Marooned*, p. 67.
97. Goldman, *Disillusionment*, pp. 139–40.
98. *Vestnik propagandy*, 8, 12 July 1920.
99. Liebman, *Leninism under Lenin*, p. 250.
100. *KT*, 25 May 1920.
101. Goldman, *Disillusionment*, p. 135; Dvinov, *Moskovskii sovet*, pp. 91–2.
102. Russell, *Practice and Theory*, pp. 72–3.
103. *KM*, cols. 42, 46 and 48.
104. *KM*, cols. 40–2, 44–6 and 50.
105. *KM*, col. 48.
106. *KM*, cols. 39–41 and 47; L. Haden-Guest (ed.), *British Labour Delegation to Russia, 1920: Official Report* (London, 1920) p. 60.
107. *KM*, cols. 39, 46 and 49.
108. *KT*, 20 March 1920.
109. *KT*, 20 March 1920.
110. *KT*, 24 March 1920; *Stenotchety MS*, 2 (1920) p. 24.
111. *KT*, 22 April 1920.
112. *KM*, col. 5.
113. *KT*, 20 April 1920.
114. *KM*, col. 674.
115. *KT*, 16 May 1920.
116. *KT*, 22 May 1920.
117. *Kommunist*, 4 (June 1918) p. 7.
118. *Perepiska*, IV, p. 256.
119. Paul Bellis, *Marxism and the USSR: The Theory of Proletarian Dictatorship and the Marxist Analysis of Soviet Society* (London: Macmillan, 1979)

p. 39, who states that Lenin's only detailed reference to the question is in 'Will the Bolsheviks Retain State Power?', Lenin *PSS*, 34, pp. 287–339.

120. Lenin *PSS*, p. 257.
121. Karl Kautsky, *The Dictatorship of the Proletariat* (Ann Arbor, 1964) p. 46.
122. N. Bukharin and E. Preobrazhenskii, *The ABC of Communism* (London: Penguin, 1969) pp. 129, 231 and 236–7.
123. *Velikaya oktyabr'skaya sotsialisticheskaya revolyutsiya: dokumenty i materialy. Revolyutsionnoe dvizhenie v Rossii posle sverzheniya samoderzhaviya* (Moscow, 1957) p. 108.
124. *Pod. i pob.*, p. 130.
125. O. G. Obichkin, *Ustavy mestnykh organizatsii RSDRP* (Moscow, 1976) p. 132.
126. *Pod. i pob.*, p. 130.
127. M. S. Koloditskii, 'Bor'ba Moskovskoi partiinoi organizatsii za prevrashchenie sovetov v organy vosstaniya i diktatury proletariata (iyul'–sentyabr' 1917g.)', *Avtoref. diss.* (Moscow, 1967) p. 14.
128. *Ustav MPO 1918*, p. 7.
129. *P*, 27 July 1918.
130. *P*, 18 September 1918.
131. *P*, 22 August, 10 September, 19 November 1918.
132. *P*, 5 January 1919.
133. *P*, 11 July 1919.
134. *VIMS*, 18 November 1920.
135. *Otchet MK za iyul' 1920g.*, p. 4.
136. *KM*, col. 658.
137. Myasnikov, *Izb. proiz.*, p. 294.
138. *VIII s"ezd RKP*, p. 543, fn. 71; V. V. Romanov, 'Bor'ba V. I. Lenina protiv antipartiinoi gruppy "Demokraticheskogo tsentralizma"' *Avtoref. diss.* (Moscow, 1969) pp. 30–9.
139. *P*, 28 January 1919.
140. *P*, 28 January 1919.
141. Lenin, *PSS*, 37, pp. 428–9.
142. TsK circular letter of 8 February 1919, *Perepiska*, VI, p. 58.
143. For example, at the 13 February 1919 Presnenskii delegate conference (*P*, 18 February 1919). The Lefortovo RK supported the DC call for a reform of soviet institutions, *P*, 30 January 1919.
144. *VIII s"ezd RKP*, pp. 166–7.
145. Ibid., p. 192.
146. Ibid., p. 199.
147. Ibid., p. 429.
148. *XVI mosk. gubpartkonf.*, p. 23.
149. Ibid., p. 21.
150. *VIII konf. RKP*, pp. 191–9.
151. Ibid., p. 130.
152. Ibid., p. 67.
153. Ibid., pp. 68–9.
154. Ibid., pp. 116–7.
155. *IX s"ezd RKP*, pp. 52–3 and 139.
156. *II kongress kommunisticheskogo internatsionala: stenograficheskii otchet* (Moscow, 1920) p. 574.

157. For recent approaches to the question see Ota Sik, *The Communist Power System* (New York: Praeger, 1981); Maria Hirszowicz, *The Bureaucratic Leviathan: A Study in the Sociology of Communism* (Oxford: Martin Robertson, 1980); Ferenc Feher, *et al.*, *Dictatorship Over Needs* (Oxford: Basil Blackwell, 1983).

158. Haden-Guest (ed.), *British Labour Delegation*, p. 65.

159. *Kommunist*, 1 (1918) p. 9.

160. L. H. Siegelbaum, *The Politics of Industrial Mobilisation in Russia, 1914–1917; A Study of the War-Industries Committees* (London: Macmillan, 1983). The term 'institutional proliferation' is used by Olga A. Narkiewiecz in her review of this book, *Soviet Studies*, XXXVII, 1 (1985) p. 142.

161. A. M. Anikst, *Vospominaniya o Lenine* (Moscow, 1933) p. 8.

162. Lenin, *PSS*, 45, p. 250.

163. *Dva goda diktatury proletariata*, p. 15; *Stat. ezhegodnik*, pp. 46–7.

164. *KT*, 5 May 1920.

165. *VIMS,* 14 June 1919.

166. Lenin, *PSS*, 42, pp. 43 and 47.

167. Chugaev (ed.), *Rabochii klass*, doc. no. 52.

168. *Kommunar*, 18 October 1918.

169. Chugaev (ed.), *Rabochii klass*, p. 60.

170. *VIMS*, 3 January 1919.

171. *Stenotchety MS*, 1 (1919) p. 14.

172. For example, *VIMS*, 28 January 1919.

173. Serge, *Memoirs of a Revolutionary*, p. 74.

174. Berkman, *Bolshevik Myth*, p. 308.

175. *Kommunar*, 17 December 1918.

176. *VIMS*, 13 February 1919.

177. Dumova, *Sekretar' MK*, p. 108.

178. *VIMS*, 21 June 1919.

179. *VIMS*, 15 November 1919.

180. Lenin, *PSS*, 52, p. 65.

181. Lenin, *PSS*, 42, p. 43.

182. Lenin, *PSS*, 42, p. 49. These figures apparently include teachers, nurses, etc.; cf. Table 2.4.

183. *KT*, 2 July 1921.

184. *Perepis' sluzhashchikh sovetskikh uchrezhdenii g. Moskvy 1922g.* (Moscow, 1922) p. 79.

185. Lenin, *PSS*, 45, p. 95.

186. Paul Mattick, *Anti-Bolshevik Communism* (London: Merlin Press, 1978) p. 67.

187. Dallin at the II SNKh congress in December 1918, *Trudy II s"ezda SNKh*, p. 25.

188. Kritsman, *Geroicheskii period* p. 152.

189. Ibid., pp. 147–8.

190. *VIII s"ezd RKP*, pp. 21–2.

191. Sorinin, *Kommunist*, 4, p. 7; Ol'minskii in *VIMS*, 7 October 1918.

192. *VIII s"ezd RKP*, p. 212.

193. *VIMS*, 17 April 1919.

194. *VIII s"ezd RKP*, pp. 212–13.

195. *VIMS*, 17 April 1919.

196. *VIII s"ezd RKP*, pp. 21–2.
197. Ibid., p. 188.
198. See, for example, Trotsky, *Revolution Betrayed*, p. 292.
199. *VIMS*, 11 February 1919.
200. *VIII s"ezd RKP*, pp. 198–9.
201. *Moskovskii pechatnik*, 1, 15 January 1921, p. 4.
202. Marx, 'Civil War in France', *Selected Works*, pp. 289–90.
203. Lenin, *PSS*, 38, pp. 96–7.
204. Garvi, *Zapiski*, p. 333.
205. Corrigan *et al.*, *Socialist Construction*, p. 64.
206. *VIMS*, 30 May 1919.
207. *VIMS*, 1 July 1919.
208. *VIMS*, 17 December 1918.
209. *VIMS*, 11 January 1919.
210. *VIMS*, 4 April 1919.
211. *VIMS*, 5 April 1919.
212. Lenin, *PSS*, 38, p. 256.
213. *Dekrety Sovetskoi vlasti*, vol. V (Moscow, 1971) pp. 46–50; Jan S. Adams, *Citizen Inspectors in the Soviet Union* (New York: Praeger, 1977) pp. 24–5.
214. *VIMS*, 9 July 1919.
215. *VIMS*, 3 July 1919.
216. *VIMS*, 1 October 1919.
217. *VIMS*, 22 September 1919.
218. *VIII konf. RKP*, p. 121: *VIMS*, 2 December 1919.
219. *VIII konf. RKP*, p. 121.
220. *P*, 8 February 1920; Carr, *Bolshevik Revolution*, 1, p. 232.
221. *KT*, 24 March 1920.
222. *KT*, 24 March 1920; Leggett, *The Cheka*, p. 157.
223. *KT*, 18 March 1920.
224. *KT*, 12 October 1920.
225. *KT*, 8 December 1920.
226. *KT*, 26 January 1921.
227. *KT*, 18 March 1920.
228. *KT*, 5 May 1920.
229. Lenin, *PSS*, 42, p. 49.
230. Feher *et al.*, *Dictatorship Over Needs*, p. 107.
231. Lenin, *PSS*, 37, p. 347.
232. Haden-Guest (ed.), *British Labour Delegation*, p. 10.
233. N. I. Bukharin, *Selected Writings on the State and the Transition to Socialism*, Richard B. Day (ed.) (London: Spokesman Books, 1982) p. XLII.
234. A. Meyer quoted in Bauman, *Socialism: The Active Utopia*, pp. 80–1.
235. Berdyaev, *The Origins of Russian Communism*, p. 116.
236. *P*, 11 May 1918.
237. *P*, 5 January 1919.
238. *P*, 26 July 1919.
239. *Otchet MK za iyul' 1920g.*, p. 14.
240. *KT*, 2 June 1920.
241. *Otchet MK za iyul' 1920g.*, p. 11.

242. *Otchet MK za oktyabr' 1920g.*, p. 4.
243. Myasnikov, *Izb, proiz.*, p. 233.
244. *Otchet voennogo otdela*, appendix.
245. *IX s"ezd RKP*, p. 37.
246. Lenin, *PSS*, 37, pp. 370–83.
247. *P*, 23 April 1919.
248. Myasnikov, *Izb. proiz.*, p. 243.
249. *KM*, cols. 659–60.
250. Lenin, *PSS*, 43, p. 31.
251. Lenin, *PSS*, 43, p. 384.
252. Maximoff, *Guillotine at Work*, pp. 154–5.
253. *Kommunisticheskie subbotniki v Moskve i Moskovskoi gubernii v 1919–1920gg.: dokumenty i materialy* (Moscow, 1950) p. 7.
254. Ibid., p. 341; *KM*, cols. 663 and 693–4; *Tri goda diktatury proletariata* (Moscow, 1921) p. 28; *P*, 24 December 1919.
255. *P*, 9, 20 May 1920.
256. *KM*, cols. 661–2.
257. Lenin, 'Velikii pochin', *PSS*, 39, p. 25.
258. Lenin, *PSS*, 40, p. 34.
259. *VIII konf. RKP*, p. 24.
260. *P*, 28 August 1919.
261. *P*, 16 April 1920.
262. For example, for Easter Sunday 1920, *P*, 16 April 1920.
263. *KM*, col. 662.
264. *P*, 12 September 1919.
265. *KM*, col. 689.
266. *P*, 25 November 1919.
267. *P*, 27 December 1919.
268. *KM*, col. 690.
269. *Perepiska*, VIII, pp. 618–9.
270. *VIII s"ezd RKP*, p. 174.
271. *P*, 5 May 1919.
272. *P*, 18 May 1919.
273. *IX s"ezd RKP*, p. 309.
274. For example, in Sokol'nicheskii raion, *KT*, 6 November 1920.
275. *Otchet MK za iyul', avgust i sentyabr' 1921g.*, p. 16.
276. *XVI Mosk. gubpartkonf.*, p. 15.
277. Bukharin, *Programma kommunistov*, p. 49.
278. Lenin, *PSS*, 38, p. 118.
279. Harrison, *Marooned*, p. 133.
280. *P*, 16 January 1919; *KT*, 24 April 1920.
281. *KT*, 28 September 1920.
282. *KT*, 22 April 1920.
283. *KT*, 24 April 1920.
284. *Vestnik propagandy*, 3 (1919) pp. 21–2.
285. *KT*, 17 April 1920.
286. For example *KT*, 31 March 1920.
287. On *Glavpolitprosvet*, see Sheila Fitzpatrick, *The Commissariat of Enlightenment* (Cambridge: Cambridge University Press, 1970) ch. 8; L. F.

Morozov, 'Glavpolitprosvet – organ ideologicheskoi raboty v massakh (1920–1930gg.)', *VI KPSS*, 11 (1984) pp. 43–56.

288. *IX konf. RKP*, p. 133.
289. Lenin, *PSS*, 41, p. 397.
290. *KT*, 15 January 1921.
291. *V Mosk. gubpartkonf.*, p. 18.
292. *X s"ezd RKP*, pp. 155–7.
293. *Statistika truda*, 11–12 (1918) pp. 23–4; *Yunyi kommunist*, 46, 4 June 1921, p. 10.
294. *P*, 30 May 1917.
295. *VI s"ezd RKP*, p. 267.
296. *Za chetyre goda* (Moscow, 1922) p. 17.
297. Efim Tseitlin, *Pyat' let. Iz istorii Moskovskoi organizatsii RKSM* (Moscow, 1922) pp. 23–5.
298. Ibid., p. 30; *P*, 30 July 1918.
299. Aleshchenko (1976), pp. 209–12.
300. Of the 176 delegates, 88 were communists, 35 communist sympathisers, 45 non-party, and 6 others – *Ocherki istorii Moskovskoi organizatsii VLKSM* (Moscow, 1976) p. 75; *Za chetyre goda*, p. 21.
301. *I s"ezd RKSM, 29 oktyabr'-4 noyabr' 1918g: protokoly* (Moscow, 1934) p. 5; *Bol'shaya Sovetskaya Entsiklopedia (BSE)* vol. 11 (Moscow, 1930) col. 640.
302. TsK circular letter of November 1918, in *Perepiska*, V, p. 34; *VIII s"ezd RKP*, pp. 435–6.
303. S. S. Khromov (ed.), *Grazhdanskaya voina i voennaya interventsiya v SSSR: entsiklopediya* (Moscow, 1983) p. 509.
304. *P*, 21 November 1918.
305. Tseitlin, *Pyat' let*, p. 30.
306. Ibid., pp. 30–1.
307. *Molodoi kommunist*, 11 (1957) p. 73.
308. *BSE*, vol. 11, col. 641.
309. *P*, 3 October 1919.
310. *II vserossiiskii s"ezd RKSM: stenograficheskii otchet* (Moscow/Leningrad, 1924) p. 174; *Izvestiya TsK RKSM*, 1, 26 March 1920.
311. *Moskovskaya gorodskaya*, p. 182.
312. *Yunyi kommunar*, 46, 4 June 1921, p. 8.
313. *Yunyi kommunar*, 2, 1 January 1919; 3, 15 April 1920.
314. *VIMS*, 3 September, 1919.
315. Tseitlin, *Pyat' let*, pp. 31–2; *Yunyi kommunar*, 3, 15 April 1920; L. V. Lyutsareva, 'O nekotorykh formakh rukovodstva Moskovskoi partiinoi organizatsii deyatel'nost'yu komsomola v gody grazhdanskoi voiny (1919–1920)', *Uch. zap. MGPI im. Potemkina*, vol. 56 (1959) p. 42.
316. *KT*, 27 April 1920.
317. *Otchet MK za sentyabr' 1920g.*, p. 4; *KT*, 5 September 1920.
318. *KT*, 28 September 1920.
319. *KT*, 17 November 1920.
320. *P*, 18 January 1919; Lyutsareva, 'O nekotorykh', p. 34; *KT*, 6 August, 19 December 1920.
321. *VLKSM za 10 let v tsifrakh* (Moscow, 1928) p. 20.
322. *X s"ezd RKP*, p. 544.

323. *Otchet MK za iyul' 1920g.*, p. 15.
324. Lyutsareva, 'O nekotorykh', p. 38.
325. *P*, 24 August 1919.
326. *BSE*, vol. 11, col. 655; *Ocherki MO VLKSM*, p. 125; A. Avtorkhanov, *Soviet Youth – Twelve Komsomol Histories* (Munich: Institute for the Study of the USSR), series 1, 51 (July 1959) pp. 9–10.
327. *BSE*, vol. 11, col. 645.
328. *P*, 3 January 1920.
329. *P*, 28 January 1920.
330. *KPSS v rez. i resh.*, vol. 1, p. 462; *Izvestiya TsK RKP*, 15, 24 March 1920.
331. *Izvestiya TsK RKP*, 21, 18 September 1920.
332. Tseitlin, *Pyat' let*, p. 36.
333. *IX konf. RKP*, pp. 119, 127 and 132.
334. *Ocherki MO VLKSM*, pp. 126–7; *Otchet MK za sentyabr' 1920g.*, p. 4.
335. *BSE*, vol. 11, col. 647.
336. *P*, 3 October 1920.
337. *Yunyi kommunar*, 1, 11 December 1920.
338. *Byulleten' TsK RKSM*, 22 January 1921.
339. *BSE*, vol. 11, col. 649.
340. *Tri goda proletariata: itogi raboty sredi zhenshchin Moskovskoi organizatsii RKP* (Moscow, 1921) p. 26.
341. For example, Richard Stites, *The Women's Liberation Movement in Russia: Feminism, Nihilism and Bolshevism, 1860–1930* (Princeton, 1978) p. 332.
342. *KT*, 6 November 1920.
343. E. Levi, 'Moskovskaya bol'shevistskaya organizatsiya s fevralya do iyul'skikh dnei', in *Ocherki po istorii oktyabr'skoi revolyutsii v Moskve* (Moscow, 1927) p. 59.
344. Aleksandra Kollontai, p. 16 and A. Unksova, p. 19 in *Tri goda*.
345. Kollontai, *Tri goda*, p. 16.
346. *Perepiska*, V, pp. 65–8; *P*, 20 December 1918.
347. Unksova, *Tri goda*, p. 19; *P*, 22 December 1918.
348. Unksova, *Tri goda*, p. 19; *P*, 18 May, 11 July 1919.
349. *KT*, 6 November 1920.
350. Unksova, *Tri goda*, p. 19.
351. Unksova, *Tri goda*, p. 20.
352. *P*, 16 August 1919.
353. *XVI Mosk. gubpartkonf.*, p. 6.
354. Unksova, *Tri goda*, p. 21.
355. Unksova, *Tri goda*, p. 22; *Otchet MK za iyul' 1920g.*, p. 9; *Moskovskaya gubernskaya konferentsiya rabotnits i krest'yanok: rezolyutsii i stat'i* (Moscow, 1920) p. 8.
356. *KT*, 6 November 1920.
357. Myasnikov, *Izb. proiz.*, pp. 319–20.

7 The Rise of the Reform Movements

1. Esther Corey, 'Passage to Russia', *Survey*, 53 (October 1964) pp. 28 and 31.
2. Goldman, *Disillusionment*, p. 32.

3. N. N. Popov, *Ocherk istorii rossiiskoi kommunisticheskoi partii (bol'-shevikov)* (Moscow/Leningrad, 1926) p. 248.
4. *P*, 19 January 1921.
5. *X s"ezd RKP*, pp. 71–2.
6. Szamuely, *First Models*, p. 71.
7. *XVI Mosk. gubpartkonf.*, pp. 46–7.
8. Ibid., pp. 24–44.
9. *P*, 17 December 1919; *P*, 5 February 1920.
10. *IX s"ezd RKP*, pp. 91–103.
11. Richard B. Day, *Leon Trotsky and the Politics of Economic Isolation* (Cambridge: Cambridge University Press, 1973) p. 25.
12. Ibid., p. 17.
13. M. S. Zorkii (ed.), *Rabochaya oppozitsiya: materialy i dokumenty* (Moscow, 1926) p. 16.
14. *P*, 12 March 1920; Ya. Bronin, *PR*, 11 (94) (1929) pp. 9–10.
15. This was also argued by Zinoviev in *Izvestiya TsK RKP*, 13, 2 March 1920, and in the TsK theses for the IX party congress, *Izvestiya TsK RKP*, 17, 30 March 1920; *IX s"ezd RKP*, pp. 558–61.
16. *Ekonomicheskaya zhizn'*, 54, 1920.
17. *KT*, 20, 21, March 1920.
18. *KT*, 26 March 1920; *P*, 26 March 1920.
19. *P*, 30 December 1919.
20. *IX s"ezd RKP*, pp. 105–6 and 155–7.
21. Ibid., pp. 15 and 21–2.
22. O. Narkiewicz, *The Making of the Soviet State Apparatus* (Manchester: Manchester University Press, 1970) p. 10.
23. *P*, 20 May 1920.
24. *KT*, 26 March 1920.
25. *IX s"ezd RKP*, p. 322.
26. Ibid., p. 356.
27. Ibid., pp. 122 and 155.
28. V. Boborynin *et al.* (eds.), *Sokol'niki* (Moscow, 1967) p. 44.
29. *Zhel. i rev.*, p. 48.
30. For example, *P*, 31 May 1919, and for another incident, *P*, 15 June 1919.
31. *VIII s"ezd RKP*, p. 425; *Izvestiya TsK RKP*, 2, 7 June 1919, p. 4.
32. *Izvestiya TsK RKP*, 13, 2 March 1920.
33. *KT*, 18 March 1920.
34. *KT*, 4 April 1920.
35. *KT*, 4 April 1920.
36. *VIMS*, 18 February 1920.
37. *Zhel. i rev.*, p. 48.
38. *IX s"ezd RKP*, pp. 207–8.
39. Ibid., p. 311.
40. *KPSS v rez. i resh.*, p. 178.
41. *Zhel. i rev.*, p. 49.
42. *Izvestiya TsK RKP*, 29, 7 March 1920, p. 5.
43. Loc. cit.
44. *KT*, 3 April 1920.
45. *KT*, 5 May 1920.

46. *KT*, 3 July 1920.
47. *KT*, 5 May 1920.
48. Bauman, *Socialism: The Active Utopia*, p. 77.
49. *Desyat' let: sbornik materialov Yu. O. K. Sokol'nicheskogo raiona k 10–letiyu oktyabr'skoi revolyutsii* (Moscow, 1927) p. 14.
50. *KT*, 3 September 1920.
51. Lenin, *PSS*, 41, p. 283; Norman Davies, 'The Missing Revolutionary War', *Soviet Studies*, 27 (April 1975) pp. 178–95. For the historiography of the Polish war see James M. McCann, *Soviet Studies*, 36 (October 1984), pp. 475–93.
52. *KT*, 22 August 1922.
53. *KT*, 24 August 1920.
54. Manevich (ed.), *Ocherki po istorii*, p. 174.
55. *IX s''ezd RKP*, p. 60.
56. V. F. Kochegarov, 'K voprosu o bor'be Moskovskoi organizatsii RKP(b) s antipartiinymi gruppirovkami nakanune diskussii o profsoyuzakh', *Uch. zap. Mos. Gos. Zaochnyi Ped. In-t.*, 27 (1969) pp. 152–3.
57. *KT*, 19 September 1920.
58. Service, *The Bolshevik Party*, pp. 132–4, 138 and 142.
59. *Izvestiya TsK RKP*, 21, 4 September 1920, p. 2.
60. *Izvestiya TsK RKP*, 29, 7 March 1921, p. 6.
61. *Otchet MK za sentyabr' 1920g.*, p. 4.
62. *KT*, 19 September 1920; *Otchet MK za sentyabr' 1920g.*, pp. 3 and 56.
63. *KT*, 17 September 1920.
64. *KT*, 19 September 1920.
65. *KT*, 21 September 1920.
66. *IX konf. RKP*, pp. 139–55.
67. Ibid., pp. 278–82.
68. *Otchet MK za oktyabr' 1920g.*, pp. 64–6.
69. Myasnikov, *Izb. proiz.*, p. 284.
70. Kochegarov (1969), p. 155.
71. Manevich (ed.), *Ocherki po istorii*, pp. 174–5.
72. *KT*, 31 October, 12 November 1920.
73. Kochegarov (1969), p. 155.
74. Ibid., p. 158.
75. *KT*, 14 November 1920.
76. *KT*, 3 November 1920; Kochegarov (1969), p. 159.
77. *P*, 10 September 1920.
78. *KT*, 28 October 1920.
79. Kochegarov (1969), p. 160.
80. Quoted by P. Zaslavskii, *Vospominaniya o V. I. Lenine* (Moscow, 1960) pp. 182–4, and Kochegarov (1969), p. 160.
81. *KT*, 20 November 1920.
82. Trotsky, *Revolution Betrayed*, pp. 89–90.
83. *KT*, 21 November 1920.
84. Lenin, *PSS*, 42, pp. 33 and 35.
85. *Otchet o rabote Moskovskoi obshchepartiinoi konferentsii, 20–22 noyabr' 1920g.: materialy dlya dokladchikov* (Moscow, 1920) p. 5.
86. *KT*, 23 November 1920.

87. *Otchet o rabote*, pp. 4–5.
88. Ibid., p. 6. *KT*, 23 November 1920 reports the vote as 163 to 115.
89. Lenin, *PSS*, 42, p. 350.
90. *Otchet o rabote*, p. 6.
91. Lenin, *PSS*, 42, p. 556.
92. Lenin, *PSS*, 42, pp. 39–40.
93. *KT*, 23 November 1920.
94. *P*, 30 November 1920; Zorkii, *Rabochaya oppozitsiya*, p. 17; Lenin, *PSS*, 42, p. 49.
95. *KT*, 2 December 1920.
96. *KT*, 7 September 1920.
97. *Otchet MK za yanvar' 1921g.*, p. 47.
98. *Otchet MK za yanvar' 1921g*, pp. 47–8.
99. *KT*, 14 August 1920; *Otchet MK za yanvar' 1920g.*, p. 48.
100. *KT*, 4 February 1921.
101. *IX konf. RKP*, p. 188.
102. *P*, 16 November 1920. The Komsomol and Baumanskii oppositionists had only been suspended from the party.
103. *KT*, 17 August 1920.
104. *Otchet MK za iyul' 1920g.*, p. 15.
105. *Otchet MK za sentyabr' 1920g.*, p. 51.
106. *X s''ezd RKP*, p. 242.
107. *KT*, 23 December 1920.
108. *KT*, 11, 21 December 1920.
109. *KT*, 21 December 1920, 30 January 1921; *Otchet MK za yanvar' 1921g.*, p. 14.
110. *KT*, 2 February 1921.
111. *Otchet MK za sentyabr' 1920g.*, p. 4.
112. *Izvestiya TsK RKP*, 25, 1920, p. 2.
113. *Izvestiya TsK RKP*, 26, 1920, p. 17.
114. Adams, *Citizen Inspectors*, p. 27; Fainsod, *How Russia is Ruled*, pp. 183–4.
115. *KT*, 14, 15 December 1920.
116. Dvinov, *Moskovskii sovet*, p. 108.
117. 496 voting and 85 consultative delegates attended, 488 of whom were communists and 113 non-party, *KT*, 18 December 1920.
118. *KT*, 18 December 1920.
119. *KT*, 19, 21 December 1920.
120. *KT*, 18 December 1920.
121. *KT*, 31 December 1920; *Iz ist. grazh. voiny*, p. 639.
122. Aleshchenko (1976), pp. 227 and 231.
123. *Otchet Sok. RK-ta*, p. 3.

8   The Defeat of the Reform Movements

1. Dvinov, *Moskovskii sovet*, p. 95.
2. Harrison, *Marooned*, p. 223. According to Farbman, *Bolshevism in Retreat*, p. 261, the markets were indeed closed in Moscow and Petrograd in late 1920.

3. Kritsman, *Geroicheskii period*, p. 225.
4. *Izmeneniya sots. struktury*, p. 314.
5. *P*, 11 November 1919.
6. *Otchet voennogo otdela*, appendix.
7. Harrison, *Marooned*, p. 185.
8. *Otchet MK za sentyabr' 1920g.*, pp. 23–4.
9. Ibid., p. 35.
10. *KT*, 20 October 1920.
11. Mel'gunov, *Red Terror*, p. 63.
12. *Otchet MK za oktyabr' 1920g.*, p. 3.
13. *P*, 3 October 1920.
14. *KT*, 1 February 1921.
15. Liebman, *Leninism under Lenin*, p. 267.
16. S. S. Maslov, *Rossiya posle chetyrekh let revolyutsii* (Paris, 1922) p. 155.
17. *KM*, cols. 631–2.
18. Mel'gunov, *Red Terror*, p. 60.
19. The tragedy is described by Maximoff, *Guillotine at Work*, pp. 113 and 119–22; Mel'gunov, *Red Terror*, pp. 53–8.
20. *KT*, 10 October 1920.
21. Leggett, *The Cheka*, p. 156.
22. Goldman, *Disillusionment*, p. 41.
23. *KT*, 9 November 1920.
24. *KT*, 17 December 1920.
25. *Otchet MK za yanvar' 1920g.*, p. 4.
26. Berkman, *Bolshevik Myth*, p. 307.
27. *Protokoly MGSPS*, 41 (1921) p. 12.
28. *P*, 8 February 1921.
29. Maslov, *Rossiya posle*, pp. 152–3.
30. *P*, 8 February 1921.
31. Lenin, *PSS*, 42, p. 308.
32. Lenin, *PSS*, 42, p. 333.
33. *KT*, 5, 16 February 1921; *P*, 8 February 1921.
34. *KT*, 8 February 1921.
35. *Obzor deyatel'nosti MGSPS*, p. 47.
36. *KT*, 17 December 1920.
37. *KT*, 16 February 1921.
38. Maslov, *Rossiya posle*, p. 155.
39. *SV*, 5, 5 April 1921, p. 14; Maslov, *Rossiya posle*, p. 156; Maximoff, *Guillotine at Work*, p. 160.
40. *P*, 1 March 1921; *SV*, 5, 5 April 1921, p. 15.
41. *KT*, 1 March 1921.
42. *KT*, 18 January 1922.
43. Manevich (ed.), *Ocherki po istorii*, p. 175.
44. Dvinov, *Moskovskii sovet*, p. 100.
45. *SV*, 5, 5 April 1921, p. 15.
46. Dvinov, *Moskovskii sovet*, pp. 180–2.
47. Maximoff, *Guillotine at Work*, p. 185.
48. *SV*, 6, 20 April 1921, p. 15.
49. *SV*, 7, 4 May 1921.
50. *KT*, 13, 14 May 1921.

51. *SV*, 4, 18 March 1921, p. 6.
52. For example, *SV*, 4, 18 March 1921, p. 6; Maslov, *Rossiya posle*, pp. 157–8.
53. Worker hostility appears to have continued into 1922. The 'Declaration of the Twenty-two' (signed by Shlyapnikov, Kollontai *et al.*) to the Comintern EC of 26 February 1922 claimed that 'The last elections to the Moscow Soviet [January 1922] were in effect boycotted by the workers. Even those workers who voted for communists did so out of fear of repression . . .', *XI s"ezd RKP*, p. 754.
54. *KT*, 1 March 1921.
55. *KT*, 19 February 1921.
56. Lenin, *PSS*, 42, p. 350.
57. Liebman, *Leninism under Lenin*, p. 299.
58. Lenin, *PSS*, 42, p. 235.
59. *P*, 25 January 1921; *X s"ezd RKP*, pp. 685–91.
60. *P*, 1 February 1921.
61. *P*, 19 January 1921.
62. Lenin, *PSS*, 42, p. 254.
63. *Profsoyuzy Moskvy*, pp. 141–2.
64. *Partiya i soyuzy*, p. 295.
65. *KT*, 21 January 1921.
66. Lenin, *PSS*, 42, p. 239.
67. 30 December 1920 meeting of MGSPS, Lenin *PSS*, 42, pp. 203–4.
68. Lenin, *PSS*, 42, p. 244. The theses of the Platform of the Ten are in *P*, 18 February 1921; *X s"ezd RKP*, pp. 663–74.
69. Liebman, *Leninism under Lenin*, pp. 297–8; Lovell, *From Marx to Lenin*, p. 189.
70. 'Krizis partii', 19 January 1921, Lenin *PSS*, 42, p. 242.
71. Lenin, 'Eshche raz o profsoyuzakh', 25 January 1921, *PSS*, 42, p. 269.
72. *Mosk. bols. v bor'be*, p. 28.
73. The first round gave Lenin 19 votes, Trotsky 7, Bukharin and the DCs 4, Ignatov 3, Shlypanikov 1; in the second ballot Lenin's position was adopted by 22 to 14 – *Otchet MK za yanvar' 1921g.*, p. 3.
74. V. F. Kochegarov, 'Bor'ba bol'shevikov Moskovskoi gubernii za pobedu leninskoi platformy vo vremya profsoyuznoi diskussii v partii (1920–1921gg.)', *MGPI im. V. I. Lenina* (1967) pp. 137–8.
75. *Petrogradskaya pravda*, 5–6 January 1921; *P*, 13 January 1921; *KT*, 13 January 1921.
76. Kochegarov (1967), pp. 139–40.
77. *KT*, 13 January 1921; *X s"ezd RKP*, pp. 832–4.
78. In the first ballot neither the DCs nor the buffer group could obtain a majority in favour of censuring the Petrograd Address:

Sapronov	3 votes for, 18 against, 4 abstentions
Yakovleva	8 votes for, 13 against, 6 abstentions
Ignatov	3 votes for, 21 against, 2 abstentions
Trotsky	16 votes for, 10 against, 1 abstention

In the second round Trotsky's motion, a combination of the first two, was passed by 14 votes to 13, with one crucial abstention – *KT*, 15 January

1921; Lenin, *PSS*, 42, pp. 239–40.

79. Rodionova, *Gody napryazhennogo truda*, p. 19.
80. Artem (F. A. Sergeev), *Stat'i, rechi, pis'ma* (Moscow, 1983) pp. 287–8.
81. Kochegarov (1967) p. 144.
82. *Otchet MK za yanvar' 1920g.*, p. 3.
83. *KT*, 19 January 1921; *P*, 19 January 1921.
84. *KT*, 19 January 1921.
85. *P*, 18 January 1921.
86. Manevich (ed.), *Ocherki po istorii*, pp. 176–7.
87. *P*, 29 January 1921.
88. *KT*, 15 January 1921.
89. *KT*, 25 January, 10 February 1921; *P*, 26 January 1921.
90. Boborynin (ed.), *Sokol'niki*, p. 129.
91. *Mosk. bol'sheviki v bor'be*, p. 24.
92. T. F. Lyudvinskaya, *Nas leninskaya partiya vela* (Moscow, 1976) p. 188.
93. *Izvestiya VTsIK*, 29 January 1921.
94. *P*, 2 February 1921.
95. *KT*, 2 February 1921.
96. *KT*, 15 February 1921.
97. *KT*, 8 February 1921.
98. *KT*, 15, 27 February 1921.
99. *V Mosk. gubpartkonf.*, p. 5; *P*, 25 February 1921; *KT*, 19, 21 February 1921.
100. Leonard Schapiro, 'Putting the Lid on Leninism' in Leonard Schapiro (ed.), *Political Opposition in One-Party States* (London: Macmillan, 1972) p. 39.
101. Myasnikov, 'Za partiyu', *Izb. proiz.*, pp. 284–7 and 304.
102. *KT*, 15 January 1921.
103. *X s"ezd RKP*, pp. 559–71.
104. *KT*, 9 February 1921.
105. The theses were signed by E. N. Ignatov, G. Lebedev, M. Burovtsev, I. Maslov, A. Orekhov, Denisov, Kh. Semenovich, I. Abin and Berezin of Gorodskoi *raion*; G. Korzinov, Kryukov, E. Kuranova and N. Tulyakov of Baumanskii *raion*; K. Radzevilov and S. Smirnov of Rogozhsko-Simonovskii *raion*; and V. Linkevich, I. Stefashkin and I. Vasil'ev of Sokol'nicheskii *raion* – *KT*, 12, 13, 15 February 1921; *P*, 12 February 1921.
106. Rudolf Bahro, *The Alternative in Eastern Europe* (London: NLB, 1978) (trans. David Fernbach), pp. 256–7 and *passim*. Bahro defines surplus consciousness as 'an energetic mental capacity that is no longer absorbed by the *immediate* necessities and dangers of human existence and can thus orient itself to more distant problems', p. 257.
107. *KT*, 12 February 1921.
108. *P*, 16 February 1921. The concept of the intellectual exploitation of the working class was developed by Waclaw Machajski (A. Vol'skii), *The Intellectual Worker* (Geneva, 1904).
109. A. Shlyapnikov, 'O nashikh vnutripartiinykh raznoglasiyakh', *Diskussion-nyi listok*, TsK RKP(b), 1 (January 1921) p. 13.
110. Ibid., p. 14.
111. Lenin, *PSS*, 42, p. 39.

112. *KT*, 15 January 1921.
113. The Democratic Centralists' theses are in *P*, 22 January 1921; *X s"ezd RKP*, pp. 656–62.
114. Myasnikov, *Izb. proiz*,. pp. 295–6.
115. *KT*, 20 February 1921.
116. *KT*, 13 February 1921.
117. *KT*, 18 February 1921.
118. *KT*, 16 February 1921.
119. *KT*, 19 February 1921.
120. Manevich (ed.), *Ocherki po istorii*, p. 177; *P*, 20 February 1921.
121. *KT*, 15 January, 19 February 1921.
122. *KT*, 19 February 1921.
123. *V Mosk. gubpartkonf.*, p. 4.
124. Ibid., pp. 3–4.
125. Erickson (1962), p. 125; cf. John Erickson, 'Some Military and Political Aspects of the "Militia Army" Controversy 1919–20', in *Essays in Honour of E. H. Carr* (London: Macmillan, 1974) pp. 204–28.
126. *V Mosk. gubpartkonf.*, p. 6.
127. Ibid., pp. 7–17.
128. Ibid., p. 7; *P*, 22 February 1921.
129. *P*, 22 February 1921; *KT*, 22 February 1921.
130. *V Mosk. gubpartkonf.*, pp. 34–6; *KT*, 22 February 1921.
131. *X s"ezd RKP*, p. 803.
132. *V Mosk. gubpartkonf.*, pp. 39 and 41.
133. Lenin, *PSS*, 42, p. 350.
134. *KT*, 24 February 1921.
135. *KT*, 3 March 1921.
136. *KT*, 4 March 1921.
137. *KT*, 25 March 1921.
138. *KT*, 27 March 1921.
139. Lenin, *PSS*, 42, p. 350.
140. Quoted by Feher *et al.*, *Dictatorship Over Needs*, pp. 142–3.
141. *P*, 19 January 1921.
142. Lenin, *PSS*, 43, p. 42.
143. Ibid., p. 24.
144. Ibid., pp. 41–42.
145. *X s"ezd RKP*, p. 584.
146. Ibid., p. 563.
147. Speech to the Moscow Soviet, 20 November 1922, Lenin, *PSS*, 45, pp. 301–2.
148. Lenin, *PSS*, 43, p. 31.
149. *Desyat' let*, p. 20.

Conclusions

1. Quoted in Bauman, *Socialism: The Active Utopia*, p. 69.
2. Lenin, *PSS*, 45, p. 308.

Bibliography

Unpublished Materials

Archive material

Tsentral'nyi gosudarstvennyi arkhiv oktyabr'skoi revolyutsii. Fond 7952: opis' 2 Istoriya promyshlennosti i rabochii klass v SSSR; opis' 3 Guzhon (Serp i Molot).

Dissertations

Bowman, B'ann, *The Moscow Bolsheviks, February–November 1917*, PhD dissertation (Indiana, 1973).

Chase, W. J., *Moscow and its Working Class, 1918–1928: A Social Analysis*, PhD dissertation (Boston, 1979).

Dolgovyazova, M. B., *Demokraticheskie preobrazovanya v khode sotsialisticheskoi revolyutsii, oktyabr' 1917–1919: po materialam Moskovskoi gubernii*, Avtoref. diss. (Moscow, 1971).

Helgesen, M. M., *The Origins of the Party–State Monolith in Soviet Russia: Relations between the Soviets and the Party Committees in the Central Provinces, October 1917–March 1921*, PhD dissertation (Stony Brook: State University of New York, 1980).

Romanov, V. V., *Bor'ba V. I. Lenina protiv antipartiinoi gruppy 'demokraticheskogo tsentralizma'*, Avtoref. diss. (Moscow, 1969).

Unpublished papers

Gooderham, P. O., *The Regional Apparatus in the First Five-Year Plan: The Case of Leningrad*, Centre for Russian and East European Studies (CREES), University of Birmingham, Soviet Industrialisation Project Series, SIPS 24 (1983).

Mawdsley, Evan, 'When did the Civil War Start?', paper presented to the Soviet Industrialisation Project seminar, CREES (January 1985).

Wheatcroft, S. G., *Famine and Factors Affecting Mortality in the USSR: The Demographic Crises of 1914–1922 and 1930–1933*, CREES, University of Birmingham, Soviet Industrialisation Project Series, SIPS 20 (1981).

Newspapers, Journals and Periodical Publications

Bol'shevik (1918–).
Bor'ba klassov.
Byulleten' MGSPS (1921–).
Byulleten' MK RKP (1921–).
Byulleten' MSNKh (1920–).
Byulleten' statistiki truda Moskovskoi gubernii (MGSPS 1920–23).
Byulleten' TsK RKSM.

Diskussionnyi listok (TsK RKP, early 1921).
Istoricheskie zapiski.
Ekonomicheskaya zhizn'.
Izvestiya MK RKP(b) (1922–23).
Izvestiya Moskovskogo komiteta po trudovoi povinnosti (1920).
Izvestiya MOSNKh (1918).
Izvestiya Moskovskogo soyuza rabochikh i sluzhashchikh po vyrabotke pish-chevikh produktov (1918).
Izvestiya MSNKh (1920–).
Izvestiya TsK RKP(b) (1919–).
Izvestiya TsK RKSM (1920–).
Izvestiya VTsIK sovetov KRS i KD i Moskovskogo soveta.
Kommunar (TsK RKP weekly).
Kommunist (1918).
Kommunisticheskii trud (March 1920–February 1922).
Molodoi kommunist.
Moskovskii pechatnik (1921–26).
Narodnoe khozyaistvo (1918–22).
Pechatnik (1917–19).
Pravda.
Proletarskaya revolyutsiya (1922–).
Protokoly zasedanii prezidiuma MGSPS (1920–21).
Sotsial-demokrat (1917–March 1918).
Sotsialisticheskii vestnik (1921–).
Statistika truda (1918–).
Stenograficheskie otchety Mossoveta (1919–).
Trudy tsentral'nogo statisticheskogo upravleniya (1918–).
Vechernie izvestiya Moskovskogo soveta rabochikh i krasnoarmeiskikh deputatov (July 1918–March 1920).
Vechernyaya krasnaya gazeta (TsK RKP, 1918).
Vestnik propagandy (MGK and MK RKP(b), 1919–20).
Vestnik truda.
Voprosy istorii KPSS.
Yunosheskaya pravda (MK RKSM).
Yunyi kommunar (MK RKSM).

Documentary and Statistical Materials

Bernshtam, M. S. (ed.), *Issledovaniya noveishei russkoi istorii*, vol. 2, *Nezavisimoe rabochee dvizhenie v 1918 godu: dokumenty i materialy* (Paris: YMCA Press, 1981).
Bolsheviks and the October Revolution: Minutes of the Russian Social–Democratic Labour Party (Bolsheviks), August 1917–February 1918 (London: Pluto Press, 1974).
IV Moskovskaya gubernskaya konferentsiya profsoyuzov, 14–15 sentyabr' 1921 g (Moscow: MGSPS, 1921).
Chugaev, D. A. (ed.), *Rabochii klass sovetskoi Rossii v pervyi god diktatury proletariata: sbornik dokumentov i materialov* (Moscow, 1964).

Dekrety Sovetskoi vlasti (Moscow), vol. 1 (1957); vol. 2 (1959); vol. 3 (1964); vol. 4 (1968); vol. 5 (1971); vol. 6 (1973); vol. 7 (1975).

X s"ezd RKP(b), mart-aprel' 1921 g.: stenograficheskii otchet (Moscow, 1963).

IX konferentsiya RKP(b), sentyabr' 1920 g.: protokoly (Moscow, 1972).

IX s"ezd RKP(b), mart–aprel' 1920 g.: protokoly (Moscow, 1960).

Haden-Guest, L. (ed.), *British Labour Delegation to Russia, 1920: Official Report* (London, 1920).

Iz istorii grazhdanskoi voiny v SSSR: sbornik dokumentov i materialov (Moscow), vol. 1 (1960); vol. 2 (1961); vol. 3 (1961).

Kommunisticheskie subbotniki v Moskve i Moskovskoi gubernii v 1919–1920 gg.: dokumenty i materialy (Moscow, 1950).

KPSS v rezolyutsiyakh i resheniyakh s"ezdov, konferentsii i plenumov TsK, vol. 2 (Moscow, 1970).

Materialy po peresmotru partiinoi programmy (Moscow: MOB, 1917).

Materialy po statistike lichnogo sostava RKP(b) (Moscow, 1921).

MChK – iz istorii Moskovskoi chrezvychainoi komissii: dokumenty (Moscow, 1978).

Moskovskaya gorodskaya i Moskovskaya oblastnaya organizatsiya KPSS v tsifrakh (Moscow, 1972).

Moskovskaya gubernskaya konferentsiya rabotnits i krest'yanok, iyul' 1920 g.: rezolyutsii i stat'i (Moscow, 1920).

Moskovskaya organizatsiya RKP(b) v tsifrakh, 1 (Moscow, 1925).

Moskovskii sovet professional'nykh soyuzov v 1917 g.: protokoly (Moscow, 1927).

Obzor deyatel'nosti MGSPS za period mezhdu II i III gubernskimi s"ezdami, sentyabr' 1920–mai 1921 gg. (Moscow, 1921).

XI s"ezd RKP(b), mart–aprel' 1922 g: stenograficheskii otchet (Moscow, 1961).

O naselenii Moskvy (Moscow, 1980).

Otchet o deyatel'nosti MK RKP(b) za iyul' 1920 g. (Moscow, 1920).

Otchet MK RKP(b) za sentyabr' 1920 g. (Moscow, 1920).

Otchet MK RKP(b) za oktyabr' 1920 g. (Moscow, 1920).

Otchet MK RKP(b) za yanvar' 1921 g. (Moscow, 1921).

Otchet o deyatel'nosti MK-ta za iyul', avgust i sentyabr' 1921 g. (Moscow, 1921).

Otchet o rabote Moskovskoi obshchepartiinoi konferentsii, 20–22 noyabr' 1920 g.: materialy dlya dokladchikov (Moscow, 1920).

Otchet o rabote voennogo otdela MK-ta RKP za vremya sushchestvovaniya s 15– go aprelya 1919 g. (Moscow, 1920).

Otchet severnoi oblastnoi konferentsii s 3–go po 6–e aprelya 1918 g.: dve rechi G. Zinov'eva (Petrograd, 1918).

Otchet Sokol'nicheskogo raionnogo komiteta RKP za vremya s 1/IX–1920 g po 1/I–1921 g. (Moscow, 1921).

Partiya v period inostrannoi voennoi interventsii i grazhdanskoi voiny, 1918– 1920 gg.: dokumenty i materialy (Moscow, 1962).

Perepiska sekretariata TsK RKP(b) s mestnymi partiinymi organizatsiyami (Moscow), vol. 2 (1957); vol. 3 (1967); vol. 4 (1969); vol. 5 (1970); vol. 6 (1971); vol. 7 (1972).

Perepis' sluzhashchikh sovetskikh uchrezhdenii g. Moskvy (Moscow, 1922).

Pervyi bukvar' kommunista (Moscow: MK, 1920).

I s"ezd RKSM, 29 oktyabr'–4 noyabr' 1918 g: protokoly (Moscow/Leningrad, 1934).

I vserossiiskii s''ezd profsoyuzov sluzhashchikh, iyun' 1918 g. (Moscow, 1918).

Podgotovka i pobeda oktyabr'skoi revolyutsii v Moskve: dokumenty i materialy (Moscow, 1957).

V Moskovskaya gubernskaya konferentsiya RKP(b), 19–21 fevral' 1921 g.: kratkii otchet i rezolyutsii (Moscow, 1921).

VII (aprel'skaya) vserossiiskaya konferentsiya RSDRP(b): protokoly (Moscow, 1958).

VII ekstrennyi s''ezd RKP(b), mart 1918 g.: stenograficheskii otchet (Moscow, 1962).

16–ya Moskovskaya gubernskaya konferentsiya RKP(b), 23 noyabr' 1919 g.: protokoly (Moscow, 1920).

VI s''ezd RSDRP(b), avgust 1917 g.: protokoly (Moscow, 1958).

Statisticheskii ezhegodnik g. Moskvy i Moskovskoi gubernii, 2, 1914–25 (Moscow, 1927).

Statisticheskii spravochnik g. Moskvy i Moskovskoi gubernii 1927 g. (Moscow, 1928).

Trudy II vserossiiskogo s''ezda sovetov narodnogo khozyaistva, 19–27 dekabr' 1918 g.: stenograficheskii otchet (Moscow, 1919).

Uprochenie sovetskoi vlasti v Moskve i Moskovskoi gubernii: dokumenty i materialy (Moscow, 1958).

Ustav Moskovskoi gubernskoi organizatsii RKP (Moscow, 1919).

Ustav Moskovskoi organizatsii RKP, 30 iyul' 1918 g. (Moscow, 1918).

Ustav Moskovskoi organizatsii RKP(b) (Moscow, 1920).

Velikaya oktyabr'skaya sotsialisticheskaya revolyutsiya. Revolyutsionnoe dvizhenie v Rossii v aprele 1917 g.: aprel'skii krizis: dokumenty i materialy (Moscow, 1958).

VLKSM za 10 let v tsifrakh (Moscow, 1928).

VIII konferentsiya RKP(b), dekabr' 1919 g.: protokoly (Moscow, 1961).

VIII s''ezd RKP(b), mart 1919 g.: protokoly (Moscow, 1959).

Vserossiiskaya perepis' chlenov RK 1922 g., 1, (Moscow, 1922).

II kongress kommunisticheskogo internatsionala, iyul' 1920 g.: stenograficheskii otchet (Moscow, 1920).

II vserossiiskii s''ezd RKSM, 5–18 oktyabr' 1919 g.: stenograficheskii otchet (Moscow/Leningrad, 1924).

Vydro, M. Ya., *Naselenie Moskvy* (Moscow, 1976).

Zorkii, M. A. (ed.), *Rabochaya oppozitsiya: materialy i dokumenty, 1920–1926 gg.* (Moscow, 1926).

Works in Russian

Aleshchenko, N. M., *Osushchestvlenie leninskikh ukazanii v period stanovleniya Sovetskoi vlast v Moskve* (Moscow, 1968).

Aleshchenko, N. M., 'Moskovskii sovet v 1918–1920 gg.', *Istoricheskie zapiski*, 91 (1973).

Aleshchenko, N. M., *Moskovskii sovet v 1917–1941 gg.* (Moscow, 1976).

Al'perovich, S., *Chetvertyi s''ezd profsoyuzov i puti Russkogo profdvizheniya* (Moscow, 1921).

Aluf, A. S., *Professional'nye soyuzy v period voennogo kommunizma* (Moscow, 1925).

Anikeev, V. V., 'Svedeniya o bol'shevistskikh organizatsiyakh s marta po dekabr' 1917 goda', *Voprosy istorii KPSS*, 2 (1958).
Anikst, A. M., *Organizatsiya rabochei sily v 1920 g.* (Moscow, 1920).
Anikst, A. M., *Vospominaniya o Lenine* (Moscow, 1933).
Arenshtein, A. I., *Rannim Moskovskim utrom* (Moscow, 1967).
Artem (F. A. Sergeev), *Stat'i, rechi, pis'ma* (Moscow, 1983).
Avtorkhanov, A., *Proiskhozhdenie partokratii*, vol. 1, *TsK i Lenin* (Frankfurt: Posev, 1973).
Baganov, Y. I., *Moskovskie bol'sheviki v ogne revolyutsionnykh boev* (Moscow, 1976).
Boborynin, V. (ed.), *Sokol'niki* (Moscow, 1967).
Bor'ba kommunisticheskoi partii protiv neproletarskikh partii, grupp i techenii (posleoktyabr'skii period): istoriograficheskie ocherki (Leningrad, 1982).
Bubnov, A. S. (ed.), *Grazhdanskaya voina, 1918–1921* (Moscow, 1928).
Bukharin, N. I., *Ot diktatury imperializma k diktature proletariata* (Petrograd, 1918).
Bukharin, N. I., *Programma kommunistov* (Moscow, 1918).
Bukov, K. I., *V bitve velikoi* (Moscow, 1960).
Bukov, K. I. and Nagapetyan, G. A., 'Ideino-organizatsionnoe ukreplenie Moskovskoi partiinoi organizatsii v gody grazhdanskoi voiny', *Voprosy istorii KPSS*, 6 (1959).
Bychkov, L., *Vzryv v Leont'evskom pereulke* (Moscow, 1934).
Desyat' let: sbornik materialov Yu. O. K. Sokol'nicheskogo raiona k 10–letiyu oktyabr'skoi revolyutsii (Moscow, 1927).
Dinamo–25 let revolyutsionnoi bor'by (Moscow: MK, 1923).
Drobizhev, V. Z., 'Obrazovanie sovetov narodnogo khozyaistva v Moskovskom promyshlennom raione, 1917–1918gg.' in *Iz istorii velikoi oktyabr'skoi sotsialisticheskoi revolyutsii* (Moscow, 1957).
Drobizhev, V. Z., *Glavnyi shtab sotsialisticheskoi promyshlennosti* (Moscow, 1966).
Dumova, N. G., *Sekretar' MK: povest' o V. M. Zagorskom* (Moscow, 1966).
Dva goda diktatury proletariata, 1917–1919 (Moscow: VSNKh, 1919).
Dvinov, B. L., *Moskovskii sovet rabochikh deputatov, 1917–1922: vospominaniya* (New York, 1961).
Ermanskii, O. A., *Iz perezhitogo* (Moscow/Leningrad, 1927).
Garvi, P. A., *Zapiski sotsial-demokrata, 1906–1921* (Newtonville, Ma.: Oriental Research Partners, 1982).
Gimpel'son, E. G., 'Iz istorii obrazovaniya odno-partiinoi sistemy v SSSR', *Voprosy istorii KPSS*, 11 (1965).
Gimpel'son, E. G., 'Kak slozhilas' sovetskaya forma proletarskogo gosudarstva', *Voprosy istorii KPSS*, 9 (1967).
Gimpel'son, E. G., *Voennyi kommunizm: politika, praktika, ideologiya* (Moscow, 1973).
Gimpel'son E. G., *Velikii oktyabr' i stanovlenie sovetskoi sistemy upravleniya narodnym khozyaistvom* (Moscow, 1977).
Gimpel'son, E. G., 'O rabochem kontrole posle prinyatiya dekreta o natsionalizatsii promyshlennosti v SSSR', *Istoriya SSSR*, 4 (1981).
Gladkov, I. A., *Ocherki sovetskoi ekonomiki, 1917–1920gg.* (Moscow, 1956).
Gogolevskii, A. V., *Petrogradskii sovet v gody grazhdanskoi voiny* (Leningrad, 1982).

Ignat'ev, G. S., *Moskva v pervyi god proletarskoi diktatury* (Moscow, 1975).

Istoriya Moskvy, vol. 6, bk 1 (Moscow, 1957).

Istoriya rabochikh Moskvy, 1917–1945gg. (Moscow, 1983).

Izmeneniya sotsial'noi struktury sovetskogo obshchestva: oktyabr' 1917–1920gg. (Moscow, 1976).

Kabanov, V. V., 'O "neitral'nosti" kooperatsii v 1917–1920gg.' in *Bankrotstvo melkoburzhuaznykh partii Rossii, 1917–1922gg.*, pt 2 (Moscow, 1977).

Khromov, S. S. (ed.), *Grazhdanskaya voina i voennaya interventsiya v SSSR: entsiklopediya* (Moscow, 1983).

Kochegarov, V. F., 'Bor'ba bol'shevikov Moskovskoi gubernii za pobedu leninskoi platformy vo vremya profsoyuznoi diskussii v partii, 1917–1921gg.', *MGPI im. Lenina* (1967).

Kochegarov, V. F., 'K voprosu o bor'be Moskovskoi organizatsii RKP(b) s antipartiinymi gruppirovkami nakanune diskussii o profsoyuzakh', *MGPI im. Lenina*, 27 (1969).

Kollontai, A. M., *Rabochaya oppozitsiya* (Moscow, 1921).

Kostina, R. V., 'Moskovskii gorodskoi sovnarkhoz v reshenii voprosov upravleniya promyshlennoist'yu stolitsy, 1918–1920gg.', *Istoriya SSSR*, 4 (1984).

Krasnaya Moskva: sbornik statei (Moscow, 1920).

Kratov, V. L., *Chonovtsy* (Moscow, 1974).

Kritsman, L., *Geroicheskii period velikoi russkoi revolyutsii: opyt analiza t.n. "voennogo kommunizma"* (Moscow/Leningrad, 1926).

Laman, N. M. and Krechetkova, Yu. I., *Istoriya zavoda 'Elektroprovod'* (Moscow, 1967).

Latsis, M., 'Tov. Dzerzhinskii i VChK', *Proletarskaya revolyutsiya*, 9 (56) (1926).

Lenin i Moskovskie bol'sheviki (Moscow, 1977).

Lozovskii, A., *Zadachi professional'nykh soyuzov* (Moscow, 1921).

Lyudvinskaya, T. F., *Nas leninskaya partiya vela: vospominaniya* (Moscow, 1976).

Lyutsareva, L. V., 'O nekotorykh formakh rukovodstva Moskovskoi partiinoi organizatsii deyatel'nost'yu komsomola v gody grazhdanskoi voiny, 1919–1920gg., *Uch. zap. MGPI im. Potemkina*, 56 (1956).

Manevich (ed.), *Ocherki po istorii revolyutsionnogo dvizheniya i bol'shevistskoi organizatsii v Baumanskom raione* (Moscow, 1928).

Maslov, S. S., *Rossiya posle chetyrekh let revolyutsii* (Paris, 1922).

Morozov, L. F., 'Glavpolitprosvet – organ ideologicheskoi raboty v massakh, 1920–1930gg.', *Voprosy istorii KPSS*, 11 (1984).

Moskovskie bol'sheviki v bor'be s pravym i "levym" opportunizmom, 1921–1929gg. (Moscow, 1969).

Moskovskii sovet za desyat' let raboty, 1917–1927gg. (Moscow, 1927).

Moskva za 50 let Sovetskoi vlasti, 1917–1967 (Moscow, 1968).

Myasnikov, A. F. (Myasnikyan), *Izbrannye proizvedeniya* (Erevan, 1965).

Nikolaev, N., *Moskovskii rabochii i krest'yanin* (Moscow, 1921).

Obichkin, O. G., *Ustavy mestnykh organizatsii RSDRP* (Moscow, 1976).

Ocherki istorii Moskovskoi organizatsii KPSS, 1883–1965 (Moscow, 1966).

Ocherki istorii Moskovskoi organizatsii KPSS, vol. 2 (Moscow, 1983).

Ocherki istorii Moskovskoi organizatsii VLKSM (Moscow, 1976).

Pankratova, A. M., *Istoriya razvitiya fabzav. pred-va i fabzav. komitetov v Rossii*

(Moscow, 1924).

Partiya i soyuzy (k diskussii o roli i zadachakh profsoyuzov), G. Zinovev, (ed.) (Petrograd, 1921).

Peters, Ya. Kh., 'Vospominaniya o rabote VChK v pervyi god revolyutsii', *Proletarskaya revolyutsiya*, 10 (33) (1924).

Petrov, Yu. P., *KPSS – rukovoditel' i vospitatel' krasnoi armii, 1918–1920gg.* (Moscow, 1961).

Petrov, Yu. P., *Partiinoe stroitel'stvo v sovetskoi armii i flote, 1918–1961gg.* (Moscow, 1964).

Piletskii, Ya. A., *Rabochii klass i khozyaistvo Rossii v 1914–1919 godakh* (Kiev, 1919).

Pokrovskii, M. N., *Oktyabr'skaya revolyutsiya* (Moscow, 1928).

Polikarpov, V. D., *Nachal'nyi etap grazhdanskoi voiny: istoriya izucheniya* (Moscow, 1980).

Popov, I. A., 'Deyatel'nost' Moskovskoi partiinoi organizatsii po ukrepleniyu svoikh ryadov, okt. 1917–yan. 1919gg.', *Uch. zap. MOPI im. Krupskoi, Istoriya KPSS*, 215, 13 (Moscow, 1968).

Popov, N. N., *Ocherk istorii rossiiskoi kommunisticheskoi partii (bol'shevikov)* (Moscow/Leningrad, 1926).

Profsoyuzy Moskvy (Moscow, 1975).

Pyat' let raboty – yacheika RKP(b) i mestkom Glavkhozsklada RKKA, 1919–1924gg. (Moscow, 1925).

Pyat' let raboty yacheiki RKP(b) tipografii 'Krasnyi proletarii', 1919–1924gg. (Moscow, 1925).

Razgon, I. M., *Moskva v period inostrannoi interventsii i grazhdanskoi voiny* (Moscow, 1947).

Rodionova, N., *Gody napryazhennogo truda: iz istorii Moskovskoi partiinoi organizatsii, 1921–1925gg.* (Moscow, 1963).

Savitskaya, R. M., 'O rabote V. I. Lenina nad vtoroi programmoi partii', *Voprosy istorii KPSS*, 4 (1984).

Shchetinov, Yu. A., *Krushenie melkoburzhuaznoi kontrrevolyutsii v Sovetskoi Rossii, konets 1920–1921gg.* (Moscow, 1984).

Shest' let na revolyutsionnom puti: k yubileyu zavodskikh organizatsii, 1917–1923gg.. Gosudarstvennyi russko-kabel'nyi i metalloprokatnyi zavod 'Russ-kabel'' (Moscow, 1923).

Shiplin, L., *et al.*, *Bol'shevistskii put' bor'by i pobed (30 let yacheiki VKP(b) zavoda 'Dinamo')* (Moscow, 1933).

Shustova, E. I., 'Bor'ba Moskovskikh bol'shevikov za profsoyuzy i fabzavkomy v period dvoevlastiya', *Voprosy istorii KPSS*, 6 (1984).

Sorokin, P. A., *Sovremennoe sostoyanie Rossii* (Prague, 1922).

Spirin, L. M., *Klassy i partii v grazhdanskoi voine v Rossii, 1917–1920gg.* (Moscow, 1968).

Strakhov, A. V., 'Natsionalizatsiya krupnoi promyshlennosti goroda Moskvy', *Uch. zap. MGPI im. Lenina*, 200 (1964).

Tarusov, V. N., 'Deyatel'nost' Moskovskoi partiinoi organizatsii po organizatsionnomy ukrepleniyu svoikh ryadov, 1918–1922gg.', *Sbornik trudov iz istorii Moskovskoi partiinoi organizatsii*, MOPI im. Krupskoi, 239 (Moscow, 1973).

Tel'nov, S. M., 'Boevye kommunisticheskie otryady osobogo naznacheniya v bor'be s kontrrevolyutsiei, 1918g.', *Uch. zap. MOPI im. Krupskoi, Istoriya KPSS*, 215, 13 (Moscow, 1968).

Tolstikh, D A., *Deyatel'nost' Moskovskoi partiinoi organizatsii po sozdaniyu organov Sovetskoi vlasti v Moskve, okt. 1917–iyun' 1918gg.* (Moscow, 1958).

Tri goda diktatury proletariata: itogi raboty sredi zhenshchin Moskovskoi organizatsii RKP (Moscow, 1921).

Trotsky, L. D., *Mirovoe ekonomicheskoe polozhenie i nashi zadachi* (Moscow, 1921).

Tseitlin, E., *Pyat' let: iz istorii Moskovskoi organizatsii RKSM* (Moscow, 1922).

Varlamov, K. I. and Slamikhin, N. A., *Razoblachenie V. I. Leninym teorii i taktiki 'levykh kommunistov', noyabr' 1917–1918gg.* (Moscow, 1964).

Venediktov, A. V., *Organizatsiya gosudarstvennoi promyshlennosti v SSSR*, vol. 1 (Moscow, 1957).

Yaroslavskii, E. M. (ed.), *Kak provodit' chistku partii* (Moscow/Leningrad, 1929).

Yarotskii, V. Ya., 'Trud v SSSR', *Entsiklopedicheskii slovar' (Granat)*, vol. 41, pt 2.

Za chetyre goda: vospominaniya (Moscow: RKSM, 1922).

Zaslavskii, P., *Vospominaniya o V. I. Lenine*, vol. 3 (Moscow, 1960).

Zheleznodorozhniki i revolyutsiya: sbornik vospominanii i dokumentov o rabote zheleznodorozhnogo raiona Moskovskoi organizatsii RKP(b) (Moscow, 1923).

Znamenskii, O. N., *Vserossiiskoe uchreditel'noe sobranie* (Leningrad, 1976).

Works in Other Languages

Abramovitch, Raphael R., *The Russian Revolution, 1917–39* (London: George Allen & Unwin, 1962).

Adams, J. S., *Citizen Inspectors in the Soviet Union* (New York: Praeger, 1977).

Adelman, J. R., 'The Development of the Soviet Party Apparat in the Civil War: Center, Localities and Nationality Areas', *Russian History/Histoire Russe*, 9, part 1 (1982).

Avineri, Shlomo (ed.), *Marx's Socialism* (New York: Lieber–Atherton, 1973).

Avrich, Paul, *Kronstadt 1921* (Princeton: Princeton University Press, 1970).

Avrich, Paul, *The Russian Anarchists* (New York: Norton, 1978).

Avtorkhanov, A., *Soviet Youth: Twelve Komsomol Histories*, series 1, 51 (Munich: Institute for the Study of the USSR, 1959).

Bahro, Rudolf, *The Alternative in Eastern Europe* (London: New Left Books, 1978).

Bater, James H., 'Some Dimensions of Urbanisation and the Response of Municipal Government: Moscow and St Petersburg', *Russian History/Histoire Russe*, 5, pt 1 (1978).

Bater, J. H. & French, R. A. (eds), *Studies in Russian Historical Geography*, vol. 2 (London: Academic Press, 1983).

Bauman, Z., *Socialism: The Active Utopia* (London: George Allen & Unwin, 1976).

Bazhenov, N. N., 'La revolution Russe', in *Pages Actuelles*, 1914–19 (Paris, 1919).

Bellis, Paul, *Marxism and the USSR: The Theory of Proletarian Dictatorship and the Marxist Analysis of Soviet Society* (London: Macmillan, 1979).

Berdyaev, Nikolai, *The Origin of Russian Communism* (London, 1937).

Berkman, Alexander, *The Bolshevik Myth: Diary, 1920–1922* (London, 1925).

Bettelheim, Charles, *Class Struggles in the USSR: First Period, 1917–1923* (Brighton: Harvester Press, 1976).

Bienkowski, Wladyslaw, *Theory and Reality: The Development of Social Systems* (London: Alison and Busby, 1981).

Bonnell, Victoria E., *Roots of Rebellion: Workers' Politics and Organisations in St Petersburg and Moscow, 1900–1914* (Berkeley, Ca.: University of California Press, 1983).

Bradley, John, *Civil War in Russia, 1917–1920* (London: Batsford, 1975).

Brodersen, Arvid, *The Soviet Worker: Labour and Government in Soviet Society* (New York: Random House, 1966).

Brovkin, V., 'The Mensheviks' Political Comeback: The Elections to the Provincial City Soviets in Spring 1918', *The Russian Review*, vol. 42 (1983).

Bukharin, N. I., *Imperialism and World Economy* (London: Merlin Press, 1972).

Bukharin, N. I., *The Politics and Economics of the Transition Period*, K. J. Tarbuck (ed.) (London: Routledge & Kegan Paul, 1979).

Bukharin, N. I., *Selected Writings on the State and the Transition to Socialism*, Richard B. Day (ed.) (London: Spokesman Books, 1982).

Bukharin, N. I. and Preobrazhenskii, E., *The ABC of Communism* (Harmondsworth: Penguin, 1969).

Carr, E. H., *The Bolshevik Revolution, 1917–1921* (Harmondsworth: Penguin, 1966).

Casanova, José, review of Jean L. Cohen, *Class and Civil Society, Telos*, 59 (1984) pp. 187–96.

Chamberlin, W. H., *The Russian Revolution, 1917–1921* (London, 1935).

Cohen, Jean L., *Class and Civil Society: The Limits of Marxian Critical Theory* (Amherst: University of Massachusetts Press, 1982).

Cohen, Stephen, F., *Bukharin and the Bolshevik Revolution: A Political Biography, 1888–1938* (New York: Vintage Books, 1970).

Colton, Timothy, J., *Commissars, Commanders and Civilian Authority: The Structure of Soviet Military Politics* (Cambridge, Mass: Harvard University Press,, 1979).

Corey, Esther, 'Passage to Russia', *Survey*, 53 (October 1964).

Corrigan, Philip, Ramsey, Harvie and Sayer, Derek, *Socialist Construction and Marxist Theory: Bolshevism and its Critique* (London: Macmillan, 1978).

Dan, Theodore, *The Origins of Bolshevism* (New York, 1964).

Daniels, R. V., *The Conscience of the Revolution: Communist Opposition in Soviet Russia* (London: Oxford University Press, 1960).

Davies, Norman, 'The Missing Revolutionary War: The Polish Campaigns and the Retreat from Revolution in Soviet Russia, 1919–1921', *Soviet Studies*, XXVII, 2 (1975).

Davies, R. W., *The Development of the Soviet Budgetary System* (Cambridge: Cambridge University Press, 1958).

Day, Richard B., *Leon Trotsky and the Politics of Economic Isolation* (Cambridge: Cambridge University Press, 1973).

Deutscher, Isaac, *Soviet Trade Unions: Their Place in Soviet Labour Policy* (London/New York: Royal Institute of International Affairs, 1950).

Dewar, M., *Labour Policy in the USSR, 1917–1928* (London/New York: Royal Institute of International Affairs, 1956).

Dobb, M., *Soviet Economic Development Since 1917* (New York: International Publishers, 1948).

Dukes, Paul, *Red Dusk and the Morrow* (London, 1923).

Erickson, John, *The Soviet High Command: A Military–Political History, 1918–1941* (New York: St Martin's Press, 1962).

Erickson, John, 'Some Military and Political Aspects of the 'Militia Army' Controversy, 1919–1920', in *Essays in Honour of E. H. Carr* (London: Macmillan, 1974).

Fainsod, Merle, *How Russia is Ruled* (London: Oxford University Press, 1963).

Farbman, Michael S., *Bolshevism in Retreat* (London, 1923).

Feher, Ferenc, Heller, Agnes, Markus, Gyorgy, *Dictatorship Over Needs* (Oxford: Basil Blackwell, 1983).

Feher, F., 'The French Revolutions as Models for Marx's Conception of Politics', *Thesis Eleven*, 8 (January 1984).

Ferro, Marc, 'The Birth of the Soviet Bureaucratic System', in R. Carter-Elwood (ed.), *Reconsiderations on the Russian Revolution* (Cambridge, Mass: Slavica Publishers, 1976).

Fitzpatrick, Sheila, *The Commissariat of the Enlightenment* (Cambridge: Cambridge University Press, 1970).

Footman, David, *Civil War in Russia* (London: Faber, 1961).

Friedrich, C., Curtis, M., Barber, B., *Totalitarianism in Perspective: Three Views* (London: Pall Mall Press, 1969).

Getzler, I, *Martov: A Political Biography of a Russian Social Democrat* (London: Oxford University Press, 1967).

Goldman, Emma, *My Disillusionment in Russia* (London, 1923).

Gorky, M., *History of the Civil War in the USSR* (London, 1947).

Gouldner, Alvin W., *The Two Marxisms: Contradictions and Anomalies in the Development of Theory* (London: Macmillan, 1980).

Gramsci, Antonio, *Selections from the Prison Notebooks* (London: Lawrence and Wishart, 1971).

Hagen, Manfred, *Die Entfaltung politischer Öffentlichkeit in Russland, 1906–1914* (Wiesbaden, 1982).

Hamm, M. F., 'The Breakdown of Urban Modernisation: A Prelude to the Revolutions of 1917', in M. F. Hamm (ed.) *The City in Russian History* (Lexington: University Press of Kentucky, 1976).

Hammond, T. T., *Lenin on Trade Unions and Revolution, 1893–1917* (New York, 1957).

Harding, Neil, *Lenin's Political Thought*, vol. 2, *Theory and Practice in the Socialist Revolution* (London: Macmillan, 1981).

Harding, Neil (ed.), *The State in Socialist Society* (London: Macmillan, 1984).

Harrison, M. E., *Marooned in Moscow* (New York, 1921).

Hirszowicz, Maria, *The Bureaucratic Leviathan: A Study in the Sociology of Communism* (Oxford: Martin Robertson, 1980).

Janos, A. (ed.), *Authoritarian Politics in Communist Europe* (University of California Press, 1976).

Jasny, Naum, *Soviet Economists of the Twenties: Names to be Remembered* (Cambridge: Cambridge University Press, 1972).

Johnson, R., *Peasant and Proletarian: The Working Class of Moscow in the Late Ninteenth Century* (Leicester: Leicester University Press, 1979).

Kautsky, Karl, *The Dictatorship of the Proletariat* (Ann Arbor: University of Michigan Press, 1964).

Keep, John L. H., *The Russian Revolution: A Study in Mass Mobilisation,*

(London: Weidenfeld & Nicolson, 1976).

Koenker, D., *Moscow Workers and the 1917 Revolution* (Princeton, NJ: Princeton University Press, 1981).

Koenker, D., 'The Evolution of Party Consciousness in 1917: The Case of the Moscow Workers', *Soviet Studies*, 30, 1 (January 1978).

Konrad, G. and Szelenyi, I., *The Intellectuals on the Road to Class Power* (Brighton: Harvester Press, 1979).

Leggett, G., *The Cheka: Lenin's Political Police* (London: Oxford University Press, 1981).

Leites, K., *Recent Economic Developments in Russia* (Oxford, 1922).

Lewin, Moshe, *Political Undercurrents in Soviet Economic Debates* (London: Pluto Press, 1975).

Liebman, Marcel, *Leninism under Lenin* (London: Merlin Press, 1980).

Linden, C. A., *The Soviet Party-State: The Politics of Ideocratic Despotism*, (New York: Praeger, 1983).

Lovell, David W., *From Marx to Lenin: An Evaluation of Marx's Responsibility for Soviet Authoritarianism* (Cambridge: Cambridge University Press, 1984).

Lowy, M., *Georg Lukacs: From Romanticism to Bolshevism* (London: New Left Books, 1979).

Lukacs, Georg, 'Towards a Methodology of the Problem of Organisation', in *History and Class Consciousness* (London: Merlin Press, 1971).

Luke, Timothy W., *Ideology and Soviet Industrialisation* (London: Greenwood Press, 1985).

Malle, S., *The Economic Organisation of War Communism* (Cambridge: Cambridge University Press, 1985).

Mallet, S., *Bureaucracy and Technocracy in the Socialist Countries* (London: Spokesman Books, 1974).

Mandel, D., *The Petrograd Workers and the Soviet Seizure of Power: from the July Days to July 1918* (London: Macmillan, 1984).

Marx, Karl, and Engels, Frederick, *Selected Works* (London: Lawrence and Wishart, 1968).

Mattick, P., *Anti-Bolshevik Communism* (London: Merlin Press, 1978).

Maximoff, G. P., *The Guillotine at Work*, vol. 1, *The Leninist Counter-Revolution* (Orkney: Cienfuegos Press, 1979).

McCann, James M., 'Beyond the Bug: Soviet Historiography of the Soviet–Polish War of 1920', *Soviet Studies*, XXXVI, 4 (October 1984).

McInnes, N., 'Georg Lukacs', *Survey*, 70–73 (1969).

Medvedev, Roy, *On Socialist Democracy* (London: Spokesman Books, 1975).

Medvedev, Roy, *The October Revolution* (London: Constable, 1979).

Mel'gunov, S. P., *The Red Terror in Russia* (London: Dent, 1925).

Molyneux, John, *Marxism and the Party* (London: Pluto Press, 1978).

Mouffe, Chantal (ed.), *Gramsci and Marxist Theory* (London: Routledge & Kegan Paul, 1979).

Narkiewicz, O., *The Making of the Soviet State Apparatus* (Manchester: Manchester University Press, 1970).

Nove, Alec, *The Economics of Feasible Socialism* (London: George Allen & Unwin, 1983).

Ollman, B. 'Marx's Vision of Communism: A Reconstruction', *Critique*, 8 (1978).

Pipes, Richard, *Russian under the Old Regime* (Harmondsworth: Penguin, 1977).

Polan, A. J., *Lenin and the End of Politics* (London: Methuen, 1984).

Raeff, Marc, *Comprendre l'ancien régime Russe: état et sociéte en Russie impériale; essai d'interprétation* (Paris: Editions du Seuil, 1982).

Ransome, Arthur, *Six Weeks in Russia in 1919* (London, 1919).

Remington, Thomas F., *Building Socialism in Bolshevik Russia: Ideology and Industrial Organisation, 1917–1921* (Pittsburgh, Pa: University of Pittsburgh Press, 1984).

Rigby, T. H., *Communist Party Membership in the USSR, 1917–1967* (Princeton, NJ: Princeton University Press, 1968).

Rigby, T. H., *Lenin's Government: Sovnarkom, 1917–1922* (Cambridge: Cambridge University Press, 1979).

Roberts, P. C., 'War Communism: A Re-examination', *Slavic Review* (June 1970).

Rosenberg, W. G., 'Russian Labor and Bolshevik Power after October', *Slavic Review* (Summer 1985).

Rosmer, Alfred, *Lenin's Moscow* (London: Pluto Press, 1971).

Russell, Bertrand, *The Practice and Theory of Bolshevism* (London, 1920).

Schapiro, L., *The Origin of the Communist Atuocracy: Political Opposition in the Soviet State, 1917–1922* (London, 1955).

Schapiro, L. (ed.). *Political Opposition in One-Party States* (London, 1972).

Schlesinger, Rudolf, *History of the Communist Party of the USSR Past and Present* (Delhi: Orient Longman, 1977).

Schumpeter, Joseph A., *Capitalism, Socialism and Democracy* 3rd ed. (New York: Harper Brothers, 1950).

Selucky, Radoslav, *Marxism, Socialism, Freedom: Towards a General Theory of Labor-Managed Systems* (New York: St Martin's Press, 1979).

Serge, V., *Memoirs of a Revolutionary, 1901–1941* (London: Oxford University Press, 1967).

Service, R., *The Bolshevik Party in Revolution, 1917–1923: A Study in Organisational Change* (London: Macmillan, 1979).

Sik, Ota, *The Communist Power System* (New York: Praeger, 1981).

Sirianni, Carmen, *Workers' Control and Socialist Democracy: The Soviet Experience* (London: Verso, 1982).

Skocpol, Theda, *States and Social Revolutions* (Cambridge: Cambridge University Press, 1979).

Sorenson, J. B., *The Life and Death of Soviet Trade Unionism, 1917–1928* (New York: Atherton Press, 1969).

Stites, R., *The Women's Liberation Movement in Russia: Feminism, Nihilism and Bolshevism, 1860–1930* (Princeton, NJ: Princeton University Press, 1978).

Szamuely, Laszlo, *First Models of the Socialist Economic Systems: Principles and Theories*, trans. by Gy. Hajdu; trans. revised by M. Dobb, (Budapest: Akademiai Kiado, 1974).

Trotsky, Leon, *The New Course* (London: New Park Publications, 1956).

Trotsky, Leon, *The Revolution Betrayed* (London, New Park Publications, 1973).

Trotsky, Leon, *Terrorism and Communism: A Reply to Karl Kautsky* (London: New Park Publications, 1975).

Vajda, Mihaly, *The State and Socialism: Political Essays* (London: Alison and Busby, 1981).

Weeks, A. L., *The First Bolshevik: A Political Biography of Peter Tkachev* (New York: New York University Press, 1968).

Wells, H. G., *Russia in the Shadows* (London, 1920).

Wortman, Richard, 'Moscow and Petersburg: The Problem of Political Center in Tsarist Russia, 1881–1914', in Sean Wilentz (ed.), *Rites of Power: Symbolism, Ritual and Politics Since the Middle Ages* (Philadelphia: University of Pennsylvania Press, 1985).

Ziegler, Charles E., 'Worker Participation and Worker Discontent in the Soviet Union', *Political Science Quarterly* (Summer 1983).

Index